The Square Dance and
Contra Dance Handbook

The Square Dance and Contra Dance Handbook

*Calls, Dance Movements, Music
Glossary, Bibliography, Discography
and Directories*

Margot Gunzenhauser

Jefferson, North Carolina, and London : *McFarland & Company, Inc., Publishers*

To the memory of Ralph Page (1903–1985),
without whom this book would
probably never exist

Photographs by Klaus Iverson, Figment Photo.

British Library Cataloguing-in-Publication data are available

Library of Congress Cataloguing-in-Publication Data

Gunzenhauser, Margot, 1949–
    The square dance and contra dance handbook : calls, dance
movements, music, glossary, bibliography, discography, and
directories / by Margot Gunzenhauser.
        p.   cm.
    Includes bibliographical references (p.) and index. ∞
    ISBN 0-89950-855-3 (lib. bdg. : 50# alk. paper)
    1. Square dancing — Handbooks, manuals, etc.   2. Country-dance —
Handbooks, manuals, etc.   I. Title.
GV1763.G86   1996
793.3′4 — dc20   95-6009
                                                                            CIP

Manufactured in the United States of America

McFarland & Company, Inc., Publishers
    Box 611, Jefferson, North Carolina 28640

Table of Contents

List of Dances, Dance Figures, and Tunes

SQUARE DANCES

TUNES

Preface and Acknowledgments

The basic manuscript for the Danish edition of this book was written in 1981, shortly after I started teaching my first square and contra dance class in the suburbs of Copenhagen. In the United States, I had previously worked mostly with international folk dancing and English country dancing, but had also danced squares and contras at various dance camps and weekends with Ralph Page in New England and at Berea College in Kentucky.

Learning to call gave me a whole new perspective on American squares and contras, and I felt there was a need for a book that could help other people learn to dance and call. By the time the Danish edition was published in 1988, I had several years of experience and had had an opportunity to meet several American dance leaders who greatly enriched my knowledge and skills—all of which went into the book in one form or another.

The Danish edition of the book was greeted with an enthusiasm beyond anything I had imagined, and I was particularly surprised when respected leaders in the United States started encouraging me to make an expanded and revised edition available in English.

Hopefully, the publication of the book in English will make American country dancing more accessible to folk dance enthusiasts in other countries as well. Experiences in Denmark, Germany, Belgium and the Czech Republic have shown that traditional style square and contra dancing is enthusiastically accepted as part of the folk dance scene. Readers abroad who are interested in exchanging views and information are most welcome to contact me through the publishers.

Every caller comes in contact with numerous people, all of whom contribute to one's development in one way or another. It is impossible to thank each of them individually, but there are a few who deserve special mention:

- Rickey Holden, who from the beginning has been an inspiring role model, a willing fount of information, and a fascinating sparring partner.

- Izzy Young, who in the first phase of my calling career provided valuable help in the form of dance material and moral support.

- Ted Sannella, Bob Dalsemer, Tony Parkes, Roger Whynot, the late Ralph Page, and a host of other American callers who, through correspondence or personal contact, so willingly have shared their knowledge and views. In particular I would like to thank Ted Sannella and Bob Dalsemer for their perceptive and helpful comments on an early draft of part of the English language edition and for their continuing friendship and support.

- P.E. Christensen, Maj-Britt Andersson, and Aase and Carl Christian Andersen, who acted as the models for most of the drawings in the book. They have been faithful dance friends through many years.

- The callers and musicians in Denmark, who have helped to build a country dance scene just as positive and inspiring as anything that can be found in the States.

- The many dance composers, whose contributions have been central to the continued popularity of square and contra dancing. The following individuals have graciously given permission to use dances in this book: Cammy Kaynor (Cammy's La Bastringue), Eric Zorn (The New Hoosier), Eric Rounds (The Last Swim of Summer), Dick Forscher (Fairfield Fancy), Roger Knox (Belles of Auburn), Rickey Holden (Balance the Lines, Johnson's Special), Roger Whynot (Carol's Neck, Sheehan's Reel, Roger's Grand Chain, Swing to a Line), Jim Gregory (Stars and Stripes), Glen Morningstar (The Lighted Sconce), Sol Gordon (Jingle Bells, Star on the Sides and Star in the Center). Also the English Folk Dance & Song Society of London, England, kindly allowed the use of Friday Night Special (created by Sam Flinders).

• And last, but definitely not least, the many present and future dancers who form the basis for all our efforts and for the existence of this book.

This book is dedicated to the many teachers, callers, recreation leaders and others who use square dancing in their programs, with students or with organization members, or just with a group of friends. It is intended to show that, without appreciably expanding the list of calls used in those well known square dance "warhorses" of the fifties, you can provide contemporary dancing that will keep the participants active and give them pleasure in dancing, in music and in each other's company. Try these dances, see how they flow, try the music, hear how it helps the dancers move, and you will be coming back for more. The material in this book is just a taste of the many fine dances being used today.

The original purpose of this book was to share the delight I find in working with American folk dances with as many other people as possible. I hope that through you—the reader, the leader, the caller—this purpose will be fulfilled. See you on the dance floor!

Margot Gunzenhauser
Virum, Denmark
September 1995

Introduction

If you were exposed to square dancing in school, most likely the dances you did were simple and repetitive and were done to records with pre-recorded calls. The records may have been made in the 1950s or 1960s with music and calling that were less than inspiring. At the other end of the spectrum, you may be familiar with what is called "modern Western square dancing" or "club square dancing"—the kind that involves dancers dressed in western shirts and baby doll dresses, with scores of different calls fired off by the caller in seemingly random fashion. This kind of dancing looks impressive, but takes a lot of practice to learn.

The mission of this book is to show that there is another alternative. "Traditional style" square and contra dancing is a recreational activity that has undergone an enormous development within the last 25 years, and that offers participants fun and sociability at a level of difficulty that most people can pick up with a minimum of teaching.

Traditional style square and contra dancing, also sometimes referred to as "country dancing," emanates from the traditional dancing that is still being done in many small towns and rural communities around the United States. But while these local communities are content to do the same dances year in and year out, country dancing as recreation has evolved into an activity that offers more challenge and variety. It is more tailored to the needs of people who want to dance as a hobby, and for whom the dance in and of itself is as important as the chance to socialize with others.

Dances done in a country dancing context vary quite a bit in difficulty, from the simplest of circle dances to some of the very sophisticated and challenging contra dances that currently are appearing in increasing numbers. The key to the accessibility of country dancing is the use of a limited number of basic movements. Twenty or thirty concepts are sufficient to provide the base for a huge number of dances in various formations and with various levels of difficulty. This stands in contrast to the modern Western style square dance movement, which considers a list of about seventy basics to be the minimum for participation in the activity, with additional lists of comparable size forming a superstructure of additional levels.

In most parts of the United States, dancing in square sets of four couples has been the norm for generations. This is reflected in the modern Western square dance movement, which concentrates almost exclusively on square dancing, in the literal sense of the term.

Contra dancing, in which a long line is formed with the dancers facing their partners, was, until recently, found only in New England, where it had been preserved along with squares as a traditional dance form. Since about the mid-1970s, contra dancing as a recreational form has spread all over the country, until now there are many groups that dance mainly contras and barely know how to handle a square.

In common with a number of other country dance leaders, I would like to argue against the narrowing down of dance practices to only one form. Squares, contras, mixers, the Appalachian big set, and other indigenous American dance forms all have their own strengths and their own appeal which can be preserved and exploited to strengthen a dance program. This book contains a wide variety of dance types, and I would strongly encourage you to build programs that incorporate them all.

The dance material

I have tried in this book to describe a number of American folk dances in terms clear enough for anyone to use them, whether or not they have had previous experience with square and contra dancing.

One typical characteristic of American folk dances, compared with those of other countries, is their modular nature. When you learn to dance, you are learning a repertory of basic movements that can be combined in many different ways. Depending on the skill and priorities of the choreographer or caller, the resulting dance may be more or less successful. I have made an effort to select dances that function well, not only on paper but in practice—dances that really are a pleasure to dance.

Even though the number of basic movements used in the book is limited, some of the dances are significantly more difficult than others. The difficulty of a dance depends not only on the movements used but also on their sequence. Some sequences simply are easier to remember than others. Some allow time for catching up in case a mistake is made, while others are less "forgiving" and demand that the dancers be on time throughout the dance. Some sequences give few problems in spatial orientation, while others require a greater effort on the part of the dancers to avoid ending in the wrong place.

The material in this book has, insofar as possible, been arranged in order of increasing difficulty, both with regard to the order of the chapters and within each chapter itself, but most of the dances in the book are suitable for beginning or intermediate dancers.

In some cases, suggestions are included for variations or simplifications of a dance. These suggestions will give you some idea of how to experiment with changes and improvements in a dance while staying within the general limits of the style. Even though the dances in this book are presented as fixed sequences, some leeway for improvisation is generally present in American folk dancing, either in adapting the dance to specific needs or during the dance itself.

This is particularly true of dances done in a square set, where the main sequence of the dance alternates with "breaks" created on the spot by the caller. Contras and progressive circles are not normally changed during the course of the dance, but dance leaders can and do create new or revised dances depending on circumstances or whim.

The book also includes information and tips intended to help you teach the dances and, not least, to learn to call them. Whether you are already involved in country dancing or are, perhaps, a teacher or recreation leader with limited square dance experience, if you follow the suggestions here for learning to call, you will probably find that it was easier than you thought to try your hand at calling and improvising dance sequences.

The dance descriptions and how to read them

The dances are presented in chapters according to type. Most movements are explained in detail each time they occur, but in some cases (for example, ladies chain, right and left through) where it would have been cumbersome to give complete descriptions over and over, the reader is asked to refer to the Glossary at the back of the book. Some simple movements that occur very often, such as the dosido, are also not explained in detail in the more advanced dances. Each dance description consists of two parts:

• The first two columns present the *calls* in relation to the music. A leader with some experience will be able to understand many of the dances on the basis of the calls alone.

• The last two columns explain the *dance movements,* also in relation to the music.

Since the calls are always slightly ahead of the movements (see "How to Call for Square and Contra Dancing" on pages 8–11), you should not try to read the whole page from left to right, but should keep to the half that interests you at the moment, depending on whether you are trying to learn the dance itself or the calls. See "How to Practice Calling" for a more detailed explanation of how to interpret the calls.

Please also note that the numbers in the "Music" columns refer to individual beats, not to measures.

Drawings and diagrams are used to clarify the dance instructions where deemed necessary. Many helpful illustrations will also be found in the glossary.

Music

For each dance in the book, I have included a couple of suggested recordings, chosen from the tunes on the following albums:

Square Dance Tonight, Vol. 1 (Square Dance Partners 8701)
Square Dance Tonight, Vol. 2 (Square Dance Partners 8702)
Square Dance Tonight, Vol. 3 (Square Dance Partners 9001)
Kitchen Junket (Fretless 200A)
Maritime Dance Party (Fretless 201)

New England Chestnuts (Fretless 203)
New England Chestnuts 2 (Fretless 204)
New England Country Dance Music (Fretless 205)
Dancing Bow and Singing Strings (Folkways FTS-6524)
Dances from Appalachia 2 (Berea College TR16-BC00802)
Old Time Music Dance Party (Flying Fish 415)

I hope this will give you some idea of where to start in choosing recorded music.

When available, live music is a definite plus and will add a whole new dimension to your square and contra dancing. If you are lucky enough to have experienced musicians at your disposal, you probably will not need the sections of this book that deal with recorded music. If, on the other hand, you have budding musicians who are looking for appropriate material, you may want to show them the sheet music in this book, as well as the section "Materials for Musicians."

Bear in mind that improvisation and personal variations are just as much a part of American dance music as they are of American dances. No two musicians play a given tune exactly the same way, and in fact, many good musicians barely play the same tune the same way twice. The 35 tunes included in this book have been stripped down to their bare essentials, which should make them easier for beginners to learn. But anyone really interested in playing traditional American dance music should listen carefully to good recordings or find some experienced musicians who can show them the basics of good technique and introduce them to the wealth of improvisations and ornaments that make a tune come alive.

Key to the diagrams and some basic principles

In the dance diagrams, the dancers are seen from *above*. If you bear that in mind when you look at the diagrams, they should be quite easy to decipher. The little line represents the dancer's nose and shows which way he or she is facing. Arms are shown only when they are relevant to the movements diagrammed.

The terms used in the book are explained in detail in the Glossary. Check there if anything seems confusing. The dancers are referred to as "ladies" and "gents," which is the traditional terminology. Today, some callers are avoiding the term "ladies" and may prefer to say "women" and "men." Decide for yourself, based on the groups you are working with and your own feelings.

Remember that in each couple, the lady normally stands to the right of the gent, and the lady always ends on the gent's right side after swinging.

Gent

Lady

Couple holding inside hands

Couple in skater's (promenade) position

Couple making an arch with inside hands joined

Couple with both hands either out to the sides or forming a double arch in the air

Couple swinging (social dance position)

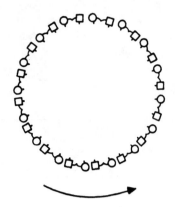

Line of direction (counterclockwise)

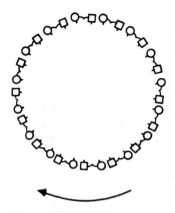

Reverse line of direction (clockwise)

Glossary

The Glossary contains definitions for over 140 terms, supplemented by illustrations for the sake of clarity. You will be able to do most of the dances in this book without problems, however, if you understand the following basic terms: allemande, balance, bend the line, cast off (I), circle, circle to a line, dosido (I), forward and back, grand right and left, half promenade, ladies chain, pass through, promenade, right and left through, star, and swing.

Directory

The Directory includes several categories of useful addresses. Separate sections are devoted to organizations and institutions; vendors of books and recordings; vendors of audio equipment; and dance camps. A mailing address and phone number along with an annotation explaining the type of information that may be available are given for each.

Materials for musicians

Many instructional books have been published for the instruments used in square and contra dance bands, but they vary in content and quality. In "Materials for Musicians," I have listed a few that may be of use, particularly if you are starting from scratch. Here you will find references for most of the instruments commonly used, including fiddle, banjo, guitar, mandolin, bass, and piano, as well as some useful general tune books.

Also included are the addresses of several suppliers of audio and video instructional tapes for those who may be interested in such courses, and the addresses of the best known folk music suppliers from whom materials can be ordered by mail.

Annotated Discography

The discography lists a large number of recordings, mostly LPs or cassette tapes, that are potentially usable for square and contra dancing. The recordings have been categorized by musical genre; by overall usability for dancing, based on an objective analysis of lengths, tempos, and types of arrangements; and by whether or not they include calls (those that do are listed in the "With calls" section even if they also include instrumental tracks). To help you quickly locate the type of material you are looking for, a separate table of contents is provided at the head of the discography. Within each section, the recordings are listed alphabetically by title.

The annotations in the discography include a personal assessment of the quality and usefulness of each recording, based on criteria explained in the introduction to the discography.

Some recordings are listed as "Mostly for listening." These have been included because they contain a high proportion of dance tunes, are played by groups associated with contra and square dancing, or have titles that imply they are usable for dancing even if they are not.

The format listed for each recording (LP, cassette, CD, etc.) is the one in which it was available to me. Many titles have been issued in more than one format.

I hope the discography will help you find enjoyable and appropriate music to dance to. Since local record stores rarely stock this type of material, you will probably find it faster, and possibly even cheaper, to order dance records directly from one of the specialized mail order houses listed in the Directory.

Annotated bibliography

The bibliography is divided into several categories: dance collections, general instructional books, instructional books on historical dance forms, history and background, calling and teaching techniques, clogging, record leaflets, syllabi, compilations, and glossaries and indexes. A table of contents provides quick access to the category of interest.

The bibliography includes only titles to which I have had personal access. Furthermore, I have made no attempt to include the many books that focus on modern Western style square dancing. There is, however, a gray area during the transitional period of the 1940s and 50s. At this time, traditional figures were being elaborated and supplemented to produce the roots of today's modern Western square dancing. Many dances and figures from this period are today considered compatible with traditional style, and several books from the period are represented here.

Any serious student of country dancing—or anyone curious enough—will want to consult both old and new works in the field. This is a good way to gain an understanding not only of the breadth and variety of dance customs, but also of the development that has taken place over time. Many of the books listed here are unfortunately out of print, but can be located in libraries and archives. Among the largest and best known archives of country dance materials in the United States are:

• The Ralph Page Collection and the library of the Country Dance and Song Society, both located at the University of New Hampshire in Durham.

• The Lloyd Shaw Foundation Archives in Albuquerque, New Mexico.

• The Library of Congress in Washington, D.C.

• The New York Public Library (main branch). But it pays to check other public and university libraries, too.

Probably the best source in the United States for purchasing books in print is the sales department of the Country Dance and Song Society. Other possibilities are Elderly Instruments, Andy's Front Hall, and Alcazar Productions.

See the "Directory" for more details about the archives and mail order houses.

The Basics of
Square and Contra Dancing

Square and contra dancing are forms of folk dancing found in the United States, and like all folk dancing, they have local and regional variants. In many regions, the term "square dancing" is used only to refer to dances done in a square formation with four couples in a set, while in other areas, it is used in a more generic way and can encompass dances done in other formations.

There are at least three kinds of square dancing going on in the United States today: real traditional dancing, particularly in rural areas; "traditional style" dancing, in which a limited number of basic movements are exploited in challenging ways to suit recreational purposes; and modern Western style square dancing, in which the repertory of basic movements is constantly being expanded, also for purposes of recreation.

Even within strictly traditional dancing, there have always been regional style differences, style differences between the urban and rural populations, and connections between different regions due to the high mobility of the American population. Throughout history, internal and external factors such as changing social needs, influences from popular culture, and other factors have contributed to changes in the ways Americans dance. Among the dances enjoyed today are ones from different stylistic periods, ones that have been popular for many years, and ones that have only recently been composed.

Three major dance formations that can be found today are:

• **Square dances,** dances done in a square set of four couples. Despite variations in stylistic details, certain basic principles are almost universal—the square formation itself, the participation of a caller, and the distinction between the main figure of the dance and the "break."

• **Contra dances,** dances done in a long row of couples, with each dancer standing across from his or her partner. Until very recently, contra dancing had virtually disappeared in most parts of the country, except in New England, where there has been an unbroken tradition up to the present time. In the last couple of decades, however, interest in contra dancing has grown enormously, and contras are now being danced by groups all over the country.

• **Big set dancing,** also called **big circle** or **Southern mountain style square dancing.** In big set dancing, which comes from Appalachia, part of the dance is done in one big circle, and part involves the couples pairing off to dance figures for four people. The term **running set** is also sometimes applied to big set dancing, but some leaders prefer to distinguish between big set, where any number of couples dance together in one big circle, and running set, where four couples dance together in a way that approximates the square dancing of other regions.

In this book I have included examples of all three of the above genres, as well as a few other formations.

A history of square and contra dancing is beyond the scope of this book. Unfortunately, much of what one reads in square dance books about the development of folk dancing in the United States is speculative at best and pure nonsense at worst. Only recently has the subject begun to attract much attention from serious researchers. Suffice it to say that the dances of America have obvious historical connections with European dance forms. Among these are the English longways dances (direct ancestors of today's contra dances) and French quadrilles (a further development of English country dances done in square sets, which eventually gave rise to today's square dances). Both of these held places of great international popularity in the seventeenth and eighteenth centuries. Dance forms that were in fashion in Europe were also fashionable in the United States, and forms danced by the aristocracy filtered down to the common people and were further developed by them, just as the higher social classes at times borrowed dance material from the masses. The influence of the longways and quadrilles occurred not only in America but all over Western Europe, where the dances were adopted and adapted in a variety of ways. So the American contras and squares of today have counterparts in the folk dances of many other countries.

THE ROLE OF THE CALLER

Probably the most unusual characteristic of American folk dancing compared with the dances of other countries is the caller. In his 1957 monograph *The History of Square Dancing*, S. Foster Damon writes that calling was already becoming common in the early 1800s. Publications from that time make it clear that Europeans who experienced the custom found it comical and vulgar. The professional itinerant dancing masters who travelled from town to town giving instruction in dance steps and etiquette also attacked the practice of calling. Good form still required that a cultivated person know the dances by heart. Quite aside from that, one can easily imagine that the dancing masters were afraid of losing their livelihood if the custom of calling became too widespread.

But regardless of what the upper crust said, the general population seems to have wholeheartedly embraced the idea of calling. In small, isolated pioneer communities there may have been only a few who could remember how the dances went, and it would have been practical for such a person to shout cues to the rest of the party. Often it was the fiddler who doubled as caller, but the caller could also be one of the dancers.

Calling developed into something of a folk art, and in many places, callers began to put nonsense and rhymes in between the dance instructions. This verbal improvisation, which is referred to as "patter," seems to have existed since the mid–1800s, if not longer.

Calling fulfills several functions:

• It forms a link between the music and the dancers.

• It reminds the dancers of what is coming next, relieving them of the responsibility of constantly thinking ahead.

• It challenges the dancers by occasionally calling something unexpected, so that the dance never becomes too monotonous.

Calling is not quite as easy at it seems, but the skills can be learned by anyone who has a sense of rhythm, a sense of humor, and a willingness to practice. See "How to call for square and contra dancing" (on pages 8–11) for a more detailed explanation of the factors that need to be taken into consideration if you want to learn to call.

SQUARE DANCE: MODERN OR TRADITIONAL?

Around the end of World War II, square dancing experienced a rise in popularity among the urban population that far exceeded the attention paid to it in the previous half century. As the modernized, postwar society developed, square dancing was transformed into a recreational activity on a par with sports and other hobbies. For the first time, professional callers emerged, and organizations and magazines were started. A process of conscious standardization was initiated, the object being to forge a common denominator out of the numerous regional forms so that people could dance together no matter where they happened to be.

In the course of the following decades, this movement evolved into a complete dance "system" that today forms the basis of modern Western style or club style square dancing. The result of this effort has been to increase the number of people involved in square dancing, but by constantly adding new basic movements to the existing repertory, a dance form has also been created that is relatively complicated and that requires a considerable amount of instruction to master.

Developments in "traditional style"

While all this was going on, there were still a number of places all over the country where people danced the way they had for generations. This kind of dancing could be found in New England, in Appalachia, and in various communities around the country, especially in small towns and rural areas. In the 1960s and early 1970s, many young people who were disillusioned with the "Establishment" moved away from the cities, came into contact with traditional dancing, and became enthusiastic about it. Lessons were unnecessary—the dances were relatively simple and relied mostly on a small number of basic movements, and in many areas it was the custom to walk through each dance before doing it. So even a beginner had a fair chance of catching on, and if a new dancer got confused, the more experienced could help. The live bands that customarily played at these dances also added an exciting dimension to the experience. A few seminal leaders made major contributions as they started to modernize the material and make it more accessible to the population at large.

As time went on, more and more dance events based on traditional principles began to be organized, and going to a "traditional style" square or contra dance—even in big cities—became a perfectly viable alternative to participating in club style square dancing. Aside from a few summer dance camps, traditional style dancing rarely involves instruction as such. People just come, dance, and learn as they go along. There are, however, some dances that are frequented by a relatively large percentage of experienced dancers, who may be looking for a certain amount of challenge, and others where beginners are in the majority. More and more people are learning to call or, just as important, to play music for square and contra dancing. Among the callers there are a number of creative choreographers capable of putting together new, exciting dance sequences that satisfy our modern desire to be as active as possible, while still keeping within the general limits of the traditional basic movements and style.

The many people who actively participate in traditional style square and contra dancing are generally not organized into formal clubs of the type prevalent within modern Western style square dancing. But the dances are often sponsored by associations of a more or less formal character. And there is a national organization that acts as a focal point for traditional dance and music: the Country Dance and Song Society. The CDSS, which was founded back in 1915 as a branch of the English Folk Dance and Song Society, has contributed to the process of preserving, developing, and researching traditional American dance forms. However, it does not (nor does it want to) carry the authoritative ring of the modern Western style movement's Callerlab, which regularly publishes lists of approved, precisely defined movements and suggestions for teaching them. The CDSS does not decide what is "correct" or "incorrect," nor does it concern itself with certification, the establishment of different levels of achievement, or the like.

Differences between the two styles

There are a number of differences between recreational square and contra dancing in traditional style on the one hand and modern Western style square dancing on the other. Some of the most important differences are the following:

• *Basic movements:* Modern Western style uses a very large number of basic movements. New movements are constantly being added, and older movements may be reevaluated and dropped or moved from one level to another. Even at the lowest levels of achievement, it takes concentration to remember all the movements, particularly as the dancers are required to execute them on demand in an unknown order. For many people it is, however, precisely this feature that makes club style square dancing exciting. Traditional style dancing involves a smaller number of basic movements, most of which are quickly learned. Additional movements may be used at times, but on the whole, choreographers concentrate on exploiting the established movements in exciting and satisfying ways.

• *Formations:* Modern Western style square dancing makes almost exclusive use of the square formation (notwithstanding recent agitation to adapt contra formation to modern Western style). Traditional style dancing, on the other hand, embraces all the major regional forms, i.e., not only squares, but also to a very great degree contras, as well as big set, mixers, progressive circles, etc. This is of importance not only because it creates more variety in the dance activity, but also because, while dancing in squares requires a multiple of eight participants, the other forms generally permit any number of couples to dance.

• *Music:* In modern Western style square dancing, the music is often given a secondary role. The rhythm is clearly the most important element, and since the melody can "get in the way" of the complicated call patterns, which are not always phrased in accordance with the number of musical beats, it is often consciously damped in the mix. Scores of records are released each year for use by club style callers; live music is virtually never used. Most of these records consist of new or older pop tunes (including country & western), played with the same kinds of arrangements as the originals and used for only a short time until being superseded by newer hits. The recordings may vary considerably with regard to their intrinsic danceability. In traditional style dancing, music plays a crucial role as a counterpart to the dance. This means that live music is preferred whenever possible, that one attempts to use the appropriate kind of music for each dance type, and that, in many cases, choreography and calling technique are consciously put to work to make the dance follow the musical phrase, so dance and music become parts of an integrated whole. The music used is primarily folk music—traditional dance tunes in various regional styles—although some bands today are becoming quite eclectic and introducing strains of jazz, swing, or foreign ethnic musics into the American dance tunes. With or without these foreign elements, the music for traditional style dancing must be played in a lively way. The rhythmic pulse must be clear, with the upbeats giving the dancers "lift" to keep their feet moving, but the melody is also very important and must be clearly heard. The caller and dancers should find the music inspiring and enjoyable in its own right.

• *Physical style:* In modern Western style square dancing, the greatest challenge is intellectual, rather than physical. Traditional style dancing is more robust in character and puts more emphasis on good "flow," i.e., the way in which the dance movements fit together to form a pleasing whole, than on learning a large number of different calls. In traditional dancing, the physical contact between dancers is just as important as the pattern they form on the floor. There is more swinging (and longer swings) than in modern Western style, and more "connectedness" between dancers, based on the handholds used and the greater frequency of certain movements that involve an element of centrifugal force.

• *Social style:* Club style square dancing tends to attract mostly couples, and it is important to participate regularly if one wants to maintain one's skills. Traditional style dancing is more open to people who come alone or sporadically. Singles are welcome, and people are encouraged to dance with many different partners. This may be done by using mixers, but in many places, the custom is simply to change partners after every dance. Furthermore, the level of complexity is such that one can drop in from time to time and still be able to dance along with the regulars.

• *"Extras":* Finally, traditional style dancers are quite uninterested in such accoutrements as special clothing, diplomas, levels, badges and the like—all things that play an important role in the world of modern Western style square dancing.

In spite of all these differences, one should remember that both kinds of dancing stem from the same roots and have a number of important features in common. This applies not only to the basic movements used but to certain stylistic elements and to the principle of listening to the caller and doing what is said. And last, but certainly not least, both types of square dancing offer an activity where people can meet one another and have an enjoyable and active evening.

Whether one prefers one or the other type of square dancing—or both—may, in the final analysis, be mainly a question of temperament. It is, however, only fair to recognize that both ways of dancing exist, and that each has positive values to offer to participants.

MUSIC FOR SQUARE AND CONTRA DANCING

In contrast to the folk dances of many other countries, square and contra dances do not necessarily have to be done to the same tune every time. There are some dances—in particular some of the classic contra dances, as well as squares done as singing calls—that have their own specific tunes. But even these can be danced to other tunes if necessary. For most other dances, the choice is open to personal taste. You will, however, find that some common sense must be applied in matching a tune to a dance. Trying to dance an Appalachian big set to a New England jig or a traditional New England contra to a driving Southern fiddle tune played in oldtime style will not give optimal results. And for any given dance, there will be some tunes that work well, while others are uninspiring or even seem to work against the dance.

In case of doubt, the best approach is to try out different tunes until you find one that you feel suits the dance in question. Most callers develop a preference for certain dance/tune combinations and use these combinations when they can. However, you should always be aware that other combinations may work out just as well. If, for example, you often use records or tapes and only occasionally work with a live band, you may find that the band's repertory does not coincide with your record collection. In that case, you must be prepared to make other selections, or, if the band is experienced, let them make appropriate selections on the basis of a short description of the type of music you want.

If you dance to different callers or bands, you will undoubtedly find that music selections for the same dance (or dance selections for the same tune) vary. To perform a dance to an unaccustomed tune can be a little disorienting, but it is even worse to be so used to dancing one particular dance to a given tune that you get confused if that tune is used for another dance. So in general it is a good idea not to become too rigid about tune selection.

A typical American dance tune consists of two parts, often referred to as the A and B parts. Each part has eight measures of two beats each, and each part is repeated twice (AABB). Thus the total is 16 beats per part or 64 beats for the entire tune.

In this book, approximate metronome speeds are given for each dance. A metronome is a sensible investment for anyone who wants to work seriously with dance. Inexpensive models are available at music stores, but if you do not have a metronome and do not want to acquire one, you can still get an idea of tempo by counting the beats in a piece of music while timing it with a watch or stopwatch. It may be sufficient to count for 30 seconds and then multiply the result by two to get the number of beats per minute.

Listen and learn

The best way to gain an understanding of square and contra dance music is to listen to it.

Even if you are able to hear live bands, you may also benefit quite a bit from listening carefully to records. In recent years a number of excellent recordings with traditional music intended specifically for dancing have been released. This is particularly true of New England music, but there are also several good records with bluegrass or oldtime music. The discography at the back of this book lists many of these records and tapes and tells where you can get them.

Northern style

Square and contra dances in New England style work best when danced to New England or Canadian music. The two most important instruments in this style are fiddle for the melody and piano for the bass and rhythm. The piano does *not* normally play the melody, although experienced musicians may sometimes take a solo break or play along with the fiddle at times. The basic fiddle/piano combo may be supplemented by accordion, hammered dulcimer, guitar, mandolin, tenor banjo, five-string banjo (more rarely), or wind instruments such as flute, recorder or pennywhistle. Around the turn of the century, town orchestras in New England used a full complement of wind instruments—cornets, clarinets, etc.—and occasional attempts have been made to recreate that sound. But wind orchestras have not caught on again to any great extent. An instrument that *has* enjoyed something of a renaissance in recent years is the hammered dulcimer, a kind of large zither played by striking the strings with two small mallets.

New England dance music has clearly been influenced both by the Scottish and Irish tune repertory and by French-Canadian playing styles. Compared to Southern dance music, the tunes are harmonically more complex, with a relatively high number of chord changes. Tunes—and the two parts of each tune—are fairly distinctive and easy to tell apart. The tempos used are relatively slow—about 116–126 beats per minute on the metronome.

In New England, both reels and jigs are played. A reel is a tune in 2/4 time, and a jig is a tune in 6/8 time. Statistically, reels are probably played more often than jigs, but a jig, with its hint of syncopation, makes a nice change of pace, and some dances seem to work best in jig time. For example, I prefer a bouncy jig for dances that use the sashay step. Hornpipes can also be found in the New England repertory, but whereas an English hornpipe, in 4/4 time, is played slowly and has the character of a schottische, American hornpipes are played much faster, as if they were reels.

Southern style

Dances from the Southern states are quite different in character from the ones in New England and require an entirely different type of music. The classic Southern string band or bluegrass band is composed of fiddle, five-string banjo, guitar, mandolin, and bass. In the old days, there was often just a fiddle, possibly supplemented by a banjo, and since the two instruments had to perform the work of an entire band, a hard-driving, rhythmical style was developed on both of them. Consequently, the fiddle and banjo are the heart of the Southern style band, just as the fiddle and piano are the heart of the Northern band. Pianos are rarely heard in Southern style bands, and accordions and wind instruments are not really appropriate, with the possible exception of a harmonica now and then.

Although the Southern repertory, too, has roots in British music, the Appalachian region was much more isolated than New England, and the ability to read music was much less common. Southern dance music seems to have undergone a more pronounced transformation to an indigenous American style. Often the tunes are less well defined. There are fewer chord changes—in fact, some fiddle tunes can be played almost all the way through using only one chord—and the difference between the A and B parts can be less obvious. Jigs are not part of the repertory, and tempos tend to be faster than in New England, ranging from about 128 to 140 beats per minute. Bluegrass music, with its close-knit band sound, can be excellent for dancing, provided it is played at an appropriate tempo. It may be a good idea to use more fiddle and banjo leads than usual, and if the guitar or mandolin does take a break, make sure that the total volume level does not drop off too sharply.

Live music

If you are lucky enough to be able to use live music for your dancing, here are a few things to bear in mind. The caller and dancers must be able to hear the rhythm, but the melody should also be clear. It is also very important that the caller's voice be clearly audible above the music. For these reasons, and in order to ensure an appropriate balance among the different instruments in the band, sound amplification is often used. Whether the instruments need to be amplified does, however, depend on the composition of the band, as well as the size and acoustics of the hall. Accordion, piano and banjo are instruments that often have sufficient volume without amplification, while guitar, mandolin, bass and some wind instruments may drown in comparison if they are not boosted. Fiddle players vary, but a single fiddle in a crowded hall will definitely need a microphone or pickup. A minimum requirement is a microphone for the caller. Few people today have the voice training to be able to call to a full hall and be heard and understood above the music without amplification.

The band should be capable of varying its tempo, depending on what is appropriate for the individual dance. It is also very important that the musicians be able to keep a set tempo throughout a given dance. The tempo should not be increased unless the caller has requested it, nor should it be allowed to drag.

You will have to decide on some signals that the caller can use to communicate with the band. Most important of all is a signal for when to stop playing; this enables the caller and band to end the dance gracefully and together. One way is by verbal message—many musicians use the expression "going out" to indicate that they are on the last repeat of the tune. Hand signals can also be used, if you make sure that the band knows what you mean by them and that all the musicians can see you give them. Agree with the band on whether your stop signal means to stop at the end of the current section (A or B) or to play the tune through to the end. Another good signal to have is one that means "cut immediately," which may, for example, be necessary in a teaching situation. Some groups also agree on signals for increasing or decreasing the tempo. However, unless the band is fairly experienced, it may be difficult for them to change the tempo on demand.

The band should always play a short introduction to allow the caller to say the first call and to give the dancers an indication of the coming tempo. In many cases, a standard four-count shuffle (referred to as "four potatoes") is enough, but sometimes an eight-count intro is desirable, depending on how much has to be said. Less experienced callers may also prefer eight counts, to give them a better chance to collect themselves. Let the band know if you have special needs.

The main principle in working with live music is to communicate with each other in a clear and pleasant way. The caller and the band are equally important to the success of the evening, and neither party should denigrate the efforts of the other. Avoid misunderstandings on stage by talking things over before the dance starts or during the intermis-sions. If a problem occurs in spite of this, try to solve it diplomatically, taking each others' needs into account and calling as little attention to the situation as possible. Ideally, the dancers should experience the caller and musicians as an integrated, cooperative unit and sense that they, too, are enjoying the evening.

DANCING STYLE

Steps

Square and contra dancing is usually done in a relaxed, natural manner that does not require much instruction in itself. The main step used is not much different from an ordinary walking step. Keep your feet close to the floor and walk with a gliding or shuffling quality, rather than a bouncy one. Children and beginners may spontaneously skip when they dance. With children, especially the youngest ones, it is best to accept this. They have a lot of energy and it is better to let them enjoy themselves than to insist on toning them down and risk having them react negatively to dancing because of it. Adult beginners who skip will usually stop doing it when they start to get tired or notice that the more experienced dancers are walking.

Other steps used in square and contra dancing are the buzz step for swinging, the balance step, and occasionally the sashay step (a sideways step in the same syncopated rhythm as that used for skipping). These steps are explained in the Glossary.

Arms and hands

Let your arms hang loosely at your sides when you are not using them. This will make it easier to take hands with other dancers as required in the course of the dance. Many of us learned in school to cross our arms when doing a dosido, but I do not know of any style of contemporary square dancing in which that is done. Putting your hands on your hips is unnecessary and looks affected, while waving your arms around can be downright hazardous to other dancers. When taking hands with other dancers, grip them firmly, but not so tightly as to cause discomfort, and don't forget to let go when moving on to the next figure!

Carriage of the body

Ideally, square and contra dancing is done not only with the feet, but with the whole body. After mastering the mechanics of the basic movements, dancers should relax and lean into the various movements with the upper body, anticipating the next movement at the end of each one executed. This improves both the flow of the dance, connection with other dancers, and personal enjoyment.

Giving weight

One very important concept in traditional style square and contra dancing is to "give weight" in any movement in which two or more dancers swing or revolve around a central point. The goal is to find the perfect balance between the dancers, creating a feeling of centrifugal force. In order to do this, there must be a slight tension in the handholds, and the dancers must be able to lean away from each other, confident that their partners will do the same. When you swing using social dance position, the gent's right hand should provide enough support for the lady's back that both dancers can lean slightly away from each other. When you do an allemande, both dancers should bend their elbows and tense their arm muscles just enough to give the movement a little centrifugal force. Even in a two-hand turn such as the type of swing recommended in this book for the big set — or for that matter, in a circle — this slight centrifugal force should be present.

The principle of giving weight also applies to movements such as the courtesy turn (the second half of a ladies chain or right and left through) and the arm-around cast off in contra dancing. These are movements in which two dancers stand not across from each other, but next to each other, and turn as a unit in place, with one dancer going forward and the other backwards.

Whether you are across from each other or next to each other, the point around which you turn should be midway between the dancers. Don't allow one dancer to stand still or pivot in place and drag or pull the other around.

As an instructor, the only way you can tell whether your dancers have learned the trick of giving weight is to get out on the dance floor and dance with them. Except in very exaggerated cases, it is usually difficult to tell from outside when this element is missing. It may take some instruction and practice to get the principle across, but giving weight properly is one of the most central and enjoyable aspects of traditional style dancing, so don't neglect it.

Eye contact

Square and contra dancing are social dance forms. Acknowledge your fellow dancers by making eye contact with your partner when you do a dosido, balance, or swing. Eye contact will also help you make the right connections when doing a ladies chain, coming out of a star, or in other figures where two dancers need to find each other.

HOW TO CALL FOR SQUARE AND CONTRA DANCING

The relationship between the caller and the dancers

The caller is the link between the dancers and the music, and must know where both are at any given time. The caller's job is to make sure that the dancers perform the dance movements at the correct time in accordance with the music. This is done by giving each call *just before* the movement is to be executed.

The dancers must be aware that the caller can vary the dance sequence. This is particularly true of the intro, break and ending of a square dance and for the big set, where the caller pieces the dance together from a repertoire of known figures. On the other hand, they should also be able to count on the caller to help them — insofar as possible — if they get lost or fall behind.

Things to remember

The main aspects of good calling technique are the following:
- call in time with the music;
- give each call just before the movement is to be executed;
- allow the correct number of steps (i.e., beats of music) for each movement;
- coordinate the beginning and end of each movement with the phrases of the music;
- use your voice to emphasize the most important information in the call;
- use variety in tone, rhythm and mode of expression;
- speak clearly;
- don't call in a mechanical way; be prepared to repeat and emphasize information — and, occasionally, to surprise the dancers.

Call in time with the music

By calling in time, the caller supports and emphasizes the rhythmic pulse of the music. Here are a few simple examples of how the calls are fitted to the musical rhythm:

Through the arch and around to place
  1   and 2 and-uh 3 and 4

Clap _____ and swing _____
  1   2   and   3   4

_____ _____ Twos go...
  1   2   3   4

As these examples show, a certain amount of rhythmic variation, including syncopation, is used, but this should always go along with the natural rhythm of the words as well as the rhythm of the music.

Give each call just before the movement is to be executed

In order to ensure that the dance can flow continuously, the caller must always be one jump ahead of the dancers. This means that each call must be given while the dancers are performing the previous movement. The overlap between the activity of the caller and that of the dancers is one of the hardest things for a beginning caller to adjust to.

In order to end each call just before the new movement starts, the caller must also know how long it will take to say the necessary words. For example, it takes four beats to say "When you meet your partner, swing" but only two to say "Meet and swing." "Right and left" takes two beats, while "Head two couples right and left through" takes four. A call like "Couple one go out to the right and circle left—go halfway 'round" eats up eight beats. As you become more experienced at calling, you will start to get a feeling for when you should begin to say the next call. But in the beginning, it may help to work out your ideas beforehand—perhaps on paper—and practice them in time to the music. Each dance in this book has a set of calls that you can use as a point of departure for your own efforts. Don't be afraid to change the wording—each caller has his or her own mode of expression—but be sure that the words you say communicate the information that the dancers need, i.e., *what* they have to do and *with whom* or *in what direction.*

How much of the music is "covered" by calls will, of course, depend partly on the content of the calls and how they are expressed. If the dance can be directed by short, concise calls, then the music will be heard uninterrupted for relatively long stretches. If more or longer expressions are necessary, more of the music will be covered, as more of the music used for executing one movement will have to be borrowed to explain the next.

Patter

As mentioned earlier, the pauses between the calls themselves can be filled by patter—more or less nonsensical filler words, often in rhyme. Patter can be quite entertaining for the dancers if the caller is creative. Whether or not to use patter depends to some extent on regional style, and also on the predilections of the individual caller. Some traditional callers were known to comment on the

dancers while they danced, but that is usually not as acceptable today as it was when the dancers were part of a tight-knit community where everyone knew each other well.

With beginning dancers it may be a good idea to keep patter to a minimum at first. Otherwise, they may have trouble figuring out how much of what you say is relevant and how much is just nonsense or repetition. Once they learn to react automatically to the calls, patter will be less confusing to them.

A beginning caller will often have enough to think about without trying to put in a lot of patter. Don't force it. As you mature and relax, patter will probably find its way into your calling almost unconsciously. You may also find that a particularly festive occasion inspires you to enhance your calling more than usual. If you are interested in learning appropriate patter, try listening to other callers you admire. Books, as well as records with calls, can also be good sources, but be wary of the artificial and stilted phrases found in some of them. Also be careful not to use expressions that are patronizing, chauvinistic, or in other ways offensive to the dancers.

Allow the correct number of steps for each movement— coordinate the beginning and end of each movement with the phrases of the music

Most movements in traditional style square and contra dancing are assigned a specific number of steps. Since the music can be broken down into phrases of 16, 8 or 4 beats, the number of steps per movement is usually also a multiple of four. This ensures that the progress of the dance coincides with the progress of the music.

Here are some of the basic movements and the number of steps used to perform them:

forward and back. . .8

circle left or right once around, with four dancers. . .8

circle left or right once around, with eight dancers. . .16

promenade halfway around, in a square. . .8

promenade all the way around, in a square. . .16

right hand star or left hand star, once around. . .8

ladies chain...8

right and left through...8

dosido once around or, in some cases, once and a half around...8

balance...4

down the center and back and cast off, in a contra...16

allemande left or allemande right, once around...8 or 4

(The timing of an allemande may depend on the choreography of the rest of the dance.)

grand right and left all the way around, in a square...24 (3 per hand)

(Almost always used in combination with allemande left or swing, to give a total of 32 steps.)

swing...4, 8, 12, 16 or as necessary to fill the available music

(Swing is the most flexible movement at the caller's disposal.)

The modular principle in square and contra dance choreography is most obvious in contras, where the dance sequence starts again each time the tune is repeated. The dance sequence must correspond precisely to the length of the tune, which is usually 64 counts.

Many New England square dance figures are constructed in a similarly tidy way. On the other hand, square dance figures from other parts of the country, including many of the old classic visiting couple figures, are often much less cut and dried. If everything goes according to a theoretical plan, it may be possible to execute the figure in perfect correspondence with the music—and the descriptions in this book are designed with that somewhat elusive goal in mind. However, it is often more important when calling such dances to adapt the timing of the calls to the dancers than to try and force them through the sequence at a predetermined rate. From this point of view, it is advisable to choose a southern fiddle tune, with its relatively loose structure, for such dances, rather than a New England tune. In any case, try to keep sight of the following guidelines:

• Make sure that the dancers are aware of the pulse of the music and that they move in time to it.

• Try to start each movement, especially each repetition of the main figure, at the beginning of a musical phrase (i.e., beats 1 and 9), even if this means that you occasionally have to let the dancers wait for a beat or two. If necessary, a call may also be given on beat 5 or 13 in this style to keep the dancers moving. But avoid starting on beats 3, 7, 11 or 15, not to mention the even-numbered beats.

---

1 2 3 4 **5** 6 7 8 **9** 10 11 12 **13** 14 15 16

• The caller should see to it that all the squares dance together and start the figure at the same time, even if some tend to get through it faster than others. Accustom the dancers to listen to the calls. They should not be allowed to run ahead of the caller, even if they know (or think they know) what is coming next.

Recorded music

Like all other kinds of folk dances, square and contra dances were originally done only to live music. And when you have a live band, they just keep playing until they are asked to stop. Only in modern times have recordings, with their pre-set lengths, come to dominate the square dance scene. Fortunately, in traditional style dancing, live music has again become the rule. But if you are working, for example, in a school or recreation program, you probably will have to rely on records or tapes as a source of music.

On many recordings intended for square dancing, the tune is played seven times through, corresponding to a standard square dance composed of an intro, break, ending, and four times through the main figure. Some recordings may be found with longer cuts, while many that otherwise would be excellent are, unfortunately, too short. You should try not to let the recordings dictate how you call. If you work with records, it is relatively easy to prolong the music by picking up the tone arm as the record nears completion and putting it down again near the beginning of the tune. This is harder with tapes, although it is possible on some machines to use the fast rewind button without stopping the tape. A better solution may be to record favorite tunes twice after each other or—if you are good at electronic splicing—to record a tune up until the next to last repetition, then repeat it again immediately from the second repetition through to the end. It is better to have too much music on hand than too little. If you do have too much music and want to end a dance before the music is finished, turn down the volume *gradually* as you end the dance, rather than suddenly punching the stop button.

Use your voice to emphasize the most important information in the call

Putting extra emphasis on key words in the call will help the dancers understand what you want them to do. For example, the words "partner" and "corner" can be hard to tell apart, especially in situations where you are improvising and the dancers do not know what is coming next. So try to say any words that can cause problems more clearly and emphatically. Similarly, if you see that not all the dancers have understood the call correctly (and if it is important that they do so), you can repeat the key words as the movement is being executed. For example:

Dosido your corner, corner — corner lady dosido

Use variety in tone, rhythm and mode of expression

Everyone knows how boring it is to listen to a speaker who never varies the volume, tone or rhythm of his or her words. The same is true of calling. Besides emphasizing the most important information, you should also vary your mode of expression sufficiently to prevent your calling from becoming monotonous. Put a little life in your calling, and the whole hall will become more lively. Some tunes seem to encourage the caller to sing along with the melody, and this is a fine and time-honored way to call. Letting your voice rest on notes of the musical chords is also a good technique. Be careful, though, not to develop a "sing-song" delivery — one that utilizes the same little "melody" over and over — or other exaggerated mannerisms of expression that will be irritating to listen to.

Speak clearly

Clear enunciation is a necessity if the dancers are to understand your calls and execute the movements you ask for. This is even more important if you are working with dancers whose native tongue is not English, or with older dancers who have hearing problems. If you are in doubt as to whether your calls are coming through clearly enough, ask the dancers. Note that sometimes when dancers say they cannot hear you, what they really mean is that they cannot understand you. The problem may be the way you speak, the way you use the microphone or the way the sound is adjusted.

You can also record yourself on tape and listen critically to the results. A recording will undoubtedly reveal a variety of things that you either are doing very nicely or need to work on. But do not be too discouraged if you feel there are many errors in your calling. Remember that mistakes that are trivial in a live situation can be blown out of proportion when they are captured on tape and are heard over and over again.

Do not call mechanically; be prepared to repeat and emphasize information — and occasionally, to surprise the dancers

As implied by much of what has already been said, calling is actually a form of two-way communication. The caller has an idea of what he or she wants to say. But there will be constant feedback from the dancers that may force the caller to react by repeating or rephrasing a call, by lengthening or shortening a dance sequence so as to keep up with the music in spite of mistakes or delays in the execution of the figures, or by taking other corrective measures that were impossible to foresee when practicing at home in the living room.

It is also important for a caller to be able to improvise a little or to vary parts of a dance, so the dancers become used to listening to the caller and do not take too much for granted. Dancers enjoy following the caller in these sequences, and if mistakes are made, they are just part of the fun.

In this connection, it cannot be overemphasized that the process of learning to dance squares and contras should not emphasize learning complete dances by heart. The idea is to learn the meaning of the *calls*. If the dancers do this, they will be ready to execute a wide range of dances using the known calls in different combinations.

HOW TO PRACTICE CALLING

Learn the words

When you start learning to call, it is best to take some easy dances first. For example, try some of the first dances in the chapters on mixers and progressive circles. Later on you can graduate to more complicated ones.

Look at the first two columns in the dance description. In the first column, the musical phrase is indicated. "A1" refers to the first time through the A part of the tune, "A2" to the second time through. "B1" is the first time through the B part of the tune, and "B2" the second time through. The rest of the numbers refer to the beats. There are 16 beats in each part (A or B) of the tune, and on the left side of the page, these are consistently divided into groups of four.

In the second column, each beat is marked by underlining. A word or syllable that is underlined is one that falls on the beat. The rest of the words must be fitted in between the beats. For example:

Look to the right and do-si-do

  1   and-uh 2 and 3 and 4

An underline without any word means that nothing is said on that beat:

_ Join hands and circle left

 1 and   2   and 3 and 4

Read the calls aloud in rhythm, being careful to put the emphasis on the underlined words. If you find this difficult, try starting by counting slowly and markedly: 1 - 2 - 3 - 4 , 5 - 6 - 7 - 8 , 1 - 2 - 3 - 4 , 5 - 6 - 7 - 8 . . . and then keeping the same rhythm as you say the words of the call. You may want to keep saying numbers on the "empty" beats to keep the rhythm going.

Most people feel funny about speaking out loud when they are not talking to anyone, but you will have to overcome that inhibition if you want to learn to call. Saying the words out loud is quite a different thing than saying them in your head. You not only have to remember what you want to say, you also have to learn to physically produce the sounds quickly and accurately enough. So find a place where you can "talk to yourself" undisturbed, or send the rest of the family on an outing for a few hours.

Put the words to the music

When the words feel comfortable to say, it's time to combine them with the music. Choose a recording with a slow tempo—the slower the better at first—and preferably a tune you are familiar with. If necessary, let the tune play one whole time through and use the last four counts of the B2 music as your intro. These are the counts you are going to need to say the first call.

Keep on calling your dance many times, until it starts to become easy and automatic. Then try a tune that is a little faster. If you have trouble finding the beat or finding the phrase, you can go back to counting 1 - 2 - 3 - 4 , and then try to insert the words.

You can also start trying to vary your calls a bit. The suggestions in this book are by no means the only way a given dance can be called. Some expressions that are natural for one caller may seem awkward to another. Furthermore, it is perfectly normal for a caller to vary the way he or she calls a given dance. And if the dance you have chosen is one that can have variations (for example, Come My Love or Sicilian Circle), you can try and put some of them in now.

Try it out on the dancers

When you feel sufficiently secure in your calling of one or a few dances, it's time to take the final step and try them out on a group of real dancers. In traditional style dancing, it is customary to walk through the dance before doing it to the music, and if the people you are calling for are not used to dancing, you will also have to teach them the meaning of the various calls. In this case, it is more important that they understand how to execute "forward and back," "dosido," "circle left" or whatever calls your dance requires than that they learn the whole dance by heart. Start the music, take a deep breath, and what do you know! You've just made your debut as a caller.

Continuing on your own

Hopefully the material in this book will give you something to work with during your first period as a caller and teacher of traditional dancing. But there are also hundreds of other good dances, some easy and some harder, in the many other books that have been published on the topic. In some of these books you will find very detailed dance descriptions and in others, much more concise ones. It may be of help to you to work out a call sheet similar to the ones in this book. Doing that will help you make sure that your timing and phrasing are correct and that nothing is missing. And you will be able to pull out the call sheet again at a later date if you want to check how you called that particular dance.

One last tip: it may take some concentration to learn the calls, not to mention actually using them in a room full of dancers. But try to relax when you call. A relaxed and smiling caller sends out good vibrations that will be returned in kind by the dancers. And whatever you do, do not read your calls. Have them clear in your head. Reading prevents you from watching the dancers, and it is essential for the caller to keep an eye on the dance floor at all times.

PROGRAMMING

Structure your program

When planning a whole evening of traditional dancing, you should try to vary the program with respect to dance type, tempo, formation, etc. Rather than using just squares or just contras, try throwing in some mixers, couple mixers, couple dances or maybe even a big set. The choice of dances should take into account the level of experience and interest of the dancers, and if, for example, you are working with beginners, you can get more mileage out of a small number of basic movements by varying the formations in which they are used.

It is always a good idea to start off with some easy dances to get everyone warmed up and give the caller a chance to size up the abilities of the crowd. Newcomers who are hesitant to join in may also be encouraged by the simplicity of the first dances.

Gradually increase the difficulty of the material, introducing new movements as you go along, but remember that the optimal learning situation is not found at the end of the evening when folks are getting tired. A better plan is to use the most challenging dances about two-thirds of the way through the evening, tapering off at the end with fun dances that require minimal teaching.

What to do if you do not have a caller

If you are going to dance without a caller, concentrate on dances from the categories represented by the first three chapters of this book (mixers, pro-

gressive circles and contras). These are dances that generally have a set sequence and are not dependent for their success on the caller's improvisations. A square can, of course, be danced as a set sequence by tacking on a set intro, break and ending, but this takes away much of the fun of dancing squares. Similarly, it is virtually impossible to dance the big set unless someone takes the responsibility for deciding which figures to do.

Arrange for partner changes

One important characteristic of traditional style square and contra dancing as it is practiced in most places today is the opportunity to dance with a number of different partners. At many dances, the unspoken custom is to change partners after every dance. If you are teaching a class or arranging dances for groups who have not danced much before, a good way to achieve partner changes without putting the burden on the individual dancers is to use mixers several times in the course of the session. At the conclusion of the mixer, you can ask the dancers to keep the partners they end up with for the next dance.

There are several reasons for emphasizing partner changes. Traditional dancing should be a welcoming environment for everyone, so one reason for partner-changing practices is to make dancers who come alone feel as welcome as those who come with a partner. In a class situation, mixers prevent the better dancers from sticking together, leaving the slower learners to fend for themselves. In the long run, mixing them up will help the whole group to become better dancers, encourage the students to take an active role in helping each other, and avoid too much polarization of skill levels or social groupings. Of course, you should make sure that free choice of partners is also possible for some dances, so that those who have brought or found a favorite partner can dance with him or her.

TEACHING TECHNIQUES

You also have to teach

As a traditional style caller, you not only are responsible for programming a session, calling the dances and choosing the music, but also for explaining the dances to the participants. The level of teaching required will vary, depending on the situation. If you are calling for a regular weekly dance, most of the people present will probably already know the basics of square and contra dancing, and you will mainly be walking them through the dances you have chosen. If, on the other hand, you are conducting a one night stand or teaching dance in a school, camp or recreation program, you will also have to teach the basic concepts to your dancers. People enjoy dancing much more than they do learning a dance, so as little time as possible should be spent on teaching and walk-throughs. Here are a few tips for making your teaching as effective and painless as possible.

Know your stuff

First of all, know the dances thoroughly before you attempt to teach or call them. You should have analyzed each dance to determine any potential pitfalls such as difficult points of transition, unusual movements, tight timing, or other features that may require special attention on the part of the dancers. Admittedly, this can be difficult to do if you are learning the dance from a book and have never had the opportunity to dance it. Pay attention to any comments or warnings given by the author, and keep your eyes open for problems as you teach the dance the first time. You may even want to make a quick note of difficulties that occur, so that you can avoid them the next time.

If you have trouble getting an overview of a given dance from the written description, it often is helpful to make a set of dolls, tokens or cards that represent the dancers, and push them around the table top one movement at a time to see where everyone winds up. It goes without saying that you also must have a clear understanding of each basic movement used in the dance and where the dancers will be after it has been executed. If you are lucky enough to have friends or family that will help you, you can get some of them together and try out any dances you are unsure of, before going off to teach them to a "real" group.

What to say

When working out verbal explanations, try to find words that will express what you mean unambiguously (this may take some trial and error). It can be an advantage to find more than one way of explaining what you want, in case the first way fails. But you also want to keep your talking to a minimum; ideally, the first explanation should be all you need.

Note that simply uttering the calls of the dance is not the same as explaining or teaching it, unless the dance is so easy that every call is self-explanatory. (If it is, you are probably working with beginners, who will not know what the calls mean until you tell them!) Not only will you need to teach any movements that are new to the dancers, you will also want to add words of orientation, such as:

with your partner / corner / opposite / neighbor
face your partner / corner / opposite / neighbor
look for your partner / corner / neighbor
across the set
up and down the set
in your own line / circle
with the same couple / a new couple
halfway around
exactly once around
all the way around and then halfway more
until you meet on the opposite side / at home
end with the ladies / gents / actives facing in / out / up / down / across
and so forth.

Try to use normal language in explaining a dance. But if you will be using special terms to call the dance once the music starts, you should mention them during the walk-through so the dancers will know what they mean.

As you prepare to teach, analyze whether any of the figures that are new to the dancers can be broken down into component parts that they already know. For instance, right and left through can be said to be made up of pass through followed by a courtesy turn, which is also the second half of ladies chain. If the dancers already know ladies chain and pass through, you can exploit this to teach them right and left through. Similarly, allemandes or circles that go once and a half around or three-quarters around can be broken down to "once around—and then halfway more" or "halfway around—and then a quarter more."

How to say it

As you teach, you should be in control of the dancers. Speak slowly and clearly. Try to keep the dancers' attention by being authoritative (but not bossy or condescending), and be prepared to use expressions like "stop," "go," "now," "freeze right there," "watch out for this next part," "here it comes," and so on.

Never give the dancers instructions for a whole series of movements before having them execute any of them. Explain the first thing you want them to do, and check that everyone has done it before giving them the next command. Wait to see that they have performed that, then give the next command, and so on. In classes or at one night stands, I generally go through the dance in this manner first, hopefully giving everyone a chance to understand what they are being asked to do. If there are problems, go through the dance again (if the problems are serious, you may have to send them back to their original positions and start all over again). Watch carefully to see if you can spot any mistakes that are putting people out of position.

Before calling the dance to the music, I usually run through it again up to tempo, giving the entire stream of calls in the natural rhythm in which they will have to be danced. This is important because it gives the dancers a chance to experience the transitions from one movement to another, which are suppressed during the first, stop-and-go walk-through. You may discover some trouble spots at this point that were not apparent the first time around. To fill in the beats between the calls, you can "doodle" some rhythmic sounds, so the dancers get an idea of the tempo and rhythm they will be dancing to. Remember that the transition from the last movement of a dance sequence to the first movement of the next sequence also sometimes requires attention.

A demonstration is worth a thousand words

In some cases, a movement or sequence can be explained much more quickly and easily by showing it than by verbalizing it. Try to develop a sense for when to go out on the floor and simply show the dancers what you want them to do.

One trick I sometimes use if a particular person or group is having trouble grasping a movement is to use them to help me demonstrate it. The idea of this is not to embarrass the dancers in question, but to get a chance to help them dance the sequence correctly. At other times, you will want to use a demonstration group that you know can do the movements. Use your judgment.

If the room is crowded, ask the people standing closest to the demonstration group to kneel down, so that others standing farther away also can see.

The pros and cons of linearity

Dancers, especially beginners, tend to want to go through a dance from beginning to end, including every movement in the correct sequence, even if it brings them right back where they started (for example, a promenade all the way around the set at the end of a square dance figure). Departing from this principle *can* cause confusion, because the kinetic feedback from the walk-through stays with the dancers when the music starts. But even with beginners, if the dance includes a movement or sequence that requires extensive teaching, it can be an advantage to teach that part first. Then, when you go through the entire dance and come to the difficult part, you will be able to have them do "that part we were practicing just before" without losing too much momentum. With experienced dancers, the tricky sequence may be the only part you need to teach, but only if the rest of the dance is so standardized that you are sure they will be able to execute it without a walk-through. Generally, it is best to do at least one quick walk-through of the whole dance before starting.

Style

In the process of teaching a dance, you have the opportunity—if appropriate—to mention style details that will help the dancers give and get maximum pleasure from their activity. These include items such as handholds, giving weight, which way to turn, timing, etc. Here again, what to do depends on the type of group and occasion. You have the most leeway in a class situation, where you may as well teach correct styling from the outset to develop good habits. However, beware of harping on style details to the extent that they become the main goal of your time together and preempt the dancing. Do a little at a time, and be prepared to have to repeat things more than once before all the dancers catch on to them.

At one night stands, it is very important to maintain a relaxed and fun atmosphere, and since the participants may not be dancing again in the near future, it is not necessary to spend an inordinate amount of effort getting them to do everything exactly correctly. You will probably want to restrict your style teaching to items that either will appreciably increase their pleasure in dancing or will reduce the likelihood of anyone getting hurt.

It is never their fault

Never scold the dancers for having trouble with a dance. If they do not understand it or cannot do what you ask, you have either chosen a dance that is above their capabilities or failed to adequately communicate what it is you want them to do. What you can and should do is give the dancers positive feedback so they will know what they are doing right and feel confident and successful. Remember: if the dancers succeed, you have succeeded.

"...The Americans are acknowledged to excel in social dancing, and to have been leading the style for some years past. In no other country is it so generally cultivated as in this."

—from William B. DeGarmo, *The Dance of Society: A Critical Analysis of all the Standard Quadrilles, Round Dances, 102 Figures of Le Cotillon, etc. (New York, 1879).*

...Too much of a good thing

Square and contra dances should not be done stiffly. There is room for individual expression within the traditional style. Just keep two important things in mind: not to get in the way of other dancers and always to be back in place in time for the next call. If dancers do not uphold these two ground rules, the caller or instructor is within rights to call it to their attention.

The converse of this principle is that ornamental variations such as twirls do not need to be standardized and introduced as an integral part of the dance. They will come quickly enough as a spontaneous expression from the dancers, and should only be used when they do not interfere with the following movements and will not confuse the person you are dancing with.

Mixers: An Easy Start

In any teaching situation, it is a good idea to start with the most elementary things and work your way up to the more complicated ones. If you are going to teach square and contra dancing you will need a good repertory of easy material that is useful for working with beginners and at one night stands, as well as for warming up with more experienced dancers. There are also times when it is a welcome change of pace to put a relatively easy dance in between more challenging material.

Why mixers?

Many of the best easy American dances are mixers, or dances where one gets a new partner for every repetition of the dance sequence. Mixers have a number of advantages. The dancers come in contact with many different partners, become acquainted with the idea of changing partners (a common occurrence in square dancing), and at the same time, the simple dance gains interest by being done with a different partner each time through.

Mixers and other easy dances can be used to teach most of the movements needed for the more complicated contras and squares—and the dancers will have a good time while they are learning. It is often possible to use simple dances to teach one or two basic movements at a time and let the dancers master them before moving on.

Finally, these dances are also a good starting place for the aspiring caller, since they are repetitive and fairly simply structured. So even if you make a mistake, there is a limit to how much damage you can do.

The dances and how to use them

This chapter contains a number of mixers that have been used with success at classes, one night stands, and regular open dances. Which of the dances you should choose in a given situation depends, among other things, on:

- the participants' level of experience
- the participants' level of interest (did they come specifically to dance, or is the dancing just an element of entertainment at a party?)
- the participants' age level
- the rest of the program (a mixer may be used to introduce a movement that you will need for a later dance)

People enjoy themselves most if they can learn the dances with a minimum of instruction, so try to set the level of difficulty accordingly. If you are an experienced dancer yourself, some of the dances in this chapter may seem a little tame. Experience shows that, in the right circumstances, people enjoy them anyway.

How long should the mixer be continued? The rule of thumb should be to keep the dance going until it is clear that the whole group has caught on to the pattern—and then a little more. Do not let the dance go on so long that it begins to be boring. If you are using recorded music and the cut is too long, turn the volume down gradually towards the end of the round you want to be the last, and end off the dance by saying "And thank your partner" or something to that effect.

Generally speaking, a mixer can go on longer if the group is large, so that one gets a new partner for each round, than if it is small, so people are coming back to their original partners over and over again. Ten to fifteen times through may be appropriate for a dance with a short sequence, and seven to ten times through for a longer dance.

Programming

When you plan your program, take into account that some dances resemble each other more than others. If you want to use several mixers in the course of an evening or season, try to pick ones that are sufficiently distinct from one another.

For private parties and similar occasions where you are working with non-dancers and want to keep teaching to a minimum, dances like EZ Mixer, Little Mixer, Circassian Circle and Oh, Susannah can be quite useful.

MIXER

One big circle of couples facing in line of direction

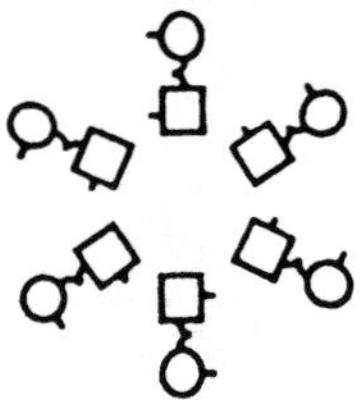

EZ MIXER

MUSIC	CALLS	MUSIC	DESCRIPTION
Intro:	Everyone ready? Promenade		
A1 1-4	__ __ And back away	**A1** 1-4	Take your partner by the hand and go forward 4 steps in the line of direction.
5-8	Look to the right and dosido	5-8	Turn to face your partner so the gent's back is to the center of the circle, and walk backwards 4 small steps, away from each other.
9-12	__ __ __ __	9-16	Look diagonally to the right and do a dosido with a new partner (go past each other, passing right shoulders, sideways back to back and then backwards to place, passing left shoulders) (8 steps). At the end of the dosido, take your new partner by the hand, ready to promenade again.
13-16	Take that gal and promenade		

A2: Repeat A1
B1: Repeat A1
B2: Repeat A1

Comments

EZ Mixer is a simple little dance of unknown origin that is useful at one night stands, private parties, and the like.

The dance is very easy, but it moves right along. Once through the dance corresponds to only 16 steps, so the sequence is danced four times in the course of a typical AABB dance tune. If you suspect that the dancers will have trouble finding the person diagonally to their right for the dosido, have them dosido their partners at first, and then teach them to look to the right.

If you have a more experienced group or want to give your students a little more challenge, you can experiment with calling something else instead of the dosido. This must be a movement that can be done in 8 counts and that flows well in context—for example, allemande right, right elbow swing or a regular buzz step swing.

Music

Virtually any tune can be used, as long as it has no irregularities (extra beats or missing beats). The tune chosen should be lively and have a good rhythmic pulse. For example: "Liberty" from *Square Dance Tonight Vol. 3* or "Ragtime Annie" from *Dancing Bow and Singing Strings*. **Tempo:** optimally about 126–130. The dance becomes trivial if done too slowly, but the tempo should be adjusted to the situation—beginners may need a slower tempo at first.

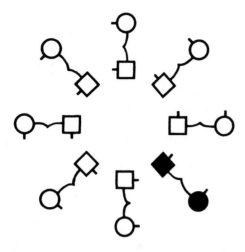

1. Starting formation for EZ Mixer.

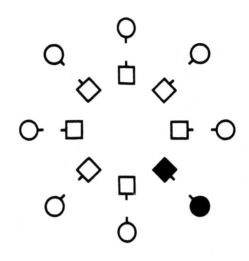

2. "Back away."

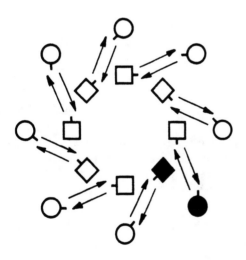

3. "Look to the right and dosido."

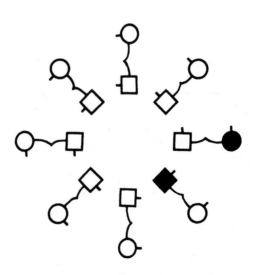

4. Promenade with a new partner.

MIXER
One big circle of couples
facing in line of direction

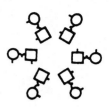

COME, MY LOVE

MUSIC	CALLS		MUSIC	DESCRIPTION

Intro: ＿ ＿ Promenade

A1 1-4 ＿ ＿ ＿ ＿

5-8 ＿ ＿ ＿ ＿

9-12 ＿ ＿ ＿ ＿

13-16 ＿ ＿ Gents turn back

A1 1-16 Take promenade position with your partner and walk forward 16 steps in the line of direction.

A2 1-4 ＿ ＿ ＿ ＿

5-8 Two-hand swing with the gal you meet

9-12 ＿ ＿ ＿ ＿

13-16 ＿ ＿ And promenade

A2 1-8 Drop hands with your partner. The gents turn around and walk in reverse line of direction while the ladies keep going forward (8 steps).

9-16 Give both hands to the nearest dancer in the opposite circle, and go once or twice around each other (clockwise) in 8 steps. Keep this person as your new partner.

B1: Repeat A1

B2: Repeat A2

Comments

Come, My Love is another easy mixer, adapted from a play party game. It can be used with both adults and children and is well suited as a warm-up dance or fun relaxer.

When the time comes to find a new partner in A2 9-16, there will almost always be someone left out, but that's just part of the fun. Don't panic — just go to the middle of the circle, where there will be someone else in the same predicament that you can team up with. By the time the promenade is over, everyone should be back in the dance.

The caller can add variation to the dance by occasionally saying "*ladies* turn back" instead of "gents turn back." Once the dancers have caught on to the sequence, you can also cut each movement to half as many beats: eight for the promenade, four for "gents turn back" and four for "two-hand swing."

Music

A lively tune with a good pulse works well for this dance. Try "Flop-Eared Mule" from *Square Dance Tonight Vol. 3* or "Polkas" from *New England Country Dance Music* with the Green Mountain Volunteers. **Tempo:** about 122–128, depending on how experienced the dancers are. If you have a live band or a record or tape player with variable speed control, you can start the dance off slowly and gradually speed it up.

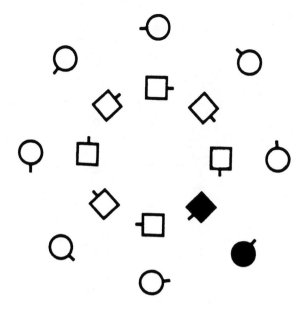

"Gents turn back."

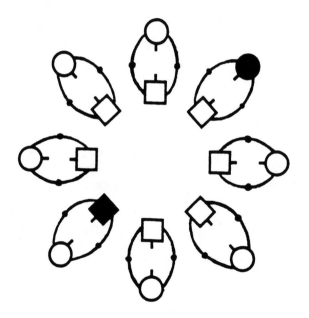

"Two-hand swing with the gal you meet."

MIXER
One big circle of couples,
everyone facing the center

LITTLE MIXER

MUSIC	CALLS		MUSIC	DESCRIPTION
Intro:	__ __ Circle left			
A1 1-4	__ __ __ __		**A1** 1-8	Join hands in a circle and go to the left 8 steps.
5-8	__ __ Circle right			
9-12	__ __ __ __		9-16	Still in your circle, go 8 steps back, to the right.
13-16	Everyone into the center and back			
A2 1-4	__ __ __ __		**A2** 1-4	Go 4 steps in towards the center...
5-8	__ __ Corner swing		5-8	...and 4 steps backwards to place.
9-12	__ __ __ __		9-16	Take social dance position with your corner (i.e., the lady on your left if you are a gent) and do a buzz step swing (8 counts). End with each lady on her new partner's right, ready to circle left.
13-16	__ Join hands and circle left			

B1: Repeat A1

B2: Repeat A2

Comments

I worked out this simple sequence one night at a private party when we needed something very easy, and it has proved useful ever since.

Instead of using a buzz step swing in A2 9-16, the dance can be additionally simplified either by using a walk-around swing in social dance position, in which everyone starts on the right foot and simply walks forward instead of doing the buzz step, or by dropping the social dance position entirely and using a right elbow swing. Just make sure that the lady ends up to the right of the gent she swung.

Music

Almost any tune is all right, provided it has no irregularities. For example, "Soldier's Joy" from *Square Dance Tonight Vol. 1* or the medley called

"Slow Contra Tempo" on *Dances from Appalachia 2*. **Tempo:** depends on the situation, but not too slow. About 126.

Swing.

MIXER
One big circle of couples,
everyone facing the center

OH, SUSANNAH

MUSIC		CALLS
Intro:		Ladies to the center and back
A1	1-4	— — — —
	5-8	Now the gents go forward and back
	9-12	— — — —
	13-16	— Grand right and left
A2	1-4	— — — —
	5-8	— — — —
	9-12	— — — —
	13-16	— — Promenade
B1	1-4	— — — —
	5-8	— — — —
	9-12	— — — —
	13-16	All the ladies forward and back

MUSIC		DESCRIPTION
A1	1-8	All the ladies go 4 steps in towards the center and 4 steps backwards to place.
	9-16	All the gents go forward and back (8 steps).
A2	1-16	Face your partner (gents face line of direction, ladies reverse line of direction) and give right hands. Pass by, letting go of your partner, and give your left hand to the next person you meet. Keep going forward, alternately giving right and left hands (16 steps).
B1	1-16	Take promenade position with the next person you meet and walk forward 16 steps in the line of direction.

Comments

There are several dances called Oh, Susannah; this one is still another play party adaptation, and it works very nicely to the tune of the same name. Note that the dance has only 48 counts, corresponding to two verses and a chorus of the song if you feel like singing it. If you are using recorded music, you will either want to find a tune that is played AAB (or ABB or ABC), extend the dance with another 16 counts (for example, dosido corner and dosido partner before starting the grand right and left) or just let the dance start over "too soon." If you want to avoid the mild chaos that can result when not everyone immediately finds a new partner after the grand right and left, have the dancers count their partners as number one and do the promenade with the seventh person that they meet.

Music

I sometimes use the tune "Oh, Susannah" for this dance, but it can also be done to other tunes, for example, "Barlow Knife" from *Square Dance Tonight Vol. 1* or "Sally Ann" from *Dancing Bow and Singing Strings*, both of which are 48-count tunes. **Tempo:** This dance should be done at a relaxed tempo, say 120-126.

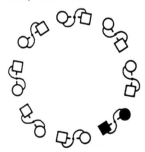

Starting position for the grand right and left.

MIXER
One big circle of couples
facing in line of direction

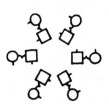

BROWN-EYED MARY

MUSIC	CALLS	MUSIC	DESCRIPTION
Intro:	__ __ Promenade		

	MUSIC	CALLS		MUSIC	DESCRIPTION
A1	**1-4**	__ __ __ __	**A1**	**1-16**	Take promenade position with your partner and walk forward 16 steps in the line of direction.
	5-8	__ __ __ __			
	9-12	__ __ __ __			
	13-16	Turn your partner by the right hand 'round			
A2	**1-4**	Corner by the left as she comes 'round	**A2**	**1-4**	Take a right-hand pigeon wing grip with your partner and go halfway around each other so the lady ends up facing in the line of direction and the gent in the reverse line of direction (4 steps).
	5-8	Partner again with the right hand 'round		**5-8**	Let go of your partner and take a left-hand pigeon wing grip with your corner (for the gent, that is the lady who originally was *behind* him, for the lady, it is the gent who originally was *in front of* her). Go halfway around each other so you are facing your partners again (4 steps).
	9-12	Back to your corner, promenade		**9-12**	Let go of your corner, take a right-hand pigeon wing grip with your partner, and go halfway around each other so you are facing your corners (4 steps).
	13-16	__ __ __ __		**13-16**	Let go of your partner, go back to your corner, and take promenade position, ready to go forward as a couple in the line of direction (4 steps).

B1: Repeat A1
B2: Repeat A2

Comments

Like Come, My Love, this dance is actually a play party game. I usually call it about as described above; you can also say "allemande right your partner" and "allemande left your corner" for the hand turns in A2 if you want to accustom the dancers to that terminology. The dance is simple, but the hand turns (which are great practice once you've taught the dancers to give weight) require a careful walk-through.

The easiest way is to have the dancers form a circle with everyone facing the center. Make sure all the ladies are on their partners' right. Have everyone notice who their corner is, then let them change to promenade position and look for their corners again. Now you can walk through the allemandes, taking it slowly until everyone understands what to do. Once the dancers get the hang of the sequence, I often shorten the promenades to eight, or even four, counts making the dance more challenging and a little less predictable.

Music

I like to use a southern fiddle tune for this dance, for example, "Cotton Baggin'" from *Square Dance Tonight Vol. 2* or "Leather Britches" from *Dancing Bow and Singing Strings*. **Tempo:** about 120 for beginners, but more experienced dancers will appreciate a faster tempo.

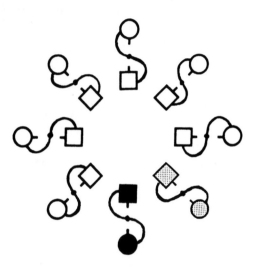

"Turn your partner by the right hand 'round."

"Corner by the left as she comes 'round."

Pigeon wing grip.

MIXER
One big circle of couples,
everyone facing the center

CIRCASSIAN CIRCLE

MUSIC		CALLS
Intro:		Everyone go forward and back
A1	1-4	_ _ _ _
	5-8	_ _ Now do it again
	9-12	_ _ _ _
	13-16	Ladies only forward and back
A2	1-4	_ _ _ _
	5-8	Now the gents go forward and
	9-12	Turn to the left and swing the next
	13-16	_ _ _ _
B1	1-4	_ _ _ _
	5-8	_ _ _ _
	9-12	_ _ _ _
	13-16	_ _ And promenade
B2	1-4	_ _ _ _
	5-8	_ _ _ _
	9-12	_ _ _ _
	13-16	All join hands, go forward and back

MUSIC		DESCRIPTION
A1	1-8	All join hands and go 4 steps in towards the center and 4 steps backwards to place.
	9-16	Go forward and back again (8 steps).
A2	1-8	All the ladies go 4 steps in towards the center and 4 steps backwards to place.
	9-16	Each gent goes 4 steps in towards the center, turns to his left and goes 4 steps forward towards his corner (the lady who was on his left in the circle).
B1	1-16	Take social dance position with your corner and swing (see Comments) (16 counts).
B2	1-16	Take promenade position with the person you swung and walk 16 steps forward in the line of direction.

Comments

Circassian Circle is actually an English dance. The version collected in Northumberland consisted of two parts: a progressive circle part and a big circle part (mixer). The dance described here is the second part, which has found favor as a simple mixer on both sides of the Atlantic. I have heard that in the old days, Circassian Circle was often done as the last dance of the evening, without the partner change (i.e., the gent returns to his partner for the swing, instead of taking his corner).

Some dancers like Circassian Circle because it gives them a chance for a good, long swing with a lot of different partners. But for the same reason, I would think twice before using this dance with a group that had not learned how to do the buzz step or, even more important, how to give weight when swinging.

If you want to use the dance anyway, there are a few ways it can be adapted. The dancers can take social dance position but do a walk around swing, with everyone starting on the right foot. This method actually can produce a swing that is nearly as satisfying as a buzz step swing, as long as the dancers give weight, and it is a lot easier to do. Another possibility, especially where children are involved, is to use a right elbow swing. Or you can have them give each other both hands and walk or skip clockwise around each other.

The swing can also be shortened by using only eight counts for the swing and eight for the promenade. In this case, the dance will start over on the B2 music (next time on the B1 music, next time on the A2 music, etc.). Not the ideal situation, but acceptable in a pinch.

Music

Almost anything is okay — reel or jig, as long as it is regular. If you want to shorten the sequence as suggested above, it may be a good idea to either find a tune with three parts (AAB, ABB or ABC) or use an old time southern tune, where the melody is not as obvious as in a New England tune. Some possibilities: "Barlow Knife" from *Square Dance Tonight Vol. 1* (AAB) or "Colored Aristocracy" from *Kitchen Junket* (AABB). **Tempo:** about 126.

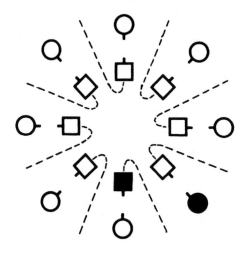

"Gents go forward, turn to the left..."

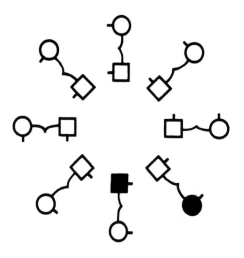

Promenade with a new partner.

MIXER
One big circle of couples
facing in line of direction

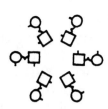

SANDY LAND

MUSIC	CALLS		MUSIC	DESCRIPTION

Intro: Everybody promenade

A1 **1-4** __ __ __ __

  5-8 Into the center, go forward and back

  9-12 __ __ __ __

  13-16 __ Grand right and left

A2 **1-4** __ __ __ __

  5-8 __ __ __ __

  9-12 __ __ __ __

  13-16 Left elbow swing with the next you meet

B1 **1-4** __ __ __ __

  5-8 On to the next with the right elbow

  9-12 __ __ __ __

  13-16 Now the next with the left elbow

B2 **1-4** __ __ __ __

  5-8 Now one more with the right elbow

  9-12 __ __ __ __

  13-16 Keep that one and promenade

A1 **1-8** Take promenade position with your partner and go 8 steps forward in the line of direction.

  9-16 Face the center, join hands in a circle, and go 4 steps in towards the center and 4 steps backwards to place.

A2 **1-16** Drop hands and face your partner (gents will be facing in the line of direction, ladies in reverse line of direction). Give your right hand to your partner, go past each other, dropping hands, give your left hand to the next person you meet, pass by, and keep going forward, alternately giving right and left hands (16 steps). You will pass five people, including your partner.

B1 **1-16** Do a left elbow swing with the sixth dancer
+B2 **1-16** you meet, going *all the way* around each other with 8 steps. Pass each other by the left shoulder and continue in the same direction as before (gents in line of direction, ladies in reverse line of direction) to the next dancer. Do a right elbow swing all the way around this person and go on to the next. Do a left elbow swing and go on to the next. Do a right elbow swing and end in promenade position, ready to start the dance again (32 steps in all).

Comments

Sandy Land is my adapted version of still another old play party game. If everyone does not get a partner for the promenade, the "lost" dancers can find a new partner most easily by going to the center of the circle, where at least one other person should be waiting.

Keep an eye on the dancers during the grand right and left. If they move faster than expected, it may work out better to let them pass one more person and start B1 with a *right* elbow swing to the next, then left, right and left.

Music

Preferably an energetic southern style fiddle tune, such as "Hawks and Eagles" from *Square* *Dance Tonight Vol. 2* or the medley called "Fast Clog Tempo" on *Dances from Appalachia 2*.
Tempo: about 126.

Right elbow swing.

MIXER
One big circle of couples,
everyone facing the center

CAMMY'S LA BASTRINGUE

MUSIC		CALLS	MUSIC		DESCRIPTION
Intro:		__ __ Into the middle			
A1	1-4	__ __ __ And back	**A1**	1-8	All join hands and go 4 steps in towards the center and 4 steps backwards to place.
	5-8	__ __ Now do it again			
	9-12	__ __ __ __		9-16	Go forward and back again (8 steps).
	13-16	__ __ And circle left			
A2	1-4	__ __ __ __	**A2**	1-8	Circle to the left 8 steps.
	5-8	The other way back, circle right			
	9-12	__ __ __ __		9-16	Circle to the right 8 steps.
	13-16	Allemande left your corners all			
B1	1-4	__ __ __ __	**B1**	1-8	Take a left-hand pigeon wing grip with your corner (the lady on the gent's left or the gent on the lady's right), and go once around each other, until each dancer is facing his or her partner (8 steps).
	5-8	Back to your partner: dosido			
	9-12	__ __ __ __		9-16	Do a dosido with your partner (go past each other, passing right shoulders, sideways back to back and then backwards to place, passing left shoulders) (8 steps).
	13-16	__ __ Corner swing			
B2	1-4	__ __ __ __	**B2**	1-8	Take social dance position with your corner and swing 8 counts.
	5-8	__ __ And promenade			
	9-12	__ __ __ __		9-16	Take promenade position with the person you swung, and walk forward 8 steps in the line of direction.
	13-16	One big circle, into the middle			

Comments

La Bastringue is a well-known French-Canadian mixer that is also popular among contra dancers in the United States. I learned this version early in my calling career from Izzy Young, of Stockholm, who had gotten it from Boston musician and caller Cammy Kaynor during one of Cammy's visits to Sweden. Not until later did I realize that several elements had been added or changed in relation to the original dance. But in the meantime, I had grown to appreciate the version presented here. I've found it quite useful with beginners, because it introduces a large number of basic figures, yet is still simple enough to be mastered quickly.

In this dance, like others in which the dancers

have to change formation from a promenade to one big circle, it is a help if the caller reminds them of it in good time (see the final call). Also note that the allemande left is intended to take a full eight counts. This is actually a bit on the high side considering the flow of the dance, and once the dancers get going, they will probably finish it early. Just call the corner swing a couple of beats earlier than shown here, and let them swing until it is time to promenade.

The original version of the dance is as follows: All forward and back twice (8 + 8), circle left and circle right, using a two-step (8 + 8), drop hands with partners and each lady moves forward towards the center of the circle and turns clockwise under her corner's raised left arm (8), swing corner (8), promenade (gent's right arm around his new partner's waist, her left hand on his right shoulder) (16).

Music

Even though the dance has been modified, I still like to use the original tune, "La Bastringue." One good recording of it is on Yankee Ingenuity's album *Heatin' Up the Hall*, in a spirited medley with "Saut de Lapin," "Beaulieu," and "Pointe au Pic." Or for variety, try "Cape Breton Symphony's Welcome to Shetland" from *Square Dance Tonight Vol. 3*. **Tempo:** About 126, possibly a little slower for beginners.

It all depends on your point of view

According to the folk dance magazine *Northern Junket*, an old saying holds that you should choose your wife not at a dance, but in the harvest field.
On the other hand, the same magazine reports that "dancing is a wonderful training for girls: it is the first way you learn to guess what a man is going to do before he does it!"

—*Northern Junket,* February 1968, and November 1967.

Used with the permission of Cammy Kaynor.

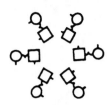

MIXER
One big circle of couples
facing in line of direction

GAY GORDONS MIXER

MUSIC		CALLS	MUSIC		DESCRIPTION
Intro:		_ _ Forward <u>all</u>			
A1	1-4	_ _ Backwards <u>now</u>	**A1**	1-4	Take Varsouvienne position with your partner (see illustration) and walk foward 4 steps in the line of direction, both starting on the right foot.
	5-8	_ _ Forward <u>again</u>		5-8	Without dropping hands, turn individually to the right and continue 4 steps *backwards*, still in the line of direction.
	9-12	_ _ Backwards <u>now</u>		9-12	Still without dropping hands, walk *forward* 4 steps, i.e., in the reverse line of direction.
	13-16	_ _ Balance <u>in</u>		13-16	Without dropping hands, turn individually to the left and continue 4 steps *backwards*, still in the reverse line of direction.
A2	1-4	_ _ Ladies cross <u>over</u>	**A2**	1-4	Join inside hands (gent's right, lady's left) with your partner. Balance, going toward each other with a pas-de-basque step, gent starting on his right foot, lady on her left, and then away from each other with a pas-de-basque step (gent left, lady right) (4 counts in all).
	5-8	_ _ Balance <u>again</u>		5-8	With 3 light steps (lady: left, right, left; gent: right, left, right), the lady rolls across in front of the gent, and the gent moves to his own right, so the lady ends up on the gent's left side. At the same time, change the handhold to gent's left, lady's right (4 counts in all, no movement on count 4).
	9-12	_ _ <u>U</u>nder you <u>go</u>		9-12	Balance toward each other with a pas-de-basque step, gent starting on his left foot, lady on her right, and then away from each other with a pas-de-basque step (gent right, lady left) (4 counts in all).
	13-16	_ _ Forward <u>all</u>		13-16	With 4 light steps (right, left, right, left), the lady turns under the gent's upraised left arm and takes Varsouvienne position with the gent behind him.

B1: Repeat A1
B2: Repeat A2

Comments

The Gay Gordons is a popular dance in Scotland, where it comes from. In the original dance, instead of balance, cross over, balance and under the arch in A2, couples do four two-steps forward with the lady turning under the gent's right arm, and then four turning polka steps in closed dance position. A mixer similar to the one presented here—presumably inspired by The Gay Gordons—was devised some years ago by Doc and Winnie Alumbaugh of California. Called the All-American Promenade, it can be found in Harris, Pittman and Waller's standard college text, *Dance a While*. One of the differences in their veresion is that couples use a simple inside handhold in A1 instead of Varsouvienne position, but I prefer the latter because it is more fun and closer to the original dance. A little demonstration of how to turn without dropping hands is usually sufficient (much better than trying to explain in words!), and it makes the dance more interesting.

With this dance, I usually restrict my "calling" to short cues as indicated above, and stop calling as soon as the dancers know the pattern.

Music

The Gay Gordons is usually danced either to the original tune of the same name or to other march-like Scottish tunes such as "Marching Down to Fyvie" or "The Meeting of the Waters." But tunes in New England or Canadian style can also be used, such as "Shelburne Reel" from *Maritime Dance Party*. One good recording using the original tune is found on the album *New England Chestnuts 2*. **Tempo:** relaxed, about 120.

Varsouvienne position.

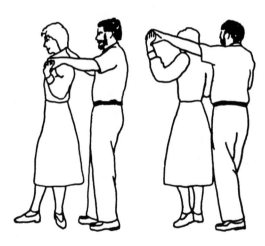

Turn individually, without dropping hands.

The lady turns under the gent's left arm and goes to the gent behind him.

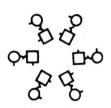

MIXER
One big circle of couples
facing in line of direction

THE DIGGING DUTCHMAN

MUSIC		CALLS
Intro:		_ _ Prom<u>e</u>nade

A1	**1-4**	_ _ _ _
	5-8	G<u>ents</u> go f<u>orward</u>, <u>on</u> to the <u>next</u>
	9-12	_ _ _ _
	13-16	L<u>adies</u> turn <u>under</u>, dosi<u>do</u>

A2	**1-4**	_ _ _ _
	5-8	L<u>ook</u> to the <u>left</u>, <u>allemande left</u>
	9-12	_ _ _ _
	13-16	B<u>ack</u> to your p<u>artner</u>: <u>see-saw</u>

B1	**1-4**	_ _ _ _
	5-8	L<u>ook</u> to the <u>right</u>, <u>allemande right</u>
	9-12	_ _ _ _
	13-16	B<u>ack</u> to your p<u>artner</u>: <u>balance there</u>

| **B2** | **1-4** | _ _ _ And <u>swing</u> |

MUSIC		DESCRIPTION
A1	**1-8**	Take skater's position with your partner and promenade 8 steps forward in the line of direction.
	9-14	Drop hands and continue promenading 6 more steps while each gent moves up to the next lady, this time taking Varsouvienne position.
	15-16	Drop left hands. The lady turns to her left under the raised right arms and the two dancers move apart from each other so that they are standing with the gent's back to the center, lady facing him, with their right arms outstretched (2 steps).

| **A2** | **1-8** | Do a dosido with your partner (go past each other, passing right shoulders, sideways back to back and then backwards to place, passing left shoulders) (8 steps). |
| | **9-16** | Look diagonally to the left and take a left-hand pigeon wing grip with that dancer. Walk all the way around each other with 8 steps and come back to your partner. |

| **B1** | **1-8** | Do a *left*-shoulder dosido (called a "seesaw") with your partner (8 steps). |
| | **9-16** | Look diagonally to the right and take a right-hand pigeon wing grip with that dancer. Walk all the way around each other with 8 steps and come back to your partner. |

| **B2** | **1-4** | Give your right hand to your partner and balance toward and away from each other (see Glossary), starting on the right foot (4 counts). |

5-8	_ _ _ _
9-12	_ _ _ _
13-16	Everybody promenade

5-16   Take social dance position with your partner and do a buzz step swing (12 counts).

Comments

The Digging Dutchman was written by Dick Atlee and Jane Farwell of Folklore Village Farm in Wisconsin, based on Englishman Dick Witt's dance, Circle Mixer. As mixers go, it is relatively complicated, but its flow is superb, and it is a good idea to have some mixers on hand for more experienced dancers.

The transition from promenade to dosido in A1 15-16 is a finesse. By first stepping apart, the dancers can give a slight pull into the following dosido. Experienced dancers will appreciate this, while beginners may not catch it. If the whole group is less experienced, you may want to drop it and just have them release hands and turn to face. You can even have them do both parts of the promenade in skater's position. (As a matter of fact, the original dance description specifies Varsouvienne position both times, but in practice, we have found it more comfortable as described here.)

If you use this dance with less experienced dancers, be prepared for a thorough walk-through. What people find confusing is the constant changing of partners in the middle part of the dance. It may help to point out to them that they only leave their partners of that round temporarily. Despite appearances, the actual partner change is quite straightforward, coming when the gents move up during the promenade.

I learned this dance serendipitously—it was on the flip side of a record we had bought for another dance, and looked interesting, so I tried it. It has been a useful part of my repertory ever since.

Music

Douglas Clark composed a catchy jig for this dance with the same title, which is found on the record *Folklore Village Farm* FLV-103. Other tunes can, however, also be used, preferably a jig such as "Jig de Philippe Bruneau" from *Square Dance Tonight Vol. 2*. **Tempo:** FLV-103 is quite fast, about 138 beats per minute, which is on the high side. I recommend turning down the speed to a maximum of 128, even slower for beginners, or, if necessary, choosing a recording at a slower tempo.

With right hands still joined, the lady turns out under the gent's arm just before doing the dosido.

Previously published in *The Folklore Village Saturday Night Book* (1981). Used with the permission of Douglas Miller, Folklore Village Farm.

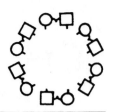

MIXER
One big circle of couples,
everyone facing the center

THE NEW HOOSIER

MUSIC	CALLS	MUSIC	DESCRIPTION

Intro: Everyone go forward and back

A1 **1-4** _ _ _ _

A1 **1-8** Join hands and go 4 steps forward into the center and 4 steps backwards to place.

5-8 _ _ And do it again

9-12 _ _ _ _

9-16 Go forward and back again (8 steps).

13-16 Allemande right your partners all

A2 **1-4** Left hand to your corner, balance there

A2 **1-4** Take a right-hand pigeon wing grip with your partner and walk once around each other with 4 steps.

5-8 Allemande left, go halfway 'round

5-8 *Keeping hands joined with your partner,* give your left hand to your corner to form one big circle of dancers, with all the gents facing the center and the ladies facing the outside. In this formation, balance by doing a pas-de-basque step forward, starting on the right foot, and then a pas-de-basque backward, starting on the left (4 counts).

9-12 Right hand to the next and balance again

9-12 Drop right hands, turn *halfway* around by the left hand in 4 steps, and give your right hand to the next dancer. You now have one big circle again, but with the ladies facing in and the gents out.

13-16 With the one on your right hand dosido

13-16 Balance again as in A2 5-8 (4 counts).

B1 **1-4** _ _ _ _

B1 **1-8** Drop hands and do a dosido with the person whose right hand you were holding (8 steps).

5-8 Swing the one behind you

9-12 _ _ _ _

13-16 _ _ And promenade

9-16 Turn around and take social dance position with the person behind you (your original corner) and do a buzz step swing (8 steps).

B2 **1-4** _ _ _ _

B2 **1-16** Promenade with the person you swung (16 steps).

5-8 _ _ _ _

9-12 — — — —

13-16 <u>All</u> join <u>hands</u>, go <u>forward</u> and <u>back</u>

Comments

Here is another mixer that is a little more complicated. I learned The New Hoosier from a caller colleague in Denmark, Stig Malmø, who had run across it in the United States during a trip there in 1984. The dance was written by Eric Zorn as a present for one of his friends who was about to move to Indiana, the Hoosier State.

The formation of a line in which the dancers are facing in alternate directions is called an "ocean wave" or "wave" in modern Western square dancing, and is now sometimes referred to as a "wavy line" in contra dancing. A *circle* of dancers facing in alternate directions as in The New Hoosier is called an "alamo style" circle. A balance done in these formations gives a good effect, and the idea is found in a number of older dances, for example, Hull's Victory (see the chapter on contra dances) as well as many contemporary dances. Some people like to balance from side to side with a nod to their two neighbours in the wave or circle. Personally, I often prefer a vigorous forward-and-back balance when it occurs in continuation of a forward movement such as the allemandes in this dance.

Music

The New Hoosier can be danced either to a New England tune or to a southern fiddle tune. Some possibilities are "Hell on the Nine Mile" from *Square Dance Tonight Vol. 1* and "Durham's Reel" from *Dances from Appalachia 2*. A particularly nice effect is achieved if one can find a tune with a melodic emphasis just where the balances occur. **Tempo:** about 128.

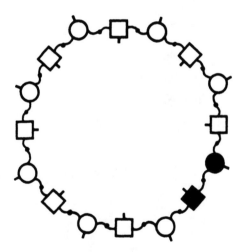

Dancers in an "alamo style" circle, ready to do the first balance.

Used with the permission of Eric Zorn.

Deportment in the ballroom

The following hints on ballroom etiquette may be of use to persons unacquainted with dancing, or who have not been accustomed to attending balls with ladies.

• It is improper for two gentlemen to dance together when ladies are present.

• While dancing, a lady should consider herself engaged to her partner, and therefore she is *not at liberty* to hold a flirtation, between figures, with another gentleman.

• If you cannot waltz gracefully, do not attempt to waltz at all.

• In waltzing, a gentleman should exercise the *utmost delicacy* in touching the waist of his partner.

• When a young lady declines dancing with a gentleman, it is her duty to give him a reason no matter how frivolous the excuse may be.

• If a lady refuses to dance with you, *bear the refusal with grace;* and if you perceive her afterwards dancing with another, *seem not to notice it.*

• Loud conversation, profanity, stamping the feet, writing on the wall, smoking tobacco, spitting or throwing anything on the floor, are *strictly forbidden.*

• The practice of chewing tobacco and spitting on the floor, is not only *nauseous* to ladies, but is *injurious* to their dresses.

—Thomas Hillgrove, *A Complete Practical Guide to the Art of Dancing* (New York: Dick & Fitzgerald, 1864) (quoted in *CDSS News,* November/December, 1985).

Progressive Circles
and Other Easy Dances

Besides circle mixers, there are a number of other dances that are relatively easy to teach and to do. Like mixers, most of these dances do not require any specific number of couples, which usually means that everyone present can participate.

Several of the dances in this chapter use a formation with couple facing couple in one large circle, like the spokes of a wheel. Since Sicilian Circle is one of the oldest and best known of these dances, the formation is sometimes referred to as "Sicilian Circle formation." Another name for this type of dance is "couple mixer," since each couple gets to dance with a new opposite couple on each repeat of the dance. Or they may be called "progressive circles," referring to the fact that, as each couple moves on to dance with the next couple, they progress around the ring.

If the number of couples present is uneven, this is no problem. Just let the "leftover" couple join the dance alone. They will have to wait out the first round, but on the next round, a couple will advance to dance with them, and as the dance progresses, a different couple will wait out each time the dance is repeated.

Progressive circles and contra dances are closely related. In fact, still another name for progressive circles is "circle contras." The main difference is that a contra is danced in a long line with a specifically designated "top" and "bottom." When a couple gets to the end, they turn around and go back the other way, which often means that they dance other movements than they did at first (see the next chapter for a more detailed explanation). In a progressive circle, on the other hand, you never change direction and consequently never change the movements you dance. If a contra is constructed in such a way that all the couples do pretty much the same things, if there are not many movements up and down the line, and if there is plenty of room in the hall, then the dance can probably be performed as a Sicilian circle, too. Fairfield Fancy is sometimes used this way.

On the other hand, there are progressive circle dances that work just as well in contra formation. An example is The Siege of Carrick, which may be useful as a contra dance for beginners. Because of the promenade at the end, people almost automatically turn around when they come to the end of the set, and this also gives an automatic crossover, so they are ready to rejoin the dance after waiting out one time.

One thing you should take into consideration when dancing progressive circles is the size and crowdedness of the hall. If the number of people present is too great for them to fit comfortably into Sicilian circle formation, you may not want to use this type of dance. Or it may be possible to form a second circle inside the first. In the latter case, be sure that people can see which circle they belong to, or you will run into problems.

PROGRESSIVE CIRCLE
Couple facing couple,
like the spokes of a wheel

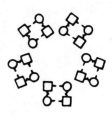

THE SIEGE OF CARRICK

MUSIC	CALLS	MUSIC	DESCRIPTION

Intro: _ _ Circle left

A1 **1-4**   _ _ _ _

5-8   _ _ Circle right

9-12   _ _ _ _

13-16   _ _ Right hand star

A1 **1-8**   Each group of two couples joins hands and circles to the left 8 steps.

9-16   Now circle to the right 8 steps, back to place.

A2 **1-4**   _ _ _ _

5-8   The other way back, left hand star

9-12   _ _ _ _

13-16   Twos arch, ones go under

A2 **1-8**   Place right hands in the center to form a right hand star and walk clockwise 8 steps.

9-16   Change to a left hand star, walk 8 steps counterclockwise back to place, and drop hands to face the other couple.

B1 **1-4**   Separate, go around to place

5-8   _ _ Clap and swing

9-12   _ _ _ _

13-16   Ones arch, twos go under

B1 **1-8**   The 2s, i.e., the couple facing in reverse line of direction, make an arch by raising their joined inside hands (gent's right, lady's left). The 1s join inside hands, go forward under the arch, drop hands, and move away from each other to continue individually around their respective opposites, back to place (8 steps).

9-16   On counts 1 and 2, everyone claps his or her own hands twice. Then take social dance position with your partner and swing for 6 counts.

B2 **1-4**   _ _ _ _

5-8   _ Clap and promenade

9-12   _ _ On to the next

13-16   _ Join hands and circle left

B2 **1-8**   As in B1, 1-8, but this time, the 1s make an arch and the 2s go through (8 steps).

9-16   On counts 1 and 2, everyone claps his or her own hands twice. Then take promenade position with your partner and promenade past the opposite couple (gents passing left shoulders) to the next couple.

Comments

I learned this dance from Izzy Young, now living in Stockholm, who got it from American caller Ralph Sweet. According to Ralph, the Siege of Carrick is a traditional Irish dance, and was originally done in contra formation.

There are several ways to form a star (see Glossary), but for this dance I recommend New England style, with each dancer loosely gripping the wrist of the person in front.

Make sure the dancers use the full eight counts of music to go through the arch and around to place. A small challenge for beginners will be getting the claps coordinated, so everyone claps together on counts 1 and 2 of the relevant phrases. Also a little more challenging than it looks on paper is the six-count promenade to the next couple, so you may want to pay extra attention to the timing of that when you teach the dance.

Music

A New England or French-Canadian tune works best for this dance. Some tunes I like are "Texas Quickstep" from *Square Dance Tonight Vol. 1* and "York County Hornpipe" from *Maritime Dance Party*. **Tempo:** about 120.

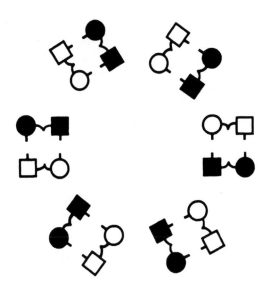

Sicilian circle formation.

Right hand star.

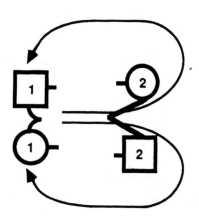

Twos arch, ones go under and around to place.

PROGRESSIVE CIRCLE
couple facing couple,
like the spokes of a wheel

BALANCE THE STAR

MUSIC	CALLS	MUSIC	DESCRIPTION

Intro: Right hands in and balance there

A1	**1-4** It's in __ out __	**A1**	**1-8** In each group of two couples, form a "hands across" right hand star by having the two ladies join right hands and the two gents join right hands (see illustration). With everyone starting on the right foot, balance by doing a pas-de-basque step in towards each other and a pas-de-basque out again. Repeat (8 counts in all).
	5-8 In __ Right hand star		
	9-12 __ __ __ __		**9-16** Keep the same handhold, walk forward 8 steps clockwise.
	13-16 Left hands in and balance again		
A2	**1-4** In __ out __	**A2**	**1-8** Change to left hands and balance in and out twice as in A1, 1-8, but this time, everyone starts on the *left* foot (8 counts).
	5-8 In __ Left hand star		
	9-12 __ __ __ __		**9-16** Keeping the same handhold, walk forward 8 steps counterclockwise, ending in original positions.
	13-16 With your opposite dosido		
B1	**1-4** __ __ __ __	**B1**	**1-8** Do a dosido with your opposite (the person directly across from you) (8 steps).
	5-8 Take that girl and bring her around		
	9-12 __ __ __ __		**9-16** Turn your back to your partner and take skater's position with the person you dosidoed. The gent now turns more or less in place while he leads the lady in a forward arc about ¾ around so that they end in his original position facing the other couple (8 steps).
	13-16 __ With your opposite dosido		
B2	**1-4** __ __ __ __	**B2**	**1-8** Do a dosido with your new opposite (who is your original partner) (8 steps).
	5-8 Take that girl, bring her around		
	9-12 Promenade, it's on to the next		**9-16** Repeat B1, 9-16, but this time, continue forward, past the other couple, with gents passing left shoulders, to meet a new couple (8 steps).
	13-16 And when you get there, you balance in		

Comments

Balance the Star was written by Raymond K. and Beatrice McLain for Christmas Country Dance School at Berea College, Kentucky, in 1973. I learned it from the Berea College Country Dancers during their tour of Denmark in 1981, and it became an immediate hit with my dancers, as it has with many other groups.

Comparing B1 9-16 with B2 9-16, you will note that the same time is alotted even though much more ground must be covered the second time. The first little "promenade" can be done at a relaxed tempo, while the second one must be done with determination! Alternatively, the extra music the first time around can be used for personal improvi-sation such as doing a few clogging steps, a special twirl, or wheeling around as a couple an extra time.

Music

"Beaumont Rag" has been established as the tune associated with this dance, and it is a fine one. The tune was recorded by Lewis Lamb and the McLain Family Band on *Dances from Appalachia* and again by the McLains on *Dances from Appalachia 3*. Other tunes can also be used, but if so, I like to keep the feeling of a rag, for example, "Black Mountain Rag" from *Square Dance Tonight Vol. 1*. **Tempo:** lively, about 130.

Handhold for the first part of the dance (balance and star).

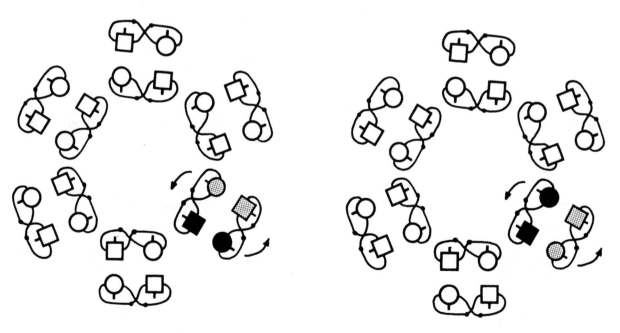

First time (B1, 9-16)   Second time (B2, 9-16)

"Take that girl and bring her around."

Used with the permission of John Ramsay, Berea College Recreation Extension.

PROGRESSIVE CIRCLE
couple facing couple,
like the spokes of a wheel

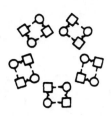

SASHAY 'ROUND THE RING

MUSIC	CALLS
Intro:	_ _ <u>Opposite swing</u>
A1 1-4	_ _ _ _
5-8	<u>Face</u> your <u>partner</u>, sashay <u>left</u>
9-12	_ _ The <u>other way back</u>
13-16	<u>Opposite couple</u>, <u>right</u> and <u>left through</u>
A2 1-4	_ _ _ _
5-8	<u>Stay</u> right <u>there</u>, sashay <u>right</u>
9-12	_ _ The <u>other way back</u>
13-16	<u>With</u> your <u>partner dosido</u>
B1 1-4	_ _ _ _
5-8	_ _ And <u>swing</u>
9-12	_ _ _ _
13-16	Go <u>forward</u> and <u>back</u>
B2 1-4	_ _ _ _
5-8	_ _ Pass <u>through</u>

MUSIC	DESCRIPTION
A1 1-8	Take social dance position with your opposite and swing 8 counts. End as a couple facing in or out of the circle, with the lady on the gent's right—your partner will now be across from you.
9-12	Take inside hands (gent's right, lady's left) with the one you swung, everyone sashays 4 steps to their own left, moving around the circumference of the large circle.
13-16	Sashay 4 steps back to the right and end facing your partners again.
A2 1-8	With the facing couple, do a right and left through (see Glossary) (8 steps).
9-12	Take inside hands with the same person you have been dancing with, and sashay 4 steps to the right, again moving around the circumference of the large circle.
13-16	Sashay 4 steps back to the left and end facing your partners again.
B1 1-8	With your original partner, who is still across from you, dosido (8 steps).
9-16	Take social dance position with your partner and swing 8 counts. End as a couple, with the lady on the gent's right. You are now back in your original position.
B2 1-8	Take inside hands (gent's right, lady's left) with your partner and go 4 steps forward towards the opposite couple and 4 steps backwards to place.

MUSIC	CALLS
9-12	[__ New <u>opposite</u>, <u>balance there</u>]
13-16	__ __ And the <u>opposite</u> <u>swing</u>

MUSIC	DESCRIPTION
9-16	Drop hands and go forward past the other couple, each person passing right shoulders with his or her opposite (8 steps). Or use 4 steps to pass through and the next 4 to do a balance with your new opposite by giving right hands and doing a pas-de-basque step towards each other and a pas-de-basque step away from each other.

Comments

Books of dances from the 1800s often include a few progressive circle dances among the contras and quadrilles. Many of the old progressive circles are "glossary" dances consisting of standard figures in a more or less random order, and as such are not particularly interesting today. There are a few that are more idiosyncratic, but since the dance descriptions typically are very concise, it is not always clear how to interpret the figures. For example, some of the dances call for a "chassé" (sashay) but this term can have a variety of interpretations. Intrigued by these cryptic old descriptions, and wanting to use the sashay step in a progressive circle formation, I put together Sashay 'Round the Ring, which undoubtedly does *not* conform to the conventions of 100–150 years ago.

In the right and left through in A2, 1-8, it may well be an advantage to take only inside hands when you turn as a couple, rather than doing a regular courtesy turn, in order to avoid having to change the handhold for the sashay that follows.

However, beginning dancers may actually find it easier to turn with the courtesy turn hold. In B2, 9-16, eight counts are available for the final pass through, but in fact only about 4 are needed. An alternative that is advisable only if the dancers are not too spread out—and preferably with dancers who have some experience—is to let them pass through and then immediately balance with their new opposites, giving a perfect lead-in to the swing with which the dance starts again. This possibility is indicated by the call in square brackets. Another, less demanding, solution that also will keep them in motion is to let them pass through *two* couples instead of only one.

Music

I like a jig for this dance, such as "Kitty Magee" from *Square Dance Tonight Vol. 1* or "Spider Island Jig" from *Maritime Dance Party*. Note that the latter is played 7½ times through, so you may want to keep track and stop before the end of the cut. **Tempo:** about 126.

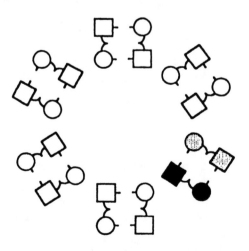

Starting position.

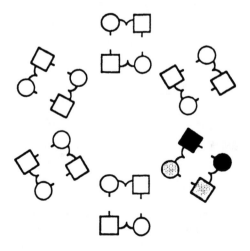

Position after "swing your opposite" (A1, 1-8)

PROGRESSIVE CIRCLE
couple facing couple,
like the spokes of a wheel

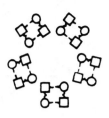

SICILIAN CIRCLE

MUSIC		CALLS	MUSIC		DESCRIPTION
Intro:		__ __ Circle left			
A1	1-4	__ __ __ __	**A1**	1-8	Each group of two couples joins hands and circles to the left 8 steps.
	5-8	The other way back, circle right			
	9-12	__ __ __ __		9-16	Now circle to the right 8 steps, back to place.
	13-16	__ __ Ladies chain			
A2	1-4	__ __ __ __	**A2**	1-8	The same two couples do a ladies chain (see Glossary) (8 steps).
	5-8	__ __ Chain them back			
	9-12	__ __ __ __		9-16	Repeat the ladies chain, back to place (8 steps).
	13-16	__ __ Right and left through			
B1	1-4	__ __ __ __	**B1**	1-8	The same two couples do a right and left through (see Glossary), thus changing places with each other (8 steps).
	5-8	__ __ Right and left back			
	9-12	__ __ __ __		9-16	Repeat the right and left through, back to place (8 steps).
	13-16	Everyone go forward and back			
B2	1-4	__ __ __ __	**B2**	1-8	Take inside hands with your partner and walk 4 steps forward towards the opposite couple and 4 steps backwards to place.
	5-8	Forward again and pass through			
	9-12	__ __ __ __		9-16	Drop hands and go forward past the other couple, each person passing right shoulders with his or her opposite (8 steps).
	13-16	On to the next and circle left			

Comments

The above description is a traditional sequence for the Sicilian Circle. Actually, if you want to be *really* traditional, you should dance forward and back and circle left in A1, instead of circle left and circle right. But since this is awkward in combination with the final pass through, most people today modify it. The order of the figures in A2 and B1 is sometimes listed in reverse, i.e., right and left

through over and back, and then ladies chain over and back, and I remember doing it that way when I first started dancing years ago. But using the order described here makes the sequence less prone to mishaps when working with less experienced dancers.

Personally, I like to use the Sicilian Circle formation as a basis for improvisation. It gives even beginning dancers a chance to try listening to the caller and executing a sequence they have not learned in advance.

I usually start by teaching circle left, circle right, right and left hand star, dosido, forward and back, and pass through. I mix and match these calls until it is clear that the group has mastered them. If appropriate, I then introduce ladies chain or right and left through and mix these more difficult movements into the sequences. The trick is to challenge the dancers just enough, but not so much that they constantly break down and become discouraged.

I often use the Sicilian Circle this way quite early in a teaching session. If done properly, it not only brings home the necessity of listening to the calls, but amuses the dancers and builds up their confidence. Improvising this way is also an excellent exercise for the beginning caller, who can practice timing, thinking ahead, and the principles of good choreography within a fairly manageable formation.

Music

Preferably a well-phrased tune, such as "Home Sweet Home" from *Square Dance Tonight Vol. 3* or "Planxty George Brabazon" from *Kitchen Junket*.
Tempo: Not too fast, especially with beginners. About 120 beats per minute.

Amazing but true—laws about dancing

Local statutes often include laws that have remained on the books long after their relevance has passed. In other cases, a certain humor seems to have been present from the start. Just consider these examples:

Ticaboo, Utah: Citizens are prohibited from eating onions when going dancing between the hours of 7 P.M. and 7 A.M.

Forestdale, Rhode Island: It is prohibited to ask anyone to square dance within four hours of having eaten garlic.

Russelville, Pennsylvania: Tickling a girl under her chin with a feather duster to get her attention at a square dance is punishable by law.

Ballantine, South Carolina: Every woman must be found to be wearing a corset when going dancing. A physician is required to inspect each female at a dance to ascertain that she complies.

Lugert, Oklahoma: Under no circumstances may a man with hair growing over his upper lip ask a female to dance.

Rock Springs, Wyoming: No woman may chew tobacco while square dancing unless she has the written permission of her husband.

Moosehead, Maine: Violin lessons may not be given on a dance floor while others are dancing.

Cotton Valley, Louisiana: No man is allowed to use handbills to advertise for a spouse at a local square dance.

Clearbrook, Minnesota: It is forbidden to go onto a dance floor while wearing a hat that would scare a timid person.

Constantia, New York: Young women may not drink coffee at a public dance after 6 P.M.

Parkersburg, West Virginia: No married woman may go dancing unless her husband stays close by, carrying a loaded gun over his left shoulder.

Palisades, Ohio: It is illegal to make silly or insulting faces at someone who is trying to learn how to square dance.

Adapted from an article by Robert W. Pelton
in American Square Dance *magazine, April 1987.*

PROGRESSIVE CIRCLE
couple facing couple,
like the spokes of a wheel

FRIDAY NIGHT SPECIAL

MUSIC	CALLS
Intro:	Twos arch, dip and dive
A1 1-4	— — — —
5-8	— — — —
9-12	— — — —
13-16	Stop right there: left hand star
A2 1-4	— — — —
5-8	— — Right hand back
9-12	— — — —
13-16	— — Ladies chain
B1 1-4	— And turn them once and a half
5-8	— — Now chain again
9-12	— — Turn once and a half
13-16	— New opposite dosido
B2 1-4	— — — —
5-8	— — And your partner swing
9-12	— — — —
13-16	Twos arch, dip and dive

MUSIC	DESCRIPTION
A1 1-16	Join inside hands with your partner. The 2s, i.e., those couples facing in the reverse line of direction, make an arch and everyone moves forward 16 steps as follows: the 1s go under the 2s' arch, then the 1s make an arch that the next 2s go through, the 2s make an arch that the next 1s go through, and the 1s make an arch that the next 2s go through.
A2 1-8	Form a "hands across" left hand star by having the two ladies join left hands and the two gents join left hands. Walk forward counter-clockwise 8 steps.
9-16	Change to a right hand star and walk clockwise 8 steps, back to place.
B1 1-8	The same two couples do a ladies chain (see Glossary). But instead of an ordinary courtesy turn, wheel around an extra 180 degrees so that you have your backs to the opposite couple (8 steps in all).
9-16	Do a ladies chain with the couple you are facing now, and again turn an extra 180 degrees (8 steps in all). The original two gents are now facing each other again, but with new partners.
B2 1-8	With your new opposite, do a dosido (8 steps).
9-16	Swing your new partner (8 counts) and face the opposite couple, ready to start again.

Comments

Friday Night Special was composed by Sam Flinders of Leicester, England, and was published by the English Folk Dance and Song Society in the book *Everyday Dances* (1969). In contrast to the other Sicilian circle dances in this chapter, it is a true mixer. *Also please note:* because of the special ladies chains, this dance must be done with an even number of couples, or disaster will result.

Note the use of a hands-across star in A2, which gives the ladies a head start into the first ladies chain. The chain, with its extra turn, must be executed in the same time normally taken for a regular ladies chain. Because of the tight timing on the ladies chains, this dance is a little more demanding than it looks, and is best attempted by dancers with some experience.

Several callers I know have attempted to adapt

Friday Night Special to make it easier or improve the flow, particularly as the original version does not include the dosido in B2 1-8, and the transition from ladies chain to partner swing plus orientation to a new facing couple is a little awkward that way. The best solution I have seen until now (suggested by Leif and Lillian Krak of Horsens, Denmark) is the one presented above, which preserves the original dance almost intact but smooths the difficult transitions at the end.

Music

Use a New England or Canadian tune, for example, "Mary Douglas Jig" from *Square Dance Tonight Vol. 2* or "Walker Street" from *Maritime Dance Party*. **Tempo:** not too fast, about 120.

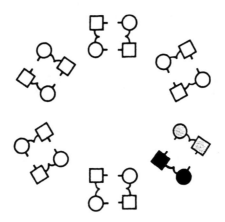

Ready for "ladies chain, turn once and a half."

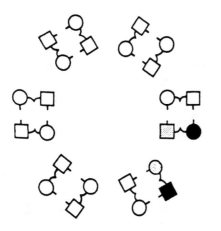

After the first ladies chain.

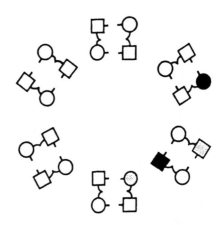

After the second ladies chain.

Previously published in *Everyday Dances* (1969). Used with the permission of the English Folk Dance and Song Society and Sam Flinders.

PROGRESSIVE CIRCLE
couple facing couple,
like the spokes of a wheel

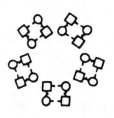

THE LAST SWIM OF THE SUMMER

MUSIC	CALLS	MUSIC	DESCRIPTION
Intro:	With your opposite dosido		
A1 1-4	__ __ __ __	**A1** 1-8	Face your opposite and do a dosido (8 steps).
5-8	Now as couples dosido		
9-12	Go once and a half around those two	9-16	Take inside hands with your partner. With
13-16	__ __ __ __	**+A2** 1-8	each couple moving as a unit, do a "dosido" all the way around the opposite couple and continue past them again, ending back to back with them (16 steps).
A2 1-4	__ __ __ __		
5-8	Swing the one behind you	9-16	Turn around and take social dance position with the person behind you. Swing 8 counts, using the buzz step, and end facing your partner, with each lady on the right of the gent she swung. One pair of dancers will be facing toward the center of the circle and the other will be facing out of the circle.
9-12	__ __ __ __		
13-16	Face across, do a ladies chain		
B1 1-4	__ __ __ __	**B1** 1-8	The same two couples do a ladies chain (see Glossary) (8 steps).
5-8	__ And chain them back again		
9-12	__ __ __ __	9-16	Repeat the ladies chain, back to place (8 steps).
13-16	Join hands and circle left		
B2 1-4	__ __ __ __	**B2** 1-8	The same two couples join hands in a circle and circle left 8 steps.
5-8	Left hand star, the other way back		
9-12	__ __ __ __	9-16	Form a left hand star and go counterclockwise once around (8 steps).
13-16	On to the next and dosido		

Comments

This dance has been in circulation for a while now, and I originally learned it under the name "The First Swing of Summer." The correct title is "The Last Swim of the Summer," and the author is Eric Rounds of Rochester, New York, who credits the movements in the first half of the dance to Roger Whynot. It's a very nice dance, just different enough to be interesting. Note that the swing in A2 9-16 is the point at which the two couples change places with each other. In the left hand star (B2

9-16), each gent will be ahead of his partner. As you come out of the star, face in your original direction and look for the next couple to dance with.

Dance Party. **Tempo:** about 120-126 beats per minute.

Music

Try "Cattle in the Cane" from *Square Dance Tonight Vol. 3* or "Cotton-Eyed Joe" from *Maritime*

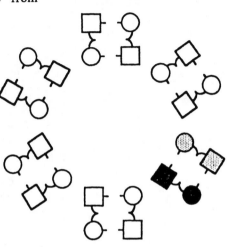

Starting position.

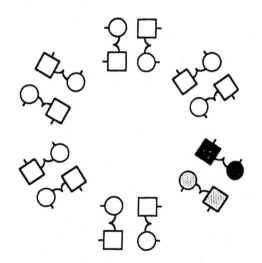

Position after "dosido as couples once and a half around."

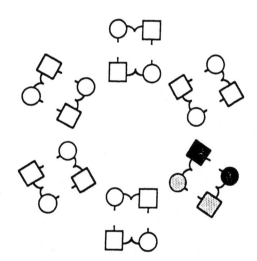

Position after "swing the one behind you."

Used with the permission of Eric Rounds.

FULL SET LONGWAYS
for 6 couples, proper

OXO SASHAY

MUSIC	CALLS	MUSIC	DESCRIPTION

Intro: One and six, sashay now

A1 1-4 _ _ _ _

5-8 _ _ And sashay back

9-12 _ _ _ _

13-16 Six on the inside, one on the outside

A1 1-8 Couple one (the couple closest to the music) give both hands to your partner and dance down the center with 8 sashay steps. At the same time, gent six and lady six each take a step backwards and dance individually up the outside with 8 sashay steps.

9-16 The four dancers who were active in A1 1-8 dance the *same way* back to place with 8 sashay steps.

A2 1-4 _ _ _ _

5-8 _ _ _ And back

9-12 _ _ _ _

13-16 Circle at the ends, star in the middle

A2 1-8 Couple six give both hands to your partner and dance up the center with 8 sashay steps. At the same time, gent one and lady one each take a step backwards and dance individually down the outside with 8 sashay steps.

9-16 The four dancers who were active in A2 1-8 dance the *same way* back to place with 8 sashay steps.

B1 1-4 _ _ _ _

5-8 _ _ Other way back

9-12 _ _ _ _

13-16 Couple one, cast off

B1 1-8 Couples one and two join hands in a circle and circle left 8 steps. At the same time, couples three and four make a right hand star and move clockwise 8 steps, and couples five and six join hands and circle left 8 steps.

9-16 The two circles turn and circle right 8 steps, while couples three and four change to a left hand star and move counterclockwise 8 steps, so everyone comes back to place.

B2 1-4 _ _ _ _

5-8 And everyone go forward and back

9-12 _ _ _ _

13-16 One on the inside, six on the outside

B2 1-8 Couple one faces the top. The gent turns to his left and the lady to her right, and they walk individually down the outside of the set, ending at the bottom position (everyone else should move up a little to make room for them) (8 steps).

9-16 Take hands along the gents' line and ladies' line, respectively, and all go 4 steps forward and 4 steps backwards to place.

Comments

Oxo Sashay is a simple dance, but it's fun because you have to stay alert. Often, couple one will complete a round of the dance and think they can relax, only to discover that they are active again as couple six.

Ideally, the dance is done with six couples, but it can also be adapted for four or five (with five, let the fifth couple do a two-hand turn with each other instead of the circles in B1).

I learned the dance from Izzy Young, now of Stockholm, as Oxo Reel. In his version, the other couples follow couple one to the foot of the set in B2 and go through an arch made by them, as in the Virginia Reel. This is, however, almost never managed in 16 counts, especially by beginners. So I changed the ending to the version described here, giving the dancers a chance to catch their breath and regroup before starting over.

In Ralph Page's book *An Elegant Collection of Contras and Squares,* another version of Oxo Reel (presumably the original one) is given. It is like Izzy Young's, but instead of the sashaying back and forth in A1 and A2, everyone goes forward and back, does a dosido with their partner, goes forward and back, and does a seesaw (left shoulder dosido) with their partner. Ralph Page writes that this version was presented by English dance leader Jack Hamilton around 1975, and that he may or may not have originated it. The name of the dance presumably refers to a brand of bouillon well known to every English housewife.

Oxo Sashay as presented here is a good example of how a dance can be passed from hand to hand, gradually being transmuted until it barely resembles the original version. In this case, only one key figure is left: the one that gives the dance its name.

Music

Preferably a jig or other bouncy tune, such as "Bouchard No. 2" from *Square Dance Tonight Vol. 1* or "East Coast Jig" from *Maritime Dance Party.* **Tempo:** should be pretty lively, about 126-130.

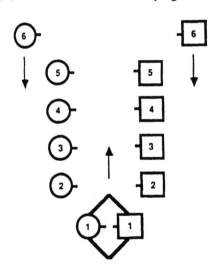

"One and six, sashay now" (A1 1-8).

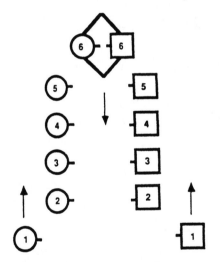

"Six on the inside, one on the outside" (A2 1-8).

FULL SET LONGWAYS
for 6 couples, proper

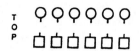

OPERA REEL

MUSIC		CALLS
Intro:		Everyone go forward and back

A1	1-4	_ _ _ _
	5-8	First old couple, sashay down
	9-12	_ _ _ _
	13-16	And everyone go forward and back

A2	1-4	_ _ _ _
	5-8	The new first couple, sashay down
	9-12	_ _ _ _
	13-16	Circle, star, right and left four

B1	1-4	_ _ _ _
	5-8	_ _ And the other way back
	9-12	_ _ _ _
	13-16	Bottom two couples, sashay up

B2	1-4	_ _ _ _
	5-8	And couple one, cast to the bottom
	9-12	_ _ _ _
	13-16	Everyone go forward and back

MUSIC **DESCRIPTION**

A1 **1-8** Join hands along your lines and go 4 steps forward and 4 steps backwards, to place.

9-16 Couple one (the couple closest to the music) give both hands to your partner, dance down the center with 8 sashay steps, and fall into place at the bottom of the line.

A2 **1-8** Join hands along your lines again and go 4 steps forward and 4 steps backwards, to place.

9-16 The couple now closest to the music give both hands to your partner, dance down the center with 8 sashay steps, and fall into place at the bottom of the line.

B1 **1-8** The two couples now closest to the top of the set join hands in a circle and circle left 8 steps. At the same time, the next two couples make a right hand star and move clockwise 8 steps, and the last two couples do a right and left four (see Glossary).

9-16 The top two couples circle right 8 steps, while the next two couples change to a left hand star and move counterclockwise 8 steps, and the last two couples repeat the right and left four, so everyone comes back to place.

B2 **1-8** The original top two couples, now at the bottom of the set, give both hands to their partners and dance up the center with 8 sashay steps, back to their original places.

9-16 Couple one faces the top. The gent turns to his left and the lady to her right, and they walk individually down the outside of the set, ending at the bottom position (everyone else should move up a little to make room for them) (8 steps)

Comments

This version of Opera Reel appears in *Community Dances Manual Book 6*, originally published in England in 1967, as an "American set dance" with no further explanation. It appears to be an elaboration of a much earlier and more stately dance by the same name found in several American sources of the mid–1800s. The dance is not really difficult, but compared to Oxo Sashay, for example, it includes enough potential confusion to keep even experienced dancers on their toes. The main challenge, of course, is to keep track of what one should be doing in B1, as well as who should be sashaying where in A1 9-16, A2 9-16 and B1 1-8.

When the original couple two sashays down in A2 9-16, they end below the original couple one, so that both couples can return to place in B2 1-8 without passing each other.

Note that the right and left four is done by two dancers of the same sex. This means that the courtesy turn hold is not used for the second half of the movement. The two dancers can put their arms around each other's waists, or they can just take inside hands. In either case, the dancer on the right goes forward and the one on the left goes backwards to execute the turn.

The *Community Dances Manual* states that the other five couples should swing their partners in B2 9-16 while couple one progresses to the bottom of the set. If so, they must be sure to stop in time to reform the lines for the forward and back in A1 1-8. Putting in or leaving out the swing will give you some leeway in adapting the dance to the level of the group.

Music

The obvious choice for this dance is the tune of the same name, an excellent recording of which is found on the album *New England Chestnuts*. Otherwise, you can use any other lively reel or jig that appeals to you. **Tempo:** about 126.

DANCE FOR COUPLES
OR SMALL GROUPS

JESSIE POLKA

MUSIC		CALLS	MUSIC		DESCRIPTION
A1	**1-2**	Left heel forward	**A1**	**1-2**	Form couples in skater's position or small groups with their arms around each other's waists. On count 1, hop on your right foot, touching your extended left heel to the floor in front of you. On count 2, jump on both feet together in place.
	3-4	Right toe back		**3-4**	On count 3, hop on your left foot, touching your right toe to the floor behind you. On count 4, hop on your left foot again, bringing the right foot in place beside it, but *not* transferring any weight to it.
	5-6	Right heel forward		**5-6**	On count 5, hop on your left foot, touching your extended right heel to the floor in front of you. On count 6, bring your right foot back to place and hop onto it.
	7-8	Left heel and cross		**7-8**	On count 7, hop on your right foot, touching your extended left heel to the floor in front of you. On count 8, hop on your right foot again, bending your left knee to cross your left foot in front of your right leg.
	9-16	Polka forward __ __ __ __ __ __		**9-16**	Dance straight ahead with 4 polka steps or two-steps, starting forward on your left foot.

Comments

Jessie Polka is a well-known polka variation said to have originated in Texas. Rickey Holden says the name is a corruption of the Mexican "Jesucita," from the name of the tune originally used. We did Jessie Polka as a couple dance in high school, but later I learned that it could also be done in groups. Izzy Young has people form short lines and then gradually move into a big star on the floor, like the spokes of a wheel, but you can also be more anarchistic and let them dance anywhere

they want to. Both children and adults enjoy the dance, which is just complicated enough to be a challenge.

This is not a dance that needs to be called as such; the cues shown above should only be used during teaching.

Music

"Jessie Polka" or any other lively polka, such as "Chickadees' Polka" from *New England Chestnuts 1.* **Tempo:** about 126.

Jessie Polka can be danced by a couple...

...or a group.

The polka step is said to have been invented by a Czech peasant girl whom a local schoolteacher observed skipping gaily around a meadow. He was so taken by her homemade dance step that he taught it to his pupils, and before long it had spread to the cities, where it became immensely popular. Whether or not this story is true, the polka certainly is a happy dance, which may be the reason why it swept through Europe and America in the mid–1800s.

The step, when danced straight ahead as in Jessie Polka, is done as follows:

The rhythm is "and-1-and-2" for "hop-step-together-step." On the first "and," hop lightly on your right foot. On "1," step forward on your left foot. On "and," close your right foot to the left (or just behind it), taking the weight. On "2," step forward again on your left foot. Repeat the step with opposite footwork, i.e., hop on the left, forward on the right, close with the left, forward on the right. Keep on doing this "hop-step-together-step" on alternate feet as long as the music or the choreography allows.

Contra Dances

Contra dancing is a form of dance traditionally associated with New England, where it survived after falling out of fashion in other parts of the country. In recent years, however, contras have enjoyed a huge renaissance and are now being done by groups all over the United States.

Formation

In a contra dance, the dancers form two long lines across from each other. The starting position is with the gentlemen on the caller's right and the ladies on the caller's left. This is logical and easily remembered if you have the dancers form a column facing the caller, with the lady, as usual, on her partner's right. When the dancers turn to face their partners, they will be standing on the correct sides. Note that in a contra, you stand *across* from your partner, not next to your partner (there are a few exceptions — see Bucksaw and Let Sleeping Dogs Lie in this chapter).

In many contra dances, the dancers in the first, third, fifth, etc. couples change places with their partners before the dance begins. In some, however, they do not. In this book as elsewhere, the dance instructions indicate whether a dance is **"improper"** (crossed over) or **"proper"**(not crossed over).

Another important concept in contra dancing is **up** and **down.** The expressions "up," "above" and "top" or "head" refer to the end of the set nearest the music and caller, while "down," "below" and "bottom" or "foot" refer to the end of the set farthest from the music.

Numbering and progression

In a "duple minor" contra dance, the couples are numbered 1, 2, 1, 2 ... starting from the top. A quick way to achieve this is to ask the dancers to take **"hands four from the top,"** i.e., form circles of

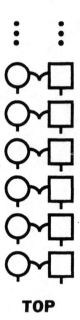

TOP

A quick and easy way to form contra lines is to have couples make a column facing the music...

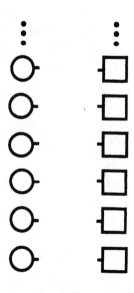

TOP

...and then have them face their partners. After a little practice, they should automatically form facing lines.

58

two couples, starting at the top. The 1s are sometimes referred to as the **active** couples and the 2s as the **inactive** couples, and each group of two couples is called a **"minor set."** (In "triple minor" dances, which were more popular in days gone by, the couples are numbered 1, 2, 3, 1, 2, 3..., but this type of dance is a little more complicated, and none are included in this book.)

Every time the dance sequence is repeated, the 1s move one place farther away from the music and the 2s move one place closer to the music. Thus, each couple meets a new other couple for each round of the dance. If you keep on going long enough, every couple will have a chance to dance both as 1s and as 2s, and everyone in the set will dance with everyone else.

When a couple gets to the end of the set, they wait out one time through without dancing. While waiting, they change their number (and, if the dance is improper, they also change places with each other) and are then ready to rejoin the dance as 1s (from the top of the set) or 2s (from the bottom).

The movement of couples along the set is called **progression,** and every contra dance must include a means of progression somewhere in its sequence. In this book, progression is noted in the dance descriptions, as it can be useful for the caller to be aware of when and how it occurs.

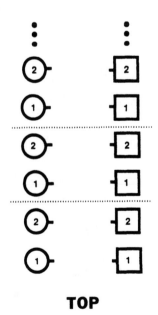

TOP

In a duple minor contra, the couples are numbered 1,2,1,2..., starting from the top. Here is the formation for a "proper" contra, where all the ladies start on the "ladies' side" and all the gents on the "gents' side."

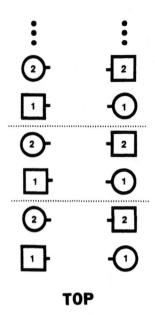

TOP

And here is the formation for an "improper" contra, where all the 1s have changed places with their partners before the dance begins.

Actives and inactives

It is important to realize from the beginning that the designation of the number 2 couples as "inactive" is not to be taken literally. In many older dances, the role of the inactive couples was much more restricted than that of the actives, but today, dances are preferred in which both couples are equally or almost equally active. It may be a good idea to remind beginning dancers that the overall goal of the 1s is to work their way down through the set, while the goal of the 2s is to get up to the top and become 1s. Thus, when reorienting at the beginning of each new round of the dance, the 1s will dance with the couple below them and the 2s with the couple above them. Remember also to emphasize that a couple *only* changes its number when it gets to the end of the set.

With the changing nature of contra dancing, more and more callers are now distinguishing between your **"partner"** and your **"neighbor"** in the minor set. Your partner is, of course, the same person throughout the dance, whereas your neighbor at any given time is the *other* person of the opposite sex in your minor set. In principle, the caller's instructions are directed to the active couple. Thus, if the call is "dosido the one below," each number 1 dancer faces the 2 below and they do a dosido. This of course, requires the 2s to face *up,* towards the 1s, but they have to figure that out for themselves. Today, the wording of calls tends increasingly to avoid this problem. For example, instead of saying "dosido the one below," many callers will now say "dosido your neighbor," implying that all four dancers should look for their neighbors.

How many couples can dance

In principle, a contra set can consist of any number of couples, with the length of the set being limited only by the size of the hall. Four couples is the absolute minimum, but in practice, the minimum should probably be set at six couples. The reason is that it is disorienting to keep changing numbers before the dance pattern has a chance to become established. Also, part of the charm of con-

tra dancing is working one's way up or down the set. Because of this, it is better to make one set of ten couples than two sets of five each, but if only five couples are present, they can still form a single set and dance.

When forming sets for a contra, remember also that long sets are all right for a dance in which everyone is equally active, but less appropriate for a dance in which the 2s have little to do. In this case, consider breaking up the dancers into two or more sets, depending on the number present.

Finally, more and more dances are being composed today in which a "double progression" occurs. This means that for each repetition of the dance sequence, each couple moves *two* places farther along the set, instead of one. The result is a much faster progression through the set and little or no waiting at the ends.

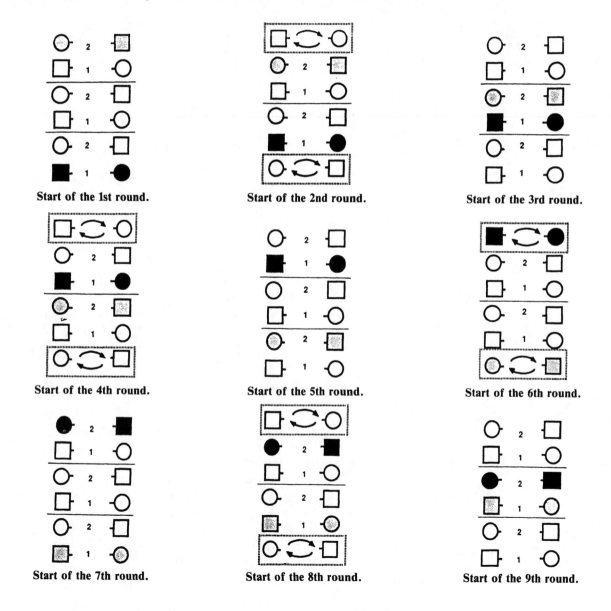

Start of the 1st round.   Start of the 2nd round.   Start of the 3rd round.

Start of the 4th round.   Start of the 5th round.   Start of the 6th round.

Start of the 7th round.   Start of the 8th round.   Start of the 9th round.

Using the illustrations on the preceding page, let's try following a single couple through a duple improper contra — for example the original top couple, shown here in black.

Each time the dance is repeated, they move one place farther down the set and dance with a new couple 2. At the start of the sixth round, the original top couple has arrived at the bottom of the set, where they wait through the dance one time (symbolized by the dotted box around them). While they wait, they must remember to change places with each other. When the seventh round starts, they are in the dance again, but have changed into 2s. Thus, they begin to work their way back up towards the top.

The diagrams also show what happens to the original last couple (shown in gray), who are moving in the opposite direction of the original top couple. The other couples are, of course, also moving up or down the set accordingly, but for the sake of simplicity they are not specially marked in the diagrams.

The structure of the dance — teaching tips

Contras are usually danced at a relaxed tempo of about 120 beats per minute, and they are always closely coordinated with the phrases of the music. The division of the tune into A and B parts and of each part into phrases of 4, 8 or 16 counts is closely followed by the structure of the dance, and the dance sequence starts again every time the tune starts again.

If you are teaching a contra and discover that it does not seem to be working out to (normally) 64 counts, stop and check that you have understood the sequence correctly and calculated the correct number of steps for each movement. If you have, and the dancers still are not finishing in time, it is best to stop and go through the dance again more slowly, until everyone seems to understand it, rather than "fudging" your way through it as you might be able to do with a square. Few things are more disorienting to an experienced contra dancer than being forced to dance out of phrase with the music. Also make sure that all the couples are progressing each time the sequence is danced. If anyone does not progress (or if a couple leaves the dance from the middle of the set, which has been known to occur with beginners), you will have

two 1s or two 2s standing next to each other, and the result can easily be chaos. Therefore, if two couples with the same number find themselves together at the beginning of a round, one couple should go to the bottom of the set and start in again there as 2s.

Responsibilities of the caller

Contra dances are relatively easy to call because the dance sequence is short and the same sequence is repeated over and over. For the same reasons, contras can be danced without a caller if necessary.

Nevertheless, the caller can contribute a good deal. First of all, the caller is responsible for planning and MCing an appropriate program — choosing the dances and the order in which they will be done and presenting them in an entertaining manner. Second, the caller is responsible for teaching and or walking through the dances, the goal being to explain them as clearly and efficiently as possible. Well-timed and succinctly worded calls used the first few times through the dance help establish its pattern. As couples advance to the top of the set and become active, they have to make some adjustments in the movements they were dancing. Inexperienced dancers may have trouble with this, and an alert caller can be ready to help them if necessary. One of the things you can do is to help beginners know when to start in as actives by saying "Ready at the top" just before starting to call the next round. But remember to say it only *every other time,* i.e., after the couple in question has already waited through one sequence of the dance. This expression is included in the dance descriptions in this book, written in parentheses.

Once the dancers have caught on to the sequence, it is not necessary to keep calling the whole dance. With beginners in particular, you may want to continue giving some short cues, especially at difficult points of transition. But if everything is going well, you can stop calling altogether and let everyone enjoy dancing to the music. If you have live music, a traditional way to end the dance is to call again for the last time through. This is a nice way of rounding things off.

CONTRA
duple improper

FAIRFIELD FANCY

MUSIC	CALLS	MUSIC	DESCRIPTION

Intro: Dosido the one below

A1 1-4 _ _ _ _

5-8 Now dosido your partners all

9-12 _ _ _ _

13-16 Join hands and circle left

A1 1-8 1s face down, 2s up. Do a dosido with the person you are facing now (your neighbor) (8 steps).

9-16 Face your partner and do a dosido (8 steps).

A2 1-4 _ _ _ _

5-8 Circle right to a line of four

9-12 _ _ _ _

13-16 Go down the center four in line

A2 1-8 The same two couples join hands in a circle of four and circle left (8 steps).

9-16 With hands still joined, circle right. On the last 2-3 steps, the 2s drop hands with each other and the circle opens to form a line facing down the set, with the 1s in the center and a 2 at each end (8 steps).

B1 1-4 _ _ _ _

5-8 Arch in the middle, ends duck under

9-12 Everybody come on up

13-16 And ladies chain with the couple you meet

B1 1-8 Walk down the center 6 steps. On the next 2 steps, the 1s make an arch and the 2s come in towards each other, take hands, go through the arch *(progression)* and then drop hands with the 1s. The two couples are now standing back to back.

9-16 Everyone now moves 8 steps up the set (1s moving backwards, 2s forward).

B2 1-4 _ _ _ _

5-8 _ _ Chain them back

9-12 _ _ _ _

13-16 Dosido the one below

B2 1-8 Do a ladies chain (see Glossary) with the couple you are facing now (8 steps). At the ends, the couples who have no one to dance with simply turn as a couple and wait out one round of the dance.

9-16 Repeat the ladies chain, back to place (8 steps).

Comments

I learned Fairfield Fancy from Rickey Holden, and like him, have found it to be a good choice as a first contra. The movements are simple, but still interesting, and best of all, the progression is virtually foolproof. If the dancers forget to change places while waiting out at the ends, the ladies chain will immediately remind them of it. Both the sequence of movements and positioning of the dancers relative to each other are easy to understand and remember. One thing to be aware of, though, is that after the progression takes place, in the middle of the sequence, you immediately dance with a new couple, which is unusual. When going on to other contras, you may therefore have to emphasize what movement the dance begins with, so that the dancers waiting out at the ends don't try to join in too soon.

Fairfield Fancy was written in 1951 by Dick Forscher of Greenwich, Connecticut, and named for his dance group.

Music

Any good New England or French-Canadian tune. I prefer a reel, such as "Le Cultivateur" from *Square Dance Tonight Vol. 2* or "Glise à Sherbrooke" from *New England Chestnuts 2*. **Tempo:** About 120.

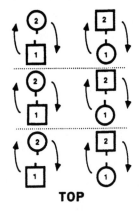

"Dosido the one below": 1s face down, 2s up.

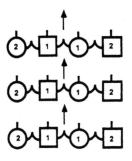

"Down the center four in line."

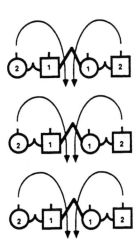

"Arch in the middle, ends duck under."

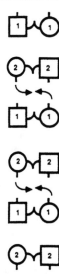

"Ladies chain with the couple you meet." (The couples that end up alone at the top and bottom of the set should turn as a couple to face in again. They will now wait out a round.)

Used with the permission of Dick Forscher.

CONTRA
duple improper

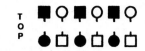

JOHNSON'S SPECIAL

MUSIC		CALLS	MUSIC		DESCRIPTION
Intro:		Actives down the outside track			
A1	1-4	— — — —	**A1**	1-8	All the 1s face the top, turn away from their partners and walk individually down the outside of the set 6 steps. On the next 2 steps, they turn towards each other to face up.
	5-8	Turn around and come on back			
	9-12	— — — —		9-16	All the 1s walk 6 steps up the outside to place. On the next 2 steps, they continue in towards the center of the set to stand between their 2s, and all four dancers face down the set.
	13-16	Into the center to a line of four			
A2	1-4	Go down the center four in line	**A2**	1-8	Take hands in your line of four and walk forward 6 steps towards the bottom of the set. On the next 2 steps, drop hands and turn to face the top, each pair of dancers turning towards each other.
	5-8	Turn alone and come on back			
	9-12	— — — —		9-16	Join hands again and walk 6 steps forward, towards the top. On the next 2 steps, bend the line, i.e., the two middle dancers drop hands with each other and move backward, while the two end dancers move slightly forward, to end as two facing couples *(progression)*.
	13-16	Bend the line and ladies chain			
B1	1-4	— — — —	**B1**	1-8	The same two couples do a ladies chain across the set (see Glossary) (8 steps).
	5-8	— — And chain them back			
	9-12	— — — —		9-16	Repeat the ladies chain, back to place (8 steps).
	13-16	Join hands and circle left			
B2	1-4	— — — —	**B2**	1-8	The same two couples for a circle of four and circle left (8 steps).
	5-8	The other way back, circle right			
	9-12	— — (Ready at the top)		9-16	Circle right, back to place (8 steps).
	13-16	— Actives down the outside			

Comments

This is also a dance I have found to be very useful as one of the first contras I teach. The progression is painless and there is good contact between the two couples dancing together. The A part, with its trips down the center and back, is typical for the contra formation and contributes to the feeling that this is a different type of dance than a progressive circle.

I learned Johnson's Special from Rickey Holden, who composed it in the 1950s.

Music

Use a New England or Canadian tune—I prefer a reel such as "La Grande Chaine" from *Square Dance Tonight Vol. 2* or "Ross's Reel No. 4" from *New England Chestnuts 2*. **Tempo:** about 120.

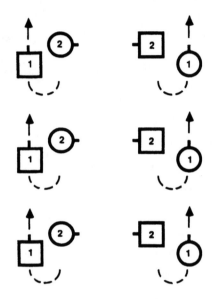

"Actives down the outside."

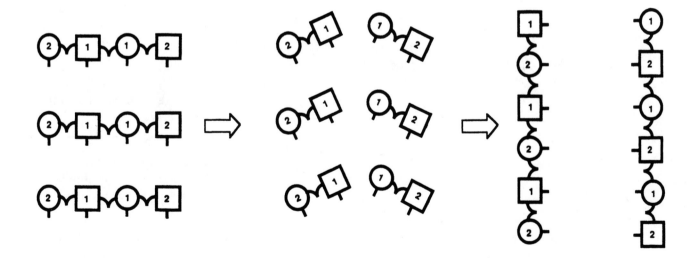

"Come on back and bend the line."

Previously published in *The Contra Dance Book*; 1956 by Rickey Holden; used with his permission.

CONTRA
duple improper

YANKEE REEL

MUSIC		CALLS	MUSIC		DESCRIPTION
Intro:		Right hand star with the couple below			
A1	1-4	— — — —	**A1**	1-8	Form a right hand star with the couple who are your neighbors and walk 8 steps clockwise.
	5-8	Left hand star, the other way back			
	9-12	— — — —		9-16	Change to a left hand star and walk 8 steps counterclockwise, back to place.
	13-16	Actives, down the center you go			
A2	1-4	Below two couples, separate and	**A2**	1-8	The 1s take inside hands and walk down the center 8 steps, past two standing couples.
	5-8	Come back up the outside track			
	9-12	— — — —		9-16	Drop hands, turn away from each other (gent to the left, lady to the right), and walk individually up the *outside* of the set, back to place (8 steps).
	13-16	— — Meet and swing			
B1	1-4	— — — —	**B1**	1-8	The 1s continue into the center of the set, take social dance position and swing 8 counts with the buzz step (end facing down, with the lady on the gent's right).
	5-8	— Now swing the one below			
	9-12	— — — —		9-16	Take social dance position with your neighbor and swing 8 counts (buzz step). End facing across, with the lady on the gent's right *(progression)*.
	13-16	Put her on the right, half promenade			
B2	1-4	— — — —	**B2**	1-8	With the person you swung, promenade across the set (gents passing left shoulders) and turn to face the center of the set (8 steps).
	5-8	Right and left through, back to place			
	9-12	— — (Ready at the top)		9-16	Come back to place by doing a right and left through (see Glossary) (8 steps).
	13-16	Right hand star with the couple below			

Comments

This is another good contra for beginners, composed by Ted Sannella in the early 1950s and published in his book *Balance and Swing* (1982).

The 1s dancing at the bottom of the set will have to make believe there are two pairs of 2s to pass in A2 1-8. Otherwise they may either come back too soon or come too far back up the set and end in the wrong position. As a matter of fact, it is a good idea to have all the 1s pay attention to the identity of the first 2s they pass, so they know what position to come back to.

There is a tendency for people to rush the half promenade in B2 1-8. Try to get them to use the full 8 counts of music.

As Ted Sannella writes, the dance is also enjoyable for more experienced dancers, who should not have trouble with the above mentioned details but who will find satisfaction in making a smooth transition from partner swing to neighbor swing in B1.

Music

A New England or Canadian tune is best for this dance. Try "Reel Fernando" from *Square Dance Tonight Vol. 2* or "Hornpipes" from *New England Country Dance Music* with the Green Mountain Volunteers. **Tempo:** about 120.

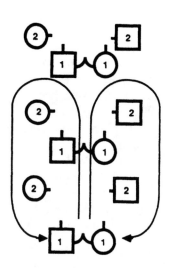

"Actives down the center, below two couples, and come up the outside" (the path of only one couple is shown, but the other 1s move correspondingly).

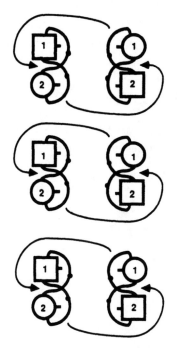

Half promenade across the set.

CONTRA
duple improper

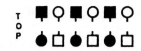

THE BELLES OF AUBURN

MUSIC	CALLS
Intro:	With the <u>one below</u>, sashay <u>down</u>
A1 1-4	_ _ _ _
5-8	_ _ _ And <u>back</u>
9-12	_ _ _ _
13-16	With the <u>same person</u>, <u>balance there</u>
A2 1-4	_ _ _ _
5-8	_ _ _ And <u>swing</u>
9-12	_ _ _ _
13-16	Put her on the <u>right</u> in <u>lines of four</u>
B1 1-4	Go <u>down</u> the <u>center</u> <u>four</u> in <u>line</u>
5-8	<u>Turn</u> as a <u>couple</u> and <u>come</u> on <u>back</u>
9-12	_ _ _ _
13-16	<u>Bend</u> the <u>line</u>, ladies <u>chain</u>
B2 1-4	_ _ _ _
5-8	_ _ And <u>chain</u> them <u>back</u>
9-12	_ _ (Ready at the <u>top</u>)
13-16	With the <u>one below</u> you sashay <u>down</u>

MUSIC	DESCRIPTION
A1 1-8	The 1s step into the middle so that they are standing back to back and each is facing his or her neighbor. Take both hands with your neighbor and sashay 8 steps down the set.
9-16	Keeping hands, sashay 8 steps the other way, back to place.
A2 1-16	With the same person, balance (pas-de-basque towards each other, pas-de-basque away from each other) (4 counts) and swing (social dance position, buzz step) 12 counts. Or balance twice (8 counts) and swing 8 counts.
B1 1-4	Finish the swing facing down the set with the lady on the gent's right, forming a line of four with the opposite pair of dancers. As a line of four, walk down the center 4 steps.
5-8	The two middle dancers drop hands. Turn 180 degrees as a couple with the one you swung (ladies go *forward*, gents *backward*) to face the top (4 steps).
9-16	Take hands in line again and walk 6 steps forward, towards the top of the set. On the next 2 steps, bend the line, i.e., the two middle dancers drop hands with each other and move backwards, while the two end dancers move slightly forward, so you end as two facing couples *(progression)*.
B2 1-8	The same two couples do a ladies chain across the set (see Glossary) (8 steps).
9-16	Repeat the ladies chain, back to place (8 steps).

Comments

The Belles of Auburn was created by Roger Knox in 1958, when he accidentally tacked another standard ending onto the first half of the dance The Beaux of Oakhill. Like some other callers, I think the result, which Ralph Page dubbed The Belles of Auburn after the town where Ralph was calling that night, is better than the original dance. The dance was published in Ralph Page's magazine, *Northern Junket*, and is also in Ted Sannella's book *Balance and Swing*.

People like to do the sashay step now and then—it's particularly popular among the younger and more energetic dancers—and it's nice to have some dances that go especially well with the many sprightly jigs in the New England repertory.

The progression in this dance is not difficult, coming as it does with a "bend the line," but it is important that the dancers form their lines of four correctly in B1 1-4 and turn as couples, not individually, in B1 5-8. In practice, the trickiest part of this dance often is getting the 1s to move down to the next 2s for the sashay at the beginning of the dance. If they do that correctly and on time, the rest of the dance is fairly straightforward.

In B1 9-16, you can also use 4 steps to return up the set and 4 to bend the line. This timing follows the phrase of the music more closely, but is a little more difficult for inexperienced dancers.

Music

To me, the sashay step, with its syncopated rhythm, spells "jig"—for example, "Mary Douglas Jig" from *Square Dance Tonight Vol. 2*. The dance can also be done to a tune in 2/4 time, but if so, I would choose one that has a bouncy quality, such as the "Hornpipes" medley from *New England Country Dance Music* with the Green Mountain Volunteers. **Tempo:** about 126.

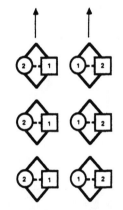

"With the one below, sashay down."

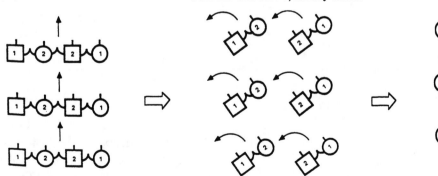

"Down the center four in line..."   "...turn as a couple..."   "...and come on back."

Previously published in *Balance and Swing* (1982 by Ted Sannella) and in *Contras: As Ralph Page Called Them* (1990 by Roger Knox). Used with the permission of Ted Sannella and Roger Knox.

CONTRA
duple improper

BALANCE THE LINES

MUSIC		CALLS
Intro:		Allemande left with the one below

A1 1-4 Turn once and a half 'til the gents face out

5-8 And the ladies in, now balance there

9-12 __ __ Turn by the left

13-16 Ladies chain across the set

A2 1-4 __ __ __ __

5-8 Chain them back, you're not through yet

9-12 __ __ __ __

13-16 Now over you go with a half promenade

B1 1-4 __ __ __ __

5-8 __ __ And promenade back

9-12 __ __ __ __

13-16 Same four, left hand star

MUSIC		DESCRIPTION

A1 1-8 1s face down, 2s up. Take a left-hand pigeon wing grip with your neighbor and go once and a half around each other with 8 steps, thus changing places. End with the lady facing in and the gent out, and without dropping hands, take a right-hand pigeon wing grip with the next person in line to form a long wave at the side of the set.

9-12 In this formation, do a balance (pas-de-basque forward, pas-de-basque back) (4 counts).

13-16 Drop right hands and turn once around with the person whose left hand you are holding (allemande left) (4 steps).

A2 1-8 Do a ladies chain across the set (see Glossary) (8 steps). As the lady starts to chain, the gent she did the allemandes with will continue to turn a couple of steps counterclockwise to face across so he can receive the opposite lady for the courtesy turn.

9-16 Repeat the ladies chain, back to place (8 steps).

B1 1-8 Keep the handhold from the courtesy turn. Promenade across the set (gents passing left shoulders) and turn to face the center of the set (8 steps).

9-16 Repeat the half promenade, back to place (8 steps).

B2 **1-4** __ __ __ __

      5-8 And the <u>other</u> way <u>back</u> with a <u>right</u> hand <u>star</u>

      9-12 __ __ (Ready at the <u>top</u>)

    13-16 <u>Allemande</u> <u>left</u> the <u>one</u> <u>below</u>

B2 **1-8** The same two couples form a left hand star and move counterclockwise 8 steps.

    9-16 Change to a right hand star and move clockwise 8 steps, back to place.

Comments

The dance presented here is Rickey Holden's simplified version of Balance Those Lines by the innovative choreographer Herbie Gaudreau, published in the latter's book *Modern Contra Dancing* (1971).

The challenging part of the dance is the A1 part, which must be done precisely and with determination. After that, the dancers can "relax" for the rest of the sequence.

In A1 1-8, the dancers are asked to do an allemande left *once and a half* around in eight counts. Establish the positioning first, by having them do an allemande left exactly once around, and then halfway more. Now check to see that all the ladies are facing the center of the set, and the gents are facing out. The second allemande will be done once around in four counts, bringing the dancers back to the same position. You will probably have to practice this part of the dance a few times up to tempo to get the timing down (and you may also need a little extra practice calling it). Quick allemandes like these, which were unusual when this dance was written, have become common in contemporary contra dancing, but beginning dancers will probably find them a little challenging.

The other figures are timed conventionally, and there should be no need to rush them. In particular, make sure that a full eight counts are used for each half promenade: four to change places and four to turn around. Also note that the stars in B2 start with a *left* hand star. Many people will automatically start to do a right hand star. When coming out of the right hand star preparatory to starting the dance again, everyone should move smoothly to meet their new neighbors along the line. To do this, the ladies should look for their new neighbors over their left shoulders and be particularly careful not to go too far in the star.

Music

Use a New England or Canadian tune, either a reel or a jig. Some possibilities are "The Long Campaign" from *Square Dance Tonight Vol. 3* and "New England Medley" from *New England Country Dance Music* with the Green Mountain Volunteers. **Tempo:** about 120.

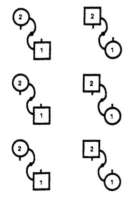

"Allemande left with the one below."

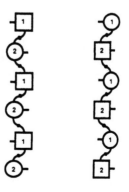

Ready for "balance in line."

Original version published in *Modern Contra Dancing* (1971 by Herbie Gaudreau); new version devised by Rickey Holden. Used with the permission of Jon Sanborne, *American Square Dance* magazine, and Rickey Holden.

CONTRA
duple improper

GREEN MOUNTAIN VOLUNTEERS

MUSIC	CALLS
Intro:	On the <u>right</u> sashay, on the <u>left</u> you <u>balance</u>

A1	**1-4**	__ __ __ And <u>swing</u>
	5-8	__ __ Sashay <u>back</u>
	9-12	__ __ __ __
	13-16	On the <u>left</u> sashay, on the <u>right</u> you <u>balance</u>

A2	**1-4**	__ __ __ And <u>swing</u>
	5-8	__ __ Sashay <u>back</u>
	9-12	__ __ __ __
	13-16	<u>Actives</u>, <u>down</u> the <u>center</u> you <u>go</u>

B1	**1-4**	__ __ __ __
	5-8	<u>Turn</u> <u>alone</u> and <u>come</u> on <u>back</u>
	9-12	__ Cast <u>off</u> with the <u>one</u> you <u>swung</u>
	13-16	__ __ <u>Right</u> and <u>left</u> <u>through</u>

B2	**1-4**	__ __ __ __
	5-8	__ __ __ And <u>back</u>
	9-12	__ __ (Ready at the <u>top</u>)
	13-16	On the <u>right</u> sashay, on the <u>left</u> you <u>balance</u>

MUSIC		DESCRIPTION
A1	**1-16**	The line on the caller's right (seen from the top) takes hands and dances towards the bottom of the set with 8 sashay steps and then back to place with 8 sashay steps). *At the same time*, each dancer in the left-hand line does a balance with his or her neighbor and then they swing (4+12 counts).
A2	**1-16**	Repeat A1, 1-16, but this time, the line on the caller's left does the sashay and the line on the right does the balance and swing.
B1	**1-8**	1s take inside hands with your partner and walk 6 steps down the center. On the next 2 steps, turn toward each other to face up.
	9-12	Join hands again and walk 4 steps up the center, until you meet the couple who were your neighbors.
	13-16	Each pair of neighbors puts their arms around each other's waists and turns as a couple 270 degrees (1s going *forward*, 2s *backwards*—see illustration) to reform the long lines (4 steps, *progression*).
B2	**1-8**	The same two couples do a right and left through (see Glossary) across the set (8 steps).
	9-16	Repeat the right and left through, back to place (8 steps).

Comments

Green Mountain Volunteers (or Green Mountain Jig, as it also is called) is a traditional dance found, for example, in *The Country Dance Book* by Beth Tolman and Ralph Page (1937). Like The Belles of Auburn, it makes use of the sashay step and is a lively dance well suited to a tune in jig time. Compared to The Belles of Auburne, however, Green Mountain Volunteers includes slightly more difficult figures, and the first part of the dance, in which the two lines do different things at the same time, is a little more difficult for the caller to direct. So I recommend saving this dance for groups with some experience.

The above description of the A part is the way I interpreted the rather sketchy instructions in *The Country Dance Book* when I started calling. Later, I discovered that the intention was for the dancers to sashay down in *couples,* as in The Belles of Auburn, with the active dancer moving into the center of the set to face his or her neighbor. Another (traditional) variation is for the "sashaying" couples to simply promenade down the set, turn as a couple, and promenade back. If you want to avoid arguments, choose one of these solutions, but I like our way of doing the dance well enough to have retained it. It makes an unusual figure that looks particularly good in performance.

Instead of a single balance in the A part, you may prefer to have the dancers balance twice and then swing only eight counts. This makes the dance slightly less strenuous and may also give the dancers a better chance to collect themselves and execute each of the figures properly, especially if they are still learning to master the balance and or the buzz step swing.

The second half of the dance — down the center, come back, cast off and right and left through (and back) — is a classic ending for older contra dances, so common that I used to take it for granted. However, the cast off in particular will take a little practice before the dancers feel comfortable with it. Remember that the actives (1s), regardless of sex, always move *forward,* continuing their motion as they come up the center, while the inactives (2s) move *backwards,* affording the 1s a pivot point. As late as the 1960s, we used to just hold hands with our neighbors for the cast off, but the arms-around-the-waist hold is universal today and gives a greater sensation of wheeling around as a couple. Please be careful, though, *not* to let gent 2 take courtesy turn hold with lady 1!

Also please note: since you have six steps to go down the center but only four to come back, the steps down the center should be smaller than those coming back. Otherwise you will be rushing to get back in time for the cast off, and some dancers may even try to do the cast off with the wrong couple. Tell them to look for the person they swung with in the A part.

Music

Preferably a jig, such as "Debbie's Jig" from *Maritime Dance Party.* Or else another bouncy tune, such as "Liberty" from *Square Dance Tonight Vol. 3.* **Tempo:** about 120-126, depending on the expertise of the group.

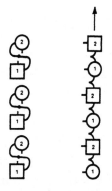

Green Mountain Volunteers starts with the line on the caller's right sashaying down the hall, while the dancers in the line on the left do a balance and swing.

Cast off.

CONTRA
duple improper

CAROL'S NECK

MUSIC	CALLS
Intro:	Active couples dosido
A1 1-4	__ __ __ __
5-8	Cross over, go below just one
9-12	__ __ __ __
13-16	Meet your own with an allemande right
A2 1-4	Go once around __ __
5-8	__ Pass by and come back up
9-12	__ __ __ __
13-16	Into the center in lines of four
B1 1-4	Go down the center four in line
5-8	Wheel in the middle and the ends cross over
9-12	Come on back in the same old track
13-16	And swing the lady on your left
B2 1-4	__ __ __ __
5-8	__ __ Right and left through

MUSIC	DESCRIPTION
A1 1-8	1s dosido your partner (8 steps).
9-16	1s go forward again and pass your partner by the right shoulder. Turn to face down the set and walk individually down the outside, passing only one person. Then come into the center to meet your partner (8 steps).
A2 1-8	1s take a right-hand pigeon wing grip with your partner and walk exactly once around each other with 8 steps.
9-16	1s drop hands, pass each other by the right shoulder and walk individually *up* the outside of your own side of the set, back to place (6 steps). On the next 2 steps, continue into the center of the set to stand between your 2s, with all four facing down.
B1 1-4	Take hands in your lines of four and walk 4 steps down the center.
5-8	The 1s drop hands with the 2s, but not with each other. The 1s wheel around 180 degrees as a couple (lady going forward, gent backwards) to face the top. At the same time, each 2 continues forward in an arc to change places with his or her partner and face the top (see diagrams) (4 steps).
9-16	Take hands in your line of four again and walk 8 steps forward, towards the top.
B2 1-8	Each gent swings with the lady on his left (social dance position, buzz step) (8 counts). End facing across, with the lady on the gent's right *(progression)*.

9-12 __ __ (Ready at the <u>top</u>)

13-16 Active <u>cou</u>ples <u>dosido</u>

9-16 The same two couples do a right and left through across the set (see Glossary) (8 steps).

Comments

Carol's Neck is by Roger Whynot, a well-known caller and choreographer from Massachusetts. I learned the dance from his booklet, *Why Not Dance with Me* (1983). In the accompanying text, Roger explains that the dance is named for a woman who participated in the dance camp where he introduced it. The original version included a "right hand high, left hand low" figure, in which two end dancers change places, with one going under the middle dancer's arm. Carol was so tall that people kept getting tangled up in her, so he changed the dance but gave it her name.

The way the lines of four turn around in B1 5-8 is to the best of my knowledge unique and was one of the things that attracted me to the dance. It's fun to do, but does require a fair amount of room up and down the set, so don't try this dance in a crowded hall!

The trickiest part of the dance is actually the A part. Some dancers find the allemande right confusing and are not sure which direction to go in afterwards. It usually helps to have them practice the trip around the 2s *without* the allemande at first, and then insert it.

The timing of the A part is a good challenge for less experienced dancers. Don't rush; executing each movement in precisely the number of beats alotted will make the dance much more enjoyable. Finally, be careful not to take too big steps on the way up in B1 9-16, or the set will quickly creep upwards.

Music

Use a well-phrased northern style tune, such as "Cape Breton Symphony's Welcome to Shetland" from *Square Dance Tonight Vol. 3* or "O'Donal Abhu" from *New England Chestnuts 2*. **Tempo:** about 120-126.

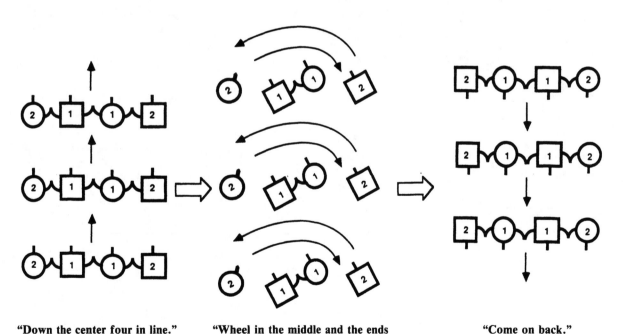

"Down the center four in line."   "Wheel in the middle and the ends cross over."   "Come on back."

Previously published in *Why Not Dance with Me*; 1983 by Roger Whynot; used with his permission.

CONTRA
duple proper

STARS AND STRIPES

MUSIC		CALLS	MUSIC		DESCRIPTION
Intro:		Right hand star with the couple below			
A1	1-4	_ _ _ _	**A1**	1-8	Form a right hand star with the couple who are your neighbors, and walk clockwise 8 steps, exactly once around.
	5-8	_ _ Actives swing			
	9-12	_ _ _ _		9-16	1s swing your partner (social dance position, buzz step) and end facing *up*, with the lady on the gent's right (8 steps).
	13-16	_ Face up, go down the outside			
A2	1-4	_ _ _ _	**A2**	1-8	The 1s now turn away from each other and walk individually down the outside of the set 6 steps. On the next 2 steps, they turn towards each other to face up.
	5-8	Turn around and come on back			
	9-12	_ _ _ _		9-16	The 1s walk 6 steps up the outside, back to place. On the next 2 steps, they continue in towards the middle of the set to stand between their 2s, and all four dancers face down the set.
	13-16	Into the center to a line of four			
B1	1-4	_ _ _ _	**B1**	1-8	Take hands in your line of four and walk forward 6 steps towards the bottom of the set. On the next 2 steps, drop hands and turn individually to face the top, each pair of dancers turning towards each other.
	5-8	Turn alone and come back home			
	9-12	_ _ _ _		9-16	Take hands again and walk 6 steps forward, towards the top. On the next 2 steps, the 1s pull back a little and the 2s, who are at the ends of the line, move forward and join hands to form a circle *(progression)*.
	13-16	Join hands and circle left			
B2	1-4	_ _ _ _	**B2**	1-8	Circle to the left 8 steps, exactly once around.
	5-8	Left hand star, go the other way back			
	9-12	_ _ _ _		9-16	Change to a left hand star and walk 8 steps counterclockwise, being sure to end with the 1s farthest from the top of the set.
	13-16	Right hand star with the next below			

Comments

Stars and Stripes was written by Jim Gregory and published in 1984 in Ralph Page's magazine, *Northern Junket,* from which I learned it.

At first glance, the dance looks simple enough, and it is not all that difficult, but it requires a little more timing and sense of positioning than, for example, Johnson's Special, which includes many of the same movements.

First of all, note that Stars and Stripes is "proper," which some dancers may find disorienting at first. Remember that they *do not* have to change places while waiting out at the ends. When teaching the dance, you may have to emphasize that the circle and star in B2 must be executed precisely, so that everyone is in position to move on to the next couple for the right hand star in A1 1-8. The transition from left hand star to right hand star should be seamless, with lady 1 and gent 2 looking for their new neighbors over their right shoulders. Also be sure that the right hand star moves exactly once around, so that the 2s find their correct positions in line while the 1s swing.

Music

Try "Arkansas Traveler" from *Square Dance Tonight Vol. 1* or "The Road to Boston" from *New England Chestnuts 2.* **Tempo:** about 120-126.

The bearers of tradition

Traditional square and contra dancing stayed alive in the areas wherein lived excellent fiddlers. They kept alive one of the most interesting forms of social recreation— contra dances. It faded in every other area of the country where good musicians were an unknown commodity. Lovers of contra dances owe a great debt to their old-time fiddlers who could and did play the proper music for them—and played the music in tune! It was not the dancers, the prompters, nor the callers, who kept contra dancing alive for folks to rediscover and enjoy—it was good fiddling.
—Ed Moody in *Northern Junket,* February 1968

Used with the permission of Jim Gregory.

CONTRA
duple improper

THE LIGHTED SCONCE

MUSIC		CALLS	MUSIC		DESCRIPTION
Intro:		__ Two ladies allemande right			

MUSIC		CALLS
A1	1-4	__ __ __ __
	5-8	__ And everyone swing your own
	9-12	__ __ __ __
	13-16	Circle left, go once around

MUSIC		DESCRIPTION
A1	1-8	The two ladies in each minor set take a right-hand pigeon wing grip and go once around each other in 8 steps.
	9-16	Each lady takes social dance position with her own partner and they swing 8 counts, using the buzz step. Finish the swing in original positions, with the 1s facing down the set and the 2s facing up.

MUSIC		CALLS
A2	1-4	__ __ __ __
	5-8	Twos arch, loop to a line
	9-12	__ __ Face up the set
	13-16	And four in line it's up you come

MUSIC		DESCRIPTION
A2	1-8	Take hands in a circle and circle left exactly once around (8 steps).
	9-16	Without anyone dropping hands, the 2s form an arch by lifting their joined hands. The 1s go forward, through the arch, drop hands with each other *only*, and move away from each other and around their respective neighbors to form a line facing *up* the set. The 2s will have to turn in towards each other and go under their own arms to avoid dropping hands (8 steps).

MUSIC		CALLS
B1	1-4	__ __ __ __
	5-8	Turn alone, go the other way back
	9-12	__ __ __ __
	13-16	Bend the line and ladies chain

MUSIC		DESCRIPTION
B1	1-8	In your line of four, walk forward 6 steps towards the *top* of the set. On the next 2 steps, drop hands and turn individually to face the opposite way, each pair of dancers turning toward each other.
	9-16	Join hands again and walk 6 steps forward, towards the bottom of the set. On the next 2 steps, bend the line, i.e., the two middle dancers drop hands with each other and move backward, while the two end dancers move slightly forward, to end as two facing couples *(progression)*.

B2 **1-4**   _ _ _ _

5-8   Turn and chain them back again

9-12   _ _ (Ready at the top)

13-16   _ Two ladies allemande right

B2 **1-8**   The same two couples do a ladies chain across the set (see Glossary) (8 steps).

9-16   Repeat the ladies chain, back to place (8 steps).

Comments

This nice contra dance was composed by Glen Morningstar, a caller from Michigan. The name of the dance refers to the sconces that adorn the walls of Lovett Hall in Dearborn, a hall built by Henry Ford and named for Benjamin Lovett, the dancing master Ford employed for many years, and with whom he worked to re-introduce gracious old time square dancing to American society.

The "Twos arch, loop to a line" movement in A2 9-16 is recognizable as a variation on the southern figure Mountaineer Loop (see the small circle figures in the chapter on the Big Set). In recent years, several interesting contra dances have been composed that include southern figures. The 2s should maintain hand contact as they turn under their own arms in this figure, but the grip must be loose and flexible.

The flow in the first part of The Lighted Sconce is excellent, and attention should be payed to timing the allemande right, swing, circle and "loop to a line" so that each movement ends just as the next one is about to start. This means that the ladies should not rush their allemande, and that the dancers should finish the swing and be back in place just in time to start the circle left.

Music

The Lighted Sconce can be danced to almost any good New England style tune—try "The Growling Old Man and the Grumbling Old Woman" from *Kitchen Junket*—but you might also want to try it to a well-phrased tune played in bluegrass style, such as "Durham's Reel" on *Dances from Appalachia 2*. **Tempo:** about 120.

Previously published, 1984 by Glen Morningstar; used with his permission.

CONTRA
duple proper

NEWLYWEDS' REEL

MUSIC		CALLS	MUSIC		DESCRIPTION
Intro:		— Actives turn by the right			
A1	1-4	— And balance four in line	**A1**	1-4	1s take a right-hand pigeon wing grip with your partner and turn halfway around, so that you are standing in the center of the set with the lady facing up and the gent down (4 steps). In the meantime, the 2s position themselves so gent 2 can take a left-hand pigeon wing grip with lady 1 and lady 2 with gent 1. You are now standing in a "wavy line" of four, with all the ladies facing up and the gents down.
	5-8	Now turn by the left, go twice around		5-8	In this formation, do a balance (pas-de-basque forward, pas-de-basque back) (4 counts).
	9-12	— — — —		9-16	The 1s drop hands with their partners and everyone does an allemande left exactly twice around (8 steps).
	13-16	Single file, go forward all			
A2	1-4	(Ladies up and the gents go down)	**A2**	1-8	Drop hands. Everyone walks forward individually 6 steps (ladies toward the top, gents toward the bottom of the set). On the next 2 steps, turn to face in the opposite direction.
	5-8	Turn around, go the other way back			
	9-12	Actives meet with the left hand 'round		9-12	Walk forward 4 steps toward the places you came from.
	13-16	Out to the sides and give 'em a swing		13-16	When the 1s meet their partners, they take a left-hand pigeon wing grip and go all the way around each other with 4 steps.
B1	1-4	— — — —	**B1**	1-16	Everybody swing your neighbor (social dance position, buzz step) and end in long lines with the lady on the gent's right *(progression)* (16 counts).
	5-8	— — — —			
	9-12	— — — —			
	13-16	Dosido your partners all			

B2 **1-4** __ __ __ __

    5-8 <u>La</u>dy 'round the <u>la</u>dy and the <u>gent</u> a<u>round</u> the <u>gent</u>

    9-12 __ __ (Ready at the <u>top</u>)

    13-16 <u>Ac</u>tives <u>turn</u> by the <u>right</u> hand '<u>round</u>

B2 **1-8** Everybody dosido with your partner (8 counts).

    9-16 The 2s stand in place while the 1s dance a half figure eight around them as follows: lady 1 passes between lady 2 and gent 2 and continues around lady 2, ending in the place in the "ladies' line" where her partner came from. *At the same time*, gent 1 passes between gent 2 and lady 2 and continues around gent 2, ending in the place in the "gents' line" where his partner came from (gent 1 lets lady 1 pass in front of him to start) (8 steps).

Comments

This lively contra was composed many years ago by Ted Sannella, a popular caller and prolific choreographer from the Boston area (now living in Maine), with a little help from his wife, Jean.

Above is the version I learned some years ago. After the publication of Ted's first book, *Balance and Swing,* I realized that it diverged slightly from the original, but since I feel the changes make the dance even better, I have retained them. In the original version, the single file promenade in A2 1-12 is to be done by the 1s only, and the final two figures, dosido partner and half figure eight, are to be done in reverse order, with only the 1s doing the dosido. The changes make the role of the 2s more active, although in a crowded hall it may still be a good idea to have only the 1s do the dosido in B2 1-8. I also like the transition from "lady 'round the lady and the gent around the gent" to the allemande right of the following sequence.

This is definitely not a dance for beginners, as it demands quite a lot of the dancers. They must constantly be aware of whom they are dancing with, even though they are separated from the rest of the minor set in the single file promenade (make sure

the 1s know who their partners are so they can find them for the allemande left in A2 13-16!). While the 1s are dancing this figure, by the way, the 2s can continue a couple of steps farther, to place—as long as the 1s can still find them for the swing.

A few more tips: in A1 1-4, it is very important that the 2s move into place to form the wave, and don't just stand passively waiting for something to happen. This is particularly true of gent 2, as it otherwise will be physically impossible for lady 1 to take hands with him. In A1 9-16, it is possible to do the allemande left just once around, but there is enough time to go twice around, so I would only recommend going once around as a teaching aid if the dancers are having problems. The call placed in parentheses in A2 1-4 is not strictly necessary, but may be of use as a reminder in the beginning.

See the next page for diagrams of this dance.

Music

Use a northern style tune, such as "The King's Favorite" from *Square Dance Tonight Vol. 3* or "Maggie Brown's Favorite" from *New England Chestnuts 2.* **Tempo:** about 120.

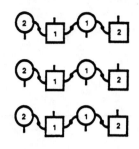

Balance four in line.

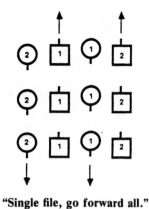

"Single file, go forward all."

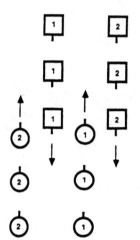

"Go the other way back."

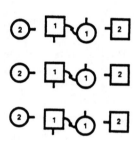

"Actives meet with the left hand 'round."

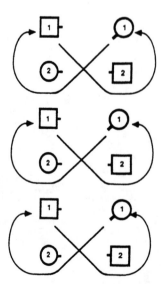

"Lady 'round the lady and the gent around the gent."

Previously published in *Balance and Swing*; 1982 by Ted Sannella; used with his permission.

CONTRA
duple improper

A BIRD IN THE HAND

MUSIC		CALLS
Intro:		__ __ Swing below
A1	**1-4**	__ __ __ __
	5-8	__ Join hands and circle left
	9-12	__ __ __ __
	13-16	Left hand star, the other way back
A2	**1-4**	__ __ __ __
	5-8	Now allemande right the next below
	9-12	Twice around __ __
	13-16	__ Two ladies dosido
B1	**1-4**	__ __ __ __
	5-8	Allemande left the one above
	9-12	Go twice around __ __
	13-16	__ __ Ladies chain
B2	**1-4**	__ __ __ __
	5-8	__ __ Chain them back
	9-12	__ __ __ __
	13-16	__ __ Swing below

MUSIC		DESCRIPTION
A1	**1-8**	Everybody swing your neighbor (social dance position, buzz step) (8 counts). Remember to end with the lady on the gent's right *(progression)*.
	9-16	The same two couples circle left 8 steps.
A2	**1-8**	Change to a left hand star and go 8 steps counterclockwise, back to place.
	9-16	From here, take a right-hand pigeon wing grip with your *next* neighbor in the line, and go twice around each other with 8 steps.
B1	**1-8**	The two ladies from the original minor set (those who did the circle and star together) do a dosido (8 steps).
	9-16	Take a left-hand pigeon wing grip with your original neighbor (the one you swung) and go twice around each other with 8 steps.
B2	**1-8**	The same two couples do a ladies chain across the set (see Glossary) (8 steps).
	9-16	Repeat the ladies chain, back to place (8 steps).

Comments

The allemande right in A2 9-16 sends the dancers outside their minor sets. Otherwise, everything takes place within the minor set, as usual. During the allemande right, the couples at the extreme ends of the set will have no one to dance with. They should be encouraged to do the allemande with their partners, but must be back in place in time for the following movements. Make sure the dancers really go twice around on both allemandes, not once and a half, which would leave them out of position. In order to do this, keep the allemandes relatively tight, with arms bent a little more than for a leisurely once-around-in-eight-counts allemande.

Music

Use a northern style tune, such as "Reel Fernando" from *Square Dance Tonight Vol. 2*. **Tempo:** about 120-126.

CONTRA
duple proper

HULL'S VICTORY

MUSIC		CALLS	MUSIC		DESCRIPTION
Intro:		__ Actives turn by the right			
A1	1-4	Halfway 'round and balance in line	**A1**	1-4	1s take a right-hand pigeon wing grip with your partner and turn halfway around, so that you are standing in the center of the set with the lady facing up and the gent down (4 steps). In the meantime, the 2s position themselves so gent 2 can take a left-hand pigeon wing grip with lady 1 and lady 2 with gent 1. You are now standing in a "wavy line" of four, with all the ladies facing up and the gents down.
	5-8	Turn by the left, go twice around		5-8	Do a balance (pas-de-basque forward, pas-de-basque back) (4 counts).
	9-12	__ __ __ __		9-16	The 1s drop hands with their partners and everyone does an allemande left exactly twice around (8 steps).
	13-16	__ Actives turn by the right			
A2	1-4	Go once around and balance again	**A2**	1-4	The 1s do an allemande right with their partners exactly once around to reform the wavy line (4 steps).
	5-8	__ __ Swing in the center		5-8	Balance as in A1 5-8 (4 counts).
	9-12	__ __ __ __		9-16	Drop hands. The 1s swing with their partners and end facing down the set, the lady on the gent's right (8 counts).
	13-16	Actives down the center you go			
B1	1-4	__ __ __ __	**B1**	1-4	The 1s join inside hands and walk down the center 4 steps.
	5-8	Turn as a couple and come on back		5-8	The 1s wheel 180 degrees as a couple (lady going forward, gent backwards) to face the top of the set (4 steps).
	9-12	__ __ Cast off		9-12	The 1s walk 4 steps up the center, until they come to their neighbors.
	13-16	__ __ Right and left four		13-16	The two dancers on each side of the set put their arms around each other's waists and turn as a couple 270 degrees (1s going *forward*, 2s *backwards*—see illustration) to reform the long lines (4 steps, *progression*).

B2   1-4   _ _ _ _

       5-8   _ _ <u>Right</u> and left <u>back</u>

      9-12   _ _ (Ready at the <u>top</u>)

     13-16   <u>Actives</u> <u>turn</u> by the <u>right</u> hand 'round

B2   1-8   The same two couples do a right and left through across the set (see Glossary) (8 steps). Since each "couple" for this figure consists of two dancers of the same sex, the courtesy turn hold is not used when you turn as a couple. Instead, use the arm-around-the-waist hold as in a cast off. The dancer on the right goes *forward* and the one on the left goes *backwards*.

      9-16   Repeat the right and left four, back to place (8 steps).

Comments

Hull's Victory is one of the classic old contra dances that it still enjoyed today. The name refers to an American naval victory over England in the War of 1812. Several variants of the A part are extant, but the above version is the one most widely danced today.

You may notice that the figures in the A1 part were borrowed by Ted Sannella for Newlyweds' Reel. As in the latter dance, the allemande left in A1 9-16 can be done only once around if necessary, but twice around is preferable. And just as in Newlyweds' Reel, it is important for the 2s to come up and meet their new 1s in order to form the wave in A1 1-4.

As mentioned in the notes to Green Mountain Volunteers, the ending "actives down the center and back, cast off and right and left through" (or right and left four) is a classic sequence found in many older contra dances. In former times, proper contras were much more common than they are today, and thus it was not unusual to do the right and left through with two men facing two women or to have two dancers of the same sex do the cast off with each other. Remember that in the cast off, the 1s still go *forward* and the 2s *backwards*. You may have to practice this a few times, but after a while, the dancers should be able to do a cast off automatically from any position.

Music

Hull's Victory is one of the dances that has its own special tune of the same name. An excellent recording can be found on the album *New England Chestnuts*, and is recommended. If necessary, the dance *can* be done to another tune, but personally, I would miss the emphasis that comes just at the times when the dancers do a balance in line—a good example of how a close correspondence between dance and tune can enhance the entire experience. **Tempo:** about 120.

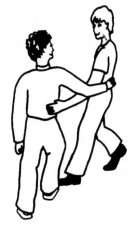 

In a proper contra, cast off may be done by two dancers of the same sex.

CONTRA
couple facing couple

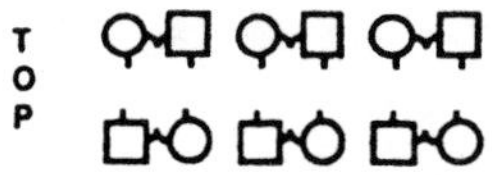

BUCKSAW

MUSIC	CALLS		MUSIC	DESCRIPTION

Intro: Allemande left your corners all

A1 1-4 _ _ _ _

5-8 _ _ Swing your own

9-12 _ _ _ _

13-16 With the opposite couple circle left

A2 1-4 _ _ _ _

5-8 _ _ Circle right

9-12 _ _ _ _

13-16 Look to the left, do a right and left through

B1 1-4 _ _ _ _

5-8 Now straight across do a right and left back

9-12 _ _ _ _

13-16 Same four, left hand star

B2 1-4 _ _ _ _

5-8 _ _ Right hand back

9-12 _ _ _ _

13-16 Allemande left your corners all

A1 1-8 Take a left-hand pigeon wing grip with your corner in the line and walk once around each other in 8 steps.

9-16 Swing your partner (social dance position, buzz step) (8 counts).

A2 1-8 With the opposite couple, circle left 8 steps.

9-16 Circle right 8 steps, back to place.

B1 1-8 Face *diagonally to the left* and do a right and left through (see Glossary) with that couple (8 steps). If there is no couple diagonally to your left, just stand still.

9-16 Face straight across the set and do another right and left through with your new opposite couple (8 steps) *(progression)*.

B2 1-8 The same two couples form a left hand star and walk 8 steps counterclockwise.

9-16 Change to a right hand star and walk 8 steps clockwise, back to place.

Comments

Here is a contra dance that is a little different. If you think of the set as a flattened circle, the progression takes place around the circle to the left, rather than step-by-step up and down the set as in a regular contra. Your partner is next to you, rather than across from you, and you also have a corner,

who remains the same throughout the dance (note that at the ends of the set, corners will be facing each other). Knowing who your corner is will help you reorient yourself each time the dance starts over.

In B1 1-8, the couples on the extreme left ends of the lines do nothing. The following right and left through brings them to the other side of the set, and they should then be careful to keep this new position after the stars in B2.

Also watch out for the transition from right hand star in B2 9-16 to the initial allemande left of the next round. This should be done smoothly, with the ladies looking over their left shoulders for their corners as they complete the star. The dancers at the extreme ends of the set will find that they are in the same stars as their corners, which may be disorienting if they are not made aware of it.

I learned Bucksaw in the early 1980s from the Green Mountain Volunteers, a performing group from Vermont that visited Denmark. Later I discovered that it was a variation on Herbie Gaudreau's innovative dance Becket Reel and that other variants also existed. Since then, other dances have been composed in this formation, sometimes referred to as "Becket formation" (see Let Sleeping Dogs Lie). I like the way the name Bucksaw reflects the "sawtooth" pattern of the right and left throughs in B1.

Music

Preferably a northern style tune such as the Canadian version of "Cotton-Eyed Joe" from *Maritime Dance Party*. But you can also try other well-phrased tunes, for example, "Ragtime Annie" from *Square Dance Tonight Vol. 1*. **Tempo:** about 126.

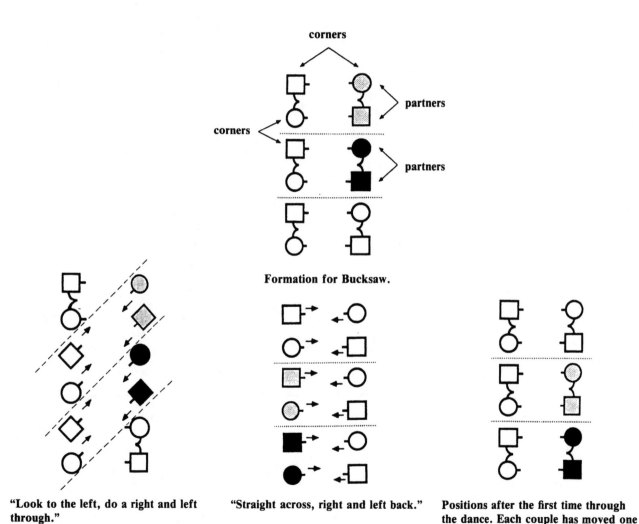

Formation for Bucksaw.

"Look to the left, do a right and left through."

"Straight across, right and left back."

Positions after the first time through the dance. Each couple has moved one place to their left.

Previously published in *Modern Contra Dancing*; 1971 by Herbie Gaudreau; used with the permission of Jon Sanborne, *American Square Dance* magazine.

CONTRA
couple facing couple

LET SLEEPING DOGS LIE

MUSIC	CALLS
Intro:	With the opposite couple, circle right
A1 1-4	_ _ _ _
5-8	Right hand star, the other way back
9-12	_ _ _ _
13-16	Allemande left your corners all
A2 1-4	Go twice around and back to your own
5-8	With your partner dosido
9-12	_ _ _ _
13-16	Right hand to your partner, "baby grand"
B1 1-4	_ _ _ _
5-8	Back to place and swing your own
9-12	_ _ _ _
13-16	Look to the left, do a half promenade
B2 1-4	_ _ _ _
5-8	Now straight across with a right and left through
9-12	_ _ _ _
13-16	And with that couple circle right

MUSIC	DESCRIPTION
A1 1-8	With the couple across from you, circle right 8 steps.
9-16	Change to a right hand star and walk 8 steps clockwise, back to place.
A2 1-8	Take a left-hand pigeon wing grip with your corner and walk *twice* around each other with 8 steps.
9-16	Come back to your partner and do a dosido (8 steps).
B1 1-8	As soon as you finish the dosido, give your right hand to your partner and dance a miniature grand right and left within your own group of two couples (8 steps).
9-16	Meet your partner at home and swing (social dance position, buzz step) (8 counts).
B2 1-8	Face *diagonally to the left* and change places with that couple by promenading to each other's places and turning to face in (8 steps). If there is no couple diagonally to your left, just stand still.
9-16	Do a right and left through (see Glossary) with your new opposite couple (8 steps) *(progression)*.

Comments

Let Sleeping Dogs Lie was composed by Inga Morton, a caller and choreographer from Lynge in Denmark. The dance is more demanding than Bucksaw, so teach the latter first to establish the ground rules.

The "baby grand" in B1 1-8 must be done quickly, since only two steps are available per hand instead of the usual three, so the dancers must be alert. Start the grand right and left as soon as you finish the dosido, think of the minor set as a tiny circle, and keep close together. The swing in B1 9-16 must not exceed the alotted time. If the dancers are late getting back from the "baby grand," they will have to shorten the swing accordingly, because the half promenade must be started on time.

Music

Use a well-phrased New England or French-Canadian tune, such as "The King's Favorite" from *Square Dance Tonight Vol. 3* or "French Canadian Reels" from *New England Country Dance Music* with the Green Mountain Volunteers. **Tempo:** relaxed, about 120.

Previously published in *Square Dance Century*; 1994 by Inga Morton; used with her permission.

Contra dance dependency syndrome

Having an interest in contra dancing may seem like a healthy and innocuous pastime at first glance, but continued exposure can lead to a dangerous dependency. The following symptoms are indications that you are becoming pathologically dependent on contra dancing:

- Preoccupation with contra dancing or with the next opportunity to contra dance.
- Increased tolerance for contra dancing; development of the ability to dance much more than others and still function adequately.
- Contra dancing with such intensity that the next morning brings amnesia about some of the events of the previous day or evening.
- Having a caller or band stashed somewhere, in case the "need to contra dance" suddenly manifests itself.
- Dancing much more than planned, or dancing much differently than planned.

If you suspect that you are suffering from contra dance dependency syndrome, you can test yourself by answering the following questions:

- Does the thought of contra dancing sometimes enter your mind when you should be thinking of something else?
- Do you sometimes feel the need to contra dance at a particular time of day?
- Do you often find that you can contra dance much more than others and not show the effects?
- Has anyone commented on your ability to contra dance?
- Have you ever contra danced in the morning?
- Do you sometimes contra dance even though you cannot afford to?
- Do you have a very definite preference to associate with people who contra dance, as opposed to those who do not?
- Have you ever wondered about your increased capacity to contra dance and that you may be somewhat proud of this ability?
- Have you ever had difficulty recalling how you got home from last night's contra dancing?
- Do you ever contra dance to calm your nerves or reduce tension?
- Do you find it difficult to enjoy a party or social gathering if no one there will be contra dancing?
- Do you contra dance to relieve physical discomfort?
- Do you ever contra dance more than you think you should?
- Is your contra dancing sometimes different than you would like it to be?

—based on Alouette Islin's suggestions published in the *Vermont Folk Arts Network Dance Calendar*, July and August 1987

Southern Mountain Style Square Dancing: Big Set

A dance form from Appalachia

The term "Southern mountain style square dancing" covers the many local variants of the regional dance style found in the southeastern United States, especially the states of Kentucky, Tennessee, North Carolina, West Virginia, Virginia, Georgia, and Alabama, portions of which are located in the Appalachian mountain range. As a region, Appalachia retained a strong folk culture longer than most other areas of the country, and this is reflected in the music and dancing we associate with the Southern mountain states.

Since Appalachia is in many ways a hotbed of genuine American folk culture, it is a little strange that Appalachian dance styles to a great degree have been overlooked in the revival of square dancing that has taken place since World War II. Many of the dance and music forms found farther west were clearly influenced by or directly evolved from the music and dance of settlers who moved west from the eastern seaboard one and two hundred years ago. In the meantime, the people of Appalachia have in many places retained and preserved their own ways of dancing.

In some parts of the region, square dancing is done in sets of four couples, similar to the square sets in other parts of the country. In other places, the custom is for all the couples present to form a single circle on the floor and the dance is then often known as "big circle" or "big set" dancing. Or both types of formations may be used in the same location, depending on the circumstances.

The English folk dance researcher and revivalist Cecil Sharp coined the term "running set" for Southern style dancing in four-couple sets after observing dancers in Kentucky in the early 1900s. In later books and articles, "running set" is sometimes used to refer to both the four-couple formation and the big set. This chapter will describe the big set.

The framework

In the case of big set, we are no longer talking about specific "dances," but about a dance *form*, in which the dance sequence never is exactly the same twice in succession. The callers have a selection of figures at their disposal and can combine them as they see fit. A good caller may have the reputation of being able to "call all night without repeating himself."

The dance tempo in this region is faster than, for example, in New England: a tempo of about 136 beats per minute is typical. At the same time, the dance is correspondingly looser in structure, especially with respect to the exactness of correlation between musical phrase and dance figure. And the music tends to emphasize rhythm more and melody less, compared with music from New England.

The choice of tune is fairly free. The dances can be quite long, and several tunes may therefore be combined into a medley, providing some variety not only for the dancers but also for the musicians. Just about any fiddle tune can be used, and while the traditional accompaniment would have been an old-fashioned string band with fiddle, banjo, and perhaps a guitar, mandolin and or bass, in many places today the bands play in the more sophisticated bluegrass style. They may even use electrified instruments and play country & western music. In fact, at some local square dances in rural areas, square dancing alternates with couple dancing, and it is an advantage for the band to be able to play popular music for couple dancing as well as square dance tunes.

Where the big set or running set is danced as part of a recreational dance program, the tendency (paradoxically) will often be toward preserving older dance customs and toward using the more traditional sounds of old-timey and bluegrass music.

Because of the relatively quick tempo and the

limitations that arise from dancing in the big set formation, the joy of this type of dancing stems not only from the choreography as such, but at least as much from the sensation of movement—the constant pulse of the dance can have an almost hypnotic effect—and from the social aspect of everyone dancing together in one big group. Still, many big set figures are attractive in their geometry, and most of them are easy enough to be quickly learned.

The caller builds up the dance

Fixed dance descriptions like the ones in the other chapters of this book would be meaningless in the case of the big set. Instead, I would like to give you a number of figures, accompanied by a few examples of how a dance sequence might be built up. Read them, and then you're on your own: improvise your own combinations, and observe the dancers (if you don't dance along with them yourself) to find out what works best. But remember, don't standardize this dance to death. It should be a little different every time you do it.

Apropos calling while you dance, this is, or was, often the custom in the southern mountains. In some places, each square would have its own caller, so that the different squares might be doing entirely different figures at the same time, and the dancers in each set might take turns acting as the caller. For a big set, however, calling from the floor is only satisfactory if everyone in the room can hear and understand you. If your group is small, it may be an excellent idea—you will gain a much better understanding of the context of the dance and how the various figures fit together with each other, and what's more, you won't have to miss out on the best part of all, the dancing. But if the group is too big, it is better to use the microphone. In the big set, only the caller knows what is coming next, so it is very important that you can be heard over the music.

Before we move on to the dance itself, I should mention that most of the figures in this chapter exist in more than one variant. It's not uncommon for the same figure to have more than one name or—even more confusing—for several different figures to have the same name. So if you consult some of the books on southern mountain dancing that are listed in the bibliography, don't be upset if you find other designations than the ones given here. I have compared several different sources and have tried to choose some of the most common, most interesting or most useful figures from them.

The basic concepts and dance style

A big set typically starts with some figures done in the big circle, with everyone dancing together. Then the couples pair off into small groups of two couples each. In some places, the couples number off before the dance starts, while in others they simply pair off extemporaneously when the time comes.

In a teaching situation, it is usually less confusing if the couples are assigned their numbers in advance. You can simply number them off, or another quick way, especially if the group is large, is to let all the dancers simultaneously form circles of two couples all the way around the big circle, with one couple in each small circle facing the center and the other with their backs to the center. The couples with their backs to the center are then designated "active," also called "odd" couples or number one couples. The others are the "inactive," "even" or number two couples. Reform the big circle by having the odd couple in each group stand to the left of their even couple, with everyone facing the center, and you will be ready to dance.

During the middle part of the dance, in which the couples are paired off, the odd couples will move one place to their left (i.e., counterclockwise in relation to the big circle) each time the caller says "On to the next." In this way they progress to a new even couple.

Theoretically, the even couples stand in place and wait for the next odd couple to reach them, but in practice, they, too, move to their left (i.e., clockwise) to meet the next odd couple. The progression is repeated several times; each time the dancers regroup, they do whatever figure the caller designates.

The dance ends by having everyone form one big circle again to dance a few more figures in this formation.

A notable characteristic of Southern mountain style dancing is that the dancers are in almost constant motion. The rule is to circle left if nothing else is happening. Should the dancers conclude a figure before the next call is given, they never stand still and wait, but continue to circle left until the call.

Since the tempo is quick, keep your steps small and light and your feet close to the ground. Dance in time with the music and keep your body relaxed—don't hop, skip or kick up your feet. You will be in style and your energy reserve will last longer.

One final point is that the buzz step is not

traditionally danced in this region. People today take social dance position when they swing, but use a walk-around type of swing (starting on the right foot) and may use more of an up-and-down motion in the knees. A certain amount of weight is given, but the highly centrifugal style of the New England buzz step is not found.

Several proponents of the traditional big set have held that the swing (which in some areas is done only once or twice around) should be done as a clockwise two-hand turn, rejecting both the buzz step and social dance position. There is some debate as to how widespread this style was in the past, although it seems likely to have existed in earlier years, when social dance position was considered too "forward."

The two-hand swing does fit nicely into the dance style and flow of the big set and I recommend trying it if you are using big set in a recreational dance program, especially with young people. Remember to give a little weight on the swing by keeping your elbows bent and leaning slightly away from each other. The center of the swing must, as always, be between the two dancers, so that both are moving around a central axis, rather than one dancer orbiting around the other.

If, on the other hand, you are a dance leader interested in reproducing authentic contemporary dance styles from the southern Appalachian area, you will probably want to look beyond this book to more specific references, such as Bob Dalsemer's *West Virginia Square Dances* (1982) or, even better, attend dances in the region to gain firsthand experience.

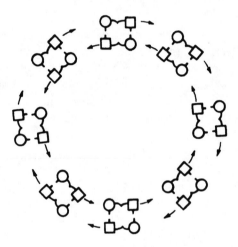

Starting formation for small circle figures.

"On to the next."

Clogging

Clogging is a kind of step dancing that, like the big set, is indigenous to the Southern mountains. Depending on local custom, it may also be referred to as "buckdancing," "flatfooting," "jigging," etc. Originally a spontaneous solo dance form, clogging steps were (and still are) made up by individual dancers, no two of whom dance exactly alike. The steps danced are improvised in accordance with the inspiration afforded by the music. Southern Appalachian clogging is assumed to derive from Irish and English forms of step dancing, possibly combined with black dance, Native American dance, or both, but its exact evolution is foggy.

In the 1930s, clogging began to be danced during the big set/running set as well as by individuals on the sidelines. A distinction was then made, where square dancing was concerned, between "clogging" and "smooth dancing," the latter term referring to the light, smooth step mentioned above.

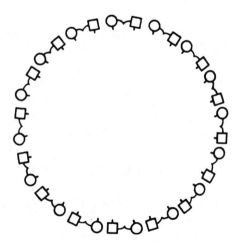

Starting formation for big circle figures.

An explanation of how to clog is, unfortunately, beyond the scope of this book, but several good manuals are available for the curious (see the Annotated Bibliography). With its complicated stepwork, clogging is a good deal more difficult to master than ordinary square dancing, but clogging has nonetheless gained tremendous popularity since the early 1970s. Since then, it has spread all over the country and has undergone some transitions of its own. Many people are now learning to clog as a separate dance form, often without any connection to square dancing at all, and a form called "precision clogging" has evolved, in which groups of dancers standing individually perform prechoreographed routines.

The calls

Southern mountain style callers often use a lot of patter; some of them call almost nonstop while the figures are being executed. Some of the calls in this chapter include examples of rhyming patter, and many more examples can be found in some of the older square dance books. If you have the temperament for improvising patter, some of the big set figures that take time to execute will give you ample opportunity.

Compared to most of the other dances in this book, it generally is not too important exactly where in the melody you give the calls for big set dancing. But they must still be given in time with the music, and a new call should start at the beginning of a 4-count musical phrase. In some cases (e.g., "Balance in") the timing of the movement will result in a call being given a precise number of beats after the previous one. In many other cases, however, the caller should keep an eye on the dancers and give the next call just when they are ready to do it. For this reason, I have not, in most cases, indicated exactly how many beats should come between the calls for each figure. But I have, as usual, underlined the words that should fall on the musical beat.

Recorded music for big set dancing

For the big set, you will need a recording long enough that you don't have to worry about it running out before the dance is over. This will probably mean at least 20 times through the tune(s). A few good recordings are the following, which are all between 10 and 20 minutes long:

"Big Set Tunes" on *Dances from Appalachia.*

"Hoedown Medley" on *Dances from Appalachia 3.*

"Chinese Breakdown" on *Traditional Southern Appalachian Square Dance Music.*

"Lost Indian" medley on *Dance Music, Square and Clog.*

"Band Box" medley and "Old Joe Clarke" medley on *Big Circle Mountain Dance Music.*

Complete references for these recordings are in the Discography.

Big circle figures

Let's get dancing! As mentioned above, the dance starts in one big circle of couples, with everyone facing the center. Each lady should, as usual, be on her partner's right. The gentleman's corner is the lady on his left; the lady's corner is the gent on her right. One couple should be designated as the leaders, since some of the big circle figures require this. Once the group has had some experience, you may be able to choose a leading couple while they are dancing, if you need one. Assign numbers to all the couples as explained under "The basic concepts and dance style." The leading couple should be 1s, the couple to their right 2s, the next couple 1s, and so on around the circle.

In the big set, "swing" may be done as a two-hand turn, in which the dancers move clockwise around each other with a walking step. Remember to give a little weight.

Big circle figures starting from one big circle with everyone facing in

CIRCLE LEFT, CIRCLE RIGHT

Call: All hands up and circle left...

_ _ Halfway and back

Description: Join hands and circle left. At the call "Halfway and back," circle right.

BALANCE IN

Call (e.g.): _ _ Balance in

_ _ Balance out

Do it again with a great big shout

Description: Everyone goes 4 steps towards the center and 4 steps backwards to place. Repeat. You can also let the dancers go 8 steps forward and 8 back.

RIP 'N' SNORT or DIVIDE THE RING

Call (e.g.): Leading couple rip and snort

Make it long or make it short

Description: *Without anyone dropping hands*, the couple designated leaders moves forward towards the opposite side of the circle, pulling the adjacent dancers with them. As they approach the other side, the two dancers they are aiming at raise their arms to form an arch, and the leaders go under the arch to the outside of the circle. Once outside, the leaders drop hands with each other and separate, the gent going left and the lady right, and lead the rest of the dancers around the outside of the circle, back to place. The dancers who form the arch will have to face each other and turn under their own upraised arms at the end to avoid dropping hands (keep the handhold loose and flexible).

THREAD THE NEEDLE

Call (e.g.): Leading gent, you thread the needle

You can tease 'em just a little

Description: The leading gent drops hands with his corner. All other handholds should be kept throughout the figure. The leader winds the circle in and out of itself at random by going between any two dancers he chooses. The dancers he goes between raise their joined arms to form an arch so the others can pass through, and turn under their own arms as necessary (keep the handholds loose and flexible!). Part of the fun of this figure is for the leader to keep the other dancers guessing as to where he is going to go—he can "fake" or feint and then suddenly go in another direction, etc. After several passes through the circle, the leader leads the other dancers around *clockwise* to reform the big circle with everyone facing in.

WIND UP THE BALL OF YARN

Call (e.g.): Now let's wind up that ball of yarn

Wind 'em up all nice and warm

Description: The leading gent drops hands with his corner, while all other handholds are maintained. The leader gradually leads the other dancers into the center of the ring to form a spiral. Then he turns sharply to his left and leads them out again (see diagram). When he emerges from the spiral, the leader should remember to turn to his left again and lead the dancers *clockwise* to reform the big circle with everyone facing in.

If the dancers get too jumbled up (this applies to the previous figure, Thread the Needle, also), you can call "Swing your partners one and all and promenade around the hall." Then continue with some big circle figures done from a promenade (see below), or go directly on to the small circle figures.

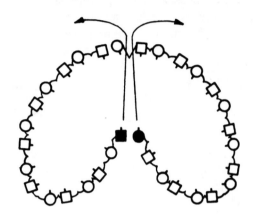

"Rip 'n' snort."

"Thread the needle."

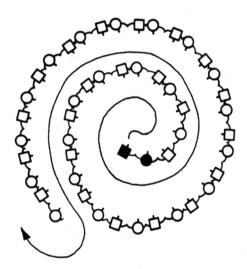

"Wind up the ball of yarn."

BASKET

Call (e.g.): a) Ladies to the inside, circle left
    Gents on the outside, circle right...
 b) __ __ And the other way back...
    Gents, find your partner and stop on her left
 c) Ladies bow and the gents know how
    Make a basket, turn it now...
 d) Reverse the basket, arms in back

d) <u>Let</u> 'er <u>rip</u>, ar<u>ound</u> that <u>track</u>...
e) <u>Break</u> that <u>ring</u> with a <u>corner</u> <u>swing</u>...
<u>Now</u> your <u>own</u>, that <u>pretty</u> little <u>thing</u>

Description: a) All the ladies go into the middle, form a circle of their own, and circle left. At the same time, the gents join hands to form a second circle outside the ladies' and circle right.
  b) Both circles turn and go back the other way, until each gent is standing to the left of his partner. Stop here, but don't drop hands!
  c) The ladies bow slightly and the gents move in and lift their joined arms over the ladies' heads and down in front of them, forming a basket. Everyone takes a small step backward to make the basket round, and then everyone dances to the left with a quick walking step.
  d) Stop and let the gents lift their arms over the ladies' heads and down behind them. Then the gents bow slightly so the ladies can lift their arms over the gents' heads and down behind them. Take a step back and dance to the left again.
  e) Everyone drops hands. Swing your corner once or twice around and then swing your partner.

"Make a basket."

"Reverse the basket, arms in back."

RIGHTS AND LEFTS

Call (e.g.):   a) Rights and lefts around the hall...
                                b) Meet your partner with an elbow swing
                                    And keep on swinging around the ring...

Description: a) Face your partner, give right hands, and do a grand right and left until you meet your partner again.

                       b) Hook right elbows with your partner and go once around each other until each of you can continue in the same direction you were going before. Drop hands with your partner, pass by and go on to the next person. Hook left elbows, go once around, pass by, and continue doing alternate right and left elbow swings with the people you meet, until you meet your partner again. The figure is usually concluded by doing an elbow swing *twice* around with your partner.

NB: This figure is best reserved for a group that is not too large, as it otherwise will take too long to complete.

SHOOFLY SWING

Call (e.g.):   Ready now for the shoofly swing
                        Lead couple into the middle of the ring
                        Turn your partner by the right, then left at the ring
                        Now your partner again with a right hand swing
                        And on to the next with a left hand swing

Description: Everyone drops hands, and the leading couple ("couple 1") moves forward a little so they are in the middle of the circle, opposite the couple that was on their right ("couple 2").

        The 1s take a right-hand pigeon wing grip with each other and go around each other with 4 steps, until lady 1 is facing gent 2. She drops hands with her partner, and while he waits in the center of the circle, she takes a left-hand pigeon wing grip with gent 2 and they go around each other with 4 steps until lady 1 is again facing her partner.

        The 1s turn again by the right with 4 steps, until lady 1 is facing gent 3. She turns him by the left with 4 steps, and the pattern is repeated — partner by the right, outside gent by the left — until couple 1 has been all the way around the circle.

        As soon as couple 1 reaches couple 4, couple 2 starts to dance the figure with couple 3. When they reach couple 5, couple 3 starts to dance with couple 4. Similarly, each couple follows up, until every couple has been all the way around the circle and back to place.

        Try to keep up the timing of 4 steps per hand on the turns. This will give the figure a good, solid rhythm that makes it especially satisfying to dance, not only for the ladies, who are in motion all the time, but also for the gents. Also note that the active gent should not stand stock still in the center while his partner is dancing with the outside gents, but should keep in motion, using the 4 steps to move on to the next position.

Variations: The figure can be done in reverse if you want a change of pace, i.e., the lady stays in the center while the gent turns alternately with his partner and the other ladies. In this case, it is called Gents Shoofly the Ring or Gents Shoofly Swing.

    It is also possible to let the gent in the outside couple turn his own partner by the right after each time he turns an active lady by the left. This makes the figure more active for everyone, but requires precise timing by all the dancers. Recommended for experienced dancers only.

Big circle figures from a promenade

PROMENADE

Call (e.g.):   Promenade, folks, don't be slow
              Big foot high and the little foot low

Description: Take promenade position with your partner and walk counterclockwise around the circle until the next command is given. The position used for promenading varies considerably from community to community—see the Glossary for some possibilities.

ROLL THE LADIES IN/OUT

Call (e.g.):   Gents, you roll the ladies in...
              Now you roll them out again

Description: While promenading and without dropping hands (based on skater's position), the lady steps forward and crosses in front of her partner to end at his left side. After a few steps, the movement is reversed to bring her back to place. In some localities, the dancers do this figure at their own whim while promenading.

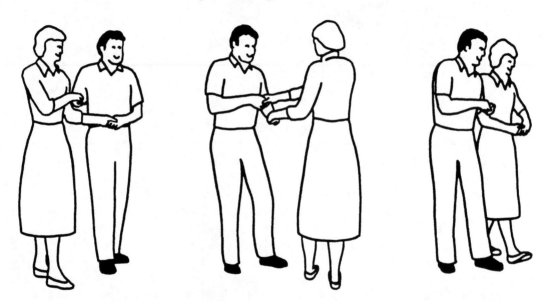

"Roll the ladies in": while promenading, the lady "rolls" across her partner to end at his left.

PROMENADE AND MOVE UP TWO/ONE/THREE

Call (e.g.):   _ _ Promenade...
              Ladies move up two and swing...
              _ _ And promenade

Description: While still promenading, the ladies drop hands with their partners and move forward as directed to the second gent they meet (or the first, third, or another number). They swing once around with a two-hand swing and resume the promenade. The movement is repeated a number of times, until partners are together again, and normally concludes with partners swinging twice around:

> Swing your <u>part</u>ner <u>high</u> and <u>low</u>
> <u>Twice</u> <u>around</u> and <u>let</u> her <u>go</u>

NB: In order to be able to get partners back together again, the caller must note the identity of one or two couples *before* starting this figure. It's embarrassing to discover midway through it that you have no idea of who was dancing with whom!

THE QUEEN'S HIGHWAY

Call: <u>Now</u> let's <u>walk</u> the <u>queen's</u> <u>highway</u>...

Description: During the promenade, the leading couple drop hands. The lady turns out to her right and starts to walk clockwise around the outside of the circle while her partner continues alone. As soon as the leading lady passes the lady behind her, the latter also turns out to the right and follows the first lady. The other ladies do the same, until all the couples have separated. As each lady meets her partner again, she turns to her right to face in promenade direction and rejoins him.

> **Variations:** As each lady meets her partner, they can take right hands and let the lady turn under the gent's right arm (lady turning to her own *left*), ending in skater's position. You can also have the ladies pass by their partners the first time and rejoin them the second time they meet. This is especially appropriate if the circle is small.

THE KING'S HIGHWAY

Call: __ Let's <u>walk</u> the <u>king's</u> <u>highway</u>...

Description: This figure is similar to The Queen's Highway, but this time the gent is the one who moves out to the right—passing *behind* his partner—and walks around the outside of the circle. When returning to place, he should also pass *behind* his partner.

Variations: When he meets his partner, the gent may join right hands with her and pull her under his right arm (lady turning to her own left), ending in skater's position. You can also have the gents pass by their partners the first time and rejoin them the second time they meet, especially if the circle is small.

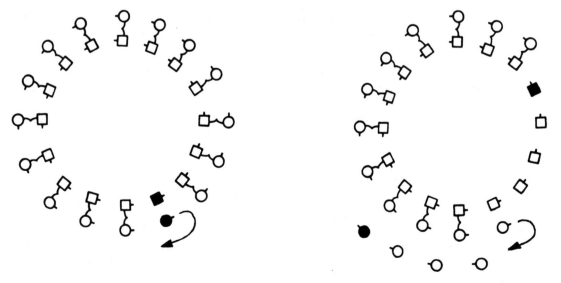

"Walk the queen's highway."

LONDON BRIDGE

Call (e.g.): London bridge, raise 'em high
Watch your head as they go by

Description: From a promenade, the leading couple drop hands, turn individually to face the opposite direction, and join inside hands (lady's right, gent's left) to form an arch over the oncoming couples, who change to an inside handhold (lady's left, gent's right). As each couple passes through the arch(es), they turn individually, make an arch, and go back the other way, following the leaders.

When the leaders have passed all the other couples, they turn individually, take inside hands, and follow the other couples under the arches. When they have passed under the last arch, they take promenade position and continue counterclockwise around the circle with a normal promenade. The other couples follow them as each couple finishes passing through the arches.

London bridge.

DIP AND DIVE

Call (e.g.): Let's do it again with a dip and dive...

Description: This figure works well as a continuation of London Bridge, or it can be done on its own. The principle is the same, but this time the leading couple alternately makes an arch for the first couple they meet and goes *under* the arch made by the next couple. When they have passed all the other couples, they turn and go back in the same manner.

Once the dancers have tried this figure a couple of times, show them the nice rhythm achieved by moving diagonally away from their partners with 4 steps as they form an arch, and diagonally towards their partners with 4 steps as they go under an arch.

A big circle figure for changing partners

Normally in a big set, you keep the same partner throughout the dance. The figure below may be used as the last in a sequence if the dancers need help taking new partners, the idea being that they keep this partner for the next dance. (Other possibilities would be to use the figure Rights and Lefts with a random number of changes, rather than going back to original partners, or to use Promenade and Move Up Two a random number of times.)

BREAK AND SWING THE NEW GIRL

Call (e.g.):   Ladies to the <u>cen</u>ter and <u>then</u> face <u>out</u>

                         <u>Gents</u> to the <u>right</u> you <u>walk</u> about...

                         <u>Swing</u> with a <u>new</u> girl, <u>prom</u>enade her

                         <u>Keep</u> her for the <u>next</u> dance, <u>she's</u> your new <u>lady</u>

Description: The ladies move into the center and form a ring, facing out, while the gents promenade individually around the outside. At the call "Swing with a new girl," each gent does a two-hand swing with the nearest lady, and then they promenade.

Small circle figures

Normally only a few big circle figures are danced before going on to the middle part of the dance, in which the couples dance in pairs. When the caller says:

      <u>Odds</u> out to <u>evens</u> and <u>couple</u> up <u>four</u>

or:

      <u>Odds</u> to the <u>right</u> and <u>circle</u> <u>four</u>

each active couple moves to join the inactive couple immediately to their right. The two couples form a small circle and begin to circle left.

The starting position for the small circle figures is one in which the active or odd couples have their backs to the middle of the big circle. This is occasionally reflected in the calls (see, for example, "Swing at the wall"), but in most cases it is not absolutely necessary. Most of the figures can be danced without any problems even if everyone is not in the correct position, but if you are working with a group over a longer period of time, teach them to keep circling left until they reach the correct starting position.

Dosido

In Southern mountain square dancing, the call **dosido** refers to completely different movements than the dosido we use for northern squares and contras. One of the simpler dosidos comes from Kentucky and is done as follows:

> The two couples are facing each other and have dropped hands. Each gent takes his partner's left hand in his own right hand and dances in place while leading her in front of him and then all the way around him back to her own place (he raises his right hand over his head in order to do this).
>
> She then gives both hands to the opposite gent, swings once around with him, goes back to her partner and swings once around with him.

Although it is not strictly necessary (practice varies from place to place), this dosido can be recommended as a rounding off movement after each small circle figure. The dance sequence thus becomes:
- on to the next
- dance figure x
- dosido
- on to the next
- dance figure y
- dosido
- on to the next
- dance figure z
- dosido

etc.

Try dancing with and without the dosido and get the reactions of the dancers. You can use the method that suits you best. You can also simplify matters and get almost the same effect by calling "Swing your corner . . . Swing your partner" after each small circle figure, which is normal practice in some places. But try the dosido—I think you will like it.

Progression and continuity

At the call:

> <u>On</u> to the <u>next</u> and <u>circle four</u>

each couple moves to the left, to dance with a new couple. They immediately form a circle and begin to circle left. At the end of each small circle figure, the dancers also circle left, until the caller says "On to the next."

How many figures should be used?

In the small circle part of the dance, a new figure may, in principle, be called each time the dancers regroup. Some traditional callers use this method, while others use only one small circle figure at a time, and take a new one for the next dance.

Personally, I usually compromise by showing the dancers two to four different figures—often supplemented by the Kentucky dosido—and working with those for a while. If this is successful, the repertory can gradually be increased.

The small circle figures described in this book are grouped by type. In some cases, I have included several figures that are quite similar to each other. But all are authentic figures that are considered different by the indigenous dancers, or that come from different areas. You can choose the variants you like best and decide whether you want to work with variations on the same theme or with figures that are as different from each other as possible. It should be noted that the family names indicated in the book are ones of my own choosing and are not standard terminology.

Kentucky dosido: the lady walks around her partner. . .

. . .swings with her opposite. . .

. . .and swings with her partner.

Small circle figures: "Divide the ring" family

MOUNTAINEER LOOP

Call: Odd couple, mountaineer loop...
(Even couple, mountaineer loop...)

Description: Mountaineer Loop is like a miniature version of the big circle figure Rip 'n' Snort (Divide the Ring). With all hands still joined, the 1s move forward and go between the 2s and under an arch formed by them. Then the 1s drop hands with each other *only,* and the gent goes left and the lady right, around the 2s and back to place. To avoid dropping hands with each other, the 2s must turn in under their own raised arms and then away from each other, keeping a loose handhold (see drawing). If desired the figure can be repeated with the 2s active.

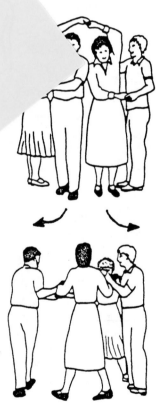

Mount.

DUCK FOR THE OYSTER

Call (e.g.): a) __ __ Duck for the oyster...
b) __ __ Dive for the clam...
c) Duck through the hole in the old tin can

Description: Duck for the Oyster can be viewed as an expanded version of Mountaineer Loop:
a) With all hands still joined, the 1s go 4 steps forward towards the 2s and under an arch made by them. But instead of continuing through the arch, the 1s then back up 4 steps to place.
b) Repeat a, but this time the 1s make an arch and the 2s go forward and back.
c) The 1s now perform the Mountaineer Loop as described above.

Variation: In part c, the 1s can keep their hands joined and turn away from each other, lifting their joined hands over their own and the 2s' heads to pull the 2s through and reform the circle—a kind of "wring the dishrag" movement. As the 2s come through the 1s' arch, they, too, must turn away from each other, under their own arms. They should do this only *after* passing through the 1s' arch.

"Wring the dishrag" ending for Duck for the Oyster.

FOUR LEAF CLOVER

Call:

> Odd couple, four leaf clover...
> __ __ Break it even...
> (Even couple, four leaf clover...
> __ __ Break it odd...)

Description:

This figure takes the "wring the dishrag" ending of Duck for the Oyster and adds something extra. The 1s go under the 2s' arch, turn away from each other and go under their own raised arms. But instead of pulling the 2s through, they lower their arms in front of them to form a cloverleaf pattern. The dancers then move clockwise until the caller says "Break it even." At this point, the 1s raise their joined arms again and pull the 2s through. The 2s turn away from each other and go under their own raised arms to reform the circle, just as in Duck for the Oyster. If desired, the figure can be repeated with the 2s active.

Four leaf clover. The cloverleaf is formed...

...and broken.

ROLL THE BARREL

Call:

                  __ __ Roll the barrel...
                  __ __ Circle right...
                  __ __ Roll the barrel...
                  __ __ Circle left...

Description: In this figure also, the 1s start by going under an arch made by the 2s, without anyone dropping hands. But this time, the 1s do not turn around at all, but stay facing out. As soon as the 1s have passed, the 2s turn toward each other and go under their own arch so they also are facing out. The "inside out" circle then moves to its own right (i.e., clockwise) until the caller again says "Roll the barrel." Then the 2s move backwards through an arch made by the 1s (the 1s must turn away from each other and bring their inside hands up to form this arch), and the circle is reformed and moves to the left (still clockwise). As in all of the "Divide the Ring" figures, it is important for the dancers to keep their handholds loose and flexible, as the figure will otherwise be uncomfortable (if not impossible) to execute.

Roll the barrel.

Small circle figures: "Figure eight" family

LADY 'ROUND THE LADY AND THE GENT ALSO

Call:
Lady 'round the <u>la</u>dy and the <u>gent</u> al<u>so</u>...
Lady 'round the <u>gent</u> but the <u>gent</u> don't <u>go</u>...
<u>Swing</u> your <u>op</u>posite __ __
And <u>now</u> your <u>own</u> __ __

Description:
Drop hands. The 2s stand still while lady 1, followed by her partner, goes between them and around lady 2, back to place. Gent 1 now stays in place while lady 1 continues between couple 2 and around gent 2 to complete the figure eight. The two couples then swing with each other's partners and with their own partners.

LADY 'ROUND THE LADY AND THE GENT AROUND THE GENT or FIGURE EIGHT

Call:
(<u>Odd</u> <u>couple</u>) <u>figure</u> <u>eight</u>
Lady 'round the <u>la</u>dy, <u>gent</u> around the <u>gent</u>...
__ __ <u>Swing</u> right <u>hands</u>
<u>Gent</u> around the <u>la</u>dy, <u>lady</u> 'round the <u>gent</u>...
__ __ <u>Swing</u> left <u>hands</u>

Description:
In this figure, lady 1 and gent 1 each simultaneously dance a figure eight pattern around couple 2, as follows:

Everyone drops hands. Lady 1 passes in front of her partner and goes between couple 2 and around lady 2, while gent 1 goes between couple 2 and around gent 2. When the 1s meet at home, they take a right-hand pigeon wing grip and go once around each other. Lady 1 then goes between couple 2 and around *gent* 2 while gent 1 goes between couple 2 and around *lady* 2. When the 1s meet at home, they take a left-hand pigeon wing grip and go once around each other to place. Since couple 2 are completely inactive, you may want to repeat the figure in reverse.

Variation: The figure can also be done as a pure figure eight, without the hand turns. In this case, the calls "Swing right hands" and "Swing left hands" are omitted.

CHASE THE RABBIT

Call (e.g.):
a) <u>Chase</u> that <u>rabbit</u>, <u>chase</u> that <u>squirrel</u>
<u>Chase</u> that <u>pretty</u> girl 'round the <u>world</u>
b) <u>Chase</u> that <u>possum</u>, <u>chase</u> that '<u>coon</u>
<u>Chase</u> that <u>silly</u> boy 'round the <u>room</u>

Description:
a) Everyone drops hands. Lady 1, followed by her partner, dances a complete figure eight around couple 2, just as in Lady 'Round the Lady and the Gent Around the Gent, but without the hand turns.
b) Gent 1 now dances the *same* figure eight (not mirror image) around couple 2, followed by his partner.
This is another figure in which the 2s do nothing, so it may be a good idea to repeat it, making the 2s active.

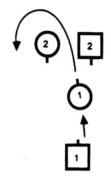

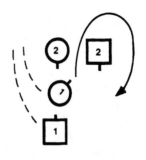

"Lady 'round the lady and the gent also."   **"Lady 'round the gent but the gent don't go."**

Lady 'round the lady and the gent also.

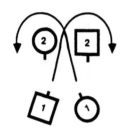 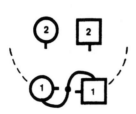 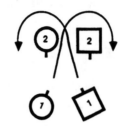 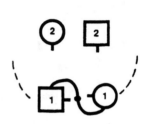

"Lady 'round the lady and the gent around the gent."   **"Swing right hands."**   **"Lady 'round the gent and the gent around the lady."**   **"Swing left hands."**

Lady 'round the lady and the gent around the gent.

Small circle figures: "Walk around" family

SWING AT THE WALL

Call:
Around that couple and swing at the wall...
Back to the center and swing in the hall...

Description:
Everyone drops hands and couple 2 stands still while the 1s separate and walk individually around the 2s (gent going to his left, lady to her right). The 1s meet behind the 2s, take both hands and swing once around so they end up facing in the same direction as the 2s, with lady 1 on her partner's left. They then separate again and go individually around the 2s, back to place (gent going to his right, lady to her left). The 1s meet at home and swing again. If you decide to have the 2s do this figure, you will want to change the call a little. For instance:

Around that couple and swing in the hall...
Back you go and swing at the wall...

SWING WHEN YOU MEET

Call:
a) Around that couple and swing when you meet...
Back to the center and swing your sweet...
b) Around that couple and swing once more...
Back to the center and swing all four...

Description: Part a is the same as the figure Swing at the Wall. In part b, the whole thing is repeated, but this time, both couples swing when the 1s return to place.

TAKE A LITTLE PEEK

Call: Around that couple and take a little peek...
Back to the center and swing your sweet...
Around that couple and peek once more...
Back to the center and swing all four...

Description: Take a Little Peek is almost the same as Swing When You Meet, but instead of going all the way around behind the 2s and swinging, the 1s only go far enough to catch a glimpse of each other behind the 2s' backs and then return to place. Part of the fun of this figure is in the implied flirting, which the 2s may try (within reason!) to hinder.

COUPLE COUPLES SWING

Call: Couple through a couple, couple 'round a couple
Couple couples swing __ couple four

Description: Everyone drops hands. The 2s stand still while the 1s go forward, between the 2s, and then separate (gent going left, lady right) to walk individually around the 2s and back to place. Then both couples swing partners. The final call, "Couple four," is just another way of saying "Circle left."

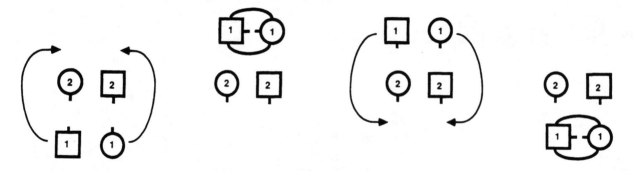

"Around that couple..."   "...and swing at the wall."   "Back to the center..."   "...and swing in the hall."

Swing at the wall.

"Around that couple and take a little peek."

LITTLE SIDE DOOR

Call: a) __ __ Circle right
        b) Little side door with the lady in the lead
        c) Gent fall through and take the lead...
        d) Lady fall through that little side door
        e) Both couples swing and circle up four

Description: a) This figure should be started from a circle right. Otherwise the transition to the first part will
            be awkward. So remember to call "Circle right" (or "Halfway and back") before starting the
            figure as such.
         b) Everyone drops hands. The 2s stand still while lady 1, followed by her partner, continues
            counterclockwise, going around gent 2.
         c) While lady 1 continues behind couple 2 and around lady 2, her partner "cheats" by going bet-
            ween the 2s, and then continues counterclockwise around gent 2. Gent 1 is now in front of his
            partner, who follows him.
         d) While gent 1 continues behind couple 2 and around lady 2 to place, his partner "cheats" by
            going between the 2s and back to her own place.
         e) Both couples swing partners and then all four circle left.

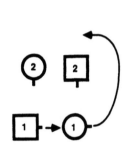 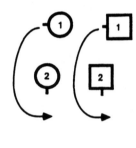 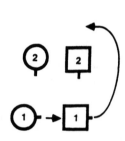 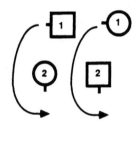

"Little side door with the lady in the lead   **"...Gent fall through..."**   **"...and take the lead..."**   **"Lady fall through that little side door."**

Small circle figures: "Swing" family

SWING YOUR MA

Call: __ __ Swing your ma
              __ __ Swing your pa
              Swing that gal from Arkansas

Description: Everyone drops hands. Gent 1 does a two-hand swing once and a half around with lady 2,
              then a two-hand swing once and a half around with gent 2, and finally a two-hand swing
              about once and a half around with his own partner, with everyone ending in place.

SWING YOUR PA

Call: __ __ Swing your pa
              __ __ Swing your ma
              And don't forget ol' Arkansas

Description: This figure is very similar to Swing Your Ma, but with lady 1 active. She swings with gent 2, then with lady 2, and finally with her partner.

ADAM AND EVE

Call: __ __ Swing old Adam
                      __ __ Swing old Eve
                      Swing old Adam before you leave
                      __ __ Partner swing

Description: Everyone drops hands. Lady 1 does a two-hand swing once around with gent 2, then about once around with lady 2, and again once around with gent 2. Then both couples swing partners.

Small circle figures: Miscellaneous

BIRDIE IN THE CAGE

Call: a) __ __ Birdie in the cage...
                      b) Birdie hop out and the crow hop in...
                      c) Crow hop out and you're gone again

Description: a) Circle left. Lady 1 goes into the middle and dances in place as the other three dancers continue to circle around her.
                      b) Lady 1 changes places with her partner, who goes into the middle and dances in place while the other three circle around him.
                      c) Gent 1 goes back to his place in the circle. Continue to circle left.
                      The dancer in the center can turn counterclockwise in place, do some clogging steps, or otherwise show off.

DOUBLE BOW KNOT

Call: Odd couple, double bow knot...
                      __ __ Circle left
                      (Even couple, double bow knot...
                      __ __ Circle left)

Description: Gent 1 drops hands with his corner. Moving clockwise, he goes under an arch made by lady 1 and gent 2 and continues around lady 1, who must turn under her own arm. The movement is repeated, but this time, gent 1 goes under an arch made by gent 2 and lady 2, and gent 2 turns under his own arm. Reform the circle and circle left.
                          The figure may be repeated with gent 2 active. He passes first between lady 2 and gent 1, and then between gent 1 and lady 1.

Variations: The active gent may go backwards under the first arch and forward under the second, he may go backwards under both, or forward under both. In any case, the following dancers always go forward.

OCEAN WAVE

Call:

Odd <u>cou</u>, <u>ocean wave</u>
a) <u>Oshee up</u> __ __
b) <u>Oshee back</u> __ __
c) <u>Oshee 'round</u> the <u>outside track</u>
__ __ __ __

Description:
a) Everyone drops hands except couple 1, who keep inside hands (gent's right, lady's left) joined. Couple 1 walks forward 4 steps, between couple 2. *At the same time,* gent 2 and lady 2 walk forward individually 4 steps, outside couple 1.

b) At this point, there are three possibilities:
Either all four dancers simply move backwards 4 steps to place.
Or all four dancers turn toward their partners and walk forward 4 steps to place.
Or couple 1 turns and walks forward back to place while gent 2 and lady 2 *continue* around the 1s, back to place, where they do a two-hand swing halfway around.

c) The movements of parts a and b are now repeated, but with couple 2 in the center and couple 1 outside.

Double bow knot.

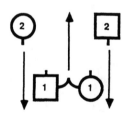

"Oshee up."

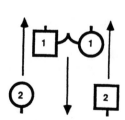 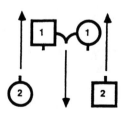 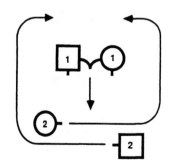

"Oshee back"—variation 1   **"Oshee back"—variation 2**   **"Oshee back"—variation 3**

Ocean wave.

RIGHT HANDS ACROSS

Call (e.g.):   a) Right <u>hands</u> across and <u>how</u> do you <u>do</u>?...
                <u>Back</u> by the <u>left</u> and <u>fine</u>, thank <u>you</u>...
            b) <u>Ladies</u> change __ __
              <u>Gents</u> the <u>same</u> __ __
            c) And <u>circle</u> <u>four</u> __ __

Description: a) The first part of this figure is just a right hand and left hand star, but note that in the South, this is always done as a "hands across" star, in which the two ladies take hands and the two gents take hands—never by gripping the wrist of the dancer in front.
            b) Drop hands. The two ladies change places by passing *left* shoulders as the dancers continue to move slightly counterclockwise. Then the two gents change places by passing *right* shoulders. While changing places, each pair of dancers should keep facing each other and maintain eye contact.
            c) Circle left.

Right hands across.

EIGHT HANDS ACROSS

Call (e.g.):   a) __ __ Eight <u>hands</u> <u>across</u>
            b) <u>Ladies</u> <u>bow</u>, <u>gents</u> <u>bow</u> under
            c) <u>Spread</u> it <u>out</u> and go like <u>thunder</u>...
            d) <u>Break</u> that <u>ring</u> with a corner <u>swing</u>
            e) __ __ Now <u>swing</u> your <u>own</u>
            f) __ __ And <u>circle</u> up <u>four</u>

Description: This figure is a miniature version of the big circle figure Basket. The circle should continue to move clockwise as the basket is being formed.

            a) The two gents take both hands, and the two ladies take both hands, with the ladies' hands under the gents'.
            b) The ladies bow slightly so the gents can raise their joined arms over the ladies' heads and down behind their backs. Then the gents bow so the ladies can lift their arms over the gents' heads and down behind their backs.
            c) In this formation, the circle moves quickly clockwise. Although the buzz step is not traditional, something like the same feeling can be achieved if everyone starts and leads on the right foot.
            d) Drop hands (being careful to slow down a little first, if necessary) and swing your corners.
            e) Swing your partners.
            f) Circle left.

Eight hands across.

Examples of dance sequences for the big set

Here are three examples of how the figures can be combined in practice. The first sequence uses simple figures only; the other two are a little more challenging.

Since the big set is danced at a relatively quick pace and lasts longer than, for example, a square, it can be experienced as strenuous, especially by beginners. It may be difficult for the caller to gauge how tired the dancers are. It is important to use some common sense, not only when planning the sequence you would like to call, but also when executing it. It is better to shorten the dance than to continue so long that the dancers are exhausted, which will certainly not endear them to the dance form.

Also bear in mind that the dancers are in almost constant motion, often in the same direction, and can become a little dizzy. Some of the small circle figures in which one couple stands still can therefore be a welcome change.

Example A, with simple figures

All hands up and circle left
Halfway and back
Everybody balance in
Balance out and do it again
Leading couple rip 'n' snort...
Odds out to evens, couple up four
Odd couple, mountaineer loop
Even couple, mountaineer loop
Dosido
On to the next and circle four
Birdie in the cage
Birdie hop out and the crow hop in
Crow hop out and you're gone again
Dosido
And on to the next
Right hands across and how do you do?
Back with the left and fine, thank you
Ladies change
Gents the same
And circle four
On to the next and dance some more
...(repeat the small circle figures as desired)

Promenade in one big ring

Let's walk the queen's highway...
Now walk the king's highway...
Join your hands in one big ring and circle left
Break that ring with a corner swing
And now your partner swing
Swing her twice, 'cause she's so nice,
Bring her off the floor and find her a place.

Example B, with slightly more difficult figures

All hands up and circle south, put a little moon-
   shine in your mouth
Halfway and back
Take your gal and promenade
Swing her in, that pretty little thing
And now you swing her out again
Let's do that London bridge...
One more time with a dip and dive
Over and under, go like thunder...
Couple up four around the floor and circle left
Duck for the oyster
Dive for the clam
Duck through the hole in the frying pan

Dosido
On to the next and couple up four,
On to the next and dance some more
Lady 'round the lady, gent around the gent
Swing right hands
Gent around the lady, lady 'round the gent
Swing left hands
Dosido
And it's on to the next and circle four
Swing your ma
Swing your pa
Swing that gal from Arkansas
Dosido
On to the next and dance some more
Couple up four around the floor
... (repeat small circle figures as desired)
Join your hands in one big ring, circle left
Ladies on the inside, circle left, gents on the out-
    side, circle right
Now the other way back in the same old track
Gents, find your partner, stop to her left
Ladies bow and the gents know how
Form a basket, turn it now
Reverse the basket, arms in back
Circle left around that track
Break that ring with a corner swing
Now your partner, take a little swing
Swing her twice and thank her again

**Example C, with big circle figures best suited to a
relatively small group**

All hands up and circle left
Halfway and back
Thread the needle...
Now let's wind up the ball of yarn...
Circle left
Rights and lefts around the hall...
Meet your partner with an elbow swing
And keep on swinging around the ring...
Meet your own and swing her twice

Couple up four around the floor
Odd couple, double bow knot
And circle left
Even couple, double bow knot
Circle left
Dosido
And it's on to the next and circle up four
Halfway and back
Do the little side door with the lady in the lead
Gent fall through and take the lead
Lady fall through that little side door
Swing your partners and couple up four
Dosido
On to the next and circle left
Ocean wave: oshee up, oshee back
Oshee 'round the outside track
Dosido
And on to the next and circle four
... (repeat small circle figures as desired)
One big circle, circle left
Ready now for the shoofly swing
Lead couple into the middle of the ring
Turn your partner by the right, then left at the ring
Partner again with a right hand swing
And on to the next with a left hand swing
And it's on you go, right around the ring...
Now all promenade in a great big ring
Ladies move up two and swing
Promenade
Ladies move up three and swing
Promenade
... (repeat with different numbers until partners
    are back together)
Ladies to the center, facing out
Gents single file, you walk about
Swing with a new girl, promenade her
Keep her for the next dance, she's your lady

Fiddling around with politics

"There are few people who know what an important part the fiddle plays in Southern politics. Of course, the country at large knows how Bob Taylor, the boy Congressman from Tennessee, fiddled his way into office two years ago, and how he failed this time because he thought he could run on his brains rather than his bow. ...But there are few who know how general and how potent the fiddle is.

Several members of the present House are expert fiddlers and fiddled their way into office. Tom Watson, the brilliant member from McDuffie, is the best fiddler in the House. He says: 'I have the best and most intelligent constituency in the States, in my opinion. My opponent was a good man and a good farmer, but was not practiced as a speaker. I felt that speaking might be considered a sort of natural gift, or due to a profession, so I did not press him on the point. But playing the fiddle was a purely acquired accomplishment, and incidental to no profession, and as many of my younger constituents are fond of dancing and like the music of the fiddle, I crowded him on that.'

'He couldn't fiddle?'

'Oh, no! And you should have seen the look of silent despair on that good man's face as he stood in a corner of a room, while I sat on a box, like a king on his throne, and made my old fiddle talk, while the boys and girls danced to my music. I made it a rule to get every girl to promise to make her partner in the reel vote for me before she would dance with him. I tell you a fiddle is a big help in a fight where you have young folks in the question.'

'What tunes did you find most popular?'

'The best vote-making tune,' said the Hon. Tom reflectively, 'that ever came out of a fiddle is Mississippi Sawyer; next to this, I think, is Yellow Gal Come Out Tonight.'

Mr. Buck, of Lumpkin ... is perhaps as good as Watson. He says: 'My constituency is a quiet one and demanded solemn tunes on the fiddle. ...One of my constituents claimed that all fiddlers went to the devil. The boys and girls told me to play ahead and they would all follow the fiddler no matter where he went. ...If you've got the right motion to your elbow and get the right twist to your fingers and good rosin on your bow, you ought to get every vote....'

...There are very few things that a man can do that are honest, and full of fun, that don't come handy to him somewhere or other in a political campaign."

—"A dispatch from the Atlanta *Constitution,*" printed in
The New Hampshire Sentinel, Keene, New Hampshire,
December 27, 1882, and quoted in *Northern Junket,*
February 1968.

Square Dances

Basic concepts

This chapter deals with square dances per se—dances executed in a square set of four couples that looks like this:

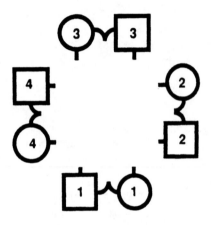

Note that the couples are numbered counterclockwise around the square, starting with the couple who have their backs to the music as number 1.

The dancer next to you who is not your partner is called your **corner**—each gent's corner is the lady on his left, and each lady's corner is the gent on her right. Your **opposite** is the dancer directly across from you. For example, gent no. 1 and lady no. 3 are opposites. Finally, a gentleman may occasionally be directed to dance with his **right hand lady** or a lady with her **left hand gent.** These two complementary terms refer to the lady in the *couple* on a gent's right or the gent in the couple on a lady's left (see illustration).

It is also important to know that couples 1 and 3 are called the **head couples** or **heads,** and couples 2 and 4 the **side couples** or **sides.**

Before starting a square dance, each dancer should make a mental note of his or her **home position.** In many dances, a partner change occurs each time the main figure is repeated, but at least one member of each couple will always come back to

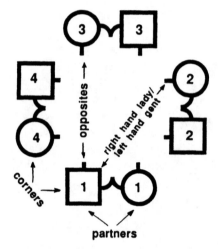

home position, and both should end up back at home when the dance is over. When you promenade, you also return to home position, which means that you never go more than once around the square—often less.

Apropos changing partners, there are a couple of rules that it is good to be aware of. If you promenade with someone, that person becomes your partner. Normally, you promenade to the gent's original place, but there are also some dances, especially newer ones, in which you promenade home to the lady's place. In such a case, the dance description—and the caller—should make it clear that this is what will happen. If you swing with someone, that person becomes your partner (remember that when you finish swinging, the gent should always be on the left and the lady on the right). On the other hand, doing, for example, a dosido or an allemande with someone is not enough for them to be considered your partner. Ladies chain is on the borderline. In the old days, ladies chain was almost always done twice in a row, so you got your own partner back. Today, ladies chain is used in a much greater variety of contexts, and is sometimes exploited to give a temporary or permanent partner change.

Finally, remember that calls directed, for example, to the head or side couples should be carried out by the dancers standing in the relevant position at the time.

Structure of a square dance

The classic structure for a square dance is:

INTRODUCTION
    MAIN FIGURE
    MAIN FIGURE
MIDDLE BREAK
    MAIN FIGURE
    MAIN FIGURE
ENDING

in which each of the listed parts takes 64 counts, i.e., once through the tune, to execute. There are, however, many variations. For instance, dances in the New England tradition are more likely to be strictly related to the music than dances from the Southern or Western states, where a figure or break often takes more or less than 64 counts. The length and placement of the breaks vary, particularly in dances from the latter areas. Sometimes there's a "mini-break" after each repetition of the figure. In other cases, the caller may choose not to use a middle break at all. The introduction and ending can also be varied in length and complexity according to local custom or the caller's whim. However, the introduction, break(s) and ending should not be eliminated entirely. Their use is very characteristic of the American style of dancing in square sets, compared to the dances of other countries.

In traditional style, the introduction, break(s) and ending are determined by the caller, who may use standard sequences or ad lib them, while the main figure for a given dance is normally fixed, and gives the dance its name.

Beginning callers are often wary of calling squares because there are more elements to coordinate than in other dance formations. Not only do you have to know the main figure, but you also have to know or be able to improvise some kind of break, and you have to keep track of how many times the figure has been danced, so you know when to insert the breaks and whether everyone is home. One way to help yourself is to plan and memorize break sequences that you know will work out in the time alotted. As your skills and confidence improve, you can start improvising your breaks, which gives you much more flexibility. You can then accomodate the breaks both to the general level of the dancers and to the situation of the

moment. One of the things that makes squares fun to dance is the surprise element of the breaks, during which the dancers must be alert and responsive to the caller's directions. So even if you have already planned and memorized your breaks beforehand, you don't need to tell the dancers that! Let them have the fun of dancing spontaneously without a walk-through. Even beginners can handle it if you keep the material at an appropriate level.

Main figures

Choreographically, square dance figures can be divided into several main categories. In this chapter, I've arranged the dances by category, with the level of difficulty increasing within each of the following three types:

• *Visiting couple:* Many of the old, traditional dances in the square dance repertory consist of figures in which the first couple (or one member of the first couple) goes to the second couple, dances a sequence with them, goes on to the next couple and dances the same sequence with them, and finally on to the last couple and dances the sequence with them, before returning home. Everyone then usually does a break of some kind, and then it's the next couple's turn to lead the figure. Some visiting couple figures are done cumulatively, so that first one, then two, then all three of the other couples are included in the figure. These dances involve less waiting out for the inactive couples. Visiting couple dances are, historically, an important component of the square dance repertory. But because of their perceived slow pace, with only two couples dancing at a time, and the fact that they are associated more with Southern or Western style dancing, visiting couple dances have fallen somewhat out of use among recreational dancers today. I've included some good visiting couple dances in this chapter—see the comments below.

• *Head couples or side couples active:* In some dances, the figure is initiated by couples 1 and 3 the first time through, and then by couples 2 and 4. If the two active couples dance primarily with each other, the situation is somewhat similar to a visiting couple dance. But in many cases, the inactive couples are quickly integrated into the figure, so everyone is dancing most of the time.

• *All four couples active:* Finally, there are figures in which all four couples are active from the start. These figures are always symmetrical in their choreography. In some cases, all four couples initiate the same actions simultaneously, with radial symmetry. In others, the head couples immediately dance with their respective side couples, so that what happens on one side of the set is a flipped mirror image of what happens on the other side.

What good are visiting couple figures?

In the old days, square dancing was an activity that was embedded in a social system, rather than an isolated recreational pursuit. When people got together for a party, they were just as interested in exchanging news, courting, and maintaining social contacts as they were in dancing per se. In some areas, dance parties might take place only occasionally, and the goal was to socialize and have fun, not to be mentally challenged by the dance. Visiting couple figures were well suited in this context. The pace of the dance was relaxed and the figures repetitive and relatively uncomplicated. If you were not sure how to execute the figure, you could dance as couple number 4. By the time it was your turn to be active, you would have had ample opportunity to both see and dance the sequence.

During the post–World War II square dance craze, visiting couple figures were still among the most common dances found. But as square dancing became more established as a recreational activity, the demands on its entertainment value grew. Today's dancers want to be in motion most of the time, whether they dance traditional style or modern.

However, visiting couple dances, if judiciously chosen, still have a value. They can be helpful in establishing basic concepts, and their relative simplicity and repetitiveness make them candidates for use with beginners or at one night stands. Because the "feel" of a visiting couple dance is different from the New England–type squares so prevalent today, doing them also adds a valuable dimension to the dance experience for more experienced dancers. Furthermore, beginning callers may find it easier to call a visiting couple square than the more tightly structured contemporary New England squares.

I have therefore started this chapter with several dances of the visiting couple type, concentrating on figures that dancers tend to enjoy.

If you and your group like the visiting couple concept, you can use the small circle figures from the chapter on Southern mountain style square dancing to generate more dances of that type.

Figures like Duck for the Oyster, Take a Little Peek, Birdie in the Cage, Eight Hands Across and the ones in the "Swing" and "Figure Eight" families are all traditional figures that are found in dance collections from all over the country as visiting couple dances for a square set. Use the description of Turkey Wing or Leave Her Alone in this chapter as a model.

Ways of presenting visiting couple figures

If you want to pep up the visiting couple dances, there are several possibilities. Sometimes you can have *both* head couples initiate the figure, rather than just one couple at a time. In this case, couple 1 dances with couple 2, and couple 3 with couple 4. Then, instead of saying "On to the next and circle four," call "Meet in the middle and circle four." The two active couples meet in the middle of the set and dance the figure with each other. They then go on to dance with the last possible couple (1 with 4, 3 with 2), after which everyone goes home to place and does the break. This method is best suited to figures with no partner change, and in which the two couples dancing together carry out the same movements (to avoid confusion as to who should lead). Because it requires the dancers to have a fairly good sense of orientation, it is best used with groups that have had some experience.

Another way to decrease waiting time is to have each couple "follow up" when the previous couple has gone past them. For example, couple 1 dances with couple 2, and then with couple 3. When they move on to couple 4, couple 2 can dance with couple 3. When couple 2 reaches couple 1 (who in the meantime have come home to place), couple 3 can start their round by dancing with couple 4, and so on. The break is not danced until everyone is back in place. This method is suggested by Lloyd Shaw in his classic book *Cowboy Dances,* (1937). Other callers, like Rod Linnell from Massachusetts, have also made use of it. In fact, the concept probably stems from the Southern mountain dance tradition, in which a similar type of follow-up is often used for dancing in four-couple sets. In some places, the couple following up dances the figure only once, after which the two circles of four revolve counterclockwise around each other while individually circling to the left, until everyone is home—a maneuver with several names, such as "bouquet waltz," "pokey-o" or just "four and four around the floor." Afterwards, a break is danced, and then the next couple leads out to start the figure.

Introductions, breaks, and endings

In most dance books, square dance figures are presented as main figures only, without any specific breaks. "Use an introduction, break and ending of your choice," the caller is instructed. To a beginning caller, this advice is of little use. How, one wonders, do you figure out what kind of break is possible or appropriate?

Fortunately, it is not that difficult to put together a break. The main things to remember are:

- the break should be choreographically distinguishable from the main figure.
- the break should gather and activate all eight dancers, especially if only some of them are active in the main figure.
- the break should not result in a change of partners or positions, but should bring everybody home to the same place where they started the break.
- if you are not going to walk through the break beforehand, it should be at a level of difficulty that the dancers can follow without special instruction. Alternatively, you may want to walk through only those parts of your intended break that are difficult or unusual, so the dancers are prepared.

Some movements typically used in breaks are:

- Circle left or circle right (all the way around = 16 counts, halfway = 8 counts)
- Everyone go forward and back (4 + 4 counts)
- Promenade (all the way around = 16 counts)
- Grand right and left (all the way around = 24 counts)
- Weave the ring (grand right and left without giving hands) (all the way around = 24 counts)
- Grand square (see the Glossary) (32 counts)

Calls like dosido, swing, and allemande are, of course, also used. Something as simple as "dosido your corners all" can gather the set after a visiting couple figure. And depending on the nature of the main figure and the skill level of the dancers, calls like ladies chain, all four ladies chain, star, etc., can also be used in a break. Be careful, though, to avoid calls that result in a change of partners, unless you are sure you can bring everbody back to place by the end of the break. Remember, for ex-

ample, that you always put the lady on the right after a swing. It is legal to follow "swing your corners all" with "run back home and swing your own," but if you follow a corner swing with circle left, you will have to find some way of getting everyone back home again.

What is the difference between a middle break and an introduction or ending? None, actually, except that it is the custom in many parts of the country to start and end a square by bowing to ("honoring") your partner and corner. Honors can be integrated into the introduction and ending in a variety of ways. You can use the first 8 or 16 counts of the tune to have the dancers honor their partners and corners. If you have live music, you can take care of the honors before the actual tune starts if the caller and band can coordinate something like the following. It's a little old-fashioned, but may be fun to try:

caller: "Honor your partner"
band plays: "da-da"
caller: "Honor your corner"
band plays: "da-da"
caller (e.g.): "All join hands and circle left"

The band then starts the tune with the A-part, without any further introduction.

When finishing off the dance, you can plan your ending so that there is plenty of time for honors (for instance, the entire last 8 or even 16 counts), or you can just round off a final swing or promenade by having the dancers honor their partners:

...Promenade around the hall
1-4:   _ _ _ _
5-8:   _ _ _ _
9-12: _ _ _ _
13-16: Bow to your partner, — that's all

A basic break can be modified to win time for honors by, for example, shortening a 16 + 16-count circle left/circle right to 8 + 8 counts, leaving out a dosido or forward and back, or shortening the sequence in some other way that still gets the dancers back home after 64 counts. Keeping your breaks to 64 counts is good discipline in the beginning and will also give you fewer problems in getting the whole dance to work out to the music — especially as many recordings intended for squares are played 7 times through 64 counts.

On pages 121–123 you can find some suggestions for 64-count breaks, arranged more or less in order of difficulty. Use them as they are or as a basis for your own improvisations.

When you put together a break (or for that matter, a new main figure), remember that the movements should flow together comfortably. Avoid sudden changes of direction as well as combinations that are awkward, such as using the same hand twice in a row (for example, right hand star followed by allemande right). Also avoid combinations that are too static or repetitive, such as:

> all four ladies forward and back
> all four gents foward and back
> head couples forward and back
> side couples forward and back

or:

> allemande left your corner
> allemande right your corner
> dosido your corner

Much better would be:

> allemande left your corner
> allemande right your *partner*
> dosido your corner

Prompt calls, patter calls singing calls, and hash

There are several styles of calling that can be encountered, particularly when it comes to dances done in square formation. **Prompt calling** is the name given to the rather spare style of calling often associated with New England dancing. Each dance command is given just before the movement is to be executed, as illustrated by the call suggestions in this book, with little extra embellishment. In **patter calling,** which is associated more with Southern and Western style dancing, the caller puts extra rhymes and filler words (patter) in between the calls. These may be stereotyped phrases or spontaneous rhymes. In a **singing call,** the caller's commands are woven into the text of a popular song, old or new, and are actually sung, rather than spoken.

The idea of singing calls goes back a long way, and the form became extremely popular during the square dance craze of the 1950s. Because of the necessity of fitting the words to the melody, the commands in a singing call are often delivered at the same time as the movement is executed, rather than beforehand as in a prompt or patter call. For this reason, singing calls gain by familiarity, and many singing calls are standards that the dancers know almost by heart.

In modern Western style square dancing today, two kinds of calls are used: singing calls and "hash," in which the caller improvises freely for a longer or shorter period of time. The dancing is usually done in "tips" of two dances each: a hash call and then a somewhat more relaxed singing call, followed by a short intermission. Hash calls have almost no relation to the music they are danced to, and are often done to recordings with as little melody as possible, just a basic rhythm. They require a good deal of concentration on the part of both the dancers and the caller, although callers have systems for enabling them to bring the dancers back to place after an improvised sequence. A standard singing call, on the other hand, is relatively simpler and more predictable, being built up in the same way as the classic prompt or patter call square, with an introduction, break, ending and four repeats of the main figure, each of which units corresponds to one time through the song.

Singing calls are a good addition to a traditional style square dance program, too. The only reason that I have not included any in this book is that they require specific tunes, and these can be difficult to come by if you are using recorded music. If you are interested in getting into this genre, many of the older titles in the bibliography include singing calls with words and music, and a recent book and tape by Bob Dalsemer, *Smoke on the Water,* is another excellent place to start.

Heads heads or heads sides?

In some square dances in which the two head couples or two side couples initiate the main figure, the order for leading off is heads, heads, sides, sides, and in others it is heads, sides, heads, sides. Why?

The key is whether the figure results in a partner change. If, for example, the ladies move one place to the right after each repetition of the figure, and the heads and sides alternate leading the figure, two of the ladies will never get to dance the figure from an active position. By having the heads lead off twice in a row, and then the sides twice, the original head ladies will be active on the first and fourth repeats, and the original side ladies on the second and third repeats.

This is also very important to remember when you are teaching a dance. After walking through the figure for the head couples, send everyone back to place, and only then walk it through for the side couples, so everyone gets a chance.

6 Breaks that use neither swing nor grand right and left

	I.a.	I.b.	I.c.	I.d.	I.e.	I.f.
A1 1-8	Circle left all the way around	Circle left halfway around	Dosido partner	Dosido corner	Forward and back	Circle left halfway around
9-16		Circle right halfway around	Gents left hand star	Forward and back	Head ladies chain	Heads right & left through
A2 1-8	Circle right all the way around	Forward and back	Gents right hand star	Dosido partner	Side ladies chain	Circle left halfway around
9-16		Forward and back	Dosido corner	Forward and back	Everyone promenade halfway round	Sides right & left through
B1 1-8	Forward and back	Dosido corner	Circle left halfway around	All four ladies chain	Head ladies chain	Circle left halfway around
9-16	Forward and back	Dosido partner	Circle right halfway around	All four ladies chain back	Side ladies chain	Forward and back
B2 1-8	Promenade your partner	Promenade your partner	Promenade your partner	Promenade your partner	Circle left halfway around	Promenade your partner
9-16					Forward and back	

6 Breaks that use swing but not grand right and left

	II.a.	II.b.	II.c.	II.d.	II.e.	II.f.
A1 1-8	Circle left all the way around	Circle left halfway around	Dosido corner	All four ladies chain	Circle left halfway around	Circle left halfway around
9-16		Circle right halfway around	Swing partner	Promenade halfway around	Circle right halfway around	Swing partner
A2 1-8	Forward and back	Dosido corner	Allemande left corner / Allemande right partner	All four ladies chain	Gents left hand star	Circle left halfway around
9-16	Forward and back	Swing partner	Allemande left corner	Promenade halfway round	Gents right hand star	Swing partner
B1 1-8	Dosido partner	Promenade your partner	Dosido partner	Dosido corner	Allemande left corner / Swing partner	Grand square
9-16	Swing partner		Swing partner	Swing partner		
B2 1-8	Promenade your partner	Forward and back	Promenade your partner	Promenade your partner	Promenade your partner	
9-16		Forward and back				

3 Breaks that use grand right and left* but not swing
3 Breaks that use both grand right and left* and swing

	III.a.	III.b.	III.c.	IV.a.	IV.b.	IV.c.
A1 1-8	Circle left halfway around	Circle left halfway around	Circle left halfway around	Circle left halfway around	Allemande left corner	Allemande right partner
					Grand right and left halfway around	Allemande left corner
9-16	Circle right halfway around	Circle right halfway around	Forward and back	Circle right halfway around		Ladies right hand star
A2 1-8	Dosido corner	Allemande left corner	Circle left halfway around	Forward and back	Dosido partner	Ladies left hand star
9-16	Dosido partner	Grand right and left all the way around	Forward and back	Dosido partner	Swing partner	Allemande right partner
B1 1-8	Allemande left corner		Allemande left corner	Grand right and left all the way around	Promenade home	Dosido corner
9-16	Grand right and left all the way around		Grand right and left halfway around		Forward and back	Swing partner
B2 1-8		Promenade your partner	Dosido partner		Dosido corner	Promenade your partner
9-16			Promenade your partner home	Swing your partner	Swing partner	

*Weave the ring (grand right and left without giving hands) can be substituted for grand right and left if desired, although traditional style dancers tend to prefer giving hands.

SQUARE
visiting couple

TURKEY WING

MUSIC	**CALLS**	**MUSIC**	**DESCRIPTION**

Intro: Couple one to the right and circle four

A1 **1-4** — — — —

5-8 The two gents swing with the right elbow

9-12 Now the opposite lady with the left elbow

13-16 Back to the middle with the right elbow

A2 **1-4** Now your own sweet honey with the left elbow

5-8 Circle up four at the side of the floor

9-12 — — — —

13-16 Now on to the next and you circle left

B1 **1-4** — — — —

5-8 The two gents swing with the right elbow

9-12 Opposite lady with the left elbow

13-16 Back to the middle with the right elbow

B2 **1-4** And your own sweet honey with the left elbow

A1 **1-8** Couple 1 moves into the center of the set to face couple 2, forms a circle with them, and all four circle left once around (8 steps). End with couple 2 in place and couple 1 in the middle of the set, facing them.

9-12 Drop hands. The two gents do a right elbow swing once around, to end facing each other's partners (4 steps).

13-16 Each gent does a left elbow swing about once and a half around with the opposite lady (4 steps).

A2 **1-4** The two gents again do a right elbow swing with each other, once around, to end facing their partners (4 steps).

5-8 Each gent does a left elbow swing once around with his own partner and turns to face the other couple, with his partner on his right (4 steps).

9-16 Reform the circle of four and circle left once around so couple 2 ends in place and couple 1 is in the middle of the set, facing them (8 steps).

B1 **1-8** Couple 1 moves to the left to face couple 3, forms a circle with them, and they circle left once around (8 steps).

9-12 The two gents do a right elbow swing (4 steps).

13-16 Each gent does a left elbow swing with his opposite (4 steps).

B2 **1-4** The two gents again do a right elbow swing (4 steps).

5-8   Circle up <u>four</u> and you <u>dance</u> some <u>more</u>

9-12   _ _ _ _
13-16   Now <u>on</u> to the <u>last</u> and circle <u>left</u>

A1   **1-4**   _ _ _ _

      5-8   The <u>two</u> gents <u>swing</u> with the <u>right</u> <u>elbow</u>

      9-12   Now the <u>opposite</u> <u>lady</u> with the <u>left</u> <u>elbow</u>

      13-16   <u>Back</u> to the <u>middle</u> with the <u>right</u> <u>elbow</u>

A2   **1-4**   <u>Now</u> your <u>honey</u> with the <u>left</u> <u>elbow</u>

      5-8   Circle up <u>four</u> as you <u>did</u> <u>before</u>

      9-12   _ _ _ _
      13-16   <u>Home</u> you <u>go</u> and <u>swing</u> your <u>own</u>

B1   **1-4**   <u>Everybody</u> <u>swing</u> your <u>own</u>
      5-8   <u>With</u> your <u>corner</u> <u>allemande</u> <u>left</u>

      9-12   Right <u>hand</u> to your <u>own</u>, grand <u>right</u> and <u>left</u>

      13-16   _ _ _ _

B2   **1-4**   <u>Hand</u> over <u>hand</u>, <u>around</u> you <u>roam</u>
      5-8   <u>Meet</u> your <u>own</u> and <u>promenade</u> <u>home</u>

      9-12   _ _ <u>Couple</u> <u>two</u>*
      13-16   <u>Go</u> <u>out</u> to the <u>right</u> and <u>circle</u> <u>left</u>...

5-8   Each gent does a left elbow swing with his partner and puts her on his right (4 steps).

9-16   Reform the circle and circle left once around so that couple 3 ends in place and couple 1 is in the middle of the set, facing them (8 steps).

A1   **1-8**   Couple 1 moves to the left to face couple 4, forms a circle with them, and they circle left once around (8 steps).

      9-12   The two gents do a right elbow swing (4 steps).

      13-16   Each gent does a left elbow swing with his opposite (4 steps).

A2   **1-4**   The two gents again do a right elbow swing (4 steps).

      5-8   Each gent does a left elbow swing with his partner and puts her on his right (4 steps).

      9-16   Reform the circle and circle left once around so that couple 4 ends in place and couple 1 is in the middle of the set, facing them (8 steps).

B1   **1-8**   Couple 1 moves home to place and all four couples swing with their partners (8 counts).

      9-12   Take a left-hand pigeon wing grip with your corner and walk counter-clockwise around each other until you are facing your partners (4 steps).

      13-16   Give your right hand to your partner,

+ B2   **1-8**   pass by, give your left hand to the next, and continue forward, alternately giving right and left hands, until you meet your partner on the other side of the set (12 steps).

      9-16   Take promenade position with your partner and walk forward 8 steps in line of direction, back to your home place.

Change this to "Couple three" and "Couple four," respectively, before the third and fourth times through the figure.

Comments

Turkey Wing, or Elbow Swing, as it is also called, is an old time figure found in many dance collections. The above description includes a short break to round out the figure and use up the rest of the music. Start with an introduction if you like, for example, I.a., II.d. or III.b.

Since the dance is a visiting couple figure, the entire sequence described above is repeated for the second, third, and fourth couples, respectively, as implied by the next to last call. As each couple becomes active, they move to face the couple on their right, dance with them as described in A1-A2 above, and then move on to the next couple, repeat the figure, etc. The initial circle left with each new couple establishes the positioning for the rest of the figure, and the active couple does *not* go back to their own place until they have danced with all three of the other couples.

Music

Preferably a Southern fiddle tune, such as "Grey Eagle" from *Square Dance Tonight Vol. 3* or "North Carolina Breakdown" from *Old Time Music Dance Party*. Note that the described sequence requires 8 × 64 counts for all four couples to complete the figure, and an extra intro will add an additional 64 counts. **Tempo:** ideally about 130, but slower for beginners.

SQUARE
visiting couple

LEAVE HER ALONE

MUSIC	CALLS	MUSIC	DESCRIPTION
Intro:	Couple one go out to the right And circle four hands 'round __		
A1 1-4	__ __ __ __	**A1** 1-8	Couple 1 moves into the center of the set to face couple 2, forms a circle with them, and all four circle left once around (8 steps). End with couple 2 in place and couple 1 in the middle of the set, facing them.
5-8	With the opposite lady dosido		
9-12	__ __ __ __	9-16	Drop hands. Gent 1 does a dosido with lady 2 and lady 1 with gent 2 (8 steps).
13-16	__ And with that lady swing		
A2 1-4	__ __ __ __	**A2** 1-8	With the same person you dosidoed, take social dance position and swing (8 counts).
5-8	Now leave her alone and swing your own		
9-12	__ __ __ __	9-16	Now swing your own partner (couple 2 at their home position, couple 1 in the center of the set) (8 counts).
13-16	Go on to the next and you circle left		
B1 1-4	__ __ __ __	**B1** 1-8	Couple 1 continues on to couple 3, forms a circle with them, and they circle left once around (8 steps). End with couple 3 in place and couple 1 in the middle of the set, facing them.
5-8	With the opposite lady dosido		
9-12	__ __ __ __	9-16	Gent 1 does a dosido with lady 3 and lady 1 with gent 3 (8 steps).
13-16	__ And with that lady swing		
B2 1-4	__ __ __ __	**B2** 1-8	With the same person you dosidoed, take social dance position and swing (8 counts).
5-8	Leave her alone and swing your own		
9-12	__ __ __ __	9-16	Now swing your partner (couple 3 at their home position, couple 1 in the center of the set) (8 counts).
13-16	And it's on to the last and circle four		
A1 1-4	__ __ __ __	**A1** 1-8	Couple 1 continues on to couple 4, forms a circle with them, and they circle left once around (8 steps). End with couple 4 in place and couple 1 in the middle of the set, facing them.
5-8	With the opposite lady dosido		

9-12   — — — —

13-16   — And with that lady swing

A2   1-4   — — — —

5-8   Leave her alone and swing your own

9-12   Swing your partner right back home

13-16   On the corner allemande left

B1   1-4   — — — —

5-8   Right to your own, grand right and left

9-12   — — — —

13-16   — — — —

B2   1-4   — — Go all the way around

5-8   — — — —

9-12   — — — —

13-16   Couple two* to the right and circle four

9-16   Gent 1 does a dosido with lady 4 and lady 1 with gent 4 (8 steps).

A2   1-8   With the same person you dosidoed, take social dance position and swing (8 counts).

9-16   Now swing your own partner (couple 4 at their home position, couple 1 in the center of the set) (8 counts). As they swing, couple 1 move home to place.

B1   1-8   Take a left-hand pigeon wing grip with your corner and walk counterclockwise around each other until you are facing your partners (4 steps).

9-16

+B2   1-16   Give your right hand to your partner, pass by, give your left hand to the next, and continue forward, alternately giving right and left hands, until you meet your partner at your home place (24 steps).

Change this to "Couple three" and "Couple four," respectively, before the third and fourth times through the figure.

Comments

Variations of this simple figure are found in several books published around 1950, including Hunt & Underwood's *Eight Yards of Calico* (1952) and Ed Durlacher's *Honor Your Partner* (1949), where he sets it to the tune of "I'm a Rambling Wreck from Georgia Tech." During this period, visiting couple figures were still much in use, and not all of them were particularly exciting by today's standards. The good flow from circle left to dosido to swing in Leave Her Alone makes it attractive to modern day dancers, and the dancers should be encouraged to keep in motion as much as possible while executing the figure.

Note that the expression "opposite" in the call refers to your opposite in the little circle of two couples, not to your original opposite in the square. Also note that after swinging your opposite in the small circle, you do *not* put the lady on the right, but put her "back where you found her."

In the above description, the main figure is filled out with a short break using a grand right and left all the way around the square. The dance can be used as described (with repetitions of the figure for couples two, three, and four, respectively), or you can add an additional intro, ending, or both, for example, I.b. or II.a.

Music

I prefer a Southern fiddle tune for this dance, such as "Hell on the Nine Mile" from *Square Dance Tonight Vol. 1* or "Walking in My Sleep" from *Old Time Music Dance Party*. Note that you will need 8 × 64 counts for all four couples to complete the figure, plus any additional breaks you add. A New England or Canadian tune can also be used, as long as you don't let it get too slow. **Tempo: 124–130.**

SQUARE
visiting couple

UNFAITHFUL NELLY GRAY

MUSIC	CALLS
Intro:	Couple one go out to the right And circle four hands 'round __
A1 1-4	__ __ __ __
5-8	Now with that couple right and left through
9-12	__ __ __ __
13-16	Right and left back that's what you do
A2 1-4	__ __ __ __
5-8	Ladies chain, do your best
9-12	__ __ __ __
13-16	Keep that gal, go on to the next
B1 1-4	__ And circle four hands 'round
5-8	With that couple, right and left through
9-12	__ __ __ __
13-16	__ __ And a right and left back
B2 1-4	__ __ __ __
5-8	Same two ladies chain across
9-12	__ __ __ __
13-16	Keep that gal, go on to the last
A1 1-4	__ And circle four hands 'round
5-8	With that couple right and left through

MUSIC	DESCRIPTION
A1 1-8	Couple 1 moves into the center of the set to face couple 2, forms a circle with them, and all four circle left once around (8 steps). End with couple 2 in place and couple 1 in the middle of the set, facing them.
9-16	Drop hands and do a right and left through (see Glossary) (8 steps).
A2 1-8	Repeat the right and left through, back to place (8 steps).
9-16	The same two couples, ladies chain (see Glossary) (8 steps).
B1 1-8	Gent 1 keeps lady 2 as his partner, takes her with him to couple 3, and the four of them circle left once around (8 steps). End with couple 3 in place and the active couple in the middle of the set, facing them.
9-16	Drop hands and do a right and left through (8 steps).
B2 1-8	Repeat the right and left through, back to place (8 counts).
9-16	The same two couples, ladies chain (8 steps)
A1 1-8	Gent 1 keeps lady 3 as his partner, takes her with him to couple 4, and the four of them circle left once around (8 steps). End with couple 4 in place and the active couple in the middle of the set, facing them.

	9-12	_ _ _ _
	13-16	_ _ <u>Right</u> and left <u>back</u>
A2	**1-4**	_ _ _ _
	5-8	_ _ <u>Ladies</u> <u>chain</u>
	9-12	_ _ _ _
	13-16	<u>Keep</u> that <u>gal</u> and <u>home</u> you <u>go</u>
B1	**1-4**	<u>Everybody</u> <u>swing</u> your <u>own</u>
	5-8	Now <u>with</u> your <u>corner</u> <u>dosido</u>
	9-12	_ _ _ _
	13-16	Go <u>back</u> to your <u>own</u> and <u>promenade</u>
B2	**1-4**	_ _ _ _
	5-8	_ _ _ _
	9-12	_ _ <u>Couple</u> <u>two</u>*
	13-16	Go <u>out</u> to the <u>right</u> and <u>circle</u> <u>four</u>

	9-16	Drop hands and do a right and left through (8 steps).
A2	**1-8**	Repeat the right and left through, back to place (8 counts).
	9-16	The same two couples, ladies chain (8 steps).
B1	**1-8**	Gent 1 and his new partner (lady 4) move back to his place, and all four couples take social dance position with their partners and swing (8 counts).
	9-16	Do a dosido with your corner (8 steps).
B2	**1-16**	Take promenade position with your partner and walk 16 steps in the line of direction, back to place.

Change this to "Couple three" and "Couple four," respectively, before the third and fourth times through the figure.

Comments

Here is another visiting couple dance using the same basic structure, but with more advanced movements. It is based on the figure traditionally danced to the tune of "Darling Nelly Gray," which was particularly popular in New England through many years. Several versions and modifications of the dance exist; in the most common one, after doing the right and left through over and back, each couple swing their own partners before the active couple moves on to the next. The ladies chain effects a partner change for a little added interest. As in Turkey Wing and Leave Her Alone, the whole sequence as described above is repeated with each of the other three couples leading. I have included a short break, and you can add an introduction, for example, I.b., I.d. or II.b.

Music

This dance can be done to both Northern and Southern tunes. For example, "Texas Quickstep" from *Square Dance Tonight Vol. 1* or "Shooting Creek" from *Old Time Music Dance Party*. You will need 8 × 64 counts to get through all four couples. **Tempo:** about 126.

SQUARE
visiting couple

DIP AND DIVE

MUSIC	CALLS		MUSIC	DESCRIPTION

Intro: Couple one to the right and circle half

A1 1-4 _ _ _ _

5-8 _ _ Dip and dive

A1 1-8 Couple 1 moves into the center of the set to face couple 2, forms a circle with them, and all four circle left *halfway* around (8 steps). End with couple 1 in couple 2's place and couple 2 in the center of the set, facing them.

9-12 _ _ _ _

9-12 Drop hands with the other couple, but keep holding hands with your partner. Couple 2 makes an arch and both couples move forward 4 steps, with couple 1 going under the arch, into the center of the set.

13-16 _ _ _ _

13-16 Couple 1 continues forward towards couple 4 and makes an arch that couple 4 goes under. *At the same time*, couple 2 wheels around or does a California twirl so so that they are again standing in their home place, facing the center of the set (4 steps).

A2 1-4 _ _ _ _

A2 1-4 Couple 4 continues forward towards couple 2 and makes an arch that couple 2 goes under. *At the same time*, couple 1 wheels around or does a California twirl so that they are standing in couple 4's place, facing the center of the set (4 steps).

5-8 _ _ _ _

5-8 Couple 2 continues forward towards couple 1 and makes an arch that couple 1 goes under. *At the same time*, couple 4 (in couple 2's place) turns to face the center of the set (4 steps).

9-12 _ _ _ _

9-12 Couple 1 continues forward towards couple 4 and makes an arch that couple 4 goes under. *At the same time*, couple 2 (in couple 4's place) turns to face the center of the set (4 steps).

13-16 __ __ __ __

13-16 Couple 4 continues forward towards couple 2 and makes an arch that couple 2 goes under. *At the same time, couple 1 (in couples 2's place) turns to face the center of the set (4 steps).*

B1 **1-4** And it's <u>on</u> to the <u>next</u> and <u>circle</u> <u>half</u>

B1 **1-4** Couple 2 continues forward towards couple 1 and makes an arch that couple 1 goes under. *At the same time, couple 4 (now at home) turns to face the center of the set (4 steps).*

5-8 <u>Dive</u> right <u>through</u>, go <u>on</u> to the <u>last</u>

5-8 Couple 1 now goes to couple 3 and circles to the left with them, halfway around, so couple 1 is in couple 3's place and couple 3 is in the center, facing them. While they do this, couple 2, now at home, turns to face the center of the set (4 steps).

9-12 __ __ And you <u>circle</u> <u>four</u>

9-12 Couple 3 makes an arch, and couple 1 goes under the arch and directly to couple 4 (4 steps).

13-16 <u>Dip</u> and <u>dive</u> ac<u>ross</u> the <u>floor</u>

13-16 Couples 1 and 4 circle left *halfway* around. End with couple 1 in couple 4's place and couple 4 in the middle of the set, facing them. While they do this, couple 3 turns to face the center of the set (4 steps).

B2 **1-4** __ __ __ __

B2 **1-4** Couple 4 makes an arch that couple 1 goes under (4 steps).

5-8 __ __ __ __

5-8 Couple 1 makes an arch that couple 2 goes under, and couple 4 turns to face in (4 steps).

9-12 __ __ __ __

9-12 Couple 2 makes an arch that couple 4 goes under, and couple 1 turns to face in (4 steps).

13-16 __ __ __ __

13-16 Couple 4 makes an arch that couple 1 goes under, and couple 2 turns to face in (4 steps).

A1 **1-4** __ __ __ __

A1 **1-4** Couple 1 makes an arch that couple 2 goes under, and couple 4 turns to face in (4 steps).

5-8 __ __ __ __

5-8 Couple 2 makes an arch that couple 4 goes under, and couple 1 turns to face in (4 steps).

9-12 <u>Home</u> you <u>go</u> and <u>swing</u> your <u>own</u>

9-12 Couple 4 makes an arch that couple 1 goes under, and couple 2, now at home, turns to face in (4 steps).

13-16 And everybody swing

A2 1-4 Allemande left your corner girl

5-8 And grand right and left, go around the world

9-12 __ __ __ __

13-16 __ __ __ __

B1 1-4 Pass your partner, all the way 'round

5-8 __ __ __ __

9-12 __ __ __ __

13-16 __ __ Promenade

B2 1-4 __ __ __ __

5-8 __ __ __ __

9-12 __ __ Couple two*

13-16 Out to the right and circle four...

13-16 Couple 1 moves on to their home place and couple 4, now at home, turns to face in (4 steps).

A2 1-4 All four couples take social dance position with their partners and swing (4 counts).

5-8 Take a left-hand pigeon wing grip with your corner and walk counterclockwise around each other until you are facing your partners (4 steps).

9-16
+ B1 1-16 Give your right hand to your partner, pass by, give your left hand to the next, and continue forward, alternately giving right and left hands, until you meet your partner at home (24 steps).

B2 1-16 Take promenade position with your partner and walk 16 steps in the line of direction, back to place.

Change this to "Couple three" and "Couple four," respectively, before the third and fourth times through the figure.

Comments

Dip and Dive is a well known traditional figure. If the description above seems complicated, it is only because the entire figure has been explained in detail. Work through it once and you will quickly get the idea. Note that the couple in the center of the set always makes the arch and the couple coming from the outside goes through, and that the dipping and diving continues just until the two inactive couples are back in place and the active couple is in the middle of the set.

Each time a couple finds themselves facing out, they turn to face the center of the set. This can be done by simply wheeling around as a couple, with the lady going forward and the gent backward. But more elegant, flowing and fun is the movement known nowadays as a California twirl. The two dancers lift their joined hands and each moves forward in a little semicircle, the gent towards the right and the lady towards the left, with the lady going under the gent's arm, to make a 180-degree turn (see the drawings).

The entire figure as described above is repeated for the second, third and fourth couples, respectively. When couple 2 is active, it will be couples 2, 3 and 1 that dance the dip and dive part of the figure. When couple 3 is active, couples 3, 4 and 2 do the dip and dive, and when couple 4 is active, couples 4, 1 and 3 do it.

Dip and Dive can also be danced on the diagonal, a little trick I learned from Rickey Holden. If couple 1 is active, they start by circling a little more than halfway around with couple 2, so couples 1, 2 and 3 (instead of 4) are lined up, and those three couples do the dip and dive. Couple 1 then goes on to couple 3, circles with them until couples 1, 3 and 4 are in line, and they do the dip and dive. Finally, couple 1 goes on to couple 4 and does a "normal" dip and dive with them and couple 2.

Finally, a little note on timing. The above description is somewhat idealized. In many cases, the dancers may take a little longer (or shorter) to complete the figure, especially if it is new to them, and you may find that different squares are moving at different paces. About all the caller can do once the figure gets started is to call to the average and try to get everyone together again for the breaks. Don't worry if you cannot execute the dance in total synchronization with the music. Just try to start each movement at the beginning of a phrase.

Music

With a dance like this, that cannot always be strictly phrased, it can be an advantage to use a Southern style tune. Try, for example, "Sourwood Mountain" from *Dancing Bow and Singing Strings*. You can also use Northern style music, such as "Kitty Magee" from *Square Dance Tonight Vol. 1*. **Tempo:** about 126.

"Dip and dive" with three couples.

"California twirl" is an elegant way of turning as a couple.

SQUARE
visiting couple

SALLY GOODIN

MUSIC	CALLS		MUSIC	DESCRIPTION

Intro: First old gent go out to the right
Turn Sally Goodin with the right hand 'round

A1 1-4 __ __ __ __

5-8 Back to your partner with the left hand 'round

9-12 __ __ __ __

13-16 Opposite lady with the right hand 'round

A2 1-4 __ __ __ __

5-8 And turn Sally Goodin with the left hand 'round

9-12 __ __ __ __

13-16 Back to your partner with the right hand 'round

B1 1-4 __ __ __ __

5-8 Now the left-hand lady with the left hand 'round

9-12 __ __ __ __

13-16 And all turn your partners with the right hand 'round

A1 1-8 Gent 1 goes to lady 2. They take a right-hand pigeon wing grip and walk clockwise around each other, until gent 1 is facing his own partner (8 steps).

9-16 Gent 1 goes back to his partner. They take a left-hand pigeon wing grip and walk counterclockwise around each other until gent 1 is facing the center of the set (8 steps).

A2 1-8 Gent 1 goes to lady 3. They take a right-hand pigeon wing grip and walk clockwise around each other until gent 1 is facing couple 2 (8 steps).

9-16 Gent 1 goes back to lady 2. They take a left-hand pigeon wing grip and walk counterclockwise around each other until gent 1 is facing his own partner (8 steps).

B1 1-8 Gent 1 goes back to his partner. They take a right-hand pigeon wing grip and walk clockwise around each other until gent 1 is facing couple 4 (8 steps).

9-16 Gent 1 goes to lady 4. They take a left-hand pigeon wing grip and walk counterclockwise around each other until gent 1 is facing his own partner (8 steps).

B2	**1-4**	_ _ _ _
	5-8	And <u>swing</u> that <u>lady</u> '<u>round</u> and '<u>round</u>
	9-12	_ _ Gent number two*
	13-16	<u>Out</u> to the <u>right</u> with the <u>right</u> hand '<u>round</u>

B2	**1-8**	Gent 1 goes home, and all four couples take a right-hand pigeon wing grip with their partners and walk clockwise around (8 steps).
	9-16	All four couples swing their partners (8 counts).

*Change this to "number three" and "number four," respectively, before the third and fourth times through the figure.

Comments

Sally Goodin is another traditional figure found in numerous variants in dance collections from all over the country. It is not exactly a visiting *couple* figure, but what is known as a "single visitor" figure, since only the gent is active. "Sally Goodin" is the gent's right-hand lady, and the sequence of turns is thus: right-hand lady, partner, opposite, right-hand lady, partner, corner, partner.

Because you do not always use the *same* hand to turn your partner and right hand lady, respectively, the active gent must be quite alert to get through the figure without any mishaps. But that's also where the fun lies. If you like the idea of this dance but find the sequence a little too difficult, try the following slightly simpler variation, which is often substituted:

> Turn your right-hand lady by the right
> Turn your partner by the left
> Turn your opposite by the right
> Turn your partner by the left
> Turn your corner by the right
> Turn your partner by the left
> Use the B2 music for a mini-break — a promenade, for example, would be appropriate.

In either case, the dance as described is repeated three more times, with each gent having a turn at being active. Or you can let *both* gents 1 and 2 be active the second time around, gents 1, 2 and 3 the third time, and gents 1, 2, 3 and 4 the last time. In the latter case, have them pass left shoulders in the center of the set when they go to their opposites.

Other possible variations are to have both head gents active at once, then both side gents, then all four. And of course, you can also let the ladies do the figure, but you will have to change the calls a little. Instead of referring to "Sally Goodin," you can direct the ladies to turn their corners, partners, opposites and left-hand gents, stressing that these terms will be absolute in relation to each lady's starting position, not relative as she moves around the square.

When you call this dance, keep an eye on the dancers and time your calls appropriately for the speed at which they are getting through the figure. The calls in the description are somewhat idealized for clarity. You can add an introduction, middle break and or ending to round out the dance, for example, III.a. or IV.c.

Music

Preferably a Southern style fiddle tune — for instance, "Sally Goodin." However, if you cannot find an appropriate recording of that, try "Grey Eagle" from *Square Dance Tonight Vol. 3* or the "Moderate Contra Tempo" medley on *Dances from Appalachia 2*. **Tempo:** about 126-130.

Relax and enjoy it

"If you get mixed up, what of it? That's where the fun comes in.
Fall back into place and wait for the rest of the call—that's all.

If you can't finish a part of a call, forget it. Start on the next figure.
Just get through in time for your 'Allemande left'
and everything will be all right.

It's just the same in square dancing as it is in life:
There isn't any use—or time—to worry over a mistake.
If you take time to correct your error, you have to take the time
from something else, and so you have two errors.
But don't forget: Your mistakes inconvenience others,
because you are dancing with a group.

If you know the calls well, try to help the others in the set.
BUT, don't under any circumstance force your help
upon those who don't want it. Dancers are resentful
of those who doubt their ability.

> —Al Muller, *All-American Square Dances*
> (Delaware Water Gap, Pennsylvania:
> Shawnee Press, 1941).

SQUARE
visiting couple

DOSIDO RIGHT

MUSIC	CALLS		MUSIC	DESCRIPTION
Intro:	Couple one promenade 'round the outside ring			
A1 1-4	_ _ _ _		**A1** 1-16	Couple 1 only, take promenade position and walk counterclockwise all the way around the outside of the square and back to place (16 steps).
5-8	_ _ _ _			
9-12	_ _ _ _			
13-16	Look to the right and dosido			
A2 1-4	_ _ _ _		**A2** 1-8	Couples 1 and 2 face each other. Gent 1 does a dosido with lady 2 and lady 1 with gent 2 (8 steps).
5-8	Go across the set with a right and left through			
9-12	_ _ _ _		9-16	Couple 1 faces couple 3 and they do a right and left through (see Glossary) (8 steps).
13-16	Turn to the right and dosido			
B1 1-4	_ _ _ _		**B1** 1-8	Couple 1, now in couple 3's place, faces couple 4. Gent 1 does a dosido with lady 4 and lady 1 with gent 4 (8 steps).
5-8	Right and left through across to place			
9-12	_ _ _ _		9-16	Couple 1 faces couple 3 and they do a right and left through, back to original places (8 steps).
13-16	All four ladies grand chain			
B2 1-4	_ _ _ _		**B2** 1-8	All four ladies do a ladies chain simultaneously, by forming a right hand star in the center and moving clockwise halfway around to the opposite gent, who picks up the lady for a courtesy turn (see Glossary) (8 steps).
5-8	_ _ Chain them back			
9-12	_ _ _ _		9-16	Repeat the four ladies chain, back to place (8 steps).
13-16	Couple two* promenade the outside track			

Change this to "Couple three" and "Couple four," respectively, before the third and fourth times through the figure.

Comments

Dosido Right was put together by Rod Linnell and Abe Kanegson, two respected and innovative callers who died in the mid-1960s. It appears in Rod Linnell's book, *Square Dances from a Yankee*

Caller's Clipboard, which was published by Louise Winston after Linnell's death.

This unusual figure is like a compressed visiting couple square. The active couple visits each of the other three couples in turn, but dances only a short movement with each of them. Progression around the square is quick, so no one has time to daydream. The challenge for the active couple is to time their actions so that they keep moving smoothly through the figures. Don't let the dance become a stop-and-go affair. The ladies chain over and back in B2 can also be done by just the inactive couples if desired, i.e., the side couples when couple 1 or 3 is active, and the head couples when couple 2 or 4 is active. I prefer the variant where all four ladies do the chain, but since four ladies chain is sometimes confusing to beginners, it's nice to know that the dance can easily be adapted to avoid that problem.

The dance as described is repeated three more times with the second, third and fourth couples leading, respectively. Afterwards, you can, if desired, repeat the sequence with *both* head couples active and then with both side couples active. You can also supplement the main figure with an intro-duction, middle break and ending. A nice touch is to use a break that ends with a promenade, so the next active couple can continue directly into the promenade that starts the main figure. Try, for example, I.c. or III.c.

Music

For this dance, Rod Linnell recommended the tune "Glise à Sherbrooke," an excellent rendition of which is found on *New England Chestnuts 2*. However, other tunes can also be used, either something in New England or Canadian style, such as the "Square Dance Tunes" medley from *New England Country Dance Music* with the Green Mountain Volunteers, or you can be adventurous and try something like "East Tennessee Blues" from *Square Dance Tonight Vol. 2*. **Tempo:** about 120-126.

Previously published in *Square Dances from a Yankee Caller's Clipboard*; 1974 by Rod Linnell and Louise Winston; used with the permission of Grace Baldwin.

SQUARE
heads or sides active

DOUBLE SASHAY

MUSIC	CALLS
Intro:	Lady <u>one</u> and your <u>opposite, forward</u> and <u>back</u>
A1 1-4	_ _ _ _
5-8	<u>Same two, cross over now</u>
9-12	_ _ _ _
13-16	<u>Ladies in the center, sashay across</u>
A2 1-4	_ _ _ _
5-8	<u>Gents in the center, sashay back</u>
9-12	_ _ _ _
13-16	Lady <u>one,</u>* gent <u>three</u>*: go <u>forward</u> and <u>back</u>
B1 1-4	_ _ _ _
5-8	<u>Same two, cross over to place</u>
9-12	_ _ _ _
13-16	And <u>everybody promenade</u>
B2 1-4	_ _ _ _
5-8	_ _ _ _
9-12	_ _ _ _
13-16	Lady <u>two</u>** and your <u>opposite, forward</u> and <u>back</u>

MUSIC	DESCRIPTION
A1 1-8	Lady 1 and gent 3 go 4 steps forward toward each other and 4 steps backwards, to place.
9-16	The same two dancers change places with each other, so lady 1 is with lady 3 and gent 3 is with gent 1 (8 steps).
A2 1-8	Ladies 1 and 3 join both hands and sashay over to the opposite side (8 counts). *At the same time,* gents 1 and 3 face each other, take a step back, and sashay individually to the opposite side, so the two ladies pass between them (8 counts).
9-16	The same four dancers sashay back to place, but this time, the two ladies take a step back and dance individually, while the two gents join hands and dance between the ladies (8 counts).
B1 1-8	Lady 1 and gent 3 go 4 steps forward toward each other and 4 steps backwards, to place.
9-16	The same two dancers change places with each other, so they come back to their partners (8 steps).
B2 1-16	All four couples take promenade position with partners and walk counterclockwise around the square, back to place (16 steps).

Change this to the relevant numbers in each case.
***Change this to "Lady three" and Lady four," respectively, before the third and fourth times through the figure.*

Comments

Double Sashay appears in *Square Dances of Today and How to Teach and Call Them,* by Richard Kraus (1950). Kraus is an educator who has produced square and folk dance materials for the school market, including his 1950 book, which is still a useful source.

Double Sashay is a nice little dance for children or one night stands. The timing in A1 9-16 and B1 9-16, where the two active dancers change places, is loose and includes plenty of time for them to get ready for the sashay or promenade that follows. If you feel the need to tighten this up, one possibility is to have the active dancers use 4 steps to cross over, then immediately take hands with their opposites and do a "heel-and-toe, heel-and-toe" with the leading foot before starting the sashay across. Young children may have trouble coordinating the shift from dancing together to dancing apart in A2. If so, you can just let everybody dance back the same way they came. But for more mature dancers,

this is clearly the fun and mildly challenging part of the dance. By the way, if there is enough room in the hall, the dancers can sashay outside the boundaries of the set in A2 1-8, as long as they get back home on the following 8 counts.

The dance as described is repeated three more times, with lady 2 and her opposite active, then lady 3 and her opposite, and finally lady 4 and her opposite. Of course, it can also be varied by having the gents initiate the action. Choose an introduction, break and ending that involves all the dancers, such as I.a., II.a. or III.a.

Music

A lively jig set such as the "Square Dance Tunes" medley from *New England Country Dance Music* with the Green Mountain Volunteers is a good choice for this dance. Or try "Dixie Hoedown" from *Square Dance Tonight Vol. 1.* **Tempo:** about 126-130.

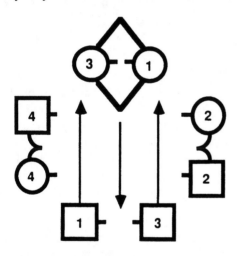

"Ladies in the center, sashay across."

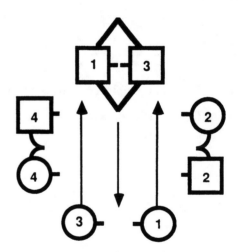

"Gents in the center, sashay back."

SQUARE
heads or sides active

JINGLE BELLS

MUSIC	CALLS	MUSIC	DESCRIPTION
Intro:	Head two couples forward and back		
A1 1-4	_ _ _ _	**A1** 1-8	Couples 1 and 3, take your partner by the hand and go 4 steps forward, into the center, and 4 steps back, to place.
5-8	Forward again and dosido		
9-12	_ _ _ _	9-16	The same two couples, dosido your opposites (gent 1 with lady 3, lady 1 with gent 3) (8 steps).
13-16	_ _ And swing right there		
A2 1-4	_ _ _ _	**A2** 1-8	The same two couples, take social dance position with your opposite and swing (8 counts). End facing the nearest side couple. Each dancer will be facing his or her corner.
5-8	Take that lady, face the sides*		
9-12	Split that couple, go around just one	9-16	Each pair of active dancers goes forward, between the inactive couple they are facing. The two active dancers then turn away from each other and continue individually around the nearest inactive dancer, back to original places (8 steps).
13-16	Come back home and dosido		
B1 1-4	_ _ _ _	**B1** 1-8	Meeting their partners at home, the active dancers continue forward to do a dosido with their partners (8 steps).
5-8	_ And with your corner swing		
9-12	_ _ _ _	9-16	Everybody swing your corner (8 counts).
13-16	Keep her, promenade the ring		
B2 1-4	_ _ _ _	**B2** 1-16	Take promenade position with the one you swung, and walk counterclockwise around the square, back to the gent's place (16 steps).
5-8	_ _ _ _		
9-12	_ _ _ _		
13-16	Head two couples** go forward and back		

*Change this to "heads" for the third and fourth times through the figure.
**Change this to "Side two couples" before the third and fourth times through the figure.

Comments

This dance was written by New York caller Sol Gordon, known in particular for his recordings of (mostly) singing calls that were used in the schools back in the 1950s and '60s. It is called Jingle Bells because he set it to that tune, but I have presented it above as a patter call.

The figure is fairly simple, but remind the dancers to put the lady on the right after they swing in A2 1-8. In A2 9-16, the inactive dancers should move apart to let the actives through.

Because of the partner change, this dance must be repeated in the sequence heads, heads, sides, sides. Fill it out with an introduction, break and ending, for example, I.a., II.b. or II.c.

Music

Both Northern and Southern style tunes can be used, for instance, "New Brunswick Hornpipe" from *Maritime Dance Party* or "Old Joe Clarke" from *Square Dance Tonight Vol. 3*. **Tempo:** 120-130, depending on the skill level of the group.

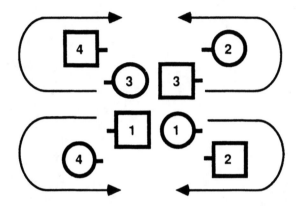

"Split that couple, go around one, and come back home."

Used with the permission of Sol Gordon.

SQUARE
heads or sides active

SILVER AND GOLD

MUSIC		CALLS
Intro:		Heads separate 'round the outside track
A1	**1-4**	— — — —
	5-8	Meet your own and dosido
	9-12	— — — —
	13-16	— — And swing right there
A2	**1-4**	— — — —
	5-8	Right and left through across the square
	9-12	— — — —
	13-16	Allemande left your corners all
B1	**1-4**	— — — —
	5-8	Go back to your own and dosido
	9-12	— — — —
	13-16	Promenade your corner lady home
B2	**1-4**	— — — —
	5-8	— — — —
	9-12	Head* two couples stand back to back
	13-16	Walk around the outside track

MUSIC		DESCRIPTION
A1	**1-8**	Couples 1 and 3 turn their backs to their partners and walk individually around the outside of the set, until they meet their partners on the opposite side (8 steps).
	9-16	The same two couples do a dosido with their partners (8 steps).
A2	**1-8**	The same two couples take social dance position with their partners and swing (8 counts).
	9-16	The same two couples face the center of the set and do a right and left through (see Glossary), back to their original places (8 steps).
B1	**1-8**	Take a left-hand pigeon wing grip with your corner and walk counter-clockwise around each other in 8 steps, until you are facing your partners.
	9-16	Everyone dosido your partner (8 steps).
B2	**1-16**	Everyone take promenade position with your *corner* and walk counter-clockwise around the square, back to the gent's home position (16 steps).

Change this to "Sides" before the third and fourth times through the figure.

Comments

Silver and Gold was written by Ted Sannella and appears in his book, *Balance and Swing*. It is a relatively easy dance, but be careful that the active couples do not swing too long in A2 1-8. Otherwise

they will have trouble completing the right and left through in time. Also note that a full 8 counts are alotted to the allemande left in B1 1-8, making it quite relaxed.

Since there is a partner change, the dance should be repeated once more with the head couples active, and then twice for the side couples. Choose your own introduction, break and ending, for example, I.f., II.e. or III.b.

but other tunes can also be used, for example, "Shandon Bells" from *Kitchen Junket* or "Home Sweet Home" from *Square Dance Tonight Vol. 3.* **Tempo:** about 120-126.

Music

Ted Sannella composed this dance specifically to go with the tune "Silver and Gold Two-Step,"

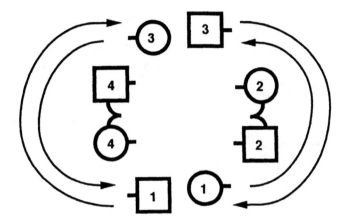

"Heads separate 'round the outside track."

Previously published in *Balance and Swing*; 1982 by Ted Sannella; used with his permission.

What size should the square be?

The dancers in a square should not be too close together, but not too far away, either, as this can make it difficult for them to complete the figures in the time alotted. Be particularly careful if there is plenty of space in the room where you're dancing: people have a tendency to spread out if they can. Also check that one couple isn't standing appreciably farther away than the other three.

As a rule of thumb, try this method of determining the ideal size for a square: with everyone standing in home position and holding hands with their partners, have the dancers extend their free arms straight out to the side. If their fingertips meet the fingertips of their corners, the square has an appropriate size.

SQUARE
heads or sides active

BLUE HAWAII

MUSIC	CALLS	MUSIC	DESCRIPTION

Intro: Head two couples pass through

A1 1-4	__ __ Separate	**A1** 1-16	Couples 1 and 3, walk forward, pass your opposite by the right shoulder, and then, moving away from your partner, walk individually around the outside of the set, back to place (16 steps).
5-8	Go all the way around the outside track		
9-12	__ __ __ __		
13-16	Face your opposite, dosido		

A2 1-4	__ __ __ __	**A2** 1-8	The same two couples, dosido your opposite (gent 1 with lady 3, lady 1 with gent 3) (8 steps).
5-8	Same four, right hand star	9-16	The same two couples form a right hand star in the center of the set and go clockwise, almost once around (8 steps).
9-12	__ __ __ __		
13-16	Find your corner and you swing		

B1 1-4	__ __ __ __	**B1** 1-8	Coming out of the star, look for your corner, take social dance position with him or her, and swing 8 counts.
5-8	New corner, allemande left	9-16	Finish the swing by putting the lady on the gent's right, and look for your new corner. Take a left-hand pigeon wing grip with your corner and go counterclockwise once around each other, back to your new partner (8 steps).
9-12	__ __ __ __		
13-16	And promenade the one you swung		

B2 1-4	__ __ __ __	**B2** 1-16	Take promenade position with your partner and walk counterclockwise all the way around the square, back to the gent's home place (16 steps).
5-8	__ __ __ __		
9-12	__ __ __ __		
13-16	Head two couples* pass through		

*Change this to "two side couples" before the third and fourth times through the figure.

Comments

This dance is based on a description I found in the book *Easy Level Squares/Mixers/Contras,* by Bob Howell and Cathie and Stan Burdick, a collection of reprints of dances that have appeared in Howell's "Easy Level" column in the magazine *American Squaredance.* No source is given for the dance, but it must originally have been a singing call to the tune of the same name.

On the face of it, Blue Hawaii looks quite similar to Jingle Bells, but watch out: the dancers will need to have a better sense of positioning for this one. Having them locate their corners before they start the star in A2 9-16 may be a help. It is also important that they put the lady on the right after the corner swing in B1 1-8.

Make sure that the dancers don't rush through the "pass through, separate, around the outside" figure in A1. They should be encouraged to time their trip around the set to arrive at home just in time for the dosido.

For the allemande left in B1 9-16, a full 8 counts are alotted, which gives anyone who has trouble finding his or her new corner a chance to recover. The dance can be simplified, if necessary, by leaving out the allemande left and just doing a longer swing.

Do the figure twice with the heads active, and then twice for the sides. You can add an additional introduction, break and ending, for instance, III.a. or IV.b.

Music

Use a Northern style tune, such as the "French-Canadian Reels" medley from *New England Country Dance Music* with the Green Mountain Volunteers or try something with more of a Southern feel, such as the medley called "Moderate Contra Tempo" on *Dances from Appalachia 2.* **Tempo:** about 120-126.

Previously published in *Easy Level Squares/Contras/Mixers*, by Bob Howell and Stan and Cathie Burdick. Used with the permission of Jon Sanborne, *American Square Dance* magazine.

SQUARE
heads or sides active

GENTS AND CORNERS

MUSIC	CALLS	MUSIC	DESCRIPTION
Intro:	Head <u>gents</u> take your <u>corners</u> to the <u>center</u> and <u>back</u>		
A1 1-4	_ _ _ _	**A1** 1-8	Gents 1 and 3 take their corners (ladies 4 and 2, respectively) by the hand and go 4 steps into the center and then 4 steps backwards to place.
5-8	<u>Same four circle left</u>		
9-12	_ _ _ _	9-16	The same four dancers go into the middle again, form a circle, and circle left once around (8 steps).
13-16	<u>Left</u> hand <u>star</u>, the <u>other way back</u>		
A2 1-4	_ _ _ _	**A2** 1-8	Change to a left hand star and walk counterclockwise once around, until you come to your partners (8 steps).
5-8	To your <u>partner now</u> with an <u>allemande right</u>		
9-12	And <u>on</u> the <u>corner</u> allemande <u>left</u>	9-12	Drop hands in the star and take a right-hand pigeon wing grip with your partner. Walk clockwise about once around each other, until you are facing your corners (4 steps).
13-16	<u>Back</u> to your <u>own</u> and <u>dosido</u>	13-16	Take a left-hand pigeon wing grip with your corner and walk counterclockwise around each other until you are facing your partners again (4 steps).
B1 1-4	_ _ _ _	**B1** 1-8	Dosido your partner (8 steps).
5-8	_ And <u>with</u> your <u>corner swing</u>		
9-12	_ _ _ _	9-16	Go back to your corner, take social dance position and swing (8 counts).
13-16	<u>Keep</u> that <u>girl</u> and <u>promenade</u>		
B2 1-4	_ _ _ _	**B2** 1-16	Take promenade position with the one you swung and walk counterclockwise around the square, back to the gent's place (16 steps).
5-8	_ _ _ _		
9-12	_ _ _ _		
13-16	Head <u>gents</u>* and <u>new</u> <u>corners</u> to the <u>center</u> and <u>back</u>		

Change this to "Side gents" before the third and fourth times through the figure.

Comments

Gents and Corners was written by Ralph Page, who for many years until his death in 1985 was the best known advocate of New England style square and contra dancing. The dance was written in the mid–1950s and was later recorded as a singing call to the tune "Trail of the Lonesome Pine" by Don Armstrong, in which form it gained much popularity.

The figures seem easy enough on the face of it, but there are two things to watch out for. First of all, it's more confusing than you might think for the gents to take their *corners* with them to the center and back, particularly as partners and corners are constantly changing on each round of the dance. Dances of this type require everyone to be alert and aware of their positions. The second thing is the allemandes in A2, which are done in 4 counts each.

The timing of this section should be stressed during the walk-through, or dancers may have a tendency to take too long on the allemandes. Conversely, they may rush unnecessarily through the following dosido, for which there are the normal 8 counts.

Repeat the sequence once more as described, and then twice for the side gents and their corners. Add an introduction, break and ending, for instance, I.e., II.b. or III.c.

Music

Normally, this dance is done to a New England or Canadian tune, such as "Fisher's Hornpipe" from *New England Chestnuts 2*. But you might also want to try something like "Cattle in the Cane" from *Square Dance Tonight Vol. 3*. **Tempo:** about 120-126.

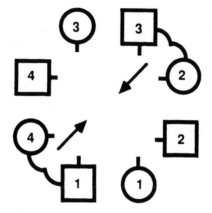

"Head gents take your corners to the center and back."

Previously published in *Balance and Swing*; 1982 by Ted Sannella; used with his permission.

SQUARE
heads or sides active

STAR ON THE SIDES AND STAR IN THE CENTER

MUSIC	CALLS	MUSIC	DESCRIPTION

Intro: The two head couples stand back to back
Separate, go 'round the track

A1 1-4 _ _ _ _

5-8 Meet your partner, pass her by

9-12 When you meet at home, pass by again

13-16 Go out to the sides* and circle four

A1 1-16 Couples 1 and 3 turn their backs to their partners and walk individually all the way around the outside of the square in 16 steps. Let the ladies pass on the inside track when you meet. When you meet again at home, pass your partner and continue individually to the side couple that was nearest your home position (i.e., the couple that includes your corner).

A2 1-4 _ _ _ _

5-8 Left hand star, the other way back

9-12 _ _ _ _

13-16 Heads** to the center with a right hand star

A2 1-8 Gent 1, lady 3 and couple 4, who are now together, form a circle, and lady 1, gent 3 and couple 2 form a circle. Circle left once around (8 steps).

9-16 Change to a left hand star and go once around, ending so that the dancers from the active couples (1 and 3) are nearest the center of the set (8 steps).

B1 1-4 _ _ _ _

5-8 Look for your corner, allemande left

9-12 Right to your own, grand right and left

13-16 _ _ _ _

B2 1-4 _ _ _ _

5-8 Meet your own and promenade home

B1 1-8 The side couples stand in place while the four active dancers go into the middle, form a right hand star, and go once around, ending when they come to their corners (8 steps).

9-12 Drop the star, take a left-hand pigeon wing grip with your corner and go about once around, until you are facing your partner (4 steps).

13-16
+B2 1-8 Give your right hand to your partner and start a grand right and left, continuing until you meet your partner on the other side of the set (12 steps).

9-12 — — — —

13-16 Side*** couples separate, 'round the outside

9-16 Take promenade position with your partner and walk counterclockwise around the set, until you get to your home place (8 steps).

Change this to "heads" for the second and fourth times through the figure.
**Change this to "Sides" for the second and fourth times through the figure.*
***Change this to "Head couples" before the third time through the figure.*

Comments

I found this dance on a Sol Gordon record under the name Two Little, Three Little Right Hand Stars. He attributes the figure to Ralph Page. The version on the record has some questionable timing and includes a right hand star with the side couple, in between the circle left and left hand star. Sol Gordon tells me that he timed the movements on the record in traditional fashion, but to adapt the dance to a standard 64-count tune and modern timing, I have tightened it up a little as presented above. If you like the idea of the right hand star, you can easily put it in, but it will require an extra 8 counts. In order to avoid starting over in the middle of a 16-count phrase, you may therefore want to extend the dance additionally. Some possibilities are: 1) Add an 8-count swing after the grand right and left, before promenading home. 2) Make the grand right and left all the way around instead of halfway, adding another 12 counts, then do a short 4-count swing at home and promenade all the way around in 16 counts.

When teaching this dance, make sure that the circle and stars are executed precisely, so that everyone is on time for the allemande left. Each figure should flow into the next; to avoid stop-and-go dancing, the dancers must think ahead and adjust their movements to the distance that needs to be covered.

There is no partner change in this dance, so it can be done in the sequence heads, sides, heads, sides. If you need to reduce the challenge level, try doing it heads, heads, sides, sides at first. Add your own introduction, break and ending or try, for example, II.d., II.e. or IV.a.

Music

The dance is a product of the New England tradition, but can also be danced to a Southern style tune, preferably one with a recognizable structure. If you adopt a version of the main figure that takes more than 64 counts, however, it may be an advantage to use a tune that is not overly structured in feel. For New England style, try "Bouchard No. 2" from *Square Dance Tonight Vol. 1* or "Reel de Montreal" from *Kitchen Junket*. **Tempo:** about 126.

Used with the permission of Sol Gordon.

Confused? Me?

PARTNER: That person who is looking for you while other couples are promenading.

CORNER: That person who will soon be your partner, but by the time you realize it is already your opposite.

—from the Alabama Square and Round Dance Association *News,* quoted in *Square Dancing,* December 1983.

SQUARE
everyone active

SHEEHAN'S REEL

MUSIC		CALLS
Intro:		All four ladies to the center and back
A1	1-4	_ _ _ _
	5-8	Now all four gents to the center and back
	9-12	_ _ _ _
	13-16	_ Four ladies, right hand star
A2	1-4	_ _ _ _
	5-8	Now the other way back with a left hand star
	9-12	_ _ Pass your partner
	13-16	_ And dosido the next
B1	1-4	_ _ _ _
	5-8	_ _ Swing with him
	9-12	_ _ _ _
	13-16	_ _ Now promenade
B2	1-4	_ _ _ _
	5-8	_ _ To the gent's home place
	9-12	_ _ _ _
	13-16	All four ladies forward and back

MUSIC		DESCRIPTION
A1	1-8	All four ladies walk 4 steps forward towards the center of the set, and 4 steps backwards, to place.
	9-16	All four gents walk 4 steps forward towards the center of the set, and 4 steps backwards, to place.
A2	1-8	The four ladies form a right hand star in the center of the set and walk clockwise once around (8 steps).
	9-16	Change to a left hand star and walk counterclockwise a little more than once around, past your partner (8 steps).
B1	1-8	With the next gent after your partner (i.e., your original corner), do a dosido (8 steps).
	9-16	Take social dance position with the same person and swing (8 counts).
B2	1-16	Take promenade position with the one you swung and walk counterclockwise around the set, until you get back to the gent's place (16 steps).

Comments

Sheehan's Reel was put together by Roger Whynot and named for a tune that he felt went well with the dance. It's a real gem for beginners and one night stands.

Because the choreography is entirely symmetrical, it can be danced without even mentioning how the couples in a square are numbered, and the simple figures can be done by most people without problems, yet the dance has good flow and is fun to do. If you want to simplify it additionally, you can have the ladies come back to their original partners each time after the left hand star. Conversely, you can add to the dance by waiting until everyone is back in place and then repeating the whole sequence in reverse, with the gents going forward and back first and doing the stars. In this case, they should promenade back to the *lady's* place after each round of the figure. I often spring this on the dancers without a walk-through, and if properly called, even one night standers can easily do it.

Add an introduction and ending, and a break if the group can handle it, for instance, I.b. or IV.a.

Music

Sheehan's Reel can be danced to a Northern style tune, but is also excellent to a good Southern style fiddle tune, such as "Old Joe Clarke" from *Square Dance Tonight Vol. 3* or the somewhat more phrased "Midway" on *Dances from Appalachia 2*. Remember to allow for extra music if you want to extend the dance as suggested above. **Tempo:** Depends on the group. About 120 for total beginners, somewhat faster for dancers with more experience.

Previously published in *Balance and Swing*; 1982 by Ted Sannella; used with the permission of Ted Sannella and Roger Whynot.

SQUARE
everyone active

STAR BREAKDOWN

MUSIC	CALLS	MUSIC	DESCRIPTION

Intro: ___ Four ladies right hand star

A1 **1-4** ___ ___ ___ ___

5-8 Left hand to your partner, once and a half

9-12 ___ ___ ___ ___

13-16 Now the gents go in with a right hand star

A1 **1-8** The four ladies form a right hand star in the center of the set and walk clockwise once around until they are facing their partners again (8 steps).

9-16 Drop the star, take a left-hand pigeon wing grip with your partner and go once and a half around each other, so the gents end up closest to the center of the set (8 steps).

A2 **1-4** ___ ___ ___ ___

5-8 Left hand to your own, turn once and a half

9-12 ___ ___ ___ ___

13-16 Go on to the next and balance there

A2 **1-8** The four gents move into the center, form a right hand star, and go once around, until they are facing their partners again (8 steps).

9-16 Drop the star, take a left-hand pigeon wing grip with your partner and go once and a half around each other, so the ladies end up closest to the center of the set, facing clockwise, and the gents are on the outside of the set, facing counterclockwise. Drop hands and move slightly forward to meet the next dancer (your original right hand lady/left hand gent) (8 steps).

B1 **1-4** ___ ___ ___ And swing

5-8 ___ ___ ___ ___
9-12 ___ ___ ___ ___
13-16 ___ Promenade around that ring

B1 **1-4** With the person you meet, balance (see Glossary) (4 counts).

5-16 With the same person, take social dance position and swing 12 counts.

B2 **1-4** ___ ___ ___ ___
5-8 ___ ___ To the lady's place
9-12 ___ ___ ___ ___
13-16 All four ladies right hand star

B2 **1-16** Take promenade position with the one you swung and walk counterclockwise around the set until you come back to the *lady's* place (16 steps).

Comments

Star Breakdown was written in 1976 by Tony Parkes, who is one of the best New England callers and choreographers of the present generation and one of the first, having become involved in square and contra dancing at a much earlier age than most. I learned the dance from the album *Kitchen Junket*, released by Tony and his band, Yankee Ingenuity, in 1977. It has since been published in Tony's book, *Shadrack's Delight* (1988), in which he mentions that the dance was inspired by an earlier routine devised by Don Durlacher.

The only part of the dance that tends to give problems is the progression of the gents to their right hand ladies at the end of A2. Dancers are rarely asked to find their right hand ladies/left hand gents, so using those terms probably will not help much. Instead, make sure during the walk-through that the allemande lefts are done precisely once and half around (it often helps to have the dancers go exactly once around, and then halfway more) and that everyone is facing in the correct direction at the end of A2. The balance should fall exactly on the downbeat of the first B part.

Fill out the dance with an introduction, break and ending, for example, II.c. or III.b.

Music

Star Breakdown is normally danced to a New England or Canadian tune, such as "Joys of Quebec" from *Kitchen Junket*, but it can also be done successfully to a Southern style tune, for example, "Black Mountain Rag" from *Square Dance Tonight Vol. 1*. **Tempo:** about 120-126.

SQUARE
everyone active

A PASSABLE SOLUTION

MUSIC	CALLS	MUSIC	DESCRIPTION
Intro:	Everyone go forward and back		

A1 1-4   — — — —

5-8   Gents star left three quarters 'round

9-12   — — — —

13-16   Find your corner, turn by the right

A1 1-8   All join hands and go 4 steps forward towards the center of the set and 4 steps backwards, to place.

9-16   The four gents form a left hand star in the center of the set and walk counterclockwise about three-quarters around, until each gent is closest to his corner lady (8 steps).

A2 1-4   — — Partner by the left

5-8   — — Corner by the right

9-12   — — Partner by the left

13-16   — — Four ladies chain

A2 1-4   Drop the star. Each gent takes a right-hand pigeon wing grip with his corner. Go around each other until you are facing your partners (4 steps).

5-8   Take a left-hand pigeon wing grip with your partner and go around each other until you are facing your corners (4 steps).

9-12   Take a right-hand pigeon wing grip with your corner and go around each other until you are facing your partners again (4 steps).

13-16   Take a left-hand pigeon wing grip with your partner and go around each other until the ladies are facing the center of the set (4 steps).

B1 1-4   — — — —

5-8   Ladies chain three quarters to your

9-12   Corner — — —

13-16   — — And promenade

B1 1-8   All four ladies do a ladies chain simultaneously, by forming a right hand star in the center and moving clockwise halfway around to the opposite gent, who picks up the lady for a courtesy turn (see Glossary) (8 steps).

9-16   Repeat the four ladies chain, but this time, the ladies move *three-quarters* of the way around the set to their corners (seen from their present positions) (8 steps).

B2 **1-4**   — — — —

      5-8   — — — —

      9-12   — — — —

      13-16   Everyone into the center and back

B2 **1-16**   Keeping the handhold from the courtesy turn, walk counterclockwise all the way around the set, back to the gent's home place (16 steps).

Comments

A Passable Solution is the result of my desire to compose a dance using an old-fashioned Texas dosido (also later called a do paso), consisting of alternate right-hand turns with the corner and left-hand turns with the partner. I finally arrived at the above sequence, which also has some similarities to the many star-type figures that were composed in the Southwest around the 1940s. Since the term do paso has now been standardized in club style square dancing to mean a left-hand turn with your partner, right-hand turn with your corner and courtesy turn with your partner, I have not used the expression do paso in the calls, but have described the movements directionally.

The four quick hand turns in A2 that constitute the do paso leave little time for hesitation. So make sure that the dancers are able to locate their partners and corners. It is also important that they know how to give weight by leaning slightly away from each other, so as to get around each other efficiently. Rickey Holden, who worked in Texas in the 1950s, says that in that region, the desire for centrifugal movement was satisfied by hand turns, rather than by the long swings that have always been so popular in New England style square dancing.

At the end of A2, the ladies move into the center for the four ladies chain, while the gents continue their forward motion from the hand turn to face in and be ready for the courtesy turn. As the ladies move in for the second ladies chain, they should check to see who their present corners are. It will also help if the gents identify their present corner ladies and are ready to help them out of the star as they come around (eye contact!).

An introduction, break and ending should be added. You may want to use something simple, such as II.a. Otherwise, an appropriate choice would be a break with a grand right and left, such as III.b.

Music

A Northern style tune will make this dance seem more phrased, a Southern style tune less so. If you want to retain the Texas feel, use a Southern/Western type tune, such as "Flop-Eared Mule" from *Square Dance Tonight Vol. 3* or "Leather Britches" from *Dancing Bow and Singing Strings*. **Tempo:** about 126-132.

SQUARE
everyone active

DUCK THROUGH AND SWING

MUSIC	CALLS	MUSIC	DESCRIPTION
Intro:	Head two couples right and left through		
A1 1-4	Side* two couples right and left through	**A1** 1-4	Couples 1 and 3 do the first half of a right and left through (see Glossary) (4 steps).
5-8	Head two couples** right and left back	5-8	Couples 1 and 3 complete their right and left through while, at the same time, couples 2 and 4 do the first half of a right and left through (4 steps).
9-12	__ __ __ __	9-12	Couples 2 and 4 complete their right and left through while, at the same time, couples 1 and 3 do the first half of a right and left through back to place (4 steps).
13-16	Heads** to the right and circle left	13-16	Couples 1 and 3 complete their right and left through (4 steps).
A2 1-4	Make a line at the sides* __ __	**A2** 1-8	Each head couple moves into the center to face the side couple on their right, forms a circle with them, and they circle left. When they are about halfway around, the head gent drops the hand of his corner in the circle and leads the other three dancers into a line at the side couple's place, facing the center of the set, with the head couple at the left-hand end of the line (8 steps).
5-8	And everyone go forward and back		
9-12	__ __ __ __	9-16	In your lines, go 4 steps forward towards the center of the set and 4 steps backwards, to place.
13-16	Forward again and pass through		
B1 1-4	Arch in the middle and the ends duck through	**B1** 1-4	Drop hands and go 4 steps forward, passing right shoulders with your opposite.
5-8	Swing the one that's facing you	5-8	Join hands again in the same lines as before (now with your backs to the center of the set). The two middle dancers in each line lift their joined hands to form an arch, and the end dancers move in towards each other

and go under the arch, into the center of the set (4 steps).

9-12 — — — —

13-16 And pro<u>men</u>ade, that's <u>what</u> you <u>do</u>

9-16 Swing the one you are facing now, i.e., the two dancers in each line who made an arch swing with each other, while those who went through the arches swing with the person coming towards them from the other side (8 counts).

B2 1-4 — — — —

5-8 — — — —

9-12 — — — —

13-16 <u>Head</u> two <u>couples</u>** <u>right</u> and left <u>through</u>

B2 1-16 Take promenade position with the one you swung and walk counterclockwise around the set, until you get back to the gent's place (16 steps).

*Change this to "head(s)" for the third and fourth times through the figure.
**Change this to "side(s)" for the third and fourth times through the figure.

Comments

Duck Through and Swing is another excellent dance by Tony Parkes, and like Star Breakdown, it can be found both on the *Kitchen Junket* album and in Tony's book, *Shadrack's Delight*. The dance was written in 1975.

The hardest part of the dance is the first 16 counts, during which the heads and sides dance overlapping right and left throughs. It is important for the caller to be on the ball and send the dancers off at the right time, as shown in the calls above. During the walk-through, you will also want to make sure that the dancers understand they are not to wait until the previous right and left through has been completed before starting the next—and also that the side couples do *not* return to place. This sequence is fairly demanding and should not be presented to beginners, who will only become frustrated. Save the dance for dancers with some experience; they'll enjoy it.

Since there is a partner change, do the dance in the sequence heads, heads, sides, sides. Note that when the sides start, the side gents are active and are therefore the ones to drop their corners' hands in A2 1-8 and lead out to a line at the *heads'* position.

Complete the dance with an intro, break and ending, for instance, II.e. or IV.c.

Music

This dance works best to a well-phrased Northern tune. I like "Mouth of the Tobique" from *Kitchen Junket* or "La Grande Chaine" from *Square Dance Tonight Vol. 2*. **Tempo:** about 120. Possibly a little faster, but not so fast that the first part becomes rushed.

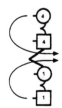 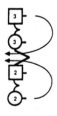 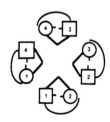

"Arch in the middle and the ends duck through..."   **"Swing the one that's facing you."**

SQUARE
everyone active

ROGER'S GRAND CHAIN

MUSIC	CALLS		MUSIC	DESCRIPTION
Intro:	The two head ladies chain to the right			
A1 1-4	— — — —		**A1** 1-8	Each head couple faces the couple on their right and does a ladies chain (see Glossary) with them, i.e., lady 1 with lady 2, and lady 3 with lady 4 (8 steps).
5-8	And all four ladies grand chain			
9-12	— — — —		9-16	All four ladies now do a ladies chain simultaneously, by forming a right hand star in the center and moving clockwise halfway around to the opposite gent, who picks up the lady for a courtesy turn (8 steps).
13-16	Now the new head* ladies chain to the right			
A2 1-4	— — — —		**A2** 1-8	At this point, lady 4 is in lady 1's original place and lady 2 in lady 3's place. They each do a ladies chain with the lady in the couple on their right (8 steps).
5-8	And all four ladies grand chain			
9-12	— — — —		9-16	All four ladies again do a ladies chain simultaneously, which brings them back to their original positions (8 steps).
13-16	— — Corner swing			
B1 1-4	— — — —		**B1** 1-8	Everyone take social dance position with your corner, swing 8 counts, and put the lady on the right.
5-8	With your new corner allemande left			
9-12	— — — —		9-16	The person you swung is now your partner. Take a left-hand pigeon wing grip with your new corner and go around each other until you are facing your new partners again (8 steps).
13-16	Go back and promenade the one you swung			
B2 1-4	— — — —		**B2** 1-16	Take promenade position with the one you swung and walk counterclockwise around the set, until you get back to the gent's place (16 steps).
5-8	— — — —			
9-12	— — — —			
13-16	Head* two ladies chain to the right			

Change this to "side ladies" for the third and fourth times through the figure.

Comments

Here is a dance that will give you plenty of practice doing the ladies chain! Just make sure the dancers are well versed in the "normal" ladies chain before throwing Roger's Grand Chain at them: it is more demanding than it may appear on paper. When the heads are directed to chain to the *right,* the sides must automatically face to their *left,* and vice versa. Since the ladies are constantly moving from place to place in the square, it is important for the gents, who stay put and have a better chance of maintaining an overview, to help guide the ladies in the right direction.

By the way, *pushing* a lady into a ladies chain with your right hand is not helping; leading gently with the left hand and offering support with that hand is. It may also help to point out to the ladies that they will be meeting the *same* other lady for the two ladies chains that are done on the diagonal.

This dance was worked out by Roger Whynot, based on an idea of Rod Linnell's in a dance he called Milton Quadrille (published in Rod Linnell's book, *Square Dances from a Yankee Caller's Clipboard*). The difference lies in the B1 part. Rod Linnell's solution was to have the four gents do a left hand star and go three-quarters of the way around, until they meet their corners, and swing with them. Roger Whynot's ending is nice because it keeps all eight dancers in motion.

Since there is a partner change, do the figure twice through with the head couples chaining to the right, and then twice with the side couples chaining to the right. Or if that is too much for the dancers to handle, you can also get away with having the heads chain to the right all four times. Add an intro, break and ending, for instance, I.c., II.f. or IV.a.

Music

This dance should definitely be done to a well-phrased tune, for example, "The New Fiddle" from *Square Dance Tonight Vol. 3* or "The Growling Old Man and the Grumbling Old Woman" from *Kitchen Junket.* **Tempo:** about 120, possibly a little faster with experienced dancers.

Previously published in *Balance and Swing*; 1982 by Ted Sannella; used with the permission of Ted Sannella and Roger Whynot.

SQUARE
everyone active

THE LAST LAUGH

MUSIC	CALLS	MUSIC	DESCRIPTION

Intro: Heads to the right and circle left

A1 1-4 __ __ Go once around

5-8 Now split that couple and go around one

A1 1-8 Each head couple moves into the center to face the side couple on their right, forms a circle with them, and they circle left exactly once around, so the side couple is in home position and the head couple is in the middle of the set, facing them (8 steps).

9-12 __ __ Make a line at the sides*

13-16 And everyone go forward and back

9-16 Each head couple goes forward, between the side dancers, who move apart to let them through. Then the head dancers turn away from their partners to go individually around the nearest side dancer and end next to that dancer, with all four in a line facing the center of the set (8 steps).

A2 1-4 __ __ __ __

5-8 Swing the lady on your left

A2 1-8 Each line of four dancers takes hands and goes forward 4 steps towards the center of the set and backwards 4 steps to place.

9-12 __ __ __ __

13-16 Right and left through, go across the set

9-16 Each gent takes social dance position with the lady on his left and they swing 8 counts. End by putting the lady on the gent's right and reforming the two lines of four (8 counts).

B1 1-4 __ __ __ __

5-8 Same two ladies, chain across

B1 1-8 With the couple across from you, do a right and left through (see Glossary) (8 steps).

9-12 __ __ __ __

13-16 Swing the lady on your left

9-16 The same two couples, do a ladies chain (see Glossary) (8 steps).

B2 1-4 __ __ __ __

5-8 Promenade home to the gentleman's place

B2 1-8 Each gent swings with the lady on his left. For the gents at the extreme left ends of the lines, this will be the lady across from you (8 counts).

9-12	_ _ _ _	
13-16	Heads** to the <u>right</u> and <u>circle</u> <u>left</u>	

9-16	Take promenade position with the one you swung, and walk counterclockwise around the set, until you get to the gent's home place (8 steps).

Change this to "heads" for the third and fourth times through the figure.
**Change this to "sides" before the third and fourth times through the figure.*

Comments

The Last Laugh is one of my own squares. I composed it in the fall of 1986, and it has been well received everywhere I have used it. The two swings with the lady on the left seem to create just enough of a surprise effect to please the dancers.

The dance has a partner change, so it should be done in the sequence heads, heads, sides, sides. Fill it out with an introduction, break and ending, for instance, I.d. or II.f.

Music

This dance works best to a New England or Canadian tune, which may be a reel or jig. Try "Woodchopper's Reel" from *Kitchen Junket* or "The New Fiddle" from *Square Dance Tonight Vol. 3*. **Tempo:** about 120-126.

SQUARE
everyone active

YEAR END TWO-STEP

MUSIC	CALLS	MUSIC	DESCRIPTION

Intro: The two head ladies chain to the right

A1 1-4 __ __ __ __

5-8 Now the two head couples* go out to the right

9-12 And circle left, go once around

13-16 __ And with your opposite swing

A1 1-8 Each head couple faces the couple on their right and does a ladies chain (see Glossary) with them, i.e., lady 1 with lady 2, and lady 3 with lady 4 (8 steps).

9-16 Each head gent and his present partner move into the center to face the side couple on their right, form a circle with them, and circle left about once around (8 steps).

A2 1-4 __ __ __ __

5-8 Put her on the right and circle to a line

9-12 __ __ __ __

13-16 Ladies chain across the floor

A2 1-8 In each circle of four, each gent takes social dance position with the lady on his left (i.e., his original partner) and they swing 8 counts. End by putting the lady on the right and reforming the circle.

9-16 Circle left. When you are about halfway around, the head gent drops the hand of his corner in the circle and leads the other three dancers into a line at the side couple's place, facing the center of the set, with the head couple at the left-hand end of the line (8 steps).

B1 1-4 __ __ __ __

5-8 Step right up and swing your own

9-12 __ __ __ __

13-16 And promenade your partner home

B1 1-8 With the couple across from you, do a ladies chain (see Glossary) (8 steps).

9-16 Swing your partner at your own home position. In order to get there, the dancers at the ends of the lines move toward each other and meet at home. The dancers in the middle will find that one member of their couple is already home. The other member crosses over to place (8 counts).

B2	**1-4**	— — — —
	5-8	— — — —
	9-12	— — — —
	13-16	Side two <u>ladies</u>** <u>chain</u> to the <u>right</u>

B2	**1-16**	Take promenade position with your partner and walk counterclockwise around the set, until you get home (16 steps).

*Change this to "two side couples" for the second and fourth times through the figure.
**Change this to "Head two ladies" before the third time through the figure.

Comments

I saw this dance in a square dance magazine once, where it was attributed to Ralph Page. In Rod Linnell's book, *Square Dances from a Yankee Caller's Clipboard,* we are told that Rod Linnell composed the dance to go with a tune Ralph had written by the same name, and surprised him with it at a dance camp in 1961. Rod Linnell's creative choreography in the 1950s and 60s helped lay the groundwork for contemporary trends within traditional square and contra dancing.

Year End Two-Step is a good dance to save for dancers with some experience. The initial call, "two head ladies chain to the right," requires the side couples immediately to face *left*. The timing of "circle to a line" in A2 9-16 is also tight, and it is therefore important that the dancers not swing longer than they are supposed to in A2 1-8. Otherwise, the ladies at the extreme right ends of the lines will have trouble getting into the ladies chain on time. Also note that the call "with your opposite swing" (A1 13-16) refers to your opposite in the circle of four, not to your original opposite in the square.

Since there is no partner change in this dance, it is best to do it in the sequence heads, sides, heads, sides. But just as with Star on the Sides and Star in the Center, you can make the dance a little easier (but less exciting) by letting the heads lead the figure twice in a row and then the sides twice in a row. Note that when the sides start, it is the side gents who lead the other dancers out to a line in the *heads'* position in A2 9-16.

Complete the dance with an introduction, break and ending, for instance, I.f., III.c. or IV.c.

Music

The tune "Year End Two-Step" can be found on the LP record *Southerners Plus Two Play Ralph Page.* But other well-phrased tunes can also be used, for example, "Le Cultivateur" from *Square Dance Tonight Vol. 2* or "Angus Campbell" from *Kitchen Junket.* **Tempo:** about 120. Possibly a little faster for experienced dancers, but not so fast that the dance becomes rushed.

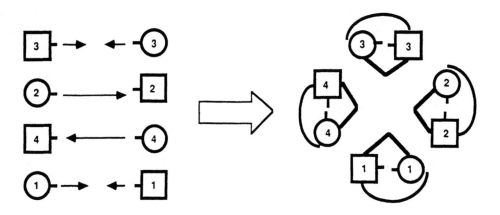

"Step right up and swing your own."

Previously published in *Balance and Swing*; 1982 by Ted Sannella; used with the permission of Ted Sannella and Roger Whynot.

SQUARE
everyone active

SWING TO A LINE

MUSIC	CALLS	MUSIC	DESCRIPTION

Intro: Heads promenade three quarters 'round

A1 **1-4**   — — — —
    5-8   And the side two couples* pass through
    9-12   Now swing right there with the one you meet

A1 **1-12**   The two head couples take promenade position with their partners and walk counterclockwise three-quarters of the way around the outside of the set, ending with couple 1 in couple 4's place and couple 3 in couple 2's place (12 steps). During the last 4 counts, the side couples pass through (go forward, passing right shoulders with your opposite), so that couple 2 is facing couple 1 and couple 4 is facing couple 3.

    13-16   — — — —
A2 **1-4**   — — — —
    5-8   Put the lady on the right, go forward and back

    13-16
+A2 **1-8**   Take social dance position with the person facing you, swing 12 counts, and end in a line of four in the side couple's place, facing the center of the set, with each lady to the right of the gent she swung.

    9-12   — — — —
    13-16   The two end ladies chain across

    9-16   Join hands in your lines and go 4 steps forward towards the center of the set and 4 steps backwards to place.

B1 **1-4**   — — — —
    5-8   Now the middle two ladies chain

B1 **1-8**   The two ladies on the extreme right ends of the lines do a ladies chain (see Glossary) with each other (8 steps).

    9-12   — — — —
    13-16   All join hands and circle left

    9-16   The remaining two ladies do a ladies chain with each other (8 steps).

B2 **1-4**   Just halfway to the gents' home place
    5-8   With your new partner swing right there

B2 **1-8**   Join hands in one big circle and circle left halfway around, until all the gents are at home (8 steps).

9-12 — — — —

13-16 <u>Sides</u>** promenade three <u>quar</u>ters 'round

9-16 Each gent swings with the lady on his right, who is his new partner (8 counts).

*Change this to "head two couples" for the second and fourth times through the figure.
**Change this to "Heads" before the third time through the figure.

Comments

Swing to a Line is another fine dance from creative choreographer Roger Whynot. It appears in Ted Sannella's book *Balance and Swing*. It is definitely not a dance for beginners, but is a lot of fun for more experienced dancers. The diagrams below should help to clarify the more unusual parts of the figure.

In B1 1-8, the two end ladies have to move farther than usual to reach each other, but if necessary, their ladies chain can be completed while the middle two ladies are starting theirs. Note that, although there is a partner change, each head couple winds up exchanging partners with the side couple on their left. This means that the dance must be repeated in the sequence heads, sides, heads, sides if you want all four gents to dance with each of the four ladies. Complete the dance with an introduction, break and ending, for instance, I.e. or IV.b.

Music

Use a Northern style tune for this dance, for instance, "Fairy Toddler Jig" from *Kitchen Junket* or "The Long Campaign" from *Square Dance Tonight Vol. 3*. **Tempo:** about 126.

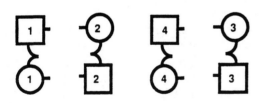

Position after "heads promenade three quarters 'round and the side two couples pass through."

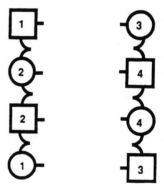

Position after "swing right there with the one you meet."

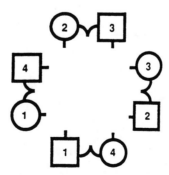

Position after the first time through the main figure.

Previously published in *Balance and Swing*; 1982 by Ted Sannella; used with the permission of Ted Sannella and Roger Whynot.

Tunes

The following pages contain musical notation for 35 traditional dance tunes that can be used for a variety of different dances. In the music presented here, the melody line is primarily intended for violin, but can also be used for guitar, mandolin, accordion, etc. Five-string banjo players will probably want to find music arranged more specifically for that instrument, unless they are experienced enough to arrange the tunes themselves. The chords can be used by anyone playing rhythm, whether on guitar, banjo, mandolin, bass, accordion or piano.

Accordion, tenor banjo and flutes can be used for New England style tunes but are not really appropriate for the Appalachian fiddle tunes. Percussion instruments like spoons, woodblock, washboard, etc. can also be included in the band, but use them with discretion or they may become tiresome. Drums and electric instruments are usually not used if a traditional sound is desired.

Traditional musicians tend to improvise, vary and ornament their tunes, rarely playing a given tune exactly the same way twice. In preparing the music for this book, I could have used transcriptions of specific performances, but in order to avoid implying that a specific, idiosyncratic version of a tune was the "right" or only way to play it, I chose instead to write out the tunes as closely as possible to their skeletal, basic forms. The first two tunes are presented in both a basic version and a more normal, elaborated version, as examples.

Many traditional American musicians play entirely by ear, although some, especially in the North, also read music. After having learned these tunes, you should try to free yourself from the written music and not let the notes dictate exactly how to play a given tune, but be open to variation and improvisation.

There are, however, certain kinds of embellishments that are typical for the different regional playing styles and others that are not. Anyone who is seriously interested in playing music for square and contra dancing should therefore listen to a variety of recordings and should try and locate experienced players who can help them learn the techniques necessary to achieve not only the notes, but the drive and rhythm inherent in good dance music. Some help may also be gained from instructional books such as the ones listed under "Materials for Musicians."

OLD JOE CLARKE

Old Joe Clarke is one of the best known Southern fiddle tunes, and although it's a simple tune, it can be very good for dancing. The bottom staff shows the basic melody and the top staff a version with simple, but typical ornamentation.

SOLDIER'S JOY

Soldier's Joy is a tune known in several European countries (under different names) as well as in the United States. Here are both the basic melody and a version with simple ornamentation as the tune might typically be played.

SALLY GOODIN

Each of the two parts of Sally Goodin is only half as long as in a "normal" dance tune, so the entire tune takes 32 counts instead of 64.

FLOP-EARED MULE

Also known as Long-Eared Mule.

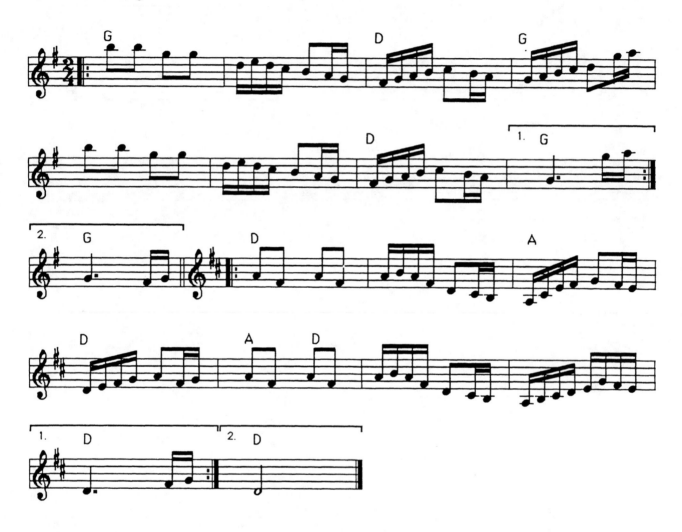

MISS McLEOD'S REEL

Also known as Hop High Ladies, Hop Light Ladies and Did You Ever See the Devil, Uncle Joe.

JUNE APPLE

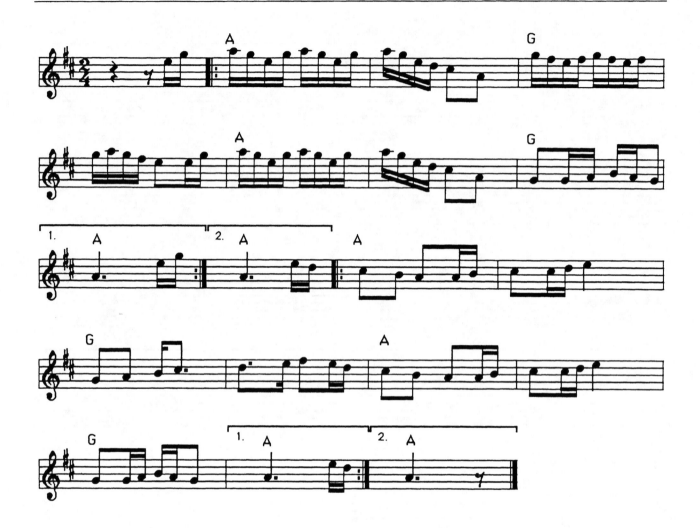

LIBERTY

Also known as Reel de Ti-Jean and The Tipsy Parson.

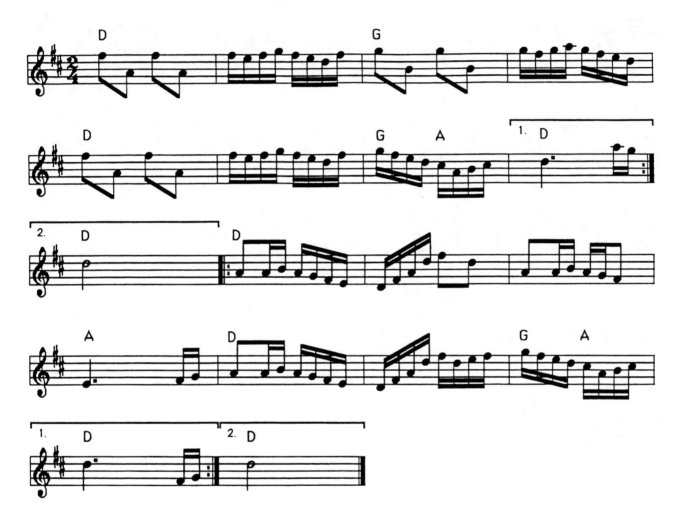

BILL CHEATHAM

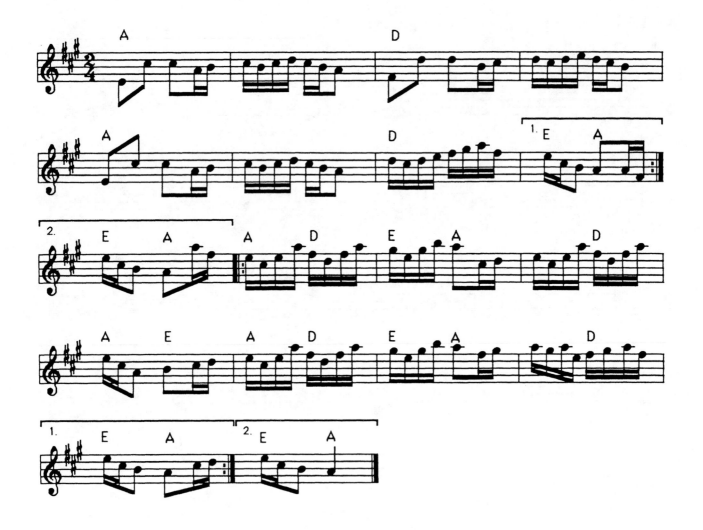

TURKEY IN THE STRAW

Also known as Old Zip Coon.

ARKANSAS TRAVELER

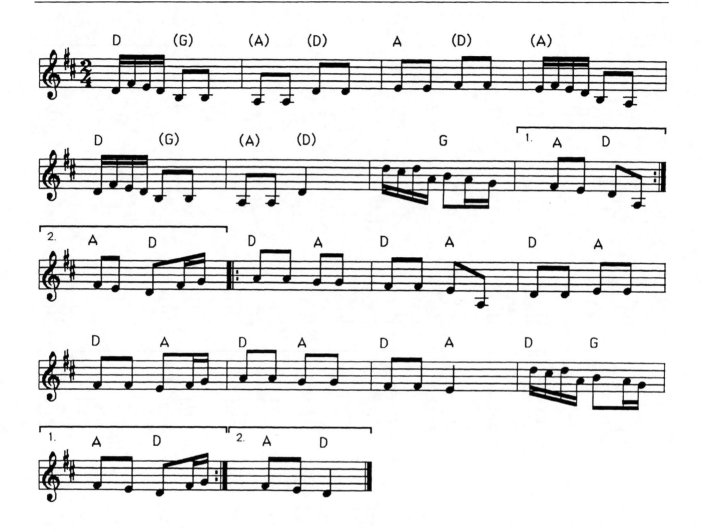

CHINESE BREAKDOWN

SALT CREEK

Also known as Salt River.

MISSISSIPPI SAWYER

RAGTIME ANNIE

Ragtime Annie has three parts instead of the usual two, but the third part is often omitted when the tune is played for dancing. The tune can thus be played AABB or AABBCC.

BILLY IN THE LOWGROUND

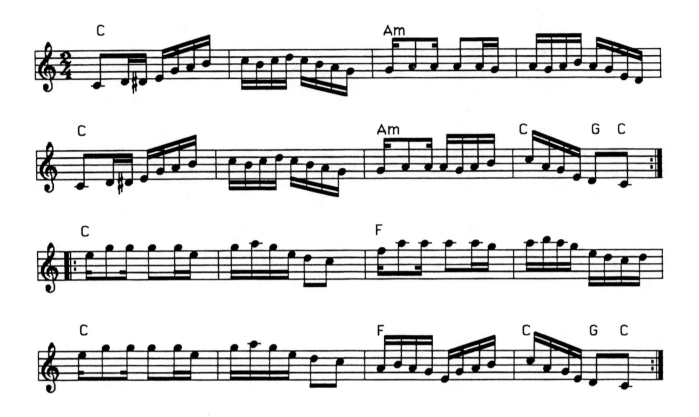

LA BASTRINGUE

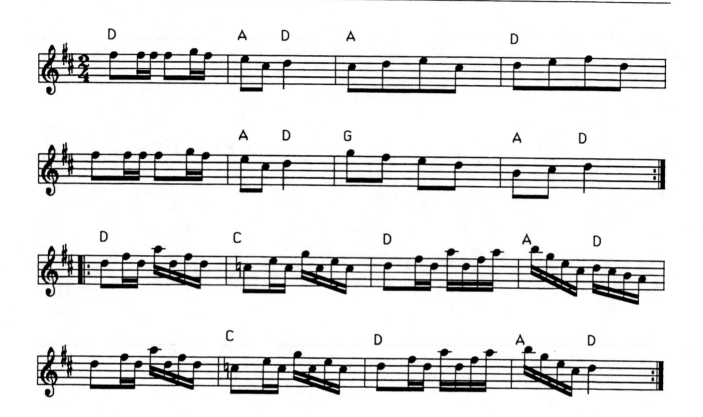

JOYS OF QUEBEC

GASPÉ REEL

Also known as Apex Reel.

SAINT ANNE'S REEL

MOUTH OF THE TOBIQUE

BATCHELDER'S REEL

Also known as Atlanta Hornpipe.

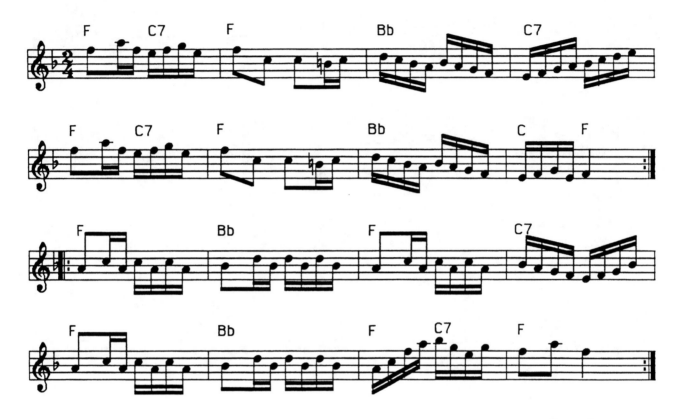

HULL'S VICTORY

BIG JOHN McNEIL

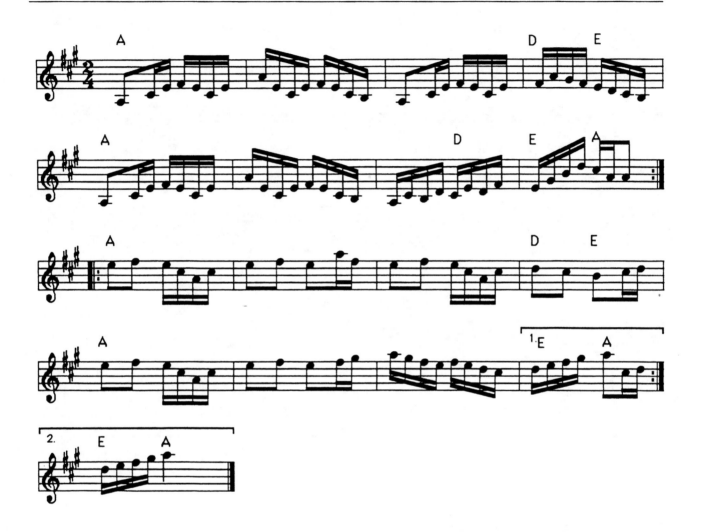

THE GROWLING OLD MAN AND WOMAN

Also known under variants of the name, such as The Growling Old Man and the Grumbling Old Woman or The Old Man and the Old Woman—or in Quebec as La Chicaneuse.

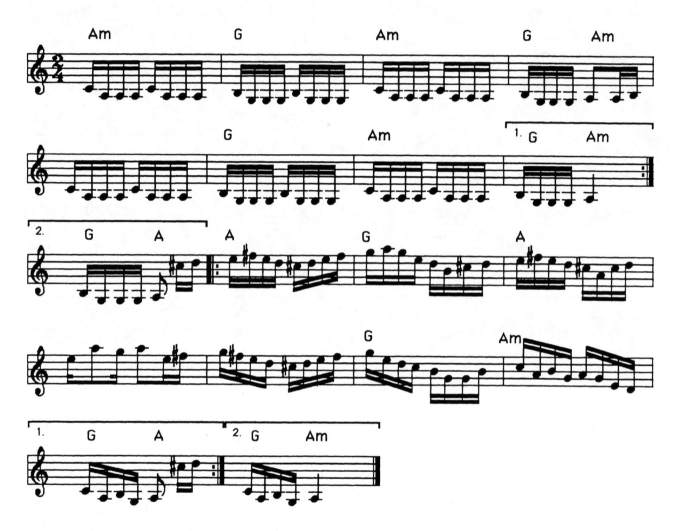

ROSS'S REEL NO. 4

OPERA REEL

Opera Reel is a little unusual, in that it has four parts, instead of the usual two. On the other hand, each part is only half as long as usual, so the result is still a 64-count tune.

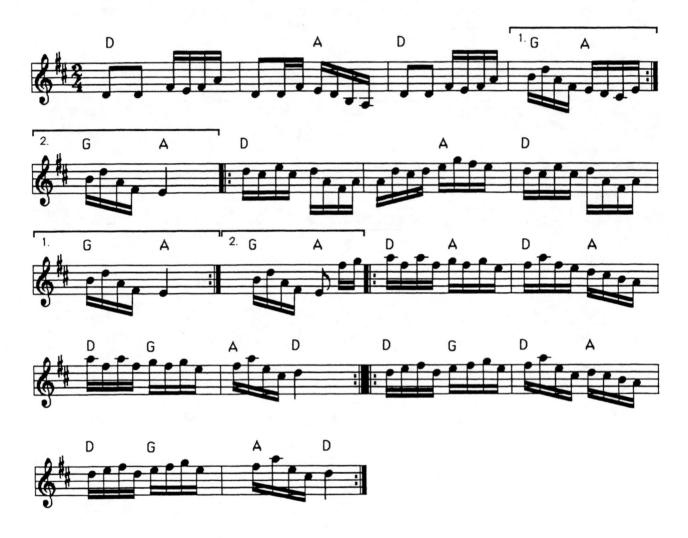

LITTLE BURNT POTATO

ROCK VALLEY

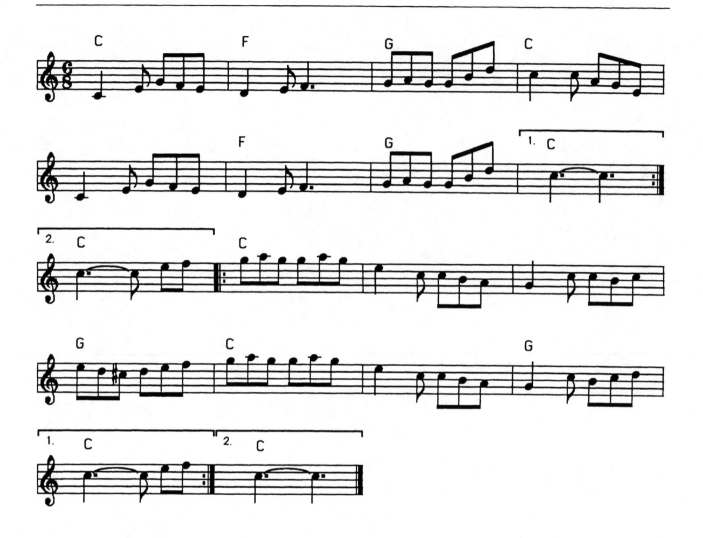

SMASH THE WINDOWS

Also known as Roaring Jelly Jig.

JENNY LIND POLKA

Also known as Heel and Toe Polka and Bonnie Polka.

BUFFALO GALS

Also known as Alabama Gals.

RED RIVER VALLEY

The verse and chorus of this song are sung to the same tune, so the same 32 counts are repeated twice.

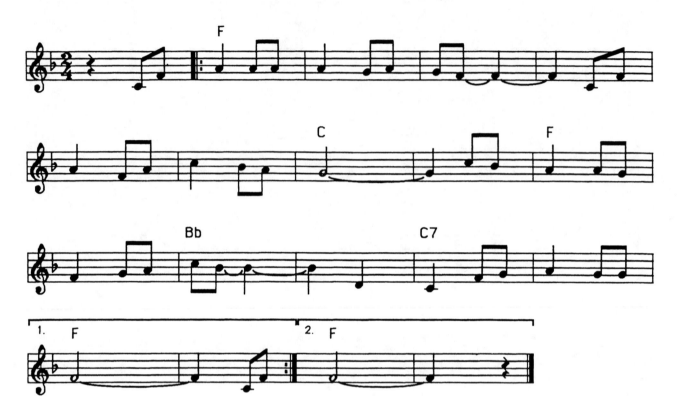

REDWING

GOLDEN SLIPPERS

THE GIRL I LEFT BEHIND ME

Also known as Brighton Camp.

The Old Fiddler

The old fiddler! What has become of him? The dear old-fashioned fiddler of our boyhood, who occupied the one chair in our kitchen, and beat such heavy time to his music on the bare oak floor. Ah! What a whole-soled thing his foot was! No dainty and inaudible pulsation of the toe, but a genuine, flat-footed "stomp," whose boisterous palpitations, heard high above the rhythmic patter of the dancers' feet, jarred and jingled the little eight-by-ten window panes at his back and thrilled every chine on the "cupboard" shelves.

There were no affectations about the old fiddler. His instrument was just a fiddle; he a fiddler, and for this homely reason alone, perhaps, it was the youthful listener felt the vibrant current of the tune in every vein, with such ecstatic spurts of inward mirthfulness at times he felt his very breath sucked up in swirls of intoxication....

And what quaint old tunes he played. "Guilderoy" was the name of one of them; the "Gray Eagle" was another, and "The Forked Deer" and "Old Fat Gal"—all favorites. Telling the names over again in fancy they all come whisking back—and the bottom of the present is knocked out, and peering through a long maelstromic vista:

> "We see the fiddler through the dust,
> Twanging the ghost of Money Musk"

We see the dancers scurrying to their places; we feel once more encased in our "best" clothes—and all mechanically our hand goes up again to stroke the bear-greased roach upon our forehead ere we salute our blushing "pardner" who, for all her shining face and chaste and rustling toilet, has still an odor of dishwater clinging to the mellow hands we love to clasp no less.

We pause impatiently as the fiddler slowly "rosums up" again; we hear the long premonitory rasping of the bow; we see the old man cross his legs with the old time abandon, and with a bewildering flourish of wrist and elbow the frolicsome old tune comes cantering over the strings like a gamesome cold down a road, and then "Salute your pardners! Corners! All hands round!" and away we go, too happy, happy, happy, to recall the half of the long vanished delight from this old, hopeless and bald-headed standpoint of today, and the magician—the maestro—the old fiddler whose deft touches either lulled or fired our blood in those old days. Ah! Where is he?

We wander wearily in quest of him. We do not find him at the banquet, the crowded concert hall, the theatre. They do not want him in the opera. The orchestra would blush to have him there. In all the wide, wide world he had nowhere to lay his head, and so the old musician wandered on, simply because

> "His instrument, perhaps, was made
> Afar from classic Italy.
> And yet we sadly, sadly fear
> Such tunes we nevermore may hear,
> Some were so sad, and some so gay—
> The tunes Dan Harrison used to play."

> —*New Hampshire Sentinel*, Keene, New Hampshire,
> September 27, 1882, quoted in *Northern Junket*,
> November 1967.

Glossary

above In a contra dance, refers to the end of the set nearest the music/caller.

active couple(s) The couple(s) who initiate the action, and to whom the caller's words are directed. In a contra, progressive circle or big set, now often called the "1's."

alamo style A circle of dancers with hands joined, with the dancers facing alternately towards and away from the center.

allemande left Two dancers take a left-hand pigeon wing grip and move once around each other counterclockwise. Some weight should be given, with the point of balance directly between the two dancers. Traditionally 8 or 4 steps. Now sometimes also 6, depending on the choreographic context. May also be called "left hands around" or "turn by the left."

allemande right Like allemande left, but with right hands joined and moving clockwise. May also be called "right hands around" or "turn by the right."

alternate duple See "improper."

arch Two dancers standing across from or next to each other join hands and lift their arms in the air.

balance There are several ways to dance a balance, which traditionally has been one of the movements with the greatest latitude for personal expression.

Two dancers face each other and take hands—they may either take right hands, both hands, or lady's right in gent's left, depending on local custom. Do *not* use the pigeon wing grip, just a normal handhold with elbows bent.

The footwork always conforms to the rhythmic pattern "1-and-2-hold, 3-and-4-hold," with both dancers starting on the right foot, but may be done in several ways.

The easiest to learn (and teach) is probably the *side-to-side balance:* on count "1," step to the right on your right foot. On count "2," swing the left foot in front of the right, bouncing slightly on the

right foot. On count "3," step to the left on your left foot. On count "4," swing the right foot in front of the left, bouncing slightly on the left foot.

The *forward-and-back balance* is, however, more widely used today and is slightly more vigorous. It is usually done with a pas-de-basque type step, as follows: on count "1," step toward each other on the right foot. On "and," transfer weight to the left toe, stepping close to the right foot. On "2," transfer weight back to the right foot, stepping in place. On "3," step away from each other on the left foot. On "and," transfer weight to the right toe, stepping close to the left foot. On "4," transfer weight back to the left foot, stepping in place. This should result in a bouncing motion toward and away from your partner. By extending your arms as you move away from each other, you will gain momentum for the swing, dosido, grand right and left or other movement that follows.

Within the basic patterns described above, some individual variation of style is possible, best learned by observing experienced contra dancers. For instance, the footwork described for a side-to-side balance can also be used in a forward-and-back direction. In practice, many dancers use a combination of the two types of footwork. In any case, make sure that the bouncy quality is retained.

The balance is a way of acknowledging your partner, and partners should therefore have eye contact during it.

balance in line or **balance four in line** Balance can occur when the dancers are in a "wavy line," i.e., four or more dancers facing in alternate directions, with hands joined in a pigeon wing grip. May be done from side to side, acknowledging the neighboring dancers as you do each half of the balance, or forward and back. I prefer a forward-and-back balance when the momentum of the preceding and or following figure flows in that direction.

ballroom position See "social dance position."

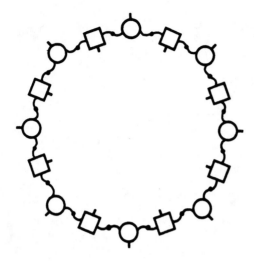

"Alamo style" circle.

Allemande left.

Arch

Balance (forward and back).

Balance (side to side).

below   In a contra dance, refers to the end of the set farthest from the music/caller.

bend the line   From a line of four dancers, all facing the same way, the two middle dancers drop hands and back up slightly, while the two end dancers come slightly forward, so that the ending position is two pairs of facing dancers.

big set   A dance form from Appalachia, done in one big circle of couples. Some of the figures are executed by the circle as a whole, and some by small groups of two couples each.

break In a square, a sequence inserted between repeats of the main figure. Provides an opportunity for improvisation (real or apparent) by the caller.

buzz step A step used for swinging, executed in the rhythm "1-and-2-and. . . ." On the downbeats (1, 2, etc.) step on the right foot, transferring full body weight and bending the knee slightly. On the upbeats ("and"), step on the left toe with the left leg extended, so that the right foot lifts slightly off the floor. The right foot should point forward in relation to the body (not to the left), and the left foot should be placed slightly to the left of or behind the right heel. The effect is to "push" the body around — some have likened the movement to propelling a child's scooter or a playground carousel.

California twirl Two dancers standing next to each other with inside hands joined turn 180 degrees by each walking forward in a small arc and letting the right-hand dancer pass in front of the left-hand dancer, under their lifted arms. The term is taken from modern Western style square dancing, but the movement was in existence before being assigned a standardized name.

call Command given by the leader to direct the dancers through a sequence. The word may be used to refer to a single command or a series of commands.

caller Dance leader who gives the commands in time with the music. A caller is usually also a teacher and often a choreographer of square and contra dances.

cast off (I) A movement used in many contra dances, especially older dances, to effect progression. Cast off typically comes after the 1s have gone down the center and back. When the 1s on their way up the set meet the 2s they were dancing with, the 1s drop hands and each of them takes inside hands with the nearest 2 — or they may place arms around each other's waists. Each pair of dancers then turns 270 degrees to reform long lines along the length of the set. Cast off takes 4 steps to execute. The 1s always go *forward* and the 2s *backwards*. Note that the courtesy turn hold is *not* used.

cast off (II) The expression cast off can also be used to mean that two dancers in a longways or contra formation turn away from each other and go individually down the outside of the set, passing one or more other dancers. In this sense, it is derived from the terminology used in English country dancing.

circle contra See "progressive circle."

circle four or **circle four hands 'round** Four dancers join hands in a ring and move to the left (i.e., clockwise). Similarly, "circle six" and "circle eight" mean that six or eight dancers, respectively, circle left.

circle left The indicated dancers join hands in a ring and move to the left (i.e., clockwise).

circle right The indicated dancers join hands in a ring and move to the right (i.e., counterclockwise).

circle to a line In a square: an indicated active couple joins hands in a ring with an inactive couple and they move to the left. When they are about halfway around, the active gent drops hands with his corner and leads the other dancers to a line at the inactive couple's original position, with the active couple on the left. Eight steps, which may also include the active couple's movement from home position towards the inactives.

In a contra, a similar action may take place, but with indicated dancers dropping hands from a circle to form a line: for example, with the actives in the middle and the inactives on the ends as in Fairfield Fancy.

clogging An American form of percussive step dancing that originated mainly in the Southern mountains. Originally (and still) done as an improvised, solo dance, but now also practiced all over the United States as a semi-standardized group and solo dance form with pre-choreographed sequences.

closer See "ending."

club style square dancing See "modern Western style square dancing."

contra dance A dance done in a double line formation, with each dancer normally standing opposite his or her partner. Also: a dance event featuring contra dances and other traditional style set dances.

corner The dancer standing next to you who is not your partner, i.e., the lady on a gent's left or the gent on a lady's right. Normally only applicable in a square or circle formation.

country dance Originally, a dance from the rural areas, as opposed to certain more formal dances of the aristocracy and bourgeoisie. Historically, however, English country dances became extremely popular among the higher social classes in the 1600s and 1700s and became an important current internationally, influencing both social and folk dance

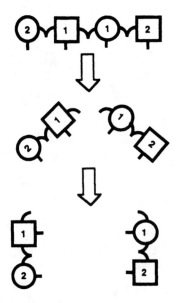

Balance four in line.

Bend the line.

Buzz step.

California twirl.

practices. Just as in the present era, new "country" dances were choreographed and disseminated by dancing masters.

country dancing In the United States and Britain, general term for the whole repertoire of national folk dances done in sets, whether square sets, contras, full set longways, circles, or other formations, but usually not including couple dances. In both the United States and Britain, dances from the other side of the Atlantic may also be found in the repertoire.

country & western dancing A repertoire of couple dances (two-step, waltz, polka, etc.) and solo dances, typically done to country and western music, often in music clubs or dance halls specifically devoted to the form. The solo dances (also sometimes referred to as "line dances") usually con-

sist of pre-choreographed steps done simultaneously by individuals arrayed in lines and columns on the floor. Or several individuals may form a "chorus line" and dance together.

couple mixer See "progressive circle."

courtesy turn A movement done by two dancers. Forms the second half of ladies chain or right and left through. With the lady standing at the gent's right, they join left hands in front (gent's palm *up,* lady's down). The gent puts his right arm around the lady's waist, and she holds her right hand palm-out behind her right hip for him to take. In this position, they turn 180 degrees around an imaginary axis exactly between them, with the lady going *forward* and the gent *backwards* 4 steps.

Cast off (I). The two dancers can put their arms around each other's waists as shown here, or just take inside hands. But don't make it into a courtesy turn.

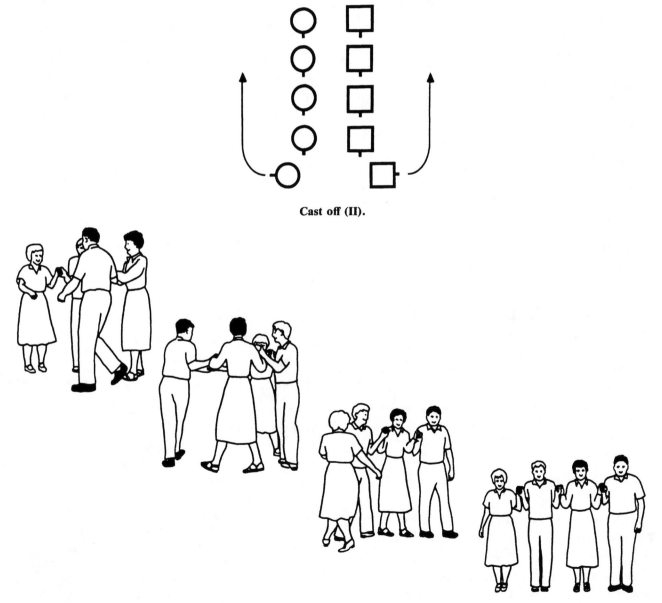

Cast off (II).

Circle to a line.

cross over Two facing dancers may be directed to cross over, meaning that they move past each other, passing right shoulders. The term is also used to refer to the fact that the 1s change places with their partners before starting an "improper" contra dance. Consequently, as each couple reaches the end of the set, they must remember to cross over to opposite places while they wait out. Some contemporary contra dances are choreographed in such a way that this crossover occurs automatically.

dip and dive A movement executed by three or more couples arranged in a column or circle, with at least one couple facing towards the remaining couples. The couples join inside hands with their partners and move toward and past each other, going alternately under and over the arches made by the oncoming couples.

When danced by three couples in a column, the middle couple makes the arch first, and couples turn as a unit (wheel around or California twirl) each time they find themselves facing away from the other two couples.

dosido (I) Two facing dancers go forward, passing each other by the right shoulder, continue sideways past each other back to back, and then backwards to place, passing left shoulders, without turning around. 8 steps.

dosido (II) In traditional dance styles of the South and West, the term "dosido" has been used to designate any of several relatively complicated movements executed by two couples, usually involving, but not limited to, a series of hand turns.

One example is the Kentucky dosido described in this book in the chapter on Southern mountain square dancing (big set). Another example is the movement now called a "do paso" in club style square dancing, which is a standardized form of a dosido from Texas.

double progression In a contra dance, indicates that each couple moves *two* places up or down the set on each round of the dance, instead of the usual one place.

down In a contra dance, the direction away from the music/caller.

down the center In a contra dance, denotes a movement between the contra lines, away from the music/caller.

down the outside In a contra, denotes a movement outside the contra lines, away from the music/caller.

duple minor In a contra dance, indicates that two couples dance together at a time. The expression comes from English country dancing, but is now also widely used in the United States. Older American dance books express the same thing by saying "couples 1, 3, 5, etc. active."

elbow swing or **elbow hook** Two dancers link arms (both right or both left) with elbows bent and go once around each other.

ending In a square, a final sequence of movements after completion of the main figure, often improvised by the caller. Also called "closer" or "final break."

even couples In Southern mountain square dancing, designates the inactive or "number 2" couples.

figure Any distinctive, often used movement; one of the building blocks of square and contra dancing (in this sense, synonymous with "call"). Or: the main sequence of movements (often, but not necessarily, amounting to 64 counts) in a square dance.

flow Flow concerns the body mechanics of the transitions from one figure to another. Good flow is a top priority among contemporary choreographers of traditional style set dances. The object is to maximize danceability, comfort and pleasurable movement by avoiding awkward or difficult transitions.

foot In a contra dance, the end of the set farthest from the music/caller.

forward and back Indicated dancers take hands with the adjacent involved dancers (if any) and move 4 steps forward and then 4 steps backwards to place. If in a circle or square, may also be called as "into the center and back."

four for nothing See "four potatoes."

four in line See "line of four" and "balance in line."

four ladies chain In a square, means that all four ladies do the ladies chain simultaneously. Instead of taking right hands with the opposite lady to start the chain, all four ladies put their right hands in the center, forming a momentary right hand star without actually taking a star grip, and move clockwise 4 steps to the opposite gent, who turns her in a courtesy turn with 4 steps. May also be called "ladies grand chain," especially in older literature. The figure can also be done with more or less than four couples, in which case each lady goes to the second gent she meets, not counting the one she starts with.

Courtesy turn.

Dosido (I).

Dip and dive.

Right elbow swing.

four potatoes Among musicians, the term for a 4-count introduction to be played before the main tune starts. Also called "four for nothing." An 8-count introduction would be "eight potatoes."

full set longways See "longways."

going out Among musicians, a term to indicate that the round they are currently playing will be the last time through the tune.

go out to the right In a square or big set, means that the indicated couple(s) should move to stand opposite the couple on their right. May also be expressed "lead (out to the) right," especially in modern Western style.

grand chain Sometimes used synonymously with "grand right and left," although more in Canada and Britain than the United States. See also "four ladies chain."

grand right and left Done in a square or circle. Partners face and give each other their right hands

as if to shake hands. Pass each other by the right shoulder, drop hands, give your left hand to the next dancer you meet, pass each other by the left shoulder, drop hands and give right hands to the next dancer, etc. Continue in this way until the next call is given. In a square, dancers should be prepared for a new call each time they meet their partners in a grand right and left. Timing: 3 steps per hand.

grand square Grand square is a relatively complicated, 32-count figure. In it, each of the eight dancers in a square describes a smaller square on the floor, corresponding to his or her own quarter of the set. While reading the description below, refer to the step-by-step diagrams for additional clarification. The terms "partner" and "opposite" indicate the *same* people throughout this description, relative to each dancer. Also note that throughout the figure, the dancers never turn their backs to the center of the square.

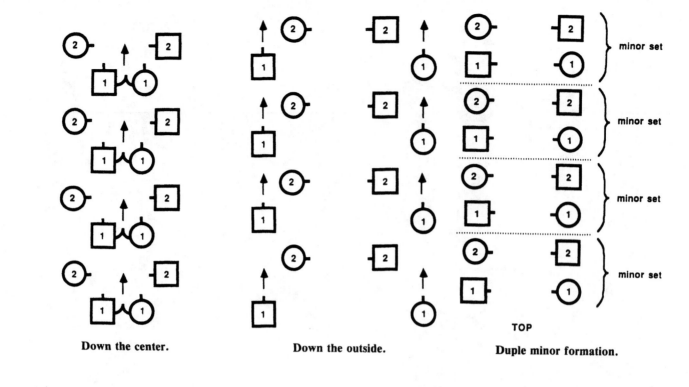

Down the center.   **Down the outside.**   **Duple minor formation.**

Counts 1-4.   **Counts 5-8.**   **Counts 9-12.**   **Counts 13-16.**

Grand square.

Grand right and left.

• The *side dancers* face their partners and back away from them 4 steps while the *head dancers* take inside hands with their partners and go 4 steps forward toward their opposites.

• The *side dancers* turn 90 degrees to face their opposites and go 4 steps forward toward them, while the *head dancers* turn 90 degrees to face their partners, take hands with their opposites, and go 4 steps backwards, away from their partners.

• The *side dancers* turn 90 degrees to face their partners, take hands with their opposites, and go 4 steps forward toward their partners, while the *head dancers* turn 90 degrees to face their opposites and go 4 steps backwards, away from them.

• The *side dancers* turn 90 degrees to face their opposites, take hands with their partners, and go 4 steps backwards, away from their opposites, to place, while the *head dancers* turn 90 degrees to face their partners and go 4 steps forward to meet them at home places.

• All the above is now repeated, but in the opposite direction, i.e., do *not* turn 90 degrees to start, but reverse the previous motion, with sides going toward their opposites and heads away from their partners.

The call for this figure is usually given as "sides face, grand square" to emphasize that the sides start by facing and dancing away from their partners, heads by going toward their opposites. If the caller says "heads face, grand square," the whole figure is done in reverse. The heads start by facing and moving away from their partners, while the sides go forward (in other words, the two halves of the figure as described are transposed).

half ladies chain and **half right and left**   In older terminology, the calls "ladies chain" and "right and left through" meant to do the movement twice, i.e., over and back. If only one time was intended, the call was "half ladies chain" or "half right and left through," respectively. The older terms may be encountered in some books; if in doubt, check how many counts are allowed for the movement (8 for once, 16 for twice).

half promenade   In a contra, indicates that two facing couples promenade to each other's places. As usual in a promenade, stay to the right, i.e., the two gents pass *left* shoulders. Be sure to use the full 8 steps (4 to change places, 4 to turn and face). May also be called in a progressive circle or square. In the latter case, the designated couples promenade *inside* the square.

hand turn   See "allemande left" and "allemande right."

hash   A style of calling squares in which the caller apparently mixes the calls completely at random, mostly encountered in club style square dancing. In fact, various systems exist for the caller to keep track of where the dancers are and get them back to place at the end of the sequence.

head   The end of the set closest to the music/caller. In contras, also called the "top."

head couples or **heads**   In a square, couples 1 and 3, i.e., the couple with their backs to the music and the couple facing the music.

hoedown   A party with square dancing. Or: a southern fiddle tune. Now also sometimes used as a synonym for square dancing or clogging or as a term for square dance music in general. In club style square dancing, a hoedown means any instrumental tune, regardless of type.

home position   In a square, the position in which a couple starts a dance and to which at least one of the dancers in the couple returns after each time through the main figure.

honor   Bow (to another dancer). Typically used at the beginning and end of a square dance.

hornpipe   A dance tune in 4/4 time. In England, hornpipes are played at a slow tempo, reminiscent of a schottische. In the U.S., many tunes called hornpipes are actually played at the same tempo as reels and are generally interchangeable with them, although some hornpipes have a more static feeling than the average reel.

improper   A contra dance in which the active couples change places with their partners before the dance begins. The expression comes from English country dancing, but is now also widely used in the United States. Older American dance books express the same thing by saying "active couples crossed over." Instead of "duple improper" you may also see the term "alternate duple."

inactive couple(s)   The couple(s) that do not initiate the action, but with whom the active couples dance. In contemporary choreography, the "inactive" couples are often just as involved in the figure as the "actives." In a contra, progressive circle, or big set, now often called the "2s."

inside hands   When two dancers are standing next to each other, their inside hands are the left hand for

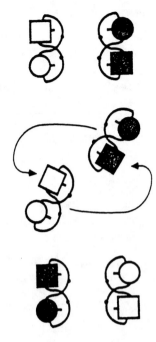

Half promenade.

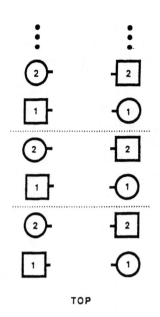

Formation for an improper contra.

the dancer on the right and the right hand for the dancer on the left.

into the center and back See "forward and back."

introduction or **intro** In a square, a sequence called before beginning the main figure of the dance. Often it will be improvised by the caller.

jig A tune in 6/8 time. In contemporary American country dancing, the term "jig" does not designate any particular type of dance, but the word may be encountered as a regional name for step dancing (clogging).

ladies chain A figure danced by two facing couples. The two ladies give right hands (as if shaking hands—do not use a pigeon wing grip), pass by each other with 4 steps and give their left hands to each other's partners (the gent offering his left hand palm up). The gent puts his right arm around the lady's waist, and she holds her right hand palm-out behind her right hip for him to take. In this position, they turn around an imaginary axis exactly between them, with the lady going *forward* and the gent *backwards*, with 4 steps, to end facing the other couple.

Note that, as the lady crosses to the opposite gent, her momentum should be continuously *forward*, but moving toward his left. She should *not* attempt to move into the spot vacated by his partner. Therefore, the gent must come slightly forward

and "pick her up," leading into the courtesy turn as she reaches him.

ladies grand chain See "four ladies chain."

lead (out to the) right See "go out to the right."

left hand gent In a square, the gentleman in the *couple* to the left of a given lady's home position (she is simultaneously his "right hand lady").

left hand star See "star."

left hands around See "allemande left."

line of direction or **line of dance** In a circle or square, the counterclockwise direction. Sometimes abbreviated in dance instructions as "LOD."

line of four A line of four dancers with hands joined, either all facing the same way or facing in alternate directions. In the latter case, it may be called a "wave" or "wavy line."

longways English term for the formation in which the dancers stand in two lines, with each dancer facing his or her partner. A longways dance may be for a specific number of couples (a "full set" longways) or for "as many as will," the latter corresponding to an American duple minor or triple minor contra dance.

minor set In a contra dance, the group of two or three couples that dances the figure together. The expression comes from English country dancing, but is now also widely used in the United States.

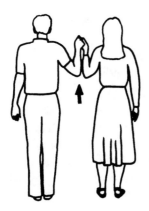

Inside hands.

mixer A dance in which you get a new partner each time the sequence is repeated. Most mixers are done in circle or Sicilian circle formation. (Note that the term is *not* used about a square dance in which the main figure results in a change of partners.)

modern Western style square dance A standardized and modernized form of square dance characterized by the use of a large number of different calls, and in several other ways different from traditional style square and contra dancing or "country dancing." Also called club style square dancing.

neighbor In a duple minor contra dance, the person of the opposite sex in your minor set who is not your partner.

numbering of couples In most American set dances, the couples are numbered to facilitate the description and calling of the dance. In a contra dance, the couples are numbered 1-2, 1-2, 1-2 ... or 1-2-3, 1-2-3 ... starting from the top, depending on whether the dance is a duple minor or triple minor. In a big set, they are numbered 1-2, 1-2, 1-2 ... counterclockwise around the circle. In a square, the couple with their backs to the music/caller is number 1, and the remaining couples are numbered 2, 3 and 4 counterclockwise around the set.

ocean wave See "wave."

odd couples In Southern mountain square dancing, designates the active or "number 1" couples.

ones See "active couple(s)."

opposite The dancer standing directly across from you. (Note that in a contra, where your partner normally stands across from you to begin, it is preferable not to use the term "opposite," but to distinguish between "partner" and "neighbor" in the minor set.)

partner In most formations, the lady on a gent's right or the gent on a lady's left. In a contra or longways dance, however, your partner is the person standing across from you when the dance starts.

pas de basque step See description under "balance."

pass through Two facing lines of two or more dancers go forward and past each other, each dancer passing right shoulders with his or her opposite. 4 steps.

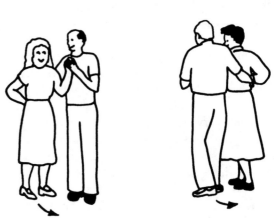

Ladies chain.

patter   Improvised fill words, often in rhyme, that the caller puts in between the dance calls.

patter call   A style of calling in which the caller chants the words in time with the music, often embellishing the dance calls with fill-in rhymes and other "patter." More typical of squares and other dances done to Southern style music than of New England style calling.

phrase   A specified, natural segment of the music. A typical traditional dance tune consists of two 16-count strains or phrases, each repeated twice, and each further subdivisible into phrases of 8 and then 4 counts.

phrasing   The art of adjusting one's calls to the structure of the music, so that the individual dance movements correspond to the natural 4-, 8- or 16-count phrases of the music.

pigeon wing grip   The hold used for hand turns (allemandes) in traditional style square and contra dancing. The two dancers both use the same hand. They place their palms against each other and clasp hands, lightly grasping each other's thumbs. Elbows are bent, and a small amount of tension in the arm muscles should be present so that the dancers can lean slightly away from each other, giving weight.

play party game   A dance, usually simple, executed to the accompaniment of the participants' singing, rather than to instrumental music. In certain areas and time periods, young people would gather for a "play party," at which such singing games would be performed, rather than for a "dance," because dancing and instrumental music were considered evil, while children's play was acceptable.

progression   In a contra, the movement of each couple one place farther up or down the set after each round of the dance. In order to achieve this, the 1s and 2s must at some point in the sequence permanently change places with each other. The expression can also be used about the similar effect that occurs in a progressive circle or big set. Progression also occurs in a full set longways dance, but here it is usually effected by having the top couple go to the bottom of the set at the end of the sequence and everyone else move up one place.

Some examples of movements that can be used to achieve progression in a contra dance are the following (there are also others):

• 1s swing with 2s and face across.
• 1s do an allemande or two-hand turn with 2s, once and a half around.

• 1s go down the center and back and cast off with 2s.
• go down the center four in line with 1s in the middle, turn alone, come back and bend the line.

progressive circle   Dance done in a large circle with couple facing couple like the spokes of a wheel. Each time the dance sequence is repeated, the couples move on to dance with a new opposite couple. May also be called a "circle contra"—since the formation resembles a contra line bent into a double circle—"Sicilian circle" or "couple mixer."

promenade   As couples, the dancers walk counterclockwise around the circle or square. Several different handholds are possible when promenading, depending partly on regional customs (see "promenade position"). If no prior preference exists, I recommend skater's position as being the most neutral.

promenade position   Different customs exist in different regions or local areas with respect to promenading. Some of the possibilities are:

• Skater's position, i.e., hands joined in front of the dancers, right hand in partner's right, left hand in left, with right hands uppermost.
• Hands joined in front with *left* hands uppermost (generally less comfortable for the ladies).
• Varsouvienne position, i.e., left hands joined in front, right hands joined behind lady's right shoulder.
• Courtesy turn position, i.e., left hands joined in front, gent's right arm around lady's waist, holding her right hand at hip (standard in New England).
• Inside arms around each other's waists.
• Gent's right arm around lady's waist, her left hand on his right shoulder.

promenade single file   A line or circle of individual dancers all face in the same direction and move forward, following one another.

prompt call   A style of calling in which only the necessary dance cues are given, just before each movement is danced, without much additional embellishment. Typically used for contras and other dances done to New England style music.

proper   A contra dance in which the active couples do not change places with their partners before the dance begins. The expression comes from English country dancing, but is now also widely used in the United States. Older American dance books express the same thing by saying "active couples not crossed over."

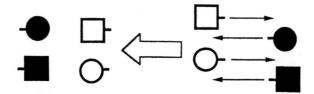

Pass through.

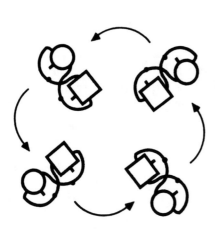

Promenade.

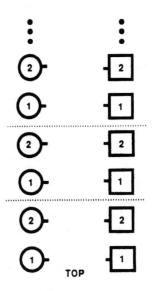

Formation for a proper contra.

quadrille A formal type of dance, done in a square set, that was popular in the 1800s. The term is sometimes used (especially by modern Western square dancers!) to denote the New England style of contemporary square dances, with their highly phrased structure.

reel A tune in 2/4 time. In contemporary American country dancing, the term "reel" does not designate any particular type of dance.

reverse line of direction or **reverse line of dance** In a circle or square, the clockwise direction. Sometimes abbreviated in dance descriptions as "RLOD."

right and left four Traditional term for a right and left through (over and back).

right and left through A figure danced by two facing couples. May be said to consist of pass through followed by a courtesy turn. Opposites pass by each other with four steps, passing right shoulders. Then each couple takes courtesy turn position and uses four steps to turn 180 degrees around an imaginary axis between the two dancers, with the lady going *forward* and the gent *backwards,* to end facing the

other couple again. In a proper contra dance, right and left through may be done by two gents facing two ladies, rather than by mixed couples. Instead of taking courtesy turn position for the turn, the dancers put their arms around each other's waists or just take inside hands. The dancer on the right moves *forward* and the one on the left moves *backwards.* 8 steps.

right hand lady In a square, the lady in the *couple* to the right of a given gent's position (he is simultaneously her "left hand gent").

right hand star See "star."

right hands around See "allemande right."

running set A traditional dance form from Appalachia that in some ways resembles the big set, but in others a square set of four couples. The term is sometimes also used to refer to the big set.

sashay A sideways movement. Or: a syncopated, sideways "gallop" step (slide step) corresponding to the first and third notes of a musical triplet. Dancing to the right, step sideways to the right on your right foot on the first note of the triplet, then close the left foot to the right, momentarily transferring weight, on the third note. Dancing to the left, use the reverse footwork.

seesaw Like dosido (I), but the dancers start by passing *left* shoulders first.

separate Instructs two designated dancers to move away from each other.

set A dance formation consisting of several couples, such as a square set, contra lines, Sicilian circle, big set, or other formation.

sets in order See "square the set."

Sicilian circle formation Couple facing couple, arrayed in a large circle like the spokes of a wheel, so one couple in each group is facing clockwise (the "2s") and the other counterclockwise (the "1s").

side couples or **sides** In a square, couples 2 and 4, i.e., the couples standing with their sides toward the music.

singing call A style of calling, especially for squares, in which the caller sings the dance cues to the tune of a popular song, accomodating the wording to the melody and rhythm of the tune.

single file See "promenade single file."

skater's position A handhold in which two dancers standing side by side join hands in front—right hand in right and left hand in left—with right hands uppermost.

social dance position Also called "ballroom position." Position used for swinging. The two dancers, normally a gent and a lady, face each other. The gent puts his right arm around the lady's waist, with his right hand supporting her back, and takes her right hand in his left. She places her left hand loosely on his right shoulder. The lady should *not* grip the gent's right overarm or squeeze his arm with her left elbow and lower arm.

When swinging, each dancer shifts slightly to his or her own left, so that the outsides of their right feet are adjacent (but not touching), and the two lean slightly away from each other, giving weight.

split that couple An indicated couple moves forward and goes between the members of another couple.

square dance A dance done by a group of four couples forming the sides of a square, with everyone facing the center. Also: a dance event featuring square dances and other traditional style set dances and or couple dancing.

square the set An expression that requests dancers in a square formation to return to places and be ready to dance. May be used preparatory to starting the dance or as a means of "regrouping" during the dance sequence if irreparable error occurs. A synonymous expression is "sets in order."

star A circle of dancers put their right hands into the center and move clockwise ("right hand star") or put their left hands into the center and move counterclockwise ("left hand star"). Typically executed by four dancers at a time, but may also be done by other numbers.

Several handholds can be used. In the Northeast, a "pack saddle grip" is used, in which each dancer lays his or her hand over the wrist of the dancer in front, loosely gripping it. This is recommended for contras and squares in New England style.

In the South, the "hands across" grip is preferred, in which each pair of two dancers diagonally across from each other take hands, gripping each other's fingers. Elbows should be bent and the dancers should lean slightly away from each other, giving a little weight (comparable to an allemande). The hands across star, which, incidentally, also is standard in English country dancing, may be preferable for certain Northern style American dances. If so, it will usually be noted in the dance description (see, for example, Friday Night Special).

swing Two dancers, normally a gent and a lady, face each other and take social dance position, i.e., the gent puts his right arm around the lady's waist, with his right hand supporting her back, and takes her right hand in his left. She places her left hand loosely on his right shoulder. The lady should *not* grip the gent's right overarm or squeeze his arm with her left elbow and lower arm.

Each dancer shifts slightly to his or her own left, so that the outsides of their right feet are adjacent (but not touching), and the two lean slightly away from each other, giving weight. They then move rapidly around each other using a buzz step (see description there) or walking step, both starting on the right foot. The central point of the swing should be exactly between the two dancers, the object being to find the point of balance between them.

Remember that the lady must finish the swing on the gent's right. She should be able to "roll out" to his right, still supported by his right arm and her left hand on his shoulder, as they finish swinging.

See also "two-hand swing."

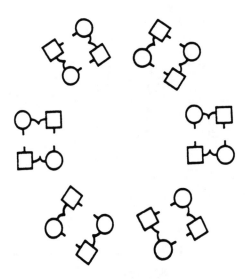

Promenade single file.

Sicilian circle formation.

Skater's position.

talk-through Short verbal run-through of a dance before starting, to remind the dancers of the figures.

timing The art of adjusting dance movements and calls to the musical structure, so that the dancers are given the proper amount of time to execute each movement in time with the music.

tip Section of a dance program, after which a short intermission is taken. Traditionally one to three dances, depending on regional and local custom. In modern Western style square dancing, a tip has been standardized at two dances—usually a hash call followed by a singing call. In contemporary contra dancing, the concept has largely fallen by the wayside, with only one or two longer intermissions included in the evening's program.

top In a contra dance, the end of the set closest to the music/caller.

triple minor In a contra dance, indicates that three couples dance together at a time. The expression comes from English country dancing, but is now also widely used in the U.S. Older American dance books express the same thing by saying "couples 1, 4, 7, etc. active."

turn alone Typically directed to two dancers moving forward as a couple. They drop hands and the two dancers turn individually towards each other 180 degrees to face in the opposite direction.

turn as a couple Two dancers standing next to each other with inside hands joined turn 180 degrees to face in the opposite direction. The dancer on the right moves *forward,* the one on the left *backwards,* with the pivot point of the turn exactly between them. May also be called "wheel around" or "wheel as a couple." Some dancers, when directed to turn as a couple, will do a California twirl. This is

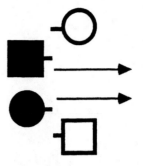

Split that couple.

Social dance position.

acceptable in most circumstances, and may even be desirable if it allows the dancers to continue their forward momentum.

turn by the left   See "allemande left."

turn by the right   See "allemande right."

turn single   An expression from English country dancing that means a 360-degree turn of an individual dancer in place with 4 steps. Should *not* be used synonymously with "turn alone."

two-hand swing or **two-hand turn**   Two dancers give each other both hands (gent palms up, lady palms down if it is a mixed couple; elbows bent) and move clockwise around each other. The dancers should lean slightly away from each other, giving some weight, and the point of turning should be exactly between the two dancers.

twos   See "inactive couple(s)."

up   In a contra dance, the direction towards the music/caller.

Varsouvienne position   With the lady standing to the right of the gent, they join their left hands in

Right and left through.

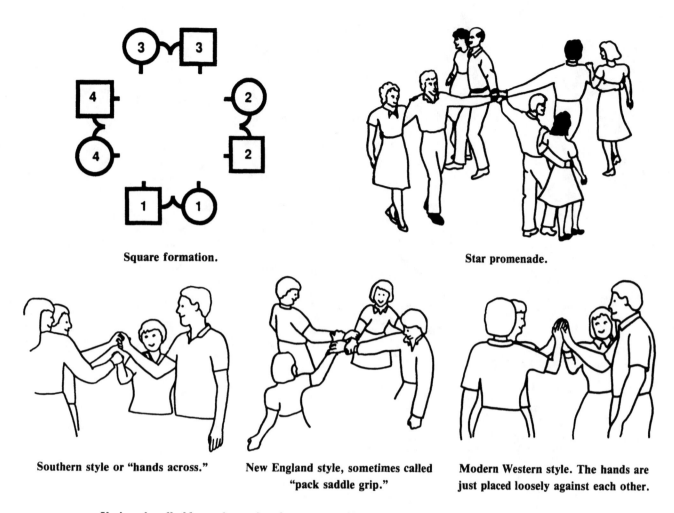

Square formation.

Star promenade.

Southern style or "hands across."

New England style, sometimes called "pack saddle grip."

Modern Western style. The hands are just placed loosely against each other.

Various handholds can be used to form a star. Above are three variants of a right hand star.

Swing, using ballroom position and buzz step.

front and their right hands just behind and above the lady's right shoulder.

visiting couple figure or **visiting couple dance**   A square dance in which the main figure causes the active couple to dance with each of the other three couples in turn, usually doing the same figure with each.

walk-through   A run-through of the figures of a dance without music, preparatory to dancing it, used to teach or review the dance.

wave   A line of dancers with hands joined, facing in alternate directions. Also called an "ocean wave" (in modern Western style square dancing) or "wavy line."

Two-hand swing.

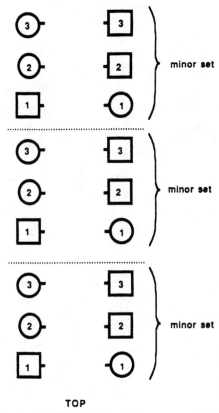

Triple minor formation.

Varsouvienne position.

wavy line   See "wave."

weave the ring   Like a grand right and left, but without giving hands.

wheel around or **wheel as a couple**   See "turn as a couple."

Wave.

Directory

ORGANIZATIONS AND INSTITUTIONS

Berea College Recreation Extension

Box 287, Berea, Kentucky 40404. Tel: (606) 986-9341

Berea College was founded in the mid–1800s to provide educational opportunities for young people from Appalachia. At the same time, the college has attempted to preserve and support Appalachian culture, including music, dance and crafts. The Recreation Extension coordinates activities within music and dance, including the well known performing group, the Berea College Country Dancers, and Christmas Country Dance School, which has been held during Christmas week for over fifty years. The Recreation Extension has published a few books and records dealing with Southern mountain dance and music styles, and organizes several annual events.

Country Dance and Song Society

17 New South Street, Northampton, Massachusetts 01060. Tel: (413) 584-9913

Founded in 1915, CDSS is the national focal point for the promotion and preservation of American and English country dancing and the music that goes along with them. It also has an interest in related dance forms (clogging and step dancing, English ceremonial dance forms, historical dances from 1600 to 1900), and in American and English folk song.

At the present time, CDSS has about 2500 individual members and over one hundred affiliated groups, located all over the United States, with a few in Canada and Europe. Most groups sponsor regular dances and occasional special events. Pinewoods Camp in Massachusetts is run by CDSS,

with week-long dance and music courses throughout the summer, and Buffalo Gap Camp in West Virginia, where several summer courses also are offered.

The organization has published several important books and recordings, and maintains a sales department with a large selection of materials on traditional music and dance. Members receive a 10 percent discount on purchases. Other benefits of membership include a bimonthly newsletter with a calendar of events and much other useful information and debate, and an annual journal containing more extensive articles on topics of interest. A directory of members and directory of associated groups, including information on the events they sponsor, is updated annually. The group directory also includes listings of known dance groups that are not yet affiliated with CDSS. The CDSS extensive library of dance and music materials was recently moved to the Ralph Page Collection at the University of New Hampshire (see below).

The John C. Campbell Folk School

Brasstown, North Carolina 28902. Tel: (704) 837-2775

This institution was founded as an educational resource for Appalachia, based on the Scandinavian "folk high schools" established in the 1800s to provide education and citizenship training for rural youth. Today, the school offers many short courses open to the general public, including an active program of dance workshops covering the full spectrum of contemporary country dance.

The Library of Congress

101 Independence Avenue SE, Washington, D.C. 20540

The Library of Congress by definition contains copies of all books published in the United States. Its dance collection is of particular interest to those searching for titles that are rare or out of print.

The Lloyd Shaw Foundation

Membership information: Ruth Ann Knapp, 2124 Passolt, Saginaw, Michigan 48603

Sales Division: P.O. Box 11, Mack's Creek, Missouri 65786. Tel: (314) 363-5432

Archives: c/o Dr. William Litchman, 1620 Los Alamos SW, Albuquerque, New Mexico 87104

The Lloyd Shaw Foundation attempts to preserve a number of indigenous American dance forms, taking as its point of departure the work of Lloyd Shaw of Colorado, an influential dance leader who was particularly active in the 1940s and 50s. The Foundation produces dance materials, including kits for school use that contain both American and international folk dances. It arranges several annual dance courses and publishes a small quarterly magazine for members. Stylistically, the LSF straddles the borderline between traditional country dancing and club style square and round dancing. Recently, the archives of the Lloyd Shaw Foundation was designated by the Library of Congress as the national repository of square and folk

dance materials. The collection is extensive and the archivist helpful to those seeking information.

The New York Public Library

Fifth Avenue and 42nd Street, New York, New York 10018

The New York Public Library, which is second only to the Library of Congress in scope, includes a large collection of dance books, including many works of historical interest as well as contemporary titles.

The Ralph Page Collection

c/o Special Collections Room, Dimond Library, University of New Hampshire, Durham, New Hampshire 03824

Based on the personal library of Ralph Page, who for many years was the leading proponent of New England square and contra dancing, this collection was placed in the custody of the University of New Hampshire after his death. With the recent addition of the library of the Country Dance and Song Society, as well as expected continuing acquisitions, this is a major resource and the most important repository of country dance materials on the East Coast.

VENDORS OF BOOKS AND RECORDINGS

Alcazar Productions, Inc.

Box 429, Waterbury, Vermont 05676. Tel: (802) 244-8657

Suppliers of recordings of folk and related music, including some dance music, as well as some books. Catalogue available.

Andy's Front Hall

P.O. Box 307, Wormer Road, Voorheesville, New York 12186. Tel: (518) 765-4193

Major folk music suppliers with a large selection of books, recordings, instruments, etc., including dance materials. Catalogue available.

Berea College Recreation Extension

Box 287, Berea, Kentucky 40404. Tel: (606) 986-9341

Stock materials related to Southern mountain style dancing as well as other books and recordings.

Country Dance and Song Society

17 New South Street, Northampton, Massachusetts 01060. Tel: (413) 584-9913

Major source for dance books, recordings and related materials. Catalogue available.

County Sales

P.O. Box 191, Floyd, Virginia 24091. Tel: (703) 745-2001

Well known source for recordings of bluegrass and oldtime music (mainly for listening purposes). Publish bimonthly newsletter with helpful reviews.

Educational Activites, Inc.

P.O. Box 392, Freeport, New York 11520

Especially for Glenn Bannerman's records with Southern mountain style dance instruction.

Elderly Instruments

1100 N. Washington, P.O. Box 14210, Lansing, Michigan 48901. Tel: (517) 372-7890

Major folk music suppliers with large selection of books, recordings, instruments and accessories, etc., including some dance materials. Catalogues available.

Folkraft Records and Tapes

P.O. Box 404, Florham Park, New Jersey 07932. Tel: (201) 377-1885

Suppliers of international folk dance records, including some good, mostly older, recordings for square and contra dancing. Catalogue available.

Hands Four Book and Record Service

13 Springs Road, Billerica, Massachusetts 01821-6502. Tel: (508) 667-7459

Suppliers of recordings and books specifically for square and contra dancing. Catalogue available.

Legacy Books

Box 494, Hatboro, Pennsylvania 19040-0494. Tel: (215) 675-6762

Publish "Come-All-Ye," a quarterly newsletter containing capsule reviews of books in the fields of folklore and folklife, social history and popular culture, including quite a few music and dance titles. Also function as a supply house for the books reviewed.

The Lloyd Shaw Foundation (Sales Division)

P.O. Box 11, Mack's Creek, Missouri 65786. Tel: (314) 363-5868

Recordings, often produced on license, for square and contra dancing. Catalogue available.

Marimac Recordings, Inc.

P.O. Box 447, Crown Point, Indiana 46307. Tel: (219) 662-7305

Producers and suppliers of recordings of oldtime music, mostly for listening. Catalogue available.

The Music Barn

P.O. Box 309, Mount Albert, Ontario L0G 1M0, Canada

Large selection of recordings of traditional Canadian music, as well as bluegrass, country & western, etc. Catalogue available.

Roundup Records

P.O. Box 154, North Cambridge, Massachusetts 02140. Tel: (717) 661-6308

Large selection of recordings in folk and bluegrass music, jazz and related genres (mainly for listening). Publish useful annotated catalogue at regular intervals and annual master catalogue.

Voyager Recordings and Publications

424 35th Avenue, Seattle, Washington 98122. Tel: (206) 323-1112

Source for recordings, including several of their own good releases, with folk and related music, mainly for listening, but some for dancing.

VENDORS OF AUDIO EQUIPMENT

Hilton Audio Products

1033-E Shary Circle, Concord, California 94518.
Tel: (510) 682-8390

Produce sound equipment specifically for
square dancing and have great expertise in the field.
Catalogue available.

Supreme Audio

P.O. Box 50, Marlborough, New Hampshire
03455-0050. Tel: (800) 445-7398 or (603) 876-3636

Specialize in sound equipment, records, etc. for
dance teachers. Large selection and helpful staff.
Catalogue available.

Worldtone Music, Inc.

230 Seventh Avenue, New York, New York 10011.
Tel: (212) 691-1934

Suppliers of sound equipment, records and
other items for folk and square dancing. Catalogue
available.

DANCE CAMPS

Most of the camps listed here are week-long, live-in gatherings where participants are offered a variety of
workshops in traditional American (and sometimes other, related) dance forms. Some of the weeks also include
workshops for musicians or callers and or workshops in singing, crafts or other aspects of folk culture. Some
are especially for families or include special children's programs. For more information, write to the addresses
listed.

California

Lark in the Morning (late July or early August):
P.O. Box 1176, Mendocino, California 95460.

Mendocino Country Dance Camp (July) and **Camp
Gualala Family Week** (July): Bay Area Country
Dance Society, P.O. Box 22165, San Francisco,
California 94122.

Colorado

Rocky Mountain Dance Roundup, La Foret, CO
(July) and **Leadership Training Institute**, Canon
City, CO (late June or early July): Lloyd Shaw
Foundation, c/o Diane Ortner, 419 NW 40th Street,
Kansas City, Missouri 64116.

Georgia

Blue Ridge Mountain Dance Roundup, Dillard, GA
(August): Lloyd Shaw Foundation, c/o Diane Ortner, 419 NW 40th Street, Kansas City, Missouri 64116.

Idaho

Lady of the Lake Summer Dance and Music Week
(June) and **Lady of the Lake Family Week**
(August), Coeur d'Alene, ID: Spokane Folklore
Society, P.O. Box 141, Spokane, Washington 99219.
Tel: (509) 747-2640.

Kentucky

Christmas Country Dance School (December):
Berea College, C.P.O. 287, Berea, Kentucky 40404.
Tel: (609) 986-9341, ext. 5143.

Kentucky Summer Dance School (June), **Leaders Lab** (July) and **Winter in the Woods** (December): Kentucky Heritage Institute for the Traditional Arts, P.O. Box 4128, Frankfort, Kentucky 40603. Tel: (502) 695-5218 or (502) 227-4466.

Massachusetts

CDSS weeks at Pinewoods, Plymouth, MA (throughout July and August): Country Dance and Song Society, 17 New South Street, Northampton, Massachusetts 01060. Tel: (413) 584-9913.

New Hampshire

Ralph Page Legacy Weekend, Durham, NH (January): Ralph Page Legacy Weekend Committee, New England Folk Festival Association, 1950 Massachusetts Avenue, Cambridge, Massachusetts 02140.

New York

Fiddle and Dance Workshops at Ashokan (July and August): R.D. 1, Box 489, West Hurley, New York 12491. Tel: (914) 338-2996.

North Carolina

John C. Campbell Folk School (various times throughout the year): John C. Campbell Folk School, Brasstown, North Carolina 28902. Tel: (704) 837-2775.

Fiddlehead Music and Dance Week (June): Trina Royar, Box 1978, Asheville, North Carolina 28802. Tel: (704) 683-1184.

Ontario

The Woods Music and Dance Camp (August): 20 Windley Avenue, Toronto, Ontario M6C 1N2, Canada.

Washington

Festival of American Fiddle Tunes (July) and **International Folk Dance and Music Festival** (August): Centrum, P.O. Box 1158, Port Townsend, Washington 98368. Tel: (206) 385-3102.

West Virginia

Augusta Heritage Arts Workshops (July and August): Davis & Elkins College, 100 Sycamore Street, Elkins, West Virginia 26241-3996. Tel: (304) 636-1903

CDSS weeks at Buffalo Gap, Capon Bridge, WV (July): Country Dance and Song Society, 17 New South Street, Northampton, Massachusetts 01060. Tel: (413) 584-9913

Materials for Musicians

If you are not sure where to start in terms of instructional materials, I would highly recommend contacting the mail order houses listed below. All three publish annotated catalogues with an up-to-date listing of the available books and tapes. The sales people, many of whom are musicians themselves, will be willing and able to advise you as to what materials best suit your needs. The first two companies also deal in folk music instruments and can give you purchasing advice:

Andy's Front Hall, P.O. Box 307, Wormer Road, Voorheesville, New York 12186. Telephone for inquiries and clerk-assisted orders: (518) 765-4193.

The Country Dance and Song Society, 17 New South Street, Northampton, Massachusetts 01060. Telephone for inquiries and clerk-assisted orders: (413) 584-9913.

Elderly Instruments, 1100 N. Washington, P.O. Box 14210, Lansing, Michigan 48901. Telephone for inquiries and clerk-assisted orders: (517) 372-7890.

Once you've learned the fundamentals on your instrument, the best way to learn how to play for dancing is by finding people who already know how to do it and learning from them. By listening to and imitating good musicians, you will not only learn basic technique, but also style and ornamentation. And they can tell you about dance and music customs in your local area. Most musicians are more than willing to help others get started, and some even give lessons on a professional basis, so don't be bashful about approaching them. An interesting note is that, although the New England style dance scene today is the fastest growing, with many new bands appearing all over the country, few instructional books exist for learning that style. This makes it even more imperative to seek out existing musicians. If you don't know where to find other musicians, try looking for them at a local contra dance or traditional style square dance. Or the Country Dance and Song Society may be able to give you some leads. You can also consider attending a dance and music camp for a week's intensive input (see the Directory).

FIDDLE

Fiddle styles vary a good deal from region to region, although there are certain basic techniques that characterize folk fiddling as opposed to classical violin. Here are several books that may be useful, including ones on northern style and on southern style.

Appalachian Fiddle

Miles Krassen (New York: Oak Publications, 1973)

Transcriptions of 58 tunes as played by traditional oldtime fiddlers. Tunes only; no chords or ac-

companiment. Introductory sections on playing technique, etc. Discography. Many of the tunes can be used for dancing. 88 pp.

Belknap's March and Other Dance Melodies

Bill Wellington (Upper Tract, West Virginia: Bill Wellington, 1983)

Notes for 13 original tunes in New England style, including not only chords but also piano accompaniment. The tunes are good, and this is the only book I have run across that includes piano music. 16 pp. A corresponding cassette tape is also available.

The Fiddle Book

Marion Thede (New York: Oak Publications, 1967)

Notes for over 150 tunes as played by traditional oldtime fiddlers. Includes extensive musical and historical commentary by the author, a "converted" classical violinist. A number of the tunes are played in non-standard tunings, and for these, Thede has written out both the notes for the tune as it should sound and notes that you can play from as if the fiddle were tuned normally. Many of the tunes can be used for dancing. 160 pp.

The Grumbling Old Woman

Donna Hinds (Amherst, Massachusetts: Chanterelle, 1981, reissued 1994)

Notes and chords for 66 dance tunes from the New England/French-Canadian repertory, some well known, others less so. For each tune, the author's source is given; often the reference is to a recording. Introductory chapter with good advice about playing technique, assuming that basic violin technique has already been mastered. Bowing is marked, which is a great help not always found in fiddle books. 40 pp.

A corresponding cassette tape is also available,

on which 28 of the tunes are demonstrated. Most are played slowly at first, and then up to tempo with typical New England piano accompaniment.

Old-Time Fiddling Across America

David Reiner and Peter Anick (Pacific, Missouri: Mel Bay Publications, Inc., 1989)

Probably the most comprehensive book currently available, this volume contains music for 66 tunes, divided into four categories covering a total of 15 regional American styles and 5 foreign ethnic styles also found in the United States. Lots of help on the all-important subject of bowing technique, as well as extensive background information on the various styles, playing techniques, individual tunes and the often well known fiddlers whose performances are transcribed. 182 pp.

A corresponding cassette tape is also available, on which all 66 tunes are demonstrated with suitable but unobtrusive backup.

Teach Yourself Bluegrass Fiddle

Matt Glaser (New York: Amsco Music Publishing Co., 1978)

Bluegrass fiddle book on a beginning level, with explanatory chapters, discography and 28 tunes. The tunes are presented both as basic melodies and fiddle versions, and there are also chords. About half the tunes can be used for dancing. 60 pp.

BANJO

The five-string banjo is mainly associated with southern dance music. There are two main playing styles: in the oldtime "frailing" or "clawhammer" style, the right hand moves as a unit, striking one or more strings on the downstroke with the nail of the first or second finger and plucking a string on the upstroke with the thumb. Bluegrass playing uses the thumb and first two fingers individually to pluck out a continuous stream of notes, and tends to be flashier and technically more demanding than frailing. A relatively modern development is "melodic" style playing, which is particularly useful for render-

ing fiddle tunes. The idea is to hit as many notes as possible of the actual melody, keeping fill-in notes to a minimum. Melodic playing can be worked out both with frailing and with bluegrass technique.

Banjo Songbook

Tony Trischka (New York: Oak Publications, 1977)

About 75 tunes, including chords, of which about half can be used for dancing. Includes tunes from both the Northern and Southern repertoires, as well as a few experimental pieces and classical pieces arranged for banjo. Chapters on technique, music theory, etc., as well as discography, short bibliography, and profiles of several well known bluegrass banjo players that include a good deal of information about their music. 144 pp.

Bluegrass Banjo

Peter Wernick (New York: Oak Publications, 1974)

Well thought out beginner's book on bluegrass banjo with about 40 tunes, of which about 10 are suitable for dancing. Includes chords. Introductory chapters on playing technique, how to care for your instrument, etc. Bibliography and discography. Also includes a "soundsheet" (flexible phonograph record) with examples. 143 pp.

Clawhammer Style Banjo: A Complete Guide for Beginning and Advanced Banjo Players

Ken Perlman (Englewood Cliffs, New Jersey: Prentice-Hall, 1983)

Comprehensive and well organized book with almost 80 fiddle tunes and other melodies from both the Northern and Southern traditions, including chords. Thorough explanations of playing technique. Bibliography and discography. 194 pp.

John Burke's Book of Old Time Fiddle Tunes for Banjo

John Burke (New York: Amsco Music Publishing Co., 1968)

About 70 tunes in "melodic clawhammer" style, some in more than one variant, intended for players who already know the basic techniques of clawhammer or frailing style banjo. Sources for each tune are given, as well as playing tips and, if applicable, song texts. Introductory chapter with general advice. Discography. Many of the tunes can be used for dancing. Also includes a "soundsheet" (flexible phonograph record) with examples. 96 pp.

Melodic Banjo

Tony Trischka (New York: Oak Publications, 1976)

About 30 tunes in "melodic" style, of which about 15–20 can be used for dancing. Also includes a chapter on standard, non-melodic banjo technique. Interviews and background information with several bluegrass musicians who helped develop the melodic style of playing. Good explanations of the various playing techniques and tunes, as well as chapters on music theory and on the banjo as an instrument. Short discography. Also includes a "soundsheet" (flexible phonograph record) with examples. 127 pp.

Teach Yourself Bluegrass Banjo

Tony Trischka (New York: Amsco Music Publishing Co., 1978)

Good beginner's book on bluegrass banjo, with 25 tunes, about half of which can be used for dancing. Both the basic melody and the banjo version are given. Also includes explanatory chapters, discography and short bibliography. 64 pp.

GUITAR

Fingerpicking the guitar is not really suited to the needs of dance music, so the books listed here deal with flatpicking. The most important thing for a guitarist to master is solid rhythm playing, using an alternating bass and appropriate bass runs. Flatpicking can also be used to play the melody, particularly in bluegrass bands where it is customary for the musicians to take turns playing the tune and backing each other up.

Flat-Pick Country Guitar

Happy Traum (New York: Oak Publications, 1973)

Good beginner's book on flatpicking, with about 40 tunes taken from both the oldtime and bluegrass repertoires. About a third of the tunes can be used for dancing. Includes chords and, where applicable, song texts. Short explanatory chapters. 111 pp.

Teach Yourself Bluegrass Guitar

Russ Barenberg (New York: Amsco Music Publishing Co., 1978)

Good beginner's book on flatpicking, with emphasis on bluegrass style. 23 tunes of increasing difficulty, of which about a third can be used for dancing. Both the basic melody and guitar version are given for each tune. Explanatory chapters and short discography. 64 pp.

MANDOLIN

The mandolin is a standard instrument in bluegrass, playing a characteristic "chop" on the offbeat and taking a turn at melody breaks. The mandolin and related instruments are now often heard in Northern style bands as well, probably due to a considerable influence from musicians who also play Celtic styles.

Bluegrass Mandolin

Jack Tottle (New York: Oak Publications, 1975)

Good beginner's book on bluegrass mandolin with about 40 tunes, of which about a third can be used for dancing. Chords included. Explanatory chapters, profiles of well known bluegrass mandolinists, and various other useful information. Also includes a "soundsheet" (flexible phonograph record) with examples. 160 pp.

Deluxe Bluegrass Mandolin Method

Ray Valla (Kirkwood, Missouri: Mel Bay Publications, 1974)

Relatively elementary beginner's book on bluegrass mandolin, with 30 tunes, including chords. Most of the tunes are fiddle tunes that can be used for dancing. Also includes chapters on theory, scale exercises, etc. A corresponding album, on which the tunes are demonstrated slowly, is also available.

Teach Yourself Bluegrass Mandolin

Andy Statman (New York: Amsco Music Publishing Co., 1978)

Beginner's book on bluegrass mandolin with 25 tunes, of which about half can be used for dancing. Both the basic melody and mandolin version, as well as the chords, are given for each tune. Explanatory chapters, relatively short bibliography but extensive discography. 64 pp.

BASS

As with rhythm guitar, bass playing for dancing is pretty much the same for both Northern and Southern style music, using an alternating bass supplemented by bass runs. You need to learn to keep a dependable and steady rhythm and to be that little bit ahead of the beat that gives the music "lift."

Bluegrass Bass

Ned Alterman & Richie Mintz (New York: Oak Publications, 1977)

Good beginner's book on bluegrass bass with about 20 tunes, of which about half can be used for dancing. Chords included. Explanatory chapters, profiles of well known bluegrass bass players, discography, and various other useful information. A disadvantage is the fact that only the bass line is given, not the actual tune. But 15 of the tunes are demonstrated on the accompanying "soundsheet" (flexible phonograph record) with a full bluegrass band. The recordings can be used for learning the tunes and for playing along with the band for practice. 109 pp.

Teach Yourself Bluegrass Bass

Roger Mason (New York: Amsco Music Publishing Co., 1978)

Beginner's book on bluegrass bass with 30 tunes, of which about half can be used for dancing. Includes the melodies and chords as well as the bass line. Explanatory chapters, discography. 48 pp.

PIANO

Until very recently, little or no instructional material was available for learning to play the piano for dancing. My guess is that most players were recruited from the ranks of those who already knew general piano technique, since the main skills involved are relatively simple chording and bass runs that they would easily be able to pick out. However, one book has now appeared that fills the breach.

Interview with a Vamper: Piano accompaniment techniques for traditional dance music

Peter Barnes (Lincoln, Mass: Canis Publishing, 1993)

One of New England's most accomplished dance musicians offers a compendium of thoughts and many practical examples of appropriate backup technique for New England-style dancing. The techniques illustrated range from basic to quite advanced, with much attention to the all-important subject of rhythm. In the absence of any accompanying tape, an ability to read (or at least decipher) music in both clefs is necessary. Discography. 139 pp.

Another way of learning how piano accompaniment should sound is to listen to recordings in which the piano is clearly heard. For example:

The Grumbling Old Woman with Donna Hinds (fiddle) and Peter Barnes and Tony Parkes (piano).
Belknap's March with Bill Wellington (fiddle) and Janet Muse (piano).
Off with the Good St. Nicholas Boat with George Wilson (fiddle) and Selma Kaplan (piano).
Castles in the Air with Rodney Miller (fiddle) and Randy Miller (piano).

Full references for these recordings are in the Discography.

OTHER INSTRUMENTS

Instructional materials for other, less common instruments, such as the hammered dulcimer, autoharp, tenor banjo, and various wind in-struments, can be found in the catalogues of the mail order houses listed at the head of this chapter.

TUNE BOOKS

I have listed only a few standard references here. There are many other tune books, covering both Northern and Southern playing styles, and including a number of books with the authors' original compositions in traditional styles. Consult the catalogues of the mail order houses to see what is currently available.

The Fiddler's Fakebook

David Brody (New York: Oak Publications, 1983)

Music and record sources for almost 500 tunes in a large variety of American and related (Canadian, British) playing styles. In many cases, the notes are transcriptions of specific players' recorded performances. This can make it hard at times to ascertain the basic melody, but it does provide a wealth of examples of typical ornamentation and personal styles worthy of imitation. Introductory chapter provides a good orientation to the material. 301 pp.

N.B. The same author has published similar books for **banjo**, **guitar** and **mandolin**, in which the tunes are written out in tablature.

New England Fiddler's Repertoire

Randy Miller & Jack Perron (Peterborough, New Hampshire: Fiddlecase Books, 1983)

Music for 168 of the most commonly played dance tunes in the New England tradition. The tunes are presented in a clear form, without too many personal elaborations, but also without chords or any other form of arrangement. The reader is assumed to be conversant with the playing style, as no explanations are given. 100 pp.

One Thousand Fiddle Tunes

(Chicago, Illinois: M.M. Cole Publishing Co., 1940)

This large collection of American and British fiddle tunes has for years been a standard source for many fiddlers, especially in the North. The book contains nothing but the bare tunes (and an occasional short dance description here and there), but for players who already know the styles, it is a good place to find additional material. 128 pp.

Square Dance Chord Book and Tune Locator, 2nd ed.

Jack Sloanaker & Tony Parkes (Plymouth, Vermont: F&W Records, 1979)

Chords only for about 500 tunes in the New England tradition, plus references to books and records where the notes (or recorded performances) can be found. Handy, with a clear presentation. Provides a supplement to the many tune books that do not include chords. 100 pp.

AUDIO AND VIDEO TAPES

The latest development in music teaching has been the appearance of tape courses—first on audio cassettes, and now increasingly on video. Both types have clear advantages, especially for beginners, in that the student can hear how the music should sound and, in the case of video, see how to perform the playing techniques. Video is the next best thing to finding a local musician, and in some cases it may even be better, since the teacher on the tape presumably has experience in breaking down techniques for others to learn. Probably the four best known suppliers of taped instruction courses are the following, all of whom sell directly to the public:

Homespun Tapes, Box 694, Woodstock, New York 12498. Tel: (914) 679-7832.

The Murphy Method, P.O. Box 2498, Winchester, Virginia 22601. Tel: (703) 877-2357.

Ridge Runner Home Lessons, P.O. Box 12215, Fort Worth, Texas 76121.

Workshop Records, P.O. Box 49507, Austin, Texas 78765. Tel: (512) 452-8348.

Audio and video tape courses can also be obtained from the folk music suppliers listed at the beginning of this chapter, particularly from Elderly Instruments and Andy's Front Hall.

Annotated Discography

TABLE OF CONTENTS

Types of recordings

In the course of time, many recordings intended for square or contra dancing have been released. They can be divided into several categories:

• Records (usually singles), with or without calls, produced by folk dance record companies, such as Folk Dancer, Folkraft, the Lloyd Shaw Foundation, the German company Walter Kögler Verlag, etc. Some of these were recorded as far back as the 1940s, while others are newer. The musicians are sometimes practicing folk musicians, but may also be generic studio "folk music bands," and the instrumentation and musical quality vary a great deal, from excellent to decidedly uninspiring.

• Commercial LPs, mostly released during the folk music boom of the 1960s, with more or less usable calls, or in some cases, entirely or partly without calls. The dances chosen tend to be traditional warhorses, and the calling is often Southern style, which may result in a need for written explanations of some calls for a correct interpretation.

• LPs and tapes released since the mid–1970s by smaller, independent labels, presenting (for the most part) excellent musicians who play for traditional dancing in real life and understand the musical needs. Most of these albums are instrumental only, but a few have calls. During the last 10 years or so, there has been a growing tendency for contra dance bands to issue tapes that showcase the talents of the band, including complex arrangements that would not be possible during a dance. Shifts in tempo and rhythm within the same cut may therefore result in music that is unsuitable for dancing. However, this category also includes most of the best dance recordings currently available.

• Singles produced for the modern Western

square dance market, most of which are so-called "flips" with instrumental music on one side and the same music with calls on the other side. Many of these are more pop than folk in feel, and the musicians are typically studio bands, since live music is very rarely used in this type of square dancing. In fact, some recordings don't even employ a band, but are clearly produced on a synthesizer. Since the musical priorities are different for traditional square dancing than they are for modern Western, it can be difficult to find useful recordings in this group, but there are some.

• Finally, danceable tunes may be found on records intended for listening, especially the numerous releases with bluegrass and old-timey music. Unfortunately, many otherwise tempting cuts are too short or too fast, but this can sometimes be remedied by splicing or by using a variable speed tape recorder.

Evaluating recordings

To evaluate the usefulness of a dance record, you will want to take the following factors into account:

• *Character and instrumentation of the tune:* Is it folk fiddling, country and western, pop? Even if the tune as such is good, you may not care for the instrumentation.

• *Execution of the tune:* The tune should be played in a manner that makes you want to get up and dance. It shouldn't be lethargic, dragged out or boring, be played so fast that definition is lost, or be rhythmically uneven. The musical execution should not suffer from poor tone quality or faulty intonation, and the technical quality should be acceptable. Furthermore, both the rhythm and melody should be clearly distinguishable, with neither one dominating the other.

• *Regularity of structure:* The tune should not have extra beats or missing beats (some folk tunes do). A tune with the standard AABB structure, in which each letter stands for 16 beats, is the easiest to work with and most generally applicable. However, tunes with other structures, such as ABAB, AABBCC, AAB, etc., can also be acceptable, depending on their intended use.

• *Length:* The standard length for dances in square formation is 7 × 64 counts, but some squares require more than that. A 6 × 64-count recording can be used for a square if you skip the introduction or the middle break (try not to eliminate the ending). For contras, most callers want tunes that run at least 7–10 times through 64 counts, but on the other hand, with contras it is a little easier to start the record or tape over and continue dancing than it is with a square. Short cuts with only 4 or 5 × 64 beats can generally only be used for mixers—especially the easy ones with a sequence that takes only 16 or 32 counts to complete—or for certain other dances of a special nature. For big set dancing, you will need a long recording, preferably not under about 20 times through.

• *Tempo:* An important factor is the tempo, which should be appropriate for the dance type. For New England squares and contras, this will normally be from about 118 to 126, for other types of squares from about 126 to 136, and for big set about 132 to 144. Music for mixers, progressive circles, full set longways dances, etc., should be evaluated on the basis of the movements involved and the dancers' level of experience. It is a great advantage to have access to a record player or tape recorder with variable speed. This feature will allow you to get much greater use out of your records and tapes, and will give you full control over the dance tempo. Remember that even the best dance can be ruined by being done at an inappropriate tempo, whether too fast or too slow.

NORTHERN STYLE, INSTRUMENTAL

Mainly for dancing

Arkansas Country Dances, Volume 1
B. Anderson, B. Beard, K. Blessing, E. Hale, M. Hudson, J. McConnell, B. Nesbitt, C. Peterson, D. Peterson, E. Peterson, A. Schlack
Arkansas Country Dance Society, no number; Cassette; (ca. 1985)

Dance music by a group of musicians whose skill level does not quite live up to their enthusiasm. To my mind, the fiddle playing in particular lacks bite and drive, and the rhythm section of the dozen-member orchestra could use more definition—the resulting sound is a bit muddy. The 12 cuts include a waltz, a march medley, a rag, a two-step, a polka, a jig, and three cuts in reel time, including a long (16 × 64, 134 bpm) medley of "Hot Time in the Old Town Tonight/Golden Slippers/Camptown Races/Redwing" that may be useful. The other tracks range in tempo from 114 to 126 and in length from 6 to 12 × 64. Occasional solos on banjo, hammered dulcimer, mandolin, and piano stand out.

Arkansas Country Dances, Volume 2
B. Anderson, B. Beard, K. Blessing, E. Hale, M. Hudson, J. McConnell, B. Nesbitt, C. Peterson, D. Peterson, E. Peterson, A. Schlack
Arkansas Country Dance Society, no number; Cassette; (ca. 1985)

This tape was released at the same time as Volume 1 (see above), and the musicians are the same, but the total impression of these nine cuts is somewhat more favorable. The tape's two schottisches, one waltz, and one slow rag are perhaps better suited to the musicians' talents, and even the two reels seem to work better than on the first tape. Also included are a cut that alternates 32 bars in waltz time with 32 beats in jig time—presumably intended for a specific dance—and two sung play party games without instrumental accompaniment (which is as they should be). The projected companion book, *Arkansas Traditional and Country Dancing*, which would have included dance descriptions and other material, has not come to my attention.

The Belle of Brattleboro
Bo Bradham and Mary Cay Brass
Self-produced, no number; Cassette; (1989)

Straight-ahead New England music for fiddle, accordion and piano in danceable arrangements, plus a waltz, a slow air, and a Bulgarian dance tune for a total of ten cuts. Tempos range from 110 to 120, lengths from 6 to (mostly) 9 × 64.

The Belle of the Contra Dance
Canterbury Country Dance Orchestra
F&W Records, no number; Cassette; (ca. 1990?)

With 14 musicians and a variety of instruments, this band has a "bigger" sound than most. The 17 tracks include three waltzes, a schottische, a song, a set of slip jigs (tunes in 9/8 time), and one cut arranged as a waltz followed by the same tune in jig time. The remaining ten tracks are danceable reels and jigs, played 5 or (mostly) 6 × 64 and at relatively slow tempos ranging from 100 to 118 bpm.

Canadian Old Tyme Music
Bob and Ginny Arbuckle, Harold and Wayne Good, Russ Gosse
World WRC1-5912/Canadian Old Tyme Music COTM 001; LP; (1988)

Six tracks of instrumental music with suggested square dances, mostly well known traditional visiting couple figures. Dance descriptions (but no glossary) are printed on the record jacket. There are three jig sets and three reel sets on the record, ranging in length from 10½ to 11½ × 64 and in tempo from 112 to 128. To my taste, the jigs never really get off the ground. The reels fare somewhat better, but the snare drum used on the reel cuts becomes tedious after a while.

Chimes of Dunkirk: Great Dances for Children
David Kaynor, Andy Davis, Mary Cay Brass, Peter Amidon, Stuart Kenney, Mary Lea, Mary Alice Amidon
New England Dancing Masters Productions, no number; Cassette; (1990)

Companion tape to the book of the same name (see Annotated Bibliography). Contains designated tunes for 12 of the 20 dances in the book, plus two all-purpose medleys and a waltz. Well played (if at times a little laid back) at slow tempos suitable for use with young children.

Everybody Swing
Various musicians
Volksdanscentrale voor Vlaanderen, no number; Cassette; (1988)

A representative selection of contemporary, mostly Northern style, dance music licensed from a variety of existing American releases (credits for the names of the records as well as those of the musicians would have been handy). All cuts are usable. Tempos range from 114 to 130 and lengths from 4 to 10 × 64.

Farewell to the Hollow
New England Tradition
CYD 101; Cassette; (1988/1991)

Fourteen cuts of excellent New England style music played on fiddle, flat-picked banjo, and piano, featuring 12 of pianist Bob McQuillen's own waltzes (several in medleys—6 cuts in all) and 4 of his other tunes, as well as other traditional reels and jigs. The tape was remixed and reissued in 1991, at which time two of the waltz tracks were added to commemorate the group's other two members, Peter Colby and April Limber, who died tragically shortly after the tape's initial release. All cuts are danceable; reels and jigs range in tempo from 122 to 128 and in length from 6 to 8 × 64.

Fluke Hits
The Fish Family Dance Band
Marimac 9012; Cassette; (1987)

Solid New England contra dance music with lots of bounce and drive. The 15 cuts are all danceable and include 2 waltzes (one Cajun style, one Norwegian), a Swedish hambo, 2 polkas played 4 × 64, and a good selection of dance medleys evenly divided between reels and jigs, most played 9 × 64. Tempos range from 116 to 130, with most between 122 and 126.

FootLoose
FootLoose
Skylark Sky 209; Cassette; (1992)

Eleven very well played cuts with a nice, light sound. Clarinet, accordion, and appropriately used drums fit right in, occasionally providing a jazzier feel than that of the average contra dance band. Includes two waltzes, a tango, an oldtimey medley, and one track that is a hybrid between a schottische and jitterbug, plus six other reel or jig medleys. Tempos range from 114 to 130, lengths mostly from 8 to 12 × 64. Several of the tunes were composed by members of the band.

Grand Picnic
Grand Picnic
Dean Street Music 101; Cassette; (1992)

Thirteen mostly danceable cuts including nine tunes composed by members of the band. Tight, rhythmic, well played music with some nice, occasionally jazzy, variation in instrumentation. Includes three waltzes, a Swedish hambo, an old-timey track with limited usability because of its slightly crooked tunes, and seven nice reel or jig medleys. Tempos mostly from 112 to 126, lengths mostly from 7 to 10 × 64, with one cut 5 × 64 at 106.

**Hold the Mustard: Contra Dance Music
   for Dancing and Listening**
Hold the Mustard
HTM-1; LP; (1987)

Somewhat reminiscent of the recordings by Wild Asparagus and Swallowtail, this album, unlike them, is arranged for dancing and provides some excellent selections. The nine tracks include four reel sets, two jig sets, a march, a waltz, and one cut with a medley of a jig and a reel. Tempos are from 116 to 126 and lengths mostly from 9 to 11 × 64 (7 × 64 for the march).

Keep on Swinging
Various musicians
Anglo-American Dance Service C9202; Cassette; (1992)

An attractive, varied selection of danceable tunes on a Belgian label, mostly licensed from existing American records. Also included in the 12 cuts are two tracks specially recorded for this tape by American musicians Steve Hickman, Laurie Andres and Larry Edelman, and one cut recorded in 1987 by the Danish group La Bastringue and not previously released as an instrumental. Tempos range from 116 to 134, with most between 120 and 124. Lengths mostly from 7 to 9 × 64, with one cut 11 × 64.

**Kitchen Junket: Traditional New England
   Square Dances and Music**
Yankee Ingenuity
Fretless FR 200A; LP; (1977)

An album full of good dance music, especially well suited for New England-style squares, plus a waltz and a polka. All 12 cuts are 7 × 64 beats, with tempos between 116 and 122. Printed on the jacket are a glossary and short, but clear, instructions for ten squares. The album was also issued as FR 200B with calls by Tony Parkes. Recently, the two versions have been re-released on a double length cassette tape; unfortunately, the dance instructions are no longer included.

Live from Contrafornia
The Glasnotes
Avocet 103; Cassette; (1990)

This tape was prepared for the 1990 American Dance Friendship Tour of American contra dancers to the Soviet Union—thus the name of the band. The 13 tracks include three waltzes, a song, and a medley of marches. The remaining eight cuts are fairly straightforward reel or jig medleys, most played 6 or 7 × 64, but one 5 × 64 and one 10 × 64. Tempos range from 118 to 128.

Maritime Dance Party
Jerry and Bobby Robichaud, Jack O'Connor, Tony
   Parkes, Sandy Davis, Donna Hinds
Fretless FR 201; LP; (1978)

This album is evenly divided between jigs and reels, and all the cuts are good, with excellent fiddling by Jerry Robichaud. The tempo is a bit high by New England standards—about 124 to 132—and is better suited to squares than contras. Most cuts are 7 × 64 beats, some a little more or less. The liner notes and a printed insert tell a little about Robichaud's background, dance customs in English-speaking Canada, and the tunes on the album, and describe three dances done at the French-American Victory Club in Waltham, Massachusetts, where Robichaud regularly plays. Recently re-issued as a double length cassette tape with FR 202, *Potluck and Dance Tonite* (see "Southern Style, with Calls"), on the other side.

New England Chestnuts
Rodney and Randy Miller, Sandy Bradley, George
   Wilson, Steve Woodruff
Fretless FR 203; LP; (1980)

    Most of the tunes on this record are associated with classic traditional contra dances, and the idea of the album was to make them all available in recorded form. Unsurpassed execution makes it tempting to use the tunes for other dances as well. There are six reels, two jigs, a waltz and a polka, and the tempos run from about 118 to 126. All cuts 7×64 beats, except the waltz, which is a little shorter. Note that "Money Musk" is a 48-count tune. Liner notes include a good overview of the nature of contra dancing plus notes on the individual tunes. Recently re-released as a double length cassette tape with FR 204, *New England Chestnuts 2*, on the other side.

New England Chestnuts 2
Rodney and Randy Miller, Sandy Bradley, George
   Wilson, Laurie Andres
Fretless FR 204; LP; (1981)

    Unsurpassed music for New England dances, especially contras. Tempos from 116 to 126 ("Gay Gordons" 106). All cuts at least 7×64 beats except "Gay Gordons" (10×32). One cut is a jig/reel/jig medley, i.e., the rhythm changes in the middle of the cut. This idea, which seems to have had its debut on this record, has become more popular among contra dance bands in recent years, but personally, I still find it a little distracting. A number of the tunes are associated with specific traditional dances, but they can also be used for other dances if desired. Recently re-released as a double length cassette tape with FR 203, *New England Chestnuts*, on the other side.

New England Contra Dance Music
Salmonberry
KAS 1; Cassette; (1991)

    Steady, solid dance music with nice long cuts (from 9 to 13×64) for contra dancing. Wind instruments provide some color without becoming too domineering. The 12 tracks include two waltzes, 6 reel medleys, 3 jig medleys, and one that starts with a jig and moves, not too distractingly, to two reels. Tempos from 112 to 120.

New England Country Dance Music
The Green Mountain Volunteers
Alcazar FR 205C; Cassette; (1983)

    This is a nice tape both for dancing and listening, as most of the cuts are medleys and a variety of rhythms are represented (reel, jig, march, schottische, waltz). The playing is lively, in spite of the fact that tempos are relatively slow—mostly about 116 to 120, but down to 110 for one of the jig sets. Cuts suitable for contras and squares are mostly played 8×64, with the "New England Medley" $10\frac{1}{2} \times 64$. Other cuts are 5 or 6×64.

Ontario Dances!
Bob and Ginny Arbuckle, Cathy Murphy, Murray
   Smith
Dancecraft LP 123322; LP; (1979)

    Eleven tracks, including two waltzes, two schottisches, and the Varsouvianna. Remaining cuts are mostly reels and one jig, with tempos ranging from 120 to 128 and lengths from 4 to 11×64. The playing seems a little heavy-handed at times (especially the piano); some cuts are more inviting than others. Judging by the record jacket, the music seems to be intended for a specific program of suggested dances, but no instruction booklet was included, and I have not been able to locate one.

Smoke on the Water: Square Dance Classics (without calls)
Peter Barnes, Steve Hickman, Bill Tomczak
Traditional Caller Productions TC 124; Cassette;
   (ca. 1988)

    Spirited arrangements of the music for ten transitional style 1950s singing calls, played on fiddle, clarinet, harmonica, and piano by three of the country's top dance musicians, leaving room for the caller to sing the melody. Unless you know the tunes, you will probably also want the called version of the tape (Traditional Caller Productions TC 124) to use as a model. An accompanying booklet by Bob Dalsemer is available with dance descriptions and tunes (see Annotated Bibliography).

Soir et Matin
Kerry Elkin, Danny Noveck, Peter Barnes
KME-1; Cassette; (1990)

Most of the ten cuts on this tape are danceable, including two waltzes, a schottische medley, and six tracks of jigs and reels. Many of the tunes are of Celtic origin and on the "notey" side; instrumentation is dominated by fiddle, tenor banjo and piano. Lengths range from 8 to 10×64 for the jig and reel tracks, and tempos from about 108 to 130 with an average of about 120—on several of the medleys, the tempo rises significantly within the cut.

Southerners Plus Two Play Ralph Page
The Southerners with Leigh Dyer and John Barber
EFDSS Records RP 500; LP; (1970)

This album was recorded in England after Ralph Page toured there in 1966. In spite of the jacket's contention that the band learned to play American style from Page, the arrangements are typically English in feel, with accordion and drums dominating, and tempos are somewhat lower than in the United States—about 110 to 116 (Page himself considered 120 the ideal tempo for contra dancing). However, for a change of pace, the album can be handy. The playing is good, and most of the cuts are 7 to 9×64, two are 6×64 and one 5×64. About half the tunes on the record were composed by Ralph Page, according to personal communication (they are not specially marked in the liner notes).

Square Dance Tunes for a Yankee Caller
The Fireside String Band
F & W Records F75-FW-6; LP; (1976)

This album was released to support the book *Square Dances from a Yankee Caller's Clipboard* by Rod Linnell and Louise Winston (see Annotated Bibliography), and is most useful in that context. The tunes are ones to which Linnell had written dances and that, in most cases, were unavailable in recorded form. The band has a full, somewhat formal sound, often a little marchy. It includes several violins playing in unison, as well as accordion, tenor banjo, etc. Similar in feel to the Canterbury Country Dance Orchestra, but a little cleaner and without the flutes. Tempos from 112 to 124, with most cuts around 120. About half the tunes are played at least 7×64, while others are done in shorter arrangements to go with specific dances.

Tradition Today
Sam Bartlett, Kerry Elkin, Gilles Losier, Tom MacKenzie, Jeremiah McLane, David Surette, Walter Weber
Vermont Performing Arts League VPAL 104; Cassette; (1991)

Solid, inspiring dance music with a very clean sound, played by some of New England's best known musicians. The 12 tracks include 7 reel sets, 2 jig sets, a waltz, a schottische, and a two-step. Tempos run from 112 to 120 for the jigs and reels, and lengths are all danceable, from 7 to 9×64. Only one cut is a little unusual: $2 \times 48 + 2 \times 96 + 2 \times 48$.

We Love Contra Dances
Pat Spaeth, Phil and Vivian Williams
Voyager VRLP 333-S; LP; (ca. 1985?)

Twelve tracks of sprightly and humorous dance music, including two waltzes, a schottische, a polka, a rag, and a march medley, as well as six cuts of jigs and reels. Except for the couple dances, lengths range from 6 to 10×64—most are at least 7×64—and tempos from 120-128.

When the Work's All Done: A Square Dance Party for Beginners & Old Hands (without calls)
Peter Barnes, Steve Hickman, Jack O'Connor, Bill Tomczak
Traditional Caller Productions TC 126; Cassette; (ca. 1990)

Produced for dancing, all ten cuts are usable, with tempos ranging from 128 to 136 and lengths from 6 to 10×64. The instrumentation, consisting of tenor banjo, clarinet, piano, woodblock, and a fiddle that sometimes tends more toward a "violin" sound, is more reminiscent of 1950s square dance records than of current contra dance band sounds, but may prove to be a welcome change of pace, depending on your taste. Impeccable musicianship and a fresh, lively sound. Four of the tunes are suitable for singing calls but can also be used for patter calling. An accompanying booklet by Bob Dalsemer is available with dance suggestions and tunes (see Annotated Bibliography).

For dancing and listening

Airplang
Rodney Miller, Russ Barenberg, Peter Barnes, Molly Mason, Tim Jackson
Rounder 0193; LP; (1985)

A showcase for fiddler Rodney Miller at his best, seconded by four other eminent New England folk musicians of the current generation, these ten cuts feature music with traditional roots in swinging arrangements. Four will be found danceable by the adventurous, ranging in tempo from 106 to 126 and in length from 6½ to 8×64. The rest make great listening.

Alive in Scandinavia
Québec Dance Band
Self-produced, no number; Cassette; (1992)

A nice tape produced in Denmark, featuring the formidable Raynald Ouellett of Québec on accordéon, ably supplemented by two versatile Danish musicians, Jes Kroman on fiddle and Morten Alfred on guitar. The 11 tracks include two waltzes as well as three or four other tracks not suitable for country dancing because of irregular tunes or special arrangements. The remaining five are great, ranging in length from 5 to 8×64 and in tempo from 120 to 126.

Black Cat Quadrille
Brattleboro Brass Band
Front Hall FHR-034C; Cassette; (1986)

Sixteen cuts of jazzy, occasionally crazy, music played by a brass ensemble (trombone, alto sax, tuba, French horn, trumpet, piccolo, flute, and percussion). The group takes its inspiration from the brass- and woodwind-heavy urban dance bands of 100 to 150 years ago, but makes no attempt to recreate their exact sound, preferring to explore the possibilities of today. Tunes range from seventeenth century classical and dance pieces to Latin- and jazz-inspired cuts to pure New England dance tunes, with the occasional surprise thrown in. Danceable cuts range in tempo from 120 to 132 and in length up to 10×64, with most, however, at 4 to 6×64. An interesting change of pace.

Call of the Wild
Wild Asparagus
Wild Asparagus WA 004; Cassette; (1993)

The fourth release from Wild Asparagus seems to me to have a more balanced tone color than some of their earlier albums; it also has a more obvious Irish influence on several tunes. This time as many as four or five of the 12 tracks are potentially usable for dancing, mostly reel sets played at tempos of about 120 to 126 and with lengths of 7 to 10×64.

Canterbury Country Dance Orchestra
Canterbury Country Dance Orchestra
F & W Records F72-FW-3; LP; (1972?)

The Canterbury Country Dance Orchestra is a relatively large group: ten musicians. Their sound, which is full and somewhat dominated by flutes, occasionally gets a little muddy on this recording. The tempo is fine for New England dancing, ranging from 116 to 128, with most cuts around 120. Most cuts are played 6×64 beats, but some are only 5×64,

and a couple are not danceable because of irregularities. "Kalendara Kolo" is the group's interpretation of a Croatian dance tune.

Canterbury Country Dance Orchestra Meets the F&W String Band
Canterbury Country Dance Orchestra and F&W String Band
F&W Records F-72-FW4; LP; (1972?)

This album brings together two groups that are large to begin with, ending up with a massed sound created by up to 18 fiddles, 15 flutes, five accordions, nine guitars, and assorted other instruments—60 musicians in all! Personally, I find the resulting sound too "big" and somewhat lacking in bite. Seven of the 14 cuts were recorded by the whole group, and the others by the Canterbury Country Dance Orchestra alone. With "only" 14 musicians, I find the latter tracks more appealing, but several of them are in special rhythms or are too short to be very useful. Tempos overall range from 104 to 128, lengths from 5 to 7×64.

Contra and Blue
Claude Ginsburg and Julie King
Self-produced, no number; Cassette; (1992)

Eleven tracks, including three original tunes by Claude Ginsburg and several by other Seattle musicians. Three of the reel sets on side two are suitable for dancing, with tempos of 112 to 122 and lengths of 6 to 7×64, and there are also two nice waltzes and a polka medley. The other cuts, several of which are very jazzy, are really for listening only.

Contra Dance Music from Western Massachusetts
The Fourgone Conclusions
Front Hall FHR-029; LP; (1983)

Lively music with a lot of little "surprises." Cuts intended for set dancing are at least 6×64 beats. Tempos about 116 to 124. The album also includes several well executed Scandinavian tunes, mostly Swedish ones, learned by members of the group on trips to Sweden.

Contrablessings
Vandy, Cammy and Edward Kaynor
Self-produced, no number; Cassette; (1990)

A full 31 cuts, recorded in 1981-82, and including nine tunes composed by Cammy Kaynor. The title of each tune or medley is announced before it is played, which is helpful on a tape with so many tracks. The music is well and clearly played—most cuts seem to be two fiddles plus piano—but of the

31 tracks, there are 14 that are waltzes, schottisches, or Swedish polskas (similar to a hambo), and a couple more that are too irregular for dancing. Of the remaining tracks, only five are played 6 or 7 × 64, and a few more are marginally usable at 4 or 5 × 64. Tempos range mostly from 114 to 124, with one cut at 108.

Contras from the Old Country
Fool's Gold
Self-produced, no number; Cassette; (1987)

Being a fan of both country dance music and klezmer music, I awaited this tape with anticipation. The 13 cuts, including two waltzes, a polka mazurka, and three other cuts not suitable for contra dancing, are played with spirit and skill, but to my taste, the integration of the two genres is not completely successful. The klezmer side seems to dominate, with the rhythm subtly moving away from the drive and lift intrinsic to American dancing. The seven potentially usable cuts range in tempo from 122 to 130 and in length from 5 to 8 × 64. Worth a shot if you are looking for something really different!

Down East ... Out West
Frank Ferrel and Gilles Losier
Voyager VRLP 329-S; LP; (ca. 1980?)

Fluid and energetic fiddling by Frank Ferrel. Of the 11 cuts, about five are danceable—most of these are played 6 × 64 at tempos of 112 to 124. The remaining tracks are great listening, but shifts between different rhythms within the same cut make them impractical for dancing.

F&W String Band
F&W String Band
F&W Records F-FW-1; LP; (1969)

This record demonstrates what a group of young people can achieve under the right leadership. The band is made up of 24 musicians—campers and staff at the Farm & Wilderness Camps in Vermont—who play for square dances during the summer. Side one offers six tracks arranged to be danceable, and most of them are. In spite of the unusually large group and amateur musicianship, the total effect is appealing. These cuts range in tempo from 112 to 120. Most are played 7 × 64, with one 9 × 64. Side two contains ten shorter cuts for listening, including a waltz, a polka, a two-step, two jigs, and five reels.

Fantastic Hornpipe
Laurie Andres, Andy Davis, Sandy Bradley
Rooster RSTR 122; LP; (1983)

Unfortunately, not many of the 13 cuts on this recording are long enough for dancing, but those that are are sure winners. Laurie Andres is probably the best known contemporary master of the accordion in country dance circles, and deservedly so. His playing is full of life, drive, and an inimitable sense of humor. The album fetaures him solo and accompanied, on both accordion and piano, in a program of polkas, jigs, hornpipes, reels, a waltz, and other tunes. Tempos mostly from 116 to 126.

Fiddle Tunes
Frank Ferrel and Graham Townsend
Voyager VRLP 320-S; LP; (1977)

Fifteen cuts of well played Canadian fiddle and piano music that begs to be danced to. Unfortunately, many of the tracks are either very short or include irregular tunes. Five reel sets played 4 or 6 × 64 at tempos of 120 to 126 are candidates for use. There is also a nice schottische and two great waltzes: Frank Ferrel's waltz fiddling is really something special.

Heatin' Up the Hall
Yankee Ingenuity
Varrick C-VR-038; Cassette; (1989)

This sparkling album showcases the talents and versatility of one of New England's longest-lived current country dance bands. The 11 cuts include two waltzes (one Venezuelan, one Finnish), a polka, a schottische in medley with a reel, and five tracks suitable for country dancing. Of these, three are in New England/French-Canadian style, one in old time Southern style, and one is a rag intended for the dance Levi Jackson Rag. Concluding the album is a called version of the old time visiting couple square Grapevine Twist, a remarkable tour de force by caller Tony Parkes. This, too, is danceable if desired, having been recorded live at a dance. Tempos from about 120 to 140; lengths of the danceable cuts mostly from 6 to 9 × 64.

Michigan Winter
The Olde Michigan Ruffwater Stringband
Michigan Seasons 001; LP; (1981)

If you are a fan of hammered dulcimer, you will be pleased to know that the 13-person band on this album includes no less than four of them! Not all the cuts are equally usable (there are, for instance, four songs), but there are a few nice dance tunes, including two good schottisches, a lively polka, and two waltzes. Most of the cuts are on the short side, only 4 or 5 × 64 beats, but tempos are suitable for dancing.

The Music of John Taggart:
  Classic Yankee Fiddle Tunes
New Hampshire Fiddlers Union
Self-produced, no number; Cassette; (1989)

The tunes on these 13 tracks were found in the manuscript autobiography of John Adams Taggart (1854–1943), a practiced and professional musician. About half of the arrangements are suitable for dancing, ranging in tempo from 112 to 132, with one cut at 102, and running mostly 6 × 64 in length. Instrumentation consists of three fiddles with guitar or piano backup.

Turning of the Tide
Fresh Fish
KME 2; Cassette; (1992)

Fourteen cuts of spirited music with a Celtic flavor, including five danceable medleys of from 6 to 9 × 64 counts (two with a more New England sound), at tempos ranging from 112-130. Also three waltzes and four other cuts that may be usable for dancing, depending on your taste.

Vermont Sampler
Sam Bartlett, Kerry Elkin, Gilles Losier, Tom
  MacKenzie, Jeremiah McLane, David Surette,
  Walter Weber
Vermont Performing Arts League VPAL 103;
  Cassette; (1991)

Fourteen cuts, including six beautifully performed songs and early American hymns, four very danceable medleys (though a little on the short side at 6 × 64), a schottische, a two-step, and a waltz. Dance tempos about 122. Note that four of the tracks also appear on VPAL 104, *Tradition Today*, including the schottische, the two-step, and two of the country dance medleys.

Yankee Dreams
Frank Ferrel, John McGann, Peter Barnes
Flying Fish FF 90572; Cassette; (1991)

A gem of a tape for any fan of New England dance music. Veteran fiddle virtuoso Frank Ferrel is backed up by two of the country's ablest dance musicians of the current generation, John McGann on guitar and mandolin and Peter Barnes on piano, in a professionally recorded performance. The 16 tracks include a waltz, two hornpipe medleys, and a few other cuts that are either too short or too slow for country dancing. Fortunately, there are also six tracks of reels, jigs, and polkas that are usable at from 6 to 9 × 64 and tempos of 120 to 130 bpm.

Mainly for listening

Airplang II: The Sequel. Acoustic and Electric
  Dance Music
Rodney Miller, Peter Barnes, John McGann
Self-produced, no number; Cassette; (1987)

Why is it that sequels never seem to completely live up to the original? This tape is more modestly produced than the first "Airplang" LP, and the music is less arranged. Three musicians with impeccable credentials offer 12 tracks of traditional tunes that, while definitely well played and often a little jazzy, also seem a little static, and therefore best suited as listening music. About 3-5 cuts are danceable, depending on taste and needs. Most of these are 6 × 64 and tempos are a little on the low side, from 106 to 116.

Belknap's March and Other Dance Melodies
Bill Wellington, Janet Muse, Carlotta Wellington,
  Paul Brier
Bill Wellington, no number; Cassette; (1983)

This tape is primarily of interest as a source of good new tunes written in traditional New England style, as well as an opportunity to hear the playing style and typical ornamentation. Of the 17 tunes on the tape, 13 were written by Bill Wellington, while the remaining four are traditional. The material is clearly played on fiddle, piano and, on some cuts, hammered dulcimer, but is on the slow side for dancing, and some unevenness in the rhythm is accentuated if the tempo is electronically increased. A companion booklet with written music for Wellington's tunes was published simultaneously.

BLT
BLT
Self-produced, no number; Cassette; (1987)

A selection of couple dance tunes (waltzes, two-steps, tangos and rags) as well as a couple of country dance medleys and assorted other tunes by one of New England's best known dance bands. 12 cuts.

Brand New Old Time Fiddle Tunes No. 1
Joe Pancerzewski, Phil and Vivian Williams
Voyager VRCS 335; Cassette; (1988)

A "sample" tape of 31 tunes composed in traditional Canadian style by Joe Pancerzewski, each played only about two times through. All the tunes have been published in one of two books by Vivian Williams: *151 Brand New Old Time Fiddle Tunes Vol. 1* and *141 Brand New Old Time Fiddle Tunes Vol 2* (Seattle, Washington: Voyager Publications).

Brand New Old Time Fiddle Tunes No. 2
Vivian Williams, Phil Williams, Ron Holdridge
Voyager VRCS 338; Cassette; (1992)

Twenty-two tracks of clearly played fiddle tunes composed in traditional Canadian and Celtic styles by Vivian Williams. Lengths are typically 2 or 3 × 64 and tempos slow, so the main value is as a sampler for musicians interested in finding new tunes. All the tunes have been published in Williams' two books *151 Brand New Old Time Fiddle Tunes Vol. 1* and *141 Brand New Old Time Fiddle Tunes Vol. 2* (Seattle, Washington: Voyager Publications).

Castles in the Air: Jigs, Reels and Airs
Rodney, Randy and Ralph Miller and Peter O'Brien
Fretless FR 119; LP; (1976)

There are many dance tunes on this record, but most of them run only 3 or 4 × 64 beats, and many of the arrangements are intended for listening rather than dancing. There are also four cuts of slow airs and songs. The few tracks that are danceable are quite good, and the album provides a model of pure New England fiddle and piano playing by excellent musicians. The use of harmonica on some tunes adds an interesting and unusual color. Tempos from 118 to 128.

Chasing the New Moon
Sarah Bauhan
CSWM 9859; Cassette; (1991)

Beautifully played music including nine tunes composed by Bauhan and featuring her skilled flute playing. Most of the tunes or arrangements on the 13 tracks are not intended for dancing, but two or three cuts feature straight-ahead, moderate-tempo reel medleys of 6 or 9 × 64 that could be used.

Contra Dance Music New England Style
Applejack with Bob McQuillen
Green Linnet SIF 1028; LP; (1980)

Bob McQuillen has been part of the New England dance scene for years, both as a musician and as a composer of scores of new tunes in traditional style. All of the 21 tunes on this album were written by him, including some, like "The Dancing Bear," that are among his best known efforts. The execution, tempos, and arrangements are fine for dancing, but since the record was conceived as a listening album, many of the 16 tracks are frustratingly short. Only three are 6 or 7 × 64 beats, and several are as short as 2 or 3 times through the tune.

Dick Richardson: Old Time New Hampshire Fiddler
Dick Richardson, Ralph Page's New Hampshire Trio, The Haltone Four, and various other musicians
Dudley Laufman, no number; Cassette; (1992)

Dudley Laufman has done the dance community a service by making available this compilation of music played by Vermont fiddler Haltone "Dick" Richardson, who was closely associated with Ralph Page and was active from 1903 to 1970. The tape's 25 cuts include numerous excerpts from the 78-rpm recordings Richardson made as a member of the Ralph Page Orchestra, Ralph Page's New Hampshire Trio, and the Haltone Four in the late 1940s and early 50s. Also included are some informative reminiscences voiced over by members of Richardson's family and a few good examples of Page's calling. A corresponding book has been published by Dudley Laufman and Corinne Nash with photographs and additional documentation (see Annotated Bibliography).

Don Messer and His Islanders: A Tribute, Tape 1
Don Messer and His Islanders
Polygram/Polytel 836 082 4; Cassette; (1988)

This tape, together with Tape 2 below, provides easy access to some of the work of the legendary Canadian fiddler Don Messer. The fluidity and relaxed authority of his playing shine through the varying technical quality of the recordings. Frustratingly, the cuts are mostly too short to use for dancing—only 3 to 5 × 64—and no liner notes are present except the tune list. Tempos range from 122 to 134.

Don Messer and His Islanders: A Tribute, Tape 2
Don Messer and His Islanders
Polygram/Polytel 836 082 4; Cassette; (1988)

Similar to Tape 1 above, but this tape has dance tunes on one side and sacred songs on the other. Presumably, all this is material that would have been heard on Messer's long-running radio show, which was a source of inspiration for many Canadian and Northeastern U.S. musicians. Tempos of the instrumental tunes range from 122 to 132 and lengths from 4 to 7 × 64.

Down East Fiddling
Gerry Robichaud, Chuck LeBlanc, Art Richard
Voyager VRLP 310-S; LP; (1973)

These 16 tracks are a fine calling card for master fiddler Robichaud, but are not much use for dancing because of their short lengths, from 2½ to

4½ × 64 (ending a tune after the A part seems to be a Canadian custom, observable on several recordings). Fortunately, Robichaud has also recorded a really fine dance album on the Alcazar/Fretless label, FR 201 *Maritime Dance Party* (see under "Northern Style, Instrumental—Mainly for dancing").

Enrichez-Vous
Erin Shrader and Edith Farrar
Sage Arts 1101; Cassette; (1991)

Beautifully played music by one of those pairs of accomplished dance musicians who can provide sufficient accompaniment with just a fiddle and piano. Unfortunately, only 3 of the 11 cuts are usable in practice. The others are either waltzes (three, nice but slow), are too short, or consist of special arrangements. The danceable cuts have a tempo of about 114.

F&W String Band 2
F&W String Band
F&W Records F-72-FW2; LP; (1972?)

This second album by the F&W String Band (with about half of the same personnel as on the first LP—see under "Northern Style, Instrumental—For dancing and listening") contains 16 tracks, including one with a complete square dance called by John Melish. All the other cuts are, however, too short to dance to, typically 3 or 4 × 64. Tempos run from 108 to 126.

Fiddle Tunes with Omer Marcoux
Omer Marcoux, Sylvia Miskoe, Justine Paul, Aimée Jobin
Sylvia Miskoe, no number; Cassette; (1981)

Recorded live with then 83-year-old French-Canadian fiddler Marcoux and his accompanists. The 14 cuts, including three waltzes and a few songs as well as dance tunes, are mostly short and primarily of interest to musicians and collectors interested in traditional French-Canadian fiddling.

Flights of Fancy
Swallowtail
Rooster Records RSTR 130; LP; (1985)

An eclectic album by a group of excellent musicians, with a variety of tone colors. Most of the music on these nine tracks is arranged for listening, although most of the tunes are dance tunes. Only one 7 × 64 reel medley is unquestionably usable for dancing, but three other tracks may be, depending on needs and taste.

Greasy Coat
The Rodney Miller Band
Sage Arts 1301; Cassette; (1990)

High-energy interpretations of traditional tunes and ones newly composed in traditional style, including eight by members of the band. A definite influence from jazz and swing is evident in this confidently played album by some top New England musicians. The 13 tracks include two waltzes and a polka but only one cut definitely usable for country dancing, a set of reels played 6 × 64 at 116 bpm. Two other cuts are "maybes," depending on taste and needs.

The Grumbling Old Woman
Donna Hébert, Peter Barnes, Tony Parkes
Hand to Mouth Music, no number; Cassette; (1981)

Reissued 1994. Companion tape to Donna Hébert's violin instruction book of the same name. Twenty-eight of the 68 tunes in the book are demonstrated, first solo at an almost excruciating tempo of about 60 bpm—about half of normal New England dance tempo. Then the tune is repeated with piano accompaniment at about 104 to 108 bpm. Helpfully, the name of each tune is announced before it is played.

In Season
Wild Asparagus
Wild Asparagus WA 001; Cassette; (ca. 1986)

Recorded by a popular dance band with an unusual sound: no fiddle is present, but the melody is borne by a variety of wind instruments (flute, recorder, oboe) and English concertina. Backup is restricted to piano and percussion (bodhran, bones, triangle, etc.) so even on the two to four cuts that are danceable (out of ten), the sound to my taste is a little thin. Many of the arrangements make use of a slow introduction building up to a faster tune, and rhythmic shifts are common. Good listening music, with one reel set and one jig set played 12 × 64 at 120 bpm.

Jacket Trimmed in Blue: Jigs, Reels, Songs and a Story
Two Fiddles
Dudley Laufman, no number; Cassette; (1992)

On side one, Laufman, one of those who, starting some 30 years ago, helped lay the ground for the present hardy contra dance scene, tells how he became acquainted with old time New England dance fiddler Arthur Hanson while working as recreation director at an old age home, and how he got Hanson playing again. The story is illustrated with examples of Hanson's favorite tunes, recreated as nearly as possible by Laufman on Hanson's own fiddle. Side two contains a selection of jigs, reels and a couple of songs, mostly traditional with a few Laufman originals. Arrangements are short and sparse and are therefore not really suitable for dancing, but interesting for study purposes.

Jersey Lightning: Traditional Fiddle Music
Jamie Gans
Self-produced, no number; Cassette; (1991)

An interesting selection of traditional tunes, including a couple of waltzes, several slow airs, and several cuts whose tempo changes make them unsuitable for dancing. Although most of the ten tracks are Northern style (several based on Irish tunes), the most impressive to me was a convincing rendition of the Southern solo fiddle piece "They Swung John Brown from a Sour Apple Tree." One reel set played 6 × 64 at 130 may be found usable for dancing. Informative liner notes are included.

Mark Hamilton: Songs and Tunes from Wolf Run
Mark Hamilton, Jim Kimball, Glenn McClure,
  Mitzie Collins
Sampler Records 9223; Cassette; (1992)

Presents the repertoire of an important western New York State tradition-bearer, who sings, fiddles, calls, and tells stories on a total of 53 cuts, backed up musically by the other musicians listed. A capsule biography of Hamilton is offered on the insert card, and a companion book is said to be in progress.

Mistwold
Canterbury Country Orchestra
F&W Records F74-FW-5; LP; (1974?)

There are some good tunes here, but the tempo in many cases is too slow for dancing. In addition, five cuts are songs and several other numbers are not intended for dancing. Most of the dance tunes are played at least 6 × 64 beats though, so if you can speed them up a little, you may find something of value.

Music from a Little Known Planet
Wild Asparagus
Wild Asparagus WA 002; Cassette; (1987)

Wild Asparagus likes to start a medley with a long, slow, specially arranged introduction and only then switch into a solid dance tune, which in most cases results in a track frustratingly unsuitable for ordinary dancing. In general, the music on these eight

tracks is highly, and inventively, arranged, providing good listening and a kind of distilled impression of why the band is so popular at dance events. As usual, wind instruments (flute, recorder, oboe) are featured more prominently than in most country dance bands, but fiddle has also been added.

New England Contra Dance Music
Alan Block/Strathspey/George Wilson/Arm &
  Hammer String Band
Kicking Mule KM 216; LP; (1977)

Despite the name, this is a record for listening, not dancing. Of the participating groups, only Arm & Hammer String Band has a full band sound, and then only on some of their cuts. Otherwise, the solid rhythm needed for dancing is missing. Additionally, most cuts are on the short side, 5 or 6 × 64 beats, while tempos are relatively high.

New Englander's Choice
Skip Gorman
Folk-Legacy C-95; Cassette; (1983)

Fifteen spirited, well fiddled cuts, many of which would be great for dancing if only they were not so short (often only 4 to 5 × 64) and most of the rest which are not arranged for country dancing. Excellent for listening, though.

Off with the Good St. Nicholas Boat
George Wilson and Selma Kaplan
Hairy People's Productions, no number; Cassette;
  (ca. 1985)

A fine tape for listening, but only usable for dancing to a limited degree, as several of the tunes are irregular and other cuts are on the short side. Of the 13 tracks, three to five are candidates for use. Two—"The Local Hero" and "Fiddle Tuned Like a Viol"—are listed on the insert in the reverse order of what is actually played.

One Hundred Years of Country Dance Music
New England Conservatory Country Fiddle Band
Columbia M 333981; LP; (1976)

Interpretations of mostly well known New England dance tunes by a large orchestra consisting of about 25 conservatory students, under the direction of Gunther Schuller. The playing is clean (of course) and fairly lively, but lacks the spontaneity and edge of true country dance fiddling. Tempos are generally slow, except for the two waltzes, and most cuts are played only 5 or 6 × 64 beats.

Spring Dance: Spirited Traditional Dance Music
Folk Like Us
North Star NS 0029 (under license from Sandy Flat
    Music); cassette; (1990)

The music on this tape is certainly spirited enough, and the tunes are dance tunes, yet they clearly are being performed by a concert band rather than one used to playing for dancing. A little more definition and "lift" in the rhythm section would help. In any case, most of the 15 cuts are too short to dance to, typically only 4 or 5×64, and some also have irregular arrangements. Instrumentation includes flutes and hammered dulcimer and tends somewhat toward the Celtic.

Step Dancing
Debby McWatty and Wendy Thompson (dancers),
    Chuck Joyce (fiddle), with unidentified piano
    player
Oak C-117; Cassette; (1982)

Judging by the picture on the insert, this tape is probably a re-release of an LP published in the 1960s or 70s. It offers ten tracks of excellent Canadian fiddle and piano playing, with step dancing on all of the cuts except the two waltzes. The playing is clean and fluid, and the dancers fit in as smoothly as if they were an additional instrument. Unfortunately, almost all the cuts have at least one change of rhythm, from slow hornpipe ("clog" or schottische rhythm) and or jig to the faster-sounding reels, and the two that do stay in reel tempo are played only 3 to 4 times through. Great listening, though.

Swallowtail
Swallowtail
Rooster C 117; Cassette; (ca. 1980?)

Artfully arranged renditions of dance tunes, mostly restricted to listening use because of variations in rhythm and tempo within the individual cuts. Like the group Wild Asparagus, which includes some of the same personnel, Swallowtail features some interesting textures provided by wind instruments, but the band also includes fiddle and a wide variety of other string instruments.

Tone Roads
Wild Asparagus
Wild Asparagus WA 003; Cassette; (1990)

Similar to Wild Asparagus' previous two releases, this tape again features solid and attractive playing, but for the most part undanceable arrangements. There are, however, a couple of reel

sets that are played relatively straight at tempos of 120 and 128, respectively, and 7 or 8×64.

**Traditional and Ethnic Square Dance Music of New
    England 1955–1957**
Various musicians
Dudley Laufman, no number; Cassette; (ca. 1988)

We cannot go back 35 to 40 years in time to witness weekly dances in small New England towns, although we might like to. But Dudley Laufman was there, and so was his tape recorder. This privately produced tape gives glimpses of dance music and calling in two localities as well as some numbers by the Nelson Square Dance Orchestra and the Haltone Four, two groups that included respected New England musicians of the 1950s. If one can look past the primitive technical quality of the recordings, there is some pretty good music here, and it is interesting to hear the callers performing in context, including walk-throughs and announcements.

Tunes from Home
Grant Lamb, Vivian and Phillip Wiliams, Richard
    Marvin
Voyager VRLP 312-S; LP; (1974)

Fine fiddling by veteran musician Grant Lamb with capable backup. The album is presented as a sampler with 20 short cuts, typically 2 to 3×64, making it more useful as a source of tunes than as a danceable record. Tempos run from 104 to 128 on the reels and jigs (there are also two waltzes, a two-step, and a special dance in which two-step and waltz music alternate with each other).

Vic Kibler: Adirondack Fiddler
Vic and Paul Kibler, Paul Van Arsdale, George
    Ward
Sampler Records 8914; Cassette; (1992)

Unlike some "tradition-bearers" who have been recorded recently, Vic Kibler (born 1919) seems to have been caught while still in his prime. The tape offers 31 tracks of attractively played fiddle tunes, many of which would be fine for dancing if they were not so short (2 to 4×64). Short biographical information on all four musicians is included, and an accompanying book edited by Thomas Bohrer is available with additional information and tune transcriptions (see Annotated Bibliography).

**The Village Green: Dance Music of Old Sturbridge
    Village**
M. Roberts, S. Astrausky, A. Bradbury, B. Foulke,

J. Schwab, J. O'Brien, W. Buckingham, P. Stevens
North Star NS 0038; Cassette; (ca. 1990?)

A program with 14 cuts of dance tunes played in what appear to be nineteenth century–inspired arrangements, of which only 3 or 4 may possibly be useful for contemporary dancing. Also includes 2 waltzes and several well known dance tunes arranged as ad lib instrumental airs.

NORTHERN STYLE, WITH CALLS

Mainly for dancing

Canadian Jigs, Reels, Waltzes: Complete Square Dances with Calls
Unidentified caller and musicians
Heritage Music Sales/Alldisc CAS 20-009; Cassette; (1988)

Apparently a reissue of an LP, this album offers six complete, called square dances—all well known traditional figures—and 11 tracks of instrumental music. The instrumentals, which include two waltzes, a schottische, and a selection of reels and jigs, feature good drive and some nice fiddling, actually better than that on the called tracks. Unfortunately, most of them are short, typically 4 or 5×64, but the tempos are appropriate, ranging from 124 to 132. No dance descriptions are included.

Kitchen Junket: Traditional New England Square Dances and Music
Yankee Ingenuity/calls: Tony Parkes
Fretless FR 200B; LP (1977)

The called version of FR 200 is a rare animal: an album of contemporary New England style squares with calls, and an excellent one at that. Tony Parkes calls the ten dances clearly and well, and the music is just right. One problem with called records is that the dancers soon learn all the sequences by heart. As a partial antidote, Parkes has seen to it that no two of the 30 intros, breaks, and endings are alike. The dances range in difficulty from easy to intermediate and are described concisely but clearly on the record jacket; a waltz and a polka round out the program. Recently re-released as a double length cassette tape with the non-called version (FR 200A) on the other side. Unfortunately, the printed dance descriptions are no longer included.

Let's Square Dance, vol. 1–5
Dick Kraus (caller) and unidentified musicians
RCA DEM 1-0081, 0082, 0083, 0084, 0085, 10″ LPs; (ca. 1955?)

A graduated series of records intended for school use and based on Kraus's book, *Square Dances of Today and How to Teach and Call Them* (see Annotated Bibliography). Each record contains nine cuts, eight called and one instrumental, and is accompanied by a booklet with clear dance descriptions. Most of the dances are squares, with occasional mixers, play parties, and a single contra thrown in. Kraus calls well and clearly, with good timing; the music is typical of the period—more studio than authentic folk—but lively, featuring fiddle, accordion, tenor banjo, piano and bass. Tempos are around 122 throughout the series, except for volume 2, which is played at 128.

Modern Style Contra Dance Party
Scott Ludwig & New England Express/calls: Dick Leger
TNT, no number; LP; (1985?)

Eight of Roger Whynot's contras, called by Dick Leger, who also gives an oral walk-through before each dance. Leger calls clearly, but the tempo of 130 would generally be considered too fast for comfortable contra dancing. This is probably because the music was taken from existing TNT records for modern Western square dancing, so both the tempo, style (pure pop) and instrumentation are typical of that genre. The dances are good, but most of them do include modern Western style movements not normally used by traditional style contra dancers. Five are double progression dances. An accompanying booklet has dance descriptions, calls, and teaching tips.

Saturday Night Square Dance
Fred Townsend (caller) and The Backwoodsmen
Oak C-104; Cassette; (1982)

Ten traditional square dances with calls, in typical Canadian style. The music is well played and similar in style to the recordings of Canadian fiddler par excellence Don Messer, and the calling is reminiscent of Roy Clifton's—clear, with quite a bit of patter. This cassette is presumably a re-release of an

LP, and there probably was a booklet included originally with dance descriptions, but none seems to be available now. Most of the dances are well known figures, but at least one is difficult to decipher without an explanation. On another cut, the figure called is not the one listed on the insert. Timing in a few places seems doubtful.

Smoke on the Water: Square Dance Classics
Peter Barnes, Steve Hickman, Bill Tomczak/
    calls: Bob Dalsemer
Traditional Caller Productions TC 123; Cassette;
    (ca. 1988)

Spirited arrangements of ten transitional style 1950s singing calls well within the reach of contemporary traditional style dancers. The music is arranged for fiddle, clarinet, harmonica, and piano and is played with authority and verve by three of the country's top dance musicians. Dalsemer's singing calls fit perfectly into the musical tapestry, providing entertainment that dancers never seem to tire of, as well as an admirable model for those wanting to fit their own calling to the uncalled version of the tape (Traditional Caller Productions TC 124). An accompanying booklet by Dalsemer with dance descriptions and tunes is available (see Annotated Bibliography).

The Square Dance Album with Calls
Graham and Eleanor Townsend/calls: Murray
    Fraser and Murray Smith
Rodeo/Banff SBS-5500; LP; (1982)

Solid, inviting dance music consisting mostly of traditional jigs and reels, with good calling. Includes the Waltz Quadrille and 11 other squares, including a number of well known traditional figures and a few more modern routines that are a little more challenging. The album does not seem to include any dance descriptions; without them, some of the dances will be difficult to interpret, especially for beginners. Tempos from 116 to 128, lengths appropriate to the dances, from 6 to 11 × 64. Timing seems to be okay for the most part.

Square Dances with Oral Instruction and Calls,
    Albums 1–4
The Top Hands/calls: Ed Durlacher
Educational Activities Honor Your Partner HYR-1
    to HYR-4; LP; (1965/1975)

This set, intended for the education and recreation market, offers five to six dances per record with complete oral talk-throughs for each dance and then the dance itself with calls and music. The record

jackets include written descriptions of the dance figures, as well as glossaries of the relevant terms for each record. Unfortunately, there are more than a few errors and omissions in the written material, although an alert listener will find the correct information in the talk-throughs in some cases. The music is pleasant, and Durlacher's calling is crystal clear—however, some may find his style and diction dated.

Viellée Québecoise
Les Mauzdits Français/calls: Francine Reeves
Arche et Ciel AEC 87002; LP; (1981)

An album of French-Canadian dance music produced in France. Four of the eight cuts are squares called in French by Francine Reeves of Québec. A booklet with detailed explanations in French is included and has suggested dances for three of the non-called cuts as well. The music on the latter tracks is irregular and would therefore be difficult to use for standard American squares and contras—unfortunately, because it is well played.

When the Work's All Done: A Square Dance Party
    for Beginners & Old Hands
Peter Barnes, Steve Hickman, Jack O'Connor, Bill
    Tomczak/calls: Bob Dalsemer
Traditional Caller Productions TC 125; Cassette;
    (ca. 1990)

The music from Traditional Caller Productions tape TC 126 is here complemented by Bob Dalsemer's calls for one mixer and nine traditional squares, evenly divided between singing calls and patter calls. Dalsemer's pleasant voice, clear calling, and musicality make this an attractive tape for groups that want pre-recorded calls, or for callers looking for role models. An accompanying booklet by Dalsemer is available with dance descriptions and tunes (see Annotated Bibliography).

For dancing and listening

Ernie Levesque Calls Canadian Square Dances
The Canadian Twin Fiddlers & The Brisson Bros.
    Band/calls: Ernie Levesque
Rodeo/Banff Records RBS 1274; LP; (1967)

Six complete square dances with calls. Levesque has a unique and personal style of calling; unfortunately his diction is not always very clear, and as far as I am able to tell, no written directions for the dances are included with the record, making some of them difficult to interpret. Music is typical

Canadian square dance music at tempos ranging from 120 to 128.

Ralph Page Calls Contras and Squares
Ralph Page (caller) and various musicians
RPMC 1; Cassette; (1989)

This tape was put together from records and, primarily, private recordings made at dance camps, as a sample of Ralph Page's calling style. Three contras and four squares are offered in their entirety; thus the tape can be danced to, although its main use will probably be as an object of study. Tempos range mostly from 116 to 120, with one cut 132. Lengths mostly from 6 to 10 × 64, with one contra 14 times through.

Square Dances with Calls
Roy Clifton (caller) and unidentified musicians
Folkways FW 8825; LP; (1959)

Twelve traditional square dances from Southeastern Canada, similar in style to the old time repertoire of the Great Lakes area in the United States. The music is typical of the 1950s, with fiddle, accordion, guitar, bass, drums and woodblock, and tempos of 120 to 128. Clifton's calls are rhythmic and well phrased; the accompanying booklet (see Annotated Bibliography) mentions that he had some problems with timing at the recording session because no dancers were present, and in fact, some of the dances would be impossible to execute as called.

Mainly for listening

Shadrack's Delight and Other Dances
Tony Parkes (caller) and various musicians
Hands Four Productions, no number; Cassette; (1988)

This unusual tape provides an opportunity to hear an expert New England style caller and study the wording, timing and phrasing of his calls, as Parkes calls each of the 43 dances in his book, *Shadrack's Delight* (see Annotated Bibliography), twice through. Two of the squares are called in their entirety to give examples of intros, breaks, and endings.

SOUTHERN STYLE, INSTRUMENTAL

Mainly for dancing

Appalachia
The Tennessee Mountain Cloggers
Ralph's Records NR 13537; LP; (ca. 1982?)

Six instrumentals, generally of a disappointing quality. Heavy-handed drums dominate the rhythm section, and the fiddling is surprisingly poor. Bluegrass banjo, electric bass, and on some cuts, guitar and pedal steel, fill out the band. One track is a waltz and one a rendition of the showpiece "Listen to the Mockingbird" that starts out very slowly and then shifts to normal dance tempo. The two fiddle tunes "Old Joe Clarke" and "Sally Goodin," are played 12 and 17 × 64, respectively, at 136 and would be good for dancing if the playing were better. "Beaumont Rag" and the march-like "Washington and Lee Swing" are a little more appealing. Each is played 6 × 64 at tempos of 130 and 136, respectively.

Big Circle Mountain Dance Music for Dancing, Clogging and Just Plain Fun
The Stoney Creek Boys
Folkraft LP-36; LP; (1972)

Bluegrass music primarily intended for big set dancing and clogging. Tempos of about 140, with Orange Blossom Special at 150 for fast clogging. There are two medleys of about 12 minutes each, one tracks that runs 7¾ × 64 beats, and one that is 7 × 80 and therefore best suited to unphrased dances or clogging. A short oral introduction gives some orientation and an example of big set calling by Glenn Bannerman. An accompanying booklet with suggestions for big set figures is unfortunately marred in several places by misprints that change the meaning of the text.

Clog Dancer's Choice
Bob Dalsemer, Jim Bienemann
Bob Dalsemer, no number; Cassette; (1982)

Privately produced cassette intended mainly as a practice tape for beginning cloggers. The ten cuts of mostly well known traditional fiddle tunes start at a tempo of 100 bpm and rise gradually to 132; best played are the faster cuts. Lengths are on the short side, ranging from 3 to 7 × 64.

Clog-In Lessons
Beverly Cotten, Clay Buckner, Doug Dorschug,
  Tommy Thompson, and various guest musicians
Flying Fish FF 237; LP; (1981)

This is one of the best instructional records that has been made for teaching clogging. Cotten goes through numerous steps spanning a considerable range of difficulty, using excellent verbal explanations as well as "sound-outs" to fiddle music played slowly enough that the learner actually has a chance of following it. The accompanying instruction booklet with detailed pictures is also a help, but most people will probably still need a living model to emulate at first—or a good videotape, of which several are now available. Side two of the record presents a variety of up-to-tempo instrumentals in old-timey, blues, and Irish styles, some with and some without clogging, giving a good idea of the symbiosis between step dancing and music.

Clogging Favorites of Ben Smathers and the Stony Mountain Cloggers
Buddy Spicher, Billy Grammer, Buck White, Roy
  Husky, Jr., Buddy Harmon
Door Knob Records DKLPS87-1014; LP; (1987)

Six relatively short tracks on side one and two long ones (18 × 64 and 10½ × 64) on side two. The music is somewhere between country western and bluegrass, leaning toward the former, with drums and piano playing a prominent role. Tempos range from 120 to 144, and several of the cuts include singing. Even the long tracks on side two will therefore probably be found more useful for clogging than for square dancing.

Country Tance I
L. Koutný, F. Kacafírek, R. Tomíček, R.
  Křemenák, J. Klocperk, J. Hořejš, Z. Vič, R.
  Bardon
Dvorana, no number; Cassette; (1992)

This tape, produced in Prague by dance organizer Jasan Bonuš, offers eight cuts of traditional American dance tunes, arranged country western style. Instrumentation includes bluegrass banjo, harmonica, capable fiddle, but also a very prominent synthesizer, electric guitar, electric bass, and drums, making for a somewhat heavy-handed rhythm section. The tunes are arranged for dancing and are mostly 7 × 64 beats at tempos of 132 to 136. Also included are a long waltz and a 16 × 64 count medley of "Comin' Round the Mountain," "Red River Valley," "Battle Hymn of the Republic" and "Marching Through Georgia." An accompanying

booklet of dance descriptions is available in Czech or English.

Country Tance II
Nota Bene
Dvorana, no number; Cassette; (1993)

Recorded by a different band than the one used for *Country Tance I*, this is a very attractive package of solid bluegrass music, sensibly arranged for dancing. Instrumentation includes fiddle, banjo, mandolin, harmonica, electric bass, and an occasional guitar solo (if the guitar is present in the rhythm section, it is lost in the mix). The playing is impressive, with solid rhythm and plenty of variation in the solo work. Most of the selections are well known fiddle tunes. Tempos from 128 to 138 and lengths from 7 to 9 × 64, except for "Levi Jackson Rag," which is played the standard five times through, and a nice arrangement of "Boil the Cabbage Down" played 10 × 96 at about 160 bpm. An accompanying booklet of dance descriptions is available in Czech or English.

Dance Music Square and Clog, Without Calls
The Midnight Plowboys/The Marc Pruett Band
Skyline Records SR 007; LP; (1981)

This album of exciting bluegrass style dance music contains only three tracks. "Cacklin' Hen" is an energetic eight-minute-long cut played at 156 bpm. The tempo and rhythmic irregularities make it most suitable for clogging routines or for fast, unphrased dancing like the big set. "Under the Double Eagle" is about 12 minutes long at 142 bpm, and the medley on side two is a full 20 minutes long—undoubtedly the longest single cut of American country dance music ever recorded—with a tempo of 140 to 148. The latter two are fine for big set dancing, and are also good for squares if the tempo is reduced a little.

Dances from Appalachia
Lewis Lamb and the McLain Family Band
Berea College Christmas Country Dance School, no
  number; LP; (1976)

Of the five tracks of bluegrass on this album, three are medleys: one is about 39 × 64 beats at a tempo of 140 and is well suited for big set dancing or other long dances, such as the Virginia Reel. A second is about 9½ minutes long at 152 bpm and a little sparse in its instrumentation. Finally, there is a useful 14-minute-long medley of march-like tunes played at a comfortable tempo of about 120. The remaining cuts are a good performance of "Beaumont Rag" (the tune associated with Balance the

Star), played 8×64 at 126; and the music for a Danish folk dance, Seven Jumps. A folder is included with short dance descriptions for the big set, running set, Balance the Star, Seven Jumps, Maggie Mixer, and a grand march sequence called Follow the Leader.

Dances from Appalachia 2
Lewis and Donna Lamb, Al White, Raymond W. McLain & David Crandall
Berea College Christmas Country Dance School TR16-BC00802; LP; (1985)

Southern dance music at reasonable tempos. The style is bluegrass and most of the tunes are traditional, but four were composed by fiddler Lewis Lamb in traditional style. The first cut on side one is a good long medley of fiddle tunes played 17×64 at about 130 bpm (too fast for contra dancing, so it is unfortunate that this is erroneously suggested on the jacket). The cut titled "Kentucky Set Running" is a 12×64 beat, ca. 140 bpm medley of four fiddle tunes that in one way or another are irregular—useful for Southern style dancing, but not phrased dances. Four other cuts are played at around 120 bpm and are usable for a variety of dances. An accompanying booklet of dance descriptions includes interesting material.

Dancing Bow and Singing Strings
Tracy Schwarz and Tracy's Family Band with Earl Yeager and Dick Staber
Folkways FTS-6524; LP; (1979)

One purpose of this record was to provide music for clogging practice, so the tunes start at a tempo of 116 and gradually rise to about 144. All cuts are at least 7×64 beats, most more. "Cindy" is irregular in structure; "Sally Ann" is played AAB, which makes it a good choice for certain dances. The fiddling is in a style that probably should be characterized as old-timey—straight-ahead, but clean and with lots of drive and the proper "lift" to move the dancers' feet—and the backup is in bluegrass style. The album is now available as a cassette tape through Smithsonian/Folkways.

Goin' to Town! Old-Time Tunes for Contras and Squares
Eloise Clark, John Bealle, Jim Johnson
Self-produced, no number; Cassette; (1990)

Fourteen cuts of old-timey music played on fiddle, banjo and guitar, including two waltzes. Tempos (124-136) and lengths (mostly 6 to 10×64) are suitable for dancing, but a bass would have

worked wonders on the overall sound, as would a little more attention to tone and intonation on the part of the fiddler. Includes copious notes on the individual tunes.

Jump Fingers! And Other Old Time Dance Tunes
Various old time dance bands from Missouri
Childgrove Country Dancers, no number; Cassette; (1993)

The first two tracks on this tape are a little disappointing, but after that the album takes off with a selection of dance tunes played mostly in old time Southern string band style at tempos and lengths appropriate for dancing. Nine different bands are represented on the 12 tracks, although several of the musicians participate in more than one group, a common occurrence in traditional dance and music communities. Cuts are long, ranging from 11 to 19×64 for the reels (there are also two waltzes), and most of the music is played with an absolute minimum of arrangement. One or two cuts are marred by background noise (everything was recorded live), and one is a called contra dance. Tempos range from 112 to 140.

Living Black and White
The Heartbeats
Marimac 9040; Cassette; (1991)

This four-woman band proves that old-time string band music does not have to be scratchy and out of tune. The tape's 14 cuts include eight tracks of superb, fluid dance music with lots of drive and lift. Two other cuts would be fine for dancing but are a little short at 5×64, and the last four are too slow (84 and 100 bpm, respectively) or too irregular for most uses. Note that a couple of the tunes have 80 or 96 counts, i.e., 5 or 6×16, which I consider danceable when used in the proper context. What may be more difficult are the tunes with irregular numbers of beats in the individual parts.

McLain Family Band Country Dance Album (Dances from Appalachia 3)
The McLain Family Band
Country Life Records CLR-16; LP; (1986)

Several of the tunes on this album were recorded specifically for dances that are described in the accompanying folder. The band plays with virtuosity in bluegrass style, with lots of drive and variation. "Boil Them Cabbage Down" is a tour de force of an old warhorse, but at a tempo of 152, it has to be slowed down considerably to be danceable. Similarly, the long "Hoedown" medley, which lasts almost ten minutes, is quite useful for long squares and the like, provided the tempo of about 144 is reduced. "Fair Jenny" has the character of an English country dance, and some numbers, such as "Big Hill," are so jazzy in feel that their use for country dancing may be questionable. "Goin' to Boston" is an a capella rendition of a play party song, an unusual find on a dance record.

Mountain Dance Music Comes Alive: Clogging and Smooth Dance Music
The Stoney Creek Boys
Educational Activities AR 82; LP; (1978)

For those who can turn down the speed of 144 somewhat, the tunes on this record provide solid bluegrass music for squares and big set dancing. Aside from the first cut, a big set sequence called by Glenn Bannerman, all the tunes are instrumental. "Ragtime Annie" is played 9×64 beats, and the remaining tunes are from 11 to 13×64, giving good flexibility for long squares or extra improvisation. Although the record implies that some of the tunes are for clogging and others for smooth dancing, they can all be used for both. An accompanying booklet explains the principles of big set dancing and describes a number of figures. The basic steps of clogging are also described, but not in sufficient detail to be of use to someone who doesn't already clog.

Music for Clogging
Jerry Lundy, Carl and Judy Pagter, Roger Williams, Bob White, Larry Nager
Papa Lou Records PL 210; LP; (1982)

Southern style music appropriate for both clogging and square dancing. Most of the banjo work is frailing, rather than three-finger picking, but the total band sound is bluegrass. Of the ten cuts, only a couple are too irregular or special to be used for squares. The remaining eight range in tempo from 124 to 146, and in length from 7 to 10×64, with one cut 5×64.

Old Time Music Dance Party
A. Robic and the Exertions (Mike Seeger, Bruce Molsky, Paul Brown, Chester McMillian, Dan Newhall)
Flying Fish FF 415; LP; (1987)

Well played old-timey music for clogging and square dancing, with a lot of drive. Of the seven cuts, one is a waltz and the remaining six are long medleys of old time southern fiddle tunes, mostly ones outside the most tried and true repertoire.

Only one track is composed of tunes so crooked that they would be difficult to use for squares. The others include both 64-count, 48-count, and 32-count tunes in various combinations, with each cut having the equivalent of from 13 to $16\frac{1}{2} \times 64$. These are fine—even preferable—for squares that do not have to be strictly phrased. Tempos from 132 to 144.

Traditional American Dance Music, Tape #2
High Strung String Band and Rick Meyers
Rick Meyers RM-102; Cassette; (1983)

Produced in conjunction with Meyers' *Traditional American Dance Book* (see Annotated Bibliography). Includes 13 instrumentals of varying lengths, sound-outs of some clogging steps, and a little "hambone" (a form of rhythmic music-making using one's own body as the instrument). Music is old-time Southern style, played at reasonable tempos of (mostly) about 120 to 126 and in appropriately long arrangements. The musicianship is a little disappointing on some cuts, but quite good on others.

Traditional Southern Appalachian Square Dance Music
The Asheville Bluegrass Band
No label, RSR-514; LP; (1977)

The four cuts on this album are fast in tempo; 138, 144, 150 and 150, respectively. They are also long, about ten minutes each. For those who can reduce the tempo, the music is quite useful for Southern style squares; otherwise, only for big set or clogging. The playing style is bluegrass and the quality good. The B part of "Liza Jane" includes two silent 4-count breaks, intended to let the dancers' (cloggers') own rhythm come forth.

For dancing and listening

America's Favorite Square Dances Without Calls
Cecil Brower and His Square Dance Fiddlers
Cumberland SRC 69509; LP; (ca. 1960?)

The tunes on this commercially produced record are traditional fiddle tunes, and the fiddling and bluegrass banjo playing is fine, but personally I find the extremely heavy drum rhythm, which nearly drowns out the melodies, irritating. Tempos are high—136 to 156—and the length of the cuts is only 5 to 6×64 beats, making it difficult to find usable tracks.

Fine Dining
Boiled Buzzards
Marimac 9043; Cassette; (1991)

Instead of the traditional old-time combination of fiddle and banjo, the Boiled Buzzards use harmonica and banjo, with guitar and bass backing up. The arrangements are very straightforward, but the music swings and has plenty of drive for dancing. The tape's 20 tracks include two songs, a waltz, and a banjo solo; unfortunately, only five of the remaining 16 cuts are played more than 5×64. Tempos run from 120 to 132.

Square Dances
Tommy Jackson (fiddle) with unidentified band
Mode Disques MDD 9278; LP; (ca. 1960?)

Nice Southern style fiddle and mandolin, with additional backup on guitar and bass, and electric guitar solos on a few tunes. The 12 tracks include a rag, a schottische, a Varsouvianna, and a fine rendition of the classic fiddle showpiece "Orange Blossom Special"; the rest of the cuts are Southern fiddle tunes. Most would be fine for dancing if they were not so short, mostly 5 to 6×64, with a few only 3½ or 4 times through.

Square Dances Without Calls
Tommy Jackson (fiddle) with unidentified band
MCA 162 (previously Decca DL7-8950; LP; originally ca. 1959)

This commercial release seems to have been intended as a combination of danceable music and listening music with popular fiddler Tommy Jackson. Of the 12 tunes, only four are played 8×64 beats or more, one 6×64, and the rest vary, down to $3½ \times 64$. The tempos are appropriate — from 120 to 132 — and Jackson's fiddling is excellent. The rest of the band consists of a good bluegrass banjo player, electric guitar, and a drummer who is a little too obtrusive for my taste.

Winter Moon
Vivian and Phil Williams, Harley Bray
Voyager VRCS 336; Cassette; (1989)

The classic Southern combination of fiddle and banjo is featured here with veteran musicians Vivian Williams (fiddle) and Harley Bray (banjo) in 21 well crafted performances. Unfortunately, only one cut is really long enough (6×64) and at the same time fast enough (120) for dancing, although seven other tracks that are played 5×64 may be useful for mixers and other short dances. Considering that the arrangements are pretty straightforward, and how little good bluegrass has been recorded with dancing in mind, I wish Williams and Bray had opted for somewhat fewer tunes and correspondingly longer cuts.

Mainly for listening

Country Dance Music
Washboard Band (Pete Seeger, Sonny Terry, Brownie McGhee, William Edward Cook, Frank Robertson)
Folkways FA 2201; 10″ LP; (1963)

In spite of the title and accompanying texts, this record is not suitable for dancing. The style of playing is bluesy and does not provide the rhythmic emphasis needed for dancing; several of the tunes are irregular; and others are played at breakneck speed. Technically, the recording is also poor, with a fluctuating sound level and unclear rhythm section.

The Falls of Richmond
Jim Taylor, Sheila Barnhill, Bruce Green, Tom Draughon, Tim Abel, Pat Sky
Pearl Mae Music 001B; Cassette; (1989)

Traditional music, mostly dance tunes, as they might have been played in army camps during the Civil War. Prominently features Jim Taylor's excellent hammered dulcimer and some fine clawhammer banjo playing by Sheila Barnhill. Extensive liner notes on the musical context of the times and on the origins and stories connected with the individual tunes. Only one cut is a possible candidate for dancing, but the tape is an excellent listening experience.

Little Rose Is Gone
Jim Taylor, Sheila Barnhill, Bruce Green, Tom Draughon
Pearl Mae Music 002CW; Cassette; (1991)

Similar in concept and execution to Taylor, et al.'s 1989 tape, *The Falls of Richmond*. Of the 13 cuts, only two are possible candidates for dancing, both reels played 6×64 at 132 bpm. Detailed and fascinating notes help round out this picture of traditional dance music of the Civil War era.

Moving Clouds
Bo Bradham and Peter Jung
Bo Bradham BB 001; Cassette; (1991)

Nice listening music; unfortunately most of the 13 cuts are too short to be usable for dancing — typically 4×64 — and some contain irregularities of tune or arrangement. Included are a waltz, two rags, a medley of solo fiddle pieces, and a medley in which a schottische is followed by two reels, as well as several cuts of straight reels. To my ear, Bradham's fiddling is much better on this tape than on his 1989 release, *The Belle of Brattleboro,* where he is almost overshadowed by Mary Cay Brass's fine piano.

The Poodles
The Poodles
Self-produced, no number; Cassette; (1986)

Although this tape was not produced for dancing, it is a good place to hear some great old-timey dance fiddling, ably backed on guitar and bass for a good, solid sound. Five of the 13 cuts fit into this category, but unfortunately only one is usable in practice at 6×64 and 132 bpm. The others are irregular tunes or tunes in medleys with songs.

Remembering
Bob Simmons, Zeke Wilson, Tex Freeland, Joe
  Yarborough
Voyager VRCS 334; Cassette; (1987)

Although fiddler Bob Simmons was 72 when this tape was recorded, and his tone probably was cleaner in his younger days, the music on these 19 tracks still reveals an impressive command, fluidity, and range of ornamental variation that makes it a worthwhile object of study for those interested in bluegrass and western swing tunes for dancing. Lengths are short, typically about four times through, and tempos vary—one of Simmons' specialties is fiddle rags, some of which are of the slow, "laid back" variety and others up-tempo. The

remaining fiddle tunes are mostly played at about 126 to 132 bpm.

Through the Ears
Green Grass Cloggers
Rounder ROU-0228; Cassette; (ca. 1985?)

This cassette gives an idea on tape of what a Green Grass Cloggers concert appearance might be like. About half of the 16 cuts are songs; most of the rest are accompanied or unaccompanied clogging numbers, but there are also two instrumentals. Spirited, well played old-timey music using various combinations of fiddle, guitar, clawhammer banjo and in one case, dobro.

Timepieces: Vintage Originals by Larry Edelman
L. Edelman, C.W. Abbott, L. Andres, S. Bradley,
  G. Canote, J. Canote, L.E. McCullough and
  various guests
D&R 128; Cassette; (1988)

As implied by the subtitle, these are original tunes composed by Edelman in traditional style. Most of them fit so seamlessly into the traditional pattern that they would immediately be accepted as "authentic." Edelman, an excellent mandolin player, has surrounded himself with a group of equally superb musicians, making the tape a good source of inspiration although most of the arrangements are not directly danceable. The 14 cuts include two waltz sets, a jig set, and a selection of other rhythms—reel, two-step, polka, and several rags.

SOUTHERN STYLE, WITH CALLS

Mainly for dancing

Appalachian Clog Dancing and Big Circle Mountain Square Dancing
Blackhawk Bluegrass Band/calls and instruction:
  Glenn Bannerman
Educational Activities AR 53; LP; (1974)

Side one contains clogging instruction, which unfortunately is of limited value: the explanations are not clear enough and the cuts with practice music are much too fast for beginners (about 140 bpm). Side two fares better, with instructions and calls for two big set dances using simple figures (Right Hand Star and Georgia Rang Tang), also played at about 140 bpm. Good bluegrass music and clear and lively calling. A descriptive booklet ac-

companies the record, but is too concise to be of much help.

Big Circle Mountain Square Dancing with Calls and Instructions
Blackhawk Bluegrass Band/calls: Glenn Bannerman
Educational Activities AR 52; LP; (1974)

Glenn Bannerman talks through some simple big circle and small circle figures and then calls them to good music—standard Southern fiddle tunes—by the Blackhawk Bluegrass Band. Between the talk-throughs and the written explanations on the record jacket, the dance descriptions are fairly clear, but a few diagrams or drawings would have been a help. Small circle figures covered are Right Hand Star, Birdie in the Cage, Duck for the Oyster, and Lady 'Round the Lady and the Gent Also. Tempos about 132 throughout.

Friday Night at the Barn: American Novelty and Big Circle Mountain Dance Music

The Stoney Creek Boys/calls: Glenn Bannerman
Educational Activities AR81; LP; (1978)

A combination of called big set sequences and non-called novelty dances (solo, couple or group dances choreographed to pop tunes). An accompanying booklet explains the dances, but it would have been nice to have an indication of the timing for the steps of the novelty dances. Nice bluegrass music at about 132 to 140 bpm for the big set dances, which introduce four small circle figures (Star Basket, Chase That Rabbit, Take a Little Peek, and Two Gents Elbow Swing) and are well and clearly called.

The Fundamentals of Square Dancing

Bob Ruff (caller) and unidentified musicians
Sets in Order American Square Dance Society LP
  6001; LP; (1967)

The first in a presumed series of albums for teaching modern Western style square dancing, this record has clear and detailed instructions on the jacket, including useful teaching tips. The first five of the 14 tracks can be characterized as exercises, although the calling and delivery are done in a way that makes them seem just as much like "real dances" as the remaining tracks. Only about 15 of the most basic calls are used, making the material accessible to traditional style dancers, although the music may not prove appealing to them, being mostly synthesizer-pop. Also note that the timing of the calls may deviate from traditional practice, being less phrased, and a few stylistic details such as handholds are different. Clear and pleasant calling by Bob Ruff.

It's Fun to Square Dance: A Wonderful Collection of Favorite Tunes with Calls

Cliffie Stone and His Orchestra/calls: Dave
  Rumbaugh
Capitol ST 1685; LP; (ca. 1960?)

Eight traditional squares plus the Virginia Reel, called clearly but in a sing-song manner that quickly becomes tiresome. The dances (including the breaks) become more complicated as the album progresses. Good fiddling with backup mostly in bluegrass style. Tempos are around 122 to 126 and the timing of the calls seems accurate. The album is supposed to include a descriptive booklet, but I have not been able to locate one.

It's Square Dance Time

Holler Hawkins and the Hayriders
Treasure TLP 825; LP; (1963?)

Nine called squares, including both simple figures and more challenging dances that make use of calls from the transitional period of the 1950s. The music is scratchy, while the calling is clear and well timed: the calls seem to have been dubbed over old 78 rpm records, with tempos for the most part around 120 to 128. Hawkins has a good voice, both on the patter calls and the three singing calls that are included. The tenth cut is instrumental music during which various dancers in the set are requested to try calling! There probably was some kind of booklet to accompany this record, but I haven't been able to locate one.

Learn Square Dancing with Ed Gilmore

Ed Gilmore (caller) and unidentified musicians
MCA-179 (formerly Decca DL7-9051); LP; (1980)

An instructional album, originally released around the late 1950s, in which Gilmore first talks through various square dance figures, starting at the very beginning, then drills them to calls without music, and finally calls practice dances to music. The stated goal is to teach new dancers enough to let them dance not only to this record, but to other modern square dance records of the time with calls. The original album included a booklet in which all the material was described, including a number of figures that are used in the dances on side two without oral explanation; this seems to have been eliminated in the reissue. The explanations and calls on the record are, however, very clear, documenting Gilmore's reputation as a master teacher and caller.

Modern Square Dances with Calls

Smoky Warren's Square Dancers/calls: Earl Bateman
Diplomat DS-2609; LP; (ca. 1960?)

Despite the title, these ten called squares are mostly well known traditional figures. And they are danced to traditional fiddle tunes and standard popular songs, although all the tunes are given other names on the album. The music, played bluegrass style, is good, and Bateman's voice is clear, if a little harsh. Tempos mostly around 126, somewhat slower on the first few dances. As far as I know, no descriptive booklet was provided with this record.

Potluck and Dance Tonite

Gypsy Gyppo String Band, Arm & Hammer String
  Band, Tracy Schwarz and band/calls: Sandy Bradley
Fretless FR 202; LP; (1979)

Seven called squares, three songs, and an instrumental. Music is old-time Southern string band style, and most of the dances are also from the Southern tradition. The accompanying booklet makes it clear why Sandy Bradley is such a popular caller—it was clearly written with a twinkle in her eye, and includes all the calls as well as explanations. Tempos run from about 126 to 134; the recording was made with dancers present, so the timing of the calls should be correct. Recently re-released on a double length cassette with FR 201, *Maritime Dance Party*, on the other side.

Square Dance
The Sunset Hoedowners with unidentified caller
Sunset SUS-5152; LP; (ca. 1960?)

Five called squares and five instrumentals. Most of the dances are easy visiting couple figures that are called only twice through instead of the normal four times, presumably due to space limitations; some of the timing seems a little off. Instrumentation is fiddle and five-string banjo plus electric guitar, tenor banjo, Hammond organ, and drums. The caller is clear but with a strange, almost condescending intonation at times. Most of the instruments are played 4 or 5×64, one 6×64. Does not seem to have included any booklet.

Square Dance Calls
Pleasant Valley Boys/calls: Carson Robison and
   Lawrence V. Loy
Metro M-504; LP; (ca. 1960?)

Eleven called squares, mostly singing calls, and one instrumental. Several of the figures incorporate couple dances (waltz, polka) or novelty dance routines. Music is on the pop side, tempos about 116 to 120. The calling is clear, but the voice (or voices—I can't distinguish them if there are two, as announced on the jacket) a little grating. Does not seem to have included any dance descriptions.

Square Dance Favorites with Calls
Juggernaut String Band, including Peter Taney,
   who calls
Nesak International 19804-2; CD; (1992)

Called versions of seven traditional squares, mostly old standbys, as well as a mixer (Pattycake Polka), the couple dance Cotton-Eyed Joe, and the Virginia Reel. The music is nice and has a bluegrass sound, even though the banjo is played clawhammer style. Dance descriptions are printed on the album insert, and Taney includes occasional explanatory comments in his calls. Most of the

choreography is problem-free, although there are some cases where the flow could be better. Taney's timing and diction are fine, but he has a habit of drawing out the last word of each call, which may prove irritating in the long run. My favorite is his swinging rendition of "Bill Bailey" as a singing call.

Square Dance Hootenanny
Buddy Durham and band/Stony Mountain Cloggers/calls: Paul Jackson
Columbia CL 2217; LP; (ca. 1960?)

Four called Southern style squares—three easy visiting couple dances and the ever-popular Texas Star—plus a few instrumentals. The music is bluegrass fiddle with acoustic backup, well played at a tempo of about 138 all the way through. What at first hearing appears to be static is actually a group of cloggers who apparently danced along during the recording session. It is not clear whether an instructional booklet accompanied the album, but it would be a help to have one in order to interpret the local dosido figure, etc.

Square Dance Party with Calls and Instructions
"Mac" Gant (caller) and His Tennessee Dew Drops
Somerset P-19000; LP; (ca. 1963?)

Three called big set dances and one standard square (Texas Star), with talk-throughs of each group of figures first. The big set dances are done with small circle figures only, including Hands Across, Cage the Bird, Duck for the Oyster, Lady 'Round the Lady, and a couple more. The new figures are gradually worked into the dance sequences, which are long: 4:25, 7:48 and 7:48 at tempos of 128 to 132. The calling and instructions are clear—Gant has an amusing, "down home" style of presenting his material—and the music is good, solid bluegrass.

Square Dance Party with Don Durlacher
Don Durlacher (caller) and unidentified musicians
Gateway Records GSLP 8007; LP; (ca. 1970?)

Seven easy dances, including a couple of old standards (Birdie in the Cage, Uptown Downtown—here called Honeycomb) and other simple figures. Music has a 1950s sound, with accordion and tenor banjo, and tempos are relatively slow: 100–114. The calling and the written descriptions on the record jacket are both clear, but the caller's style may be found a little too "cute," and the frequent use of kissing figures and the like may make the material less appropriate for some groups than intended.

Square Dance Party with Ed Gilmore

Ed Gilmore (caller) and unidentified musicians
MCA-826 (formerly on Decca); LP; (1980)

This album was released at the same time as *Learn Square Dancing with Ed Gilmore*. It contains 12 called squares, evenly divided between patter calls and singing calls, with the singing calls slightly less demanding. Most of the dances are presented as set routines; most of them were devised by Gilmore, who was a good choreographer. There are a number of interesting figures here that would be an appropriate challenge for adventurous traditional style dancers, since most of the calls used are within their repertoire. However, the accompanying booklet, with the calls and explanations, will probably be a necessary help for any contemporary dancers in interpreting some of the figures.

Square Dance with Dick Meyers and the Country Cousins (Level 2)

Dick Meyers (caller) and the Country Cousins
Gateway Records GSLP 8005; LP; (ca. 1970?)

Five dances, including the Virginia Reel and four simple squares—two patter calls and two singing calls—are first talked through (detailed instructions are also on the record jacket) and then called to the music. Side two has the same music without calls. Calling and explanations are generally clear, although some items in the written descriptions may prove cryptic to a novice. The music is some of the worst I have ever heard, entirely synthetic sounding and irritating to the ear.

Square Dance with Dick Meyers and the Country Cousins (Level 3)

Dick Meyers (caller) and the Country Cousins
Gateway Records GSLP5-8006; Cassette; (ca. 1970?)

Dick Meyers gives good walk-throughs before each dance on this tape, with clear oral explanations of the figures, and his calling is also clear. The five dances are simple, including a couple of traditional standards (Sally Goodin, Dip and Dive), an easy visiting couple routine, and two simple quadrilles. The music, however, is unfortunate in the extreme, consisting mainly of electric guitar and a poorly played synthesizer, plus some banjo and fiddle. The calling and music sound as if they were on two different planets! Side two contains the same music without calls.

Square Dance with Lee Schmidt and the Mojave Round Up (Level 5)

Lee Schmidt (caller) and the Mojave Round Up
Gateway Records GSLP5-8009; Cassette; (ca. 1970?)

Five squares called in modern club style, but consisting of material that traditional style dancers easily could execute. Includes two singing calls, one patter call, and two simple hash calls, i.e., dances without a predictable pattern. Side two has the same music without calls. Although Mojave Round Up is credited as the band on this recording, there are clearly three different styles of music on the tape, which appear to be taken from existing recordings, or perhaps they were covered for this project by a studio band. Two cuts have a relatively traditional sound, with nice fiddling, while the others are more modern/pop. The tape is presumably a re-release of an LP, which probably had an explanatory booklet, but none seems to be included now.

Square Dance with Old Time Southern Dance Music

Bucksnort Barndance Band/calls: Michael Kemp
Sunny Mountain Records EB 1008; LP; (1978)

Four called dances—a big set sequence and three well known traditional squares—and four instrumental tracks. Music is old-time Southern string band style at tempos from 126 to 138 and lengths of 10 to 15 × 64 for the instrumentals. A fairly detailed booklet is included with dance descriptions, calls, and general advice. A few of the more advanced terms could be more clearly defined. The called cuts were recorded live with dancers, and most of the timing seems to be okay, but beginners may have a little difficulty understanding the caller because the calls are shouted rather than spoken.

Square Dances

Tommy Jackson and band/calls: T. Tommy
Dot DLP 25580; LP; (ca. 1960?)

Ten Southern style squares with calls, some easy and some more complicated. Good fiddling with acoustic backup. Tempos vary from about 114 to 150! The caller is clear but sometimes a condescending note seems to creep into his voice. Dance descriptions are virtually a necessity for this album, but I have been unable to discover whether they were originally included.

Square Dances

Lawrence V. Loy (caller) with Carson Robison and
His Pleasant Valley Boys/Floyd C. Woodhull
(caller) with Woodhull's Old Tyme Masters
RCA Victor LPM-1238; LP; (1956)

Side one has eight tracks, including a rather static instrumental of "The Irish Washerwoman" played 14 × 32 at 124, and seven simple squares called in patter/semi-singing style by Loy, whose voice is clear, but a little shrill. Side two has a usable instrumental march, "Blackberry Quadrille" (8 × 64, 126) and five called squares, most of which are simple singing calls. Some of the timing on a couple of these dances seem very unrealistic. The record jacket includes explanations of the basic movements used, but not of the individual dances, and several of the figures would probably be difficult for beginners to interpret from the calls alone.

Square Dances with Calls
Lee Bedford, Jr., and Bill Mooney (callers) and
    unidentified musicians
Imperial LP-12396; LP; (ca. 1960?)

Side one features Lee Bedford, Jr., with three patter calls and three singing calls. Both the music and calling have a Southern/Western feeling, and the dances are mostly simple, well known routines. There is a lot of echo in the mix, and the band sounds far away from the caller, almost as if it were packed in cotton. Side two has Bill Mooney as caller and apparently a different band. Mooney has a more affected style than Bedford, and the band is not as convincing either. Five of the dances on this side are patter calls, including some very simple figures and one considerably more complicated Texas square, The Spinning Wheel. The sixth dance is a waltz quadrille with sung calls. If there was an instructional booklet for this album, it has not been available to me.

Square Dances with Calls
The Liberty Square Dance Club with unidentified
    caller
Liberty LRP-3218; LP; (ca. 1960?)

Twelve patter-called squares to music that is on the borderline between bluegrass and country & western. The unidentified caller has a clear and pleasant voice and a rhythmic delivery, but is often distractingly out of phrase with the music. The dance figures are a combination of well known simple visiting couple dances and other simple figures (Texas Star, Divide the Ring, Forward Six and Back) and more advanced dances, several of which have Southwestern roots.

Swing Your Partner
Uncle Bill Wiley and His Tall Corn Boys
Manhattan MAN 518; LP; (ca. 1960?)

This album offers a caller with a clear, pleasant voice and some nice, traditional-sounding music that moves right along. Half of the 12 dances are patter calls, and half are singing calls. Most of the figures are simple, well known dances, but two are relatively complicated Texas figures—El Paso Star and The Spinning Wheel—and one dance is unclear without a written description (if there was a booklet with this album, I have not located it). Many of the dances are done only two times through instead of the usual four, but the main problem with this record is that the timing seems to be off in many places, which may make it difficult to execute the dances as called.

Traditional American Dance Music, Tape #1
High Strung String Band and Rick Meyers/calls:
    Rick Meyers
Rick Meyers RM-101; Cassette; (1983)

Produced in conjunction with Meyers' *Traditional American Dance Book* (see Annotated Bibliography).

Twelve cuts are called and twelve are not, including six singing squares that are offered in both called and uncalled versions. Music is old-time Southern style, played at reasonable tempos of (mostly) about 120 to 126 and in appropriately long arrangements. The dance material is on an easy level, being intended for school use in the lower grades; the musicianship is a little disappointing on some cuts, but good on others.

MIXED STYLES, INSTRUMENTAL

Mainly for dancing

Square Dance Tonight, vol. 1
Græshopperne/Betty Bakingplate and the Bull
    Mountain Bakers
Square Dance Partners 8701; LP; (1987)

Ten tracks of traditional music arranged for dancing, each side featuring a different band.

Græshopperne (The Grasshoppers) is a bluegrass band. Betty Bakingplate plays a mixed repertoire of New England/French-Canadian music and old-time Southern tunes, featuring a solid three-person fiddle section with spirited backup on clawhammer banjo, guitar, bass, and washboard. All cuts are 9 × 64 beats except Betty Bakingplate's "Bouchard No. 2," which is 8 × 64 (jacket mistakenly states 10 × 64).

Tempos on side one range from about 126 to 132, on side two mostly from 118 to 126.

Square Dance Tonight, vol. 2
La Bastringue/Meet the Beat Boys
Square Dance Partners 8702; LP; (1987)

Nine tracks of traditional music arranged for dancing, each side featuring a different band. La Bastringue plays solidly crafted French-Canadian music on fiddles, accordéon, guitar, piano, bass, and percussion. Tempos range from about 116 to 128, lengths are 9×64. Meet the Beat Boys is an oldtimey string band with fiddle, banjo, guitar and bass. Their cuts are also 9×64 beats, except "East Tennessee Blues" (7×64) and "Breakin' Up Christmas" (21×64). Tempos are 132 to 140.

Square Dance Tonight, vol. 3
American Cafe Orchestra/Backporch Bluegrass
Square Dance Partners 9001; Cassette; (1990)

Ten tracks of traditional music arranged for dancing, each side featuring a different band. American Cafe Orchestra is a Scandinavian-American band that on this recording includes well known American musicians Ruthie Dornfeld (fiddle) and John McGann (mandolin) as well as Morten Alfred on guitar and Anders Hoffset on bass. Their tight, energetic arrangements of Northern fiddle tunes use an unusual backup style reminiscent of Western swing. Lengths 8×64, except the more Southern style "Grey Eagle," which is 13×64; tempos about 120 bpm. Backporch Bluegrass offers a selection of fiddle tunes in standard bluegrass instrumentation at danceable tempos of 122 to 130 and lengths of 10×64.

Square Dance Tonight, vol. 4
The Poodles/Labradors
Square Dance Partners 9301; Cassette; (1993)

Ten tracks of traditional music arranged for dancing, each side featuring a different band. The Poodles is an American old-time string band consisting of two fiddles, guitar, and bass. Their high-energy, superbly danceable tunes are played 10×64 beats at tempos of about 126 bpm. Labradors is a Danish band featuring fiddle, accordéon, hammered dulcimer, clawhammer banjo, and piano. Here they play French-Canadian/New England tunes at a tempo of about 116 and lengths of 10×64.

For dancing and listening

Tripping Up Stairs
John Pranio, Jan Drechsler, Bob Mills

Barley Sheaf Productions BSP-102C; Cassette; (1986)

Includes four well played 6×64 or 7×64 medleys in old-timey style (with piano rhythm) that are well suited for dancing, at tempos of 122 to 128. The remaining seven cuts are in New England or Irish style but in non-danceable arrangements.

Uncle Gizmo
Uncle Gizmo
Black Socks Press 14; Cassette; (1992)

Eleven tracks of well played music with a slightly jazzy edge. Of the 17 tunes, nine were written by guitarist Larry Unger (in traditional styles), three by other named composers, and five are traditional. There are three waltzes and three or four other cuts that are danceable. Tempos on the latter run from 104 to 132 and lengths are $7\frac{1}{2}$ or 8×64 or the equivalent.

Mainly for listening

American Cafe Orchestra
American Cafe Orchestra
Folkmus 7013; Cassette; (1987)

Among the ten cuts are a few danceable high-energy reel medleys (5 to 9×64, tempos around 130), as well as three waltzes and two schottisches, but this tape is mostly intended for listening. Ruthie Dornfeld's fiddling is, as always, masterful and many-faceted.

Egyptian Dominoes
American Cafe Orchestra
Northeastern Records NR 5011-C; Cassette; (1992)

Eclectic interpretations of American and Scandinavian traditional dance tunes and a few other pieces. Sparkling instrumental work, but the arrangements preclude the use of more than one or two cuts for dancing.

Fiddle Fever
Fiddle Fever
Flying Fish FF 247; LP; (1981)

Superb double and triple fiddling and other nice arrangements of traditionally-based material, also influenced by jazz and swing. Three of the 12 cuts are straight enough to be danceable, but all are relatively short (5×64). Includes four tunes composed by members of the band.

Somewhere in Sweden
American Cafe Orchestra
DEC 1088; Cassette; (1988)

Although not intended for dancing, this tape offers some high quality fiddling of both Northern and Southern style dance tunes by Ruthie Dornfeld, including a couple of tracks that you may find long enough to use. Nice arrangements and variation of styles in an eclectic program with guitar, bass, and harmonica.

Waltz of the Wind
Fiddle Fever
Flying Fish FF 303; LP; (1984)

A mostly listening album with roots in traditional music, including dance tunes, plus jazz and swing. Twin and triple fiddles and excellent guitar and mandolin solos contribute sweet and sassy sounds that in a few cases may be danceable. Ten tracks, including Jay Ungar's now famous tune, "Ashokan Farewell," and three other tunes composed by members of the band.

MIXED STYLES, WITH CALLS

Mainly for dancing

Square and Contra Dances with Calls
Betty Bakingplate/Græshopperne/La Bastringue/
   Meet the Beat Boys. Calls: Margot Gunzenhauser.
Square Dance Partners 8703; EP; (1987)

Extended-play 33-rpm single with four called dances—two contras and two squares—of easy to intermediate difficulty. Dances are described in the present work, but the record also includes a 12-page booklet with full instructions. The music was selected from *Square Dance Tonight Vol. 1* and *Vol. 2* (Square Dance Partners 8701 and 8702, respectively), except the cut by La Bastringue, which has since been released as an instrumental on the tape *Keep on Swinging* (Anglo-American Dance Service C9202).

Square Dance Fest
Betty Bakingplate/La Bastringue/Backporch
   Bluegrass. Calls: Margot Gunzenhauser
Square Dance Partners 9101; Cassette; (1991)

Twelve relatively easy called dances in various formations, including two mixers, three progressive circles, two full set longways, two contras, and three squares. The dances are described in Gunzenhauser's book *Square Dancing at School/Country Dancing at School* (see Annotated Bibliography), but the tape is also accompanied by a 20-page booklet with full dance descriptions. Music was selected from the first three *Square Dance Tonight* albums (Square Dance Partners 8701, 8702 and 9001, respectively).

MUSIC FOR HERITAGE DANCES

American Country Dances of the Revolutionary Era, 1775-1795
J. Cohen, L. Farrar, B. Ferns, P. Garnick,
   P. Locklear, K. Keller, R. Sweet, W. Sweet &
   F. Van Cleef
Country Dance in Connecticut CDIC-1; LP; (1976)

Music for eight specific dances from Keller and Sweet's book, *A Choice Selection of American Country Dances of the Revolutionary Era* (see Annotated Bibliography). The tunes can also be used for other dances, although two are irregular in structure. Instrumentation makes extensive use of

flutes for the lead; arrangements are purposely somewhat modern in feel rather than strictly historical. Tempos from about 114 to 124, lengths mostly 8 × 64 beats.

Early American Country Dances from the John Griffiths Collection, 1788
Spring Fever
The Hendrickson Group, THG-2; Cassette; (1989)

Specific, pleasantly played arrangements of music for ten of the dances in C.C. Hendrickson's *Early American Dance and Music: John Griffiths,*

Dancing Master, 29 Country Dances, 1788 (see Annotated Bibliography). Tempos are relaxed, from 110 to 116.

Sackett's Harbor: Nineteenth Century Dance Music from Western New York State

Jim Kimball, Betsy Gamble, Mitzie Collins, Eric Rounds, Glenn McClure, Karen Park
Sampler Records 8809; Cassette; (1988)

Twenty-four cuts of nineteenth century dance tunes from New York State, featuring the hammered dulcimer, an instrument extremely popular there at the time. Lengths are short, with only a few cuts ranging above four times through the tune. Tempos generally from about 110 to 126. A corresponding booklet with tune transcriptions, dance instructions and historical notes was scheduled for publication in the fall of 1994 by Sampler Records Ltd., Rochester, New York, which would imply that some of the arrangements on the tape may correspond to specific dances.

Social Dances from the American Revolution

Frances C. Hendrickson
The Hendrickson Group THG-104; Cassette; (1993)

Seventeen tunes for the dances in Hendrickson and Keller's book of the same name (see Annotated Bibliography), arranged and played on a Korg synthesizer based on sampled instrument sounds

(piano, viola, string bass, harp, oboe, bassoon, English horn, piccolo, flute, and drum). This is a two-cassette set, pleasantly played in appropriate dance-length arrangements, and very natural sounding. Short notes on each tune are included.

Sweet Richard

The Playford Consort
CDS 10; Cassette; (1990)

Music for ten specific dances from Keller and Sweet's *A Choice Selection of American Country Dances of the Revolutionary Era* (see Annotated Bibliography), all different from those on CDIC-1, *American Country Dances of the Revolutionary Era* except for the title tune. The instrumentation—violin, recorders, bassoon and harpsichord—seems close to what might have been heard at the time, and the arrangements and execution are appropriately stately and fine.

Young Widow

The Playford Consort
CDS 11; Cassette; (1990)

Music for 12 specific dances from Morrison's *Twenty-Four Early American Country Dances, Cotillions and Reels for the Year 1976* (see Annotated Bibliography). Same fine musicians and sound as on CDS 10, *Sweet Richard*.

SINGLES

Most square and contra dance singles are produced by companies dedicated to the dance market. Singles are a relatively expensive way to acquire dance music, and now that hardly anyone uses a record player for dance instruction anymore (except in modern Western square dancing, where 45 rpm records are still very much the norm), they may soon be disappearing completely from the catalogs of the recording companies. However, some singles are still available, and sometimes they are a good choice if you are looking for a particular special tune.

I have not been in a position to survey the vast numbers of records that, through the years, have appeared as 78, 45, or 33 rpm singles, so the suggestions below merely represent a few titles that I personally have found suitable for traditional style square and contra dancing. All the recordings listed are at least 9×64 beats. Tempos vary, but are

generally apropriate for the style of music played. Except for most of the Lloyd Shaw Foundation titles, Folkraft 1154, CDS-5, and FLV-103, the tunes listed are played Southern style; a few under "Miscellaneous" tend toward country & western.

Folkraft

Folkraft 1141	Arkansas Traveler
Folkraft 1148	Davy, Davy, Nick-Nock
Folkraft 1149	Martha Campbell—Wake Up Susan
Folkraft 1150	High Level Hornpipe—Sally Goodin
Folkraft 1151	Devil's Dream—Paddy on the Turnpike
Folkraft 1152	Miller's Reel—Soldier's Joy
Folkraft 1154	Crooked Stovepipe—Peter Street
Folkraft 1156	Cincinnati Hornpipe
Folkraft 1325	Black Mountain Rag—Back Up and Push

Folkraft 1326 Grey Eagle—Eighth of January
Folkraft 1327 Tennessee Wagoner—Boil the Cabbage
Folkraft 1335 Ann Marie Reel—Miss McCloud's Reel
Folkraft 1336 Louisville Two-Step—Coming Down from Denver

Lloyd Shaw Foundation
LS307/308 Ocean View Reel/My Love Is But a Lassie Yet/Flowers of Edinburgh
LS325/326 Maureen from Gibberland
LS335/336 Doc Boyd's Jig/Jerry's Beaver Hat
LS337/338 March of St. Timothy
LS339/340 Little Burnt Potato/Jig in A (tunes are actually performed in reverse order)
LS343/344 Combination Rag
LS347/348 The Spider Bit the Baby
LS E-27 New Brunswick Horn pipe/Rainy Reel—Crossing on the Ferry/Elegant Esther Gray
LS E-49 Black Mountain Rag
LS E-50 Hawks and Eagles/Rock the Cradle, Joe
LS E-51 Julianne Johnson/Grub Springs—Ken Loch Jig/Newfoundland Jig/Tripping Up the Stairs
LS E-52 Reel St. Sauveur/La Vieille Dame—Kansas City Reel
LS E-53 Reel de St. Jean/Eddie's Reel/Seneca Square Dance—Granny, Will Your Dog Bite?

Sets in Order American Square Dance Society
Sets in Order HD-59 Missouri Mule (=Flop-Eared Mule)
Sets in Order HD-67 Whistling Rufus
Sets in Order HD-68 New Chinese Breakdown
Sets in Order HD-70 Rubber Dolly
Sets in Order HD-84 Hell Broke Loose in Georgia
Sets in Order HD-85 Durang's Hornpipe

Miscellaneous
Blue Star 2270 Buck and Doe Run—Step and Fetch It
CDSS CDS-5 Brisk Young Lads/Two and Six-penny Girl—Starr Label Reel/Ned Kendall's Favorite
Chaparral C-409 Mountain Dew
ESP 140 Blue Moon of Kentucky
ESP 404 Patter I (=Sally Goodin)
Folklore Village Farm FLV-103 The Digging Dutchman—Levi Jackson Rag
Golden Throat GT 2002 Tupelo Stomp (=Chinese Breakdown)
Ralph Pierce Records NR 14332 Eyes of Jean (=Liza Jane)
Red Boot 316 Lonesome Road Blues
Square Tunes ST 306 Stay a Little Longer
Sundown Ranch SDR 103 Golden Slippers
Sunny Hills AC 112-5 Boil the Cabbage Down
Thunderbird TH 518 Southland
TNT 173 Stallion Gray

Annotated Bibliography

TABLE OF CONTENTS

Dance collections

The books in this section are collections of newly composed dances by specific choreographers. Most of them are aimed at experienced dance leaders looking for new material, and they therefore contain little additional information besides the dance descriptions.

Blazej, Rich. *Ferryin' with Lucy Beyond the Mist and Other Original Tunes and Dances.* Brattleboro, Vermont: Richard D. Blazej, 1984.

Twenty-one contras, two progressive circles, one mixer, and 26 tunes composed by the author in traditional style. No glossary. 25pp.

Bonner, Ken. *Ken's Contras: Dances That Flow.* Sutton Coldfield, UK: Ken Bonner, 1988.

Sixteen contras and three progressive circles written by the author in American style. For some reason, the term "contra" is used instead of "neighbor" or "contrary" (the English term for "corner"), which may be confusing at first. No glossary, but occasional movements taken from club square dancing are explained where they occur. 20 pp.

Bonner, Ken. *Ken's Contras No. 2: More Dances That Flow.* Sutton Coldfield, UK: Ken Bonner, 1993.

Seventeen contras and two progressive circles written by the author in American style. Same comments as for Bonner's first book. 20 pp.

Bullimore, Barrie. *The First Eleven* and *The Second Eleven.* Laleham, Middlesex, UK: Barrie Bullimore, 1991/1992.

Two privately printed booklets, each containing 11 dances composed by the author in American style. Eighteen contras, two progressive circles, one square, and one square set for six couples, plus variants for some of the dances. Quite a few of the dances use movements taken from the modern Western square dance repertoire, but as with some other choreographers who do this, the traditional feeling may still be maintained if the movements are used appropriately and traditional timing and phrasing are retained. Total: 10 pp.

Chapman, John and Dee. *Dancing Through the Night.* Tilehurst, Berkshire, UK: SueTerR Folk, 1987.

Twenty-eight dances composed by the

authors, including nine squares, eight contras, five mixers, three progressive circles, two couple dances, and one full set longways. The squares, which are mostly singing calls, seem inspired by modern Western style but like most of the other dances in the book, they are fairly easy. The dances in the remaining formations tend more toward English style than American, but use many concepts common to both. No glossary. 24 pp.

Country Dance and Song Society. *Gems: The Best of the Country Dance and Song Society Diamond Jubilee Music, Dance and Song Contest.* Northampton, Mass.: Country Dance and Song Society, 1993.

A collection of original dances, tunes and songs in traditional style by a variety of authors, chosen from material submitted to a contest held on the occasion of CDSS's 75th anniversary in 1990. Includes 31 dances in American style (22 contras, five progressive circles, three squares, and one triplet) and 13 in English style, as well as 30 dance tunes and two songs. No glossary. 94 pp.

Elvins, Mark. *Both Feet Again: A 2nd Collection of Contemporary Dances in a Variety of Styles.* n.p.: Cotswold Music Ltd., 1991.

Twenty dances composed by the author, including nine contras, five full set longways, four squares, and two progressive circles. Five of the dances are English in feeling; the rest would be considered American style. Short glossary lists only the terms that come from club square dancing; several other less common terms might well have been included. Music for 20 tunes. 48 pp.

Elvins, Mark. *In with Both Feet: A Collection of Contemporary Dances in a Variety of Styles.* London: English Folk Dance and Song Society, 1988.

Twelve dances by the author, including six contras, four in longways formation for three couples, and two progressive circles. Most are in a style that would be considered American. No glossary or explanatory comments; in places, the descriptions could have been clearer. Music for 13 tunes and short discography of recommended tunes from recordings. 24 pp.

Fix, Penn. *Contra Dancing in the Northwest.* Spokane, Washington?: Penn Fix, 1991.

See annotation under "General instructional books."

Freeman, John B. *The First Ten Years: 15 Contemporary Michigan Dances.* n.p.: John B. Freeman, 1989.

Twelve contras, a square, a mixer, and a triplet, composed by the author in traditional style. Helpful comments and introductory section on dance style and the notation used. No glossary. 12 pp.

Garfath, Henry. *Kindly Keep It Contra: A Collection of 101 Contra Dances.* Orpington, Kent, UK: Discofolk, 1989.

Packing 101 dances into 20 small pages requires a very compact notation, which is the case here. Many abbreviations are used, with a reference list at the back, and explanatory comments are kept to a minimum. Some general concepts and personal preferences are, however, discussed in the front and back matter. The dances, all composed by the author in American style, are arranged by choreographic category; some include movements taken from modern Western square dancing. Partial glossary only. 32 pp.

Gaudreau, Herbie. *Modern Contra Dancing.* Sandusky, Ohio: Square Dance Magazine, 1971.

Calls and descriptions for 50 contra dances written by the author. The book was aimed at modern Western style callers in an attempt to interest them in using more contras, and some of the dances include movements normally used only in the modern Western program. Gaudreau was one of the first contemporary callers to experiment extensively with creating new contra dances, and is particularly noted for choreography in which all the dancers are in motion most of the time. He was also one of the first to put modern Western movements into the contra formation and to create dances with a double progression. Includes orientation about contra dances, calling technique, and choice of music, but no glossary. 40 pp.

Gunzenhauser, Margot. *Square and Fair.* Virum, Denmark: Square Dance Partners Forlag, 1995.

About 30 dances, mostly squares and contras, written by the author in traditional style. Glossary.

Hansen, Mogens. *More Pure Invention.* Roskilde, Denmark: Mogens Hansen, 1993.

Sixteen contras, 11 squares, and 2 progressive circles, written by the author in traditional style and described in English in the form of calls with a few explanatory comments. No glossary, but includes diagrammed explanations of a couple of modern Western style calls that appear. 18 pp.

Hansen, Mogens. *Pure Invention.* Roskilde, Denmark: Mogens Hansen, 1993.

Twenty-one contras, four squares, eight progressive circles, and three mixers, written by the author in traditional style and described in English in the form of calls with a few explanatory comments. No glossary. 18 pp.

Hazell, Peggy. *Norfolk Capers: A Collection of Country Dances.* Croydon, Surrey, UK: Ring O'Bells Publishing, 1991.

Two hundred mostly easy dances in a variety of formations, composed by the author in traditional style. A familiarity with English folk dance terminology may be helpful in interpreting some of the dances, but most fall easily within the conventions of American style. No glossary. 87 pp.

Herman, Fried de Metz, editor. *The Road to Ruin and Other Country Dances Old and New.* Larchmont, New York: Fried de Metz Herman, n.d.

Presumably published in the early 1980s. Fifty original or less well known dances, most composed or researched by Herman, but with some contributions from friends. Some of the dances are in American style, others in English style. No glossary. Music for 38 tunes. 50 pp.

Hill, Becky. *Twirling Dervish and Other Contra Dances.* Cleveland Heights, Ohio: Dance Gypsy Publications, 1992.

Twenty-six contra dances composed by the author in traditional style. No glossary. 32 pp.

Hinds, Tom. *Dance All Night: 30 New Contra, Square and Circle Dances.* Silver Spring, Maryland: Tom Hinds, 1989.

Eighteen contras, six squares, and six dances in other formations, composed by the author in traditional style. Level of difficulty indicated for each dance. No glossary. 34 pp.

Hinds, Tom. *Dance All Night 2: 35 More Contra, Square and Circle Dances.* Silver Spring, Maryland: Tom Hinds, 1991.

Twenty-one contras, seven squares, and seven dances in other formations, composed by the author in traditional style. Level of difficulty indicated for each dance. As stated by the author, the dances in this book flow better and are more original than those in his first book. No glossary. 39 pp.

Hinds, Tom. *Dance All Night 3: 31 New Contra and Square Dances.* Silver Spring, Maryland: Tom Hinds, 1992.

Twenty contras, nine squares, and two dances for four facing four in a column, composed by the author in traditional style. Similar to Hinds' first two booklets, but the dances have gradually become more sophisticated and the comments on them more helpful. Level of difficulty indicated for each dance. No glossary. 35 pp.

Hubert, Gene. *Dizzy Dances.* Columbia, Missouri: Gene Hubert, 1983.

Thirty-nine contras, nine squares and two mixers written by the author or his friends in traditional style. Good introduction with orientation about terminology, the construction of contras in general, timing, etc. Some of the dances are quite original; most are best suited to dancers with some experience. No glossary. 45 pp.

Hubert, Gene. *Dizzy Dances, Volume 2.* Greensboro, North Carolina: Gene Hubert, 1986.

Twenty-five contras, one square and one mixer written by the author in traditional style, including the five most successful dances from *Dizzy Dances,* with somewhat more extensive commentary. Most are best suited for intermediate or advanced dancers. No glossary. 26 pp.

Hubert, Gene. *More Dizzy Dances, Volume 3.* n.p.: Gene Hubert, 1990.

Thirty-three more contras, eight squares, two mixers, and five tunes written by the author, one of the best known contra choreographers of the current wave. Helpful comments and background notes. No glossary. 26 pp.

Hume, Colin. *Squares with a Difference, Vol. 1.* London: Colin Hume, 1992.

Twenty-two squares and two contras by the author, an English caller with a growing reputation on both sides of the Atlantic. About a third of the squares are arranged as singing calls, including some to contemporary pop tunes. Some interesting choreography can be found here, at times borrowing basic moves and movement patterns from modern Western square dancing, but still keeping the general feel of traditional style. No glossary, but unusual movements are explained where they occur. 28 pp.

Laufman, Dudley. *Okay, Let's Try a Contra, Men on the Right, Ladies on the Left, Up and Down the Hall.* New York, N.Y.: Country Dance and Song Society, 1973.

Eighteen contras composed by the author in traditional style. For several of the dances, a variant is also given for use with a specific number of couples. Music for 41 tunes. No glossary. 38 pp.

Limet, Eric. *La Fressinette: A Collection of Dances and Tunes with a Continental Flavour.* South Croydon, Surrey, UK: Barn Dance Publications Ltd., 1992.

Thirty-five dances and 50 tunes composed by the Belgian author (previously published in French by the author, although no reference to that edition is given). The dances, in a variety of formations, use American and English figures and terminology, but many could be more original or have better flow. 37 pp.

Linnell, Rod, and Louise Winston. *Square Dances from a Yankee Caller's Clipboard.* Norwell, Massachusetts: The New England Square Dance Caller, 1974.

Calls and explanations for about fifty squares, eight contras, five original double quadrilles (a square set with two couples on each side instead of one) and four old five-figure quadrilles. Most were worked out by the author, in some cases as modifications of existing dances. Linnell was one of the first New England callers to start changing the old dances while staying within the general limits of traditional movements and style. His creativity helped pave the way for other choreographers from his own and the following generation. The book was completed by Louise Winston after Linnell's untimely death, and includes a short biography of Rod Linnell, capsule biographies of other well known callers with connections to him, a glossary, bibliography, and extensive recommendations for music. 102 pp. Companion LP—see Annotated Discography.

Morton, Inga. *Square Dance Century: A Collection of 100 Dances.* Lynge, Denmark: Sandy Books, 1994.

One hundred dances—23 squares, 24 contras, 20 progressive circles, 17 mixers, 10 dances for 5 couples, and 6 triplets—written in New England style by the author, a prolific choreographer with some interesting ideas. Dance descriptions are in English with additional explanations in Danish where deemed necessary. Glossary.

Parkes, Tony. *Shadrack's Delight and Other Dances: 43 Square, Circle and Contra Dances in the New England Style.* Bedford, Massachusetts: Hands Four Books, 1988.

Twenty-five contras, 17 squares, and one progressive circle composed by the author in New England style. Level of difficulty indicated for each dance. Well tailored dances and clear descriptions, with helpful comments on each dance. Glossary. 46 pp.

Parkes, Tony. *Son of Shadrack and Other Dances: 42 More Square, Circle and Contra Dances in the New England Style.* Bedford, Massachusetts: Hands Four Books, 1993.

Twenty-six contras, 11 squares, 3 mixers, and 2 progressive circles, composed by the author in New England style. Level of difficulty indicated for each dance. Well tailored dances and clear descriptions, with helpful comments on each dance. Credit is given for all "borrowed" ideas, whether from other callers' dances or the author's own. Glossary. 46 pp.

Richardson, Mike. *Crossing the Cascades: Contra Dances and Tunes from the Pacific Northwest.* Seattle, Washington: Mike Richardson, 1992.

Eighteen contra dances, 1 mixer, and 25 tunes, all composed by the author in traditional style, some quite interesting. No glossary. 45 pp.

Roodman, Gary M. *Additional Calculated Figures: A Set of 15 English and American Country Dances.* Binghamton, New York: Gary Roodman, 1992.

Six dances in contemporary New England style, eight in historical English style, and one progressive circle in waltz time, composed by the author, with music for a tune for each. Similar to Roodman's earlier book. Discography of records referred to. No glossary. 32 pp.

Roodman, Gary M. *Calculated Figures: A Set of 12 English and American Country Dances.* Binghamton, New York: Gary Roodman, 1987.

Eight dances in contemporary New England style (in a variety of formations), three in historical English ("Playford") style, and one waltz mixer, all composed by the author. Includes some interesting choreography, mostly for intermediate and advanced dancers. Explanatory comments are held to a minimum; in some cases more would have been helpful. For each dance, music is given for one tune and a recording is suggested, not necessarily of the same tune. Discography of records referred to. No glossary. 27 pp.

Sannella, Ted. *Balance and Swing*. New York: Country Dance and Song Society, 1982. See "General instructional books."

Sannella, Ted. *Swing the Next*. Northampton, Mass.: Country Dance & Song Society, 1994? See "General instructional books."

Schwartz, Burt. *Fantasies of a Michigan Caller*. Dearborn, Michigan: C & C Consultants, 1982.

Instructions for 22 contemporary dances in traditional style, written by the author. Schwartz has taken inspiration from both the American and English country dance traditions, and uses a large variety of formations, some of which are probably unique. Included in each dance description is an explanation of how the choreography was arrived at, and specific tunes, some of which cannot be replaced by other selections, are suggested for each dance. 45 pp.

Stix, Peter, editor. *Contra*Butions: A Selection of Dances and Tunes from the Upper Midwest*. Minneapolis, Minnesota: Peter Stix, 1992.

Sixty-one dances in New England style, mostly contras, composed by dance leaders from Minnesota and Wisconsin. Includes explanatory comments, biographical notes, and an introductory section that explains the conventions used, but no glossary. Also nine original tunes. 89 pp.

Whynot, Roger. *More of Whynot*. n.pub., n.d.

Presumably produced in England around 1985. This second booklet of Whynot's imaginative and well-flowing dances includes 15 contras and 8 squares. 24 pp.

Whynot, Roger. *Why Not Dance with Me*. n.p.: n.pub., n.d.

According to the author, this little booklet of his original dances was self-published in Edenbridge, Kent, in 1983, in connection with a calling tour of England. It contains 12 contras and 12 squares, many of which are quite interesting. No glossary and few explanatory comments, but a few movements not usually employed in traditional style square dancing are explained where they occur. 20 pp.

General instructional books

Listed here are books of a general nature that include both dance descriptions and other explanatory background material and whose primary purpose is instructional.

Amidon, Peter, Mary Cay Brass and Andy Davis. *Chimes of Dunkirk: Great Dances for Children*. Brattleboro, Vermont: New England Dancing Masters Productions, 1991.

A collection of dances for school use—8 full set longways, 4 circle mixers, 3 progressive circles, 3 contras, and 2 squares—taken from the American and English traditions. Dance descriptions are clear and well written, and the book includes much excellent advice for working with children. Music for 9 tunes, short list of resource people and institutions, glossary. 40 pp. Companion tape—see Annotated Discography.

Armstrong, Don. *The Caller/Teacher Manual for Contras*. Los Angeles, California: Sets in Order, 1973.

Although written primarily for club style callers, who rarely use contras, this book is generally regarded as a good basic text for beginning contra callers. Both the introductory sections and the dance descriptions are presented clearly and sensibly. Includes a total of 101 dances, of which about half are presented in detail, including calls, and the rest exclusively as calls with a few explanatory comments. Glossary. 96 pp.

Black, Lou. *Square Dancing Ozark Style*. Springfield, Missouri: Radiozark Enterprise Publications, 1949.

Calls and descriptions for about 20 dances, with an introductory explanation of the basic movements and of the meaning of some of the more unusual calls. The author has attempted to make the material accessible, even for beginners, and photos and diagrams are used to clarify some of the figures. Nevertheless, not all the explanations are equally successful, and the main value of the book is as a document of how these particular figures and dances were executed in the author's area at that time. Includes a section with examples of fill patter. No glossary. 38 pp.

Bonner, Charles X. *Clogging and the Southern Appalachian Square Dance*. Acworth, Georgia: The Bonner Company, 1983.

Based on the author's reading and his participation in clogging and Southern mountain square dancing in various localities, this book attempts an encyclopedic treatment of the two genres. Includes descriptions of 73 square dance figures and 40 current clogging steps and discussions of the historical antecedents for both types of dancing, competition rules and tips for cloggers, use of music, etc. Lists of recordings and dance courses. Bibliography. 254 pp.

Boyd, Neva L., and Tressie M. Dunlavy. *Old Square Dances of America.* Chicago: H.T. Fitz-Simons Company, 1932.

Sixth printing, originally published 1925. Forty-two traditional squares as danced in southern Iowa in the early decades of this century. Very clear descriptions of the basic movements and of the dances, which are categorized by choreographic type. 96 pp.

Burchenal, Elizabeth. *American Country Dances: Vol. 1: 28 Contra Dances, Largely from the New England States.* New York: G. Schirmer, Inc., 1918.

Descriptions for 19 duple and triple minor contras, 4 progressive circles, 3 full set longways and 2 mixers, collected from living New England tradition and the memories of living caller/fiddlers in the early 1900s. The amount of variation in figures is limited: for example, all the contras end with down the center and back, cast off and right and left through. Very clear glossary and dance descriptions, although in some cases the number of measures specified does not jibe with the number of counts stated. Basic prompting technique is explained. Music for at least one tune for each dance. 53 pp.

Butenhof, Ed. *Dance Parties for Beginners.* n.p.: Lloyd Shaw Foundation, 1990.

With its advice on how to work with every conceivable type of "one time only" group, this book is a good source of inspiration for any caller willing to be hired for one night stands. Included are instructions for 43 squares, 21 line/solo dances, 17 mixers, 10 contras and full set longways dances, and 8 couple dances. Glossary; lists of records, books, and organizations. 135 pp.

Callens, Philippe. *Everybody Swing!* Antwerp, Belgium: Volksdanscentrale voor Vlaanderen, 1989.

Thirty-five dances in New England style—13 contras, 8 squares, 5 mixers, 3 progressive circles, and 6 dances in other formations—with good introductory explanations of historical context, choreography, style, and music and clear dance descriptions. Most of the dances were composed within the last 30 years, and the origin and author of each is noted. Detailed glossary. Bibliography. In Dutch/Flemish. 84 pp. Companion tape—see Annotated Discography.

Callens, Philippe. *Keep on Swinging: A Collection of 24 New England Style Dances.* Lovendegem, Belgium: Anglo-American Dance Service v.z.w., 1992.

A nice collection of contemporary dances—some well known, others less so—written in New England style by a variety of callers. Contains 9 contras, 7 squares, 3 progressive circles, 3 mixers and 2 triplets. Dances are described in both English and Dutch/Flemish, with helpful comments by Callens, the primus motor of traditional square and contra dancing in Belgium. No glossary. 2×36 pp. Companion tape—see Annotated Discography.

Casey, Betty. *The Complete Book of Square Dancing (and Round Dancing).* Garden City, New York: Doubleday & Co., 1976.

Primarily oriented toward modern Western square dancing, but includes a section with 15 traditional/transitional squares. The section on contra dances is a travesty, including only two dances: the Virginia Reel and a Bucksaw-like dance, Slaunch to Donegal. The book includes some sensible background material, but considering its declared scope, it is unfortunate that no mention is made of the flourishing contemporary scene within traditional square and contra dancing. Additionally, the use of young children in the photos for the traditional section implies that the dances are suitable only for that age group. Separate glossaries for square dancing and round dancing (choreographed and "cued" couple dances). Short bibliography. 191 pp.

Cazden, Norman. *Dances from Woodland: Square Dances from the Catskills.* Bridgeport, Connecticut: Norman Cazden, 1955.

(2nd rev. ed. First ed. pub. 1945). Calls and music for 44 old time dances from the Catskill region of New York State—mostly squares, with occasional dances in other formations—chosen from among the variants known to the author. In most cases, little explanation is given other than the calls; it would have been nice to learn more about the mode and style of dancing in this area. 48 pp.

Chase, Ann Hastings. *The Singing Caller: A Book on the Square Dance with Calls and Music.* New York: Association Press, 1944.

Calls, tunes, and descriptions, presented in a clear, tabular form, for 15 squares, arranged as singing calls and intended for use by YMCAs and similar groups. No glossary—movements are explained as they occur and drawings help clarify the main figure of each dance. 78 pp.

Clossin, Jimmy, and Carl Hertzog. *West Texas Square Dances.* El Paso, Texas: Carl Hartzog, 1950.

Originally published in 1940. Calls and instructions for about 35 dances from western Texas, some of which are presented with several variations, written by two leading Texas callers of the era. An interesting picture of the regional dance repertoire during a period in which new ideas were starting to be added to the old traditional dances. Illustrations help clarify the text. Glossary and short discography. 48 pp.

Coley, Donna Mae and George T., editors. *Raymond Smith's Collection of Square Dances and Mixers: A Supplement to Raymond Smith's Square Dance Hand Book.* Dallas, Texas: Raymond Smith, 1950.

Calls and explanations for 37 squares—30 patter calls and 7 singing calls—and a number of breaks or "mixers" (Smith uses the terms synonymously). Intended as a supplement to *Raymond Smith's Square Dance Hand Book*, a much larger proportion of the dances here are newly composed figures attributable to specific choreographers. No glossary. 65 pp.

Coley, Donna Mae and George T., editors. *Raymond Smith's Square Dance Hand Book (2nd ed.).* Dallas, Texas: Raymond Smith, 1948.

First edition published in 1947. Calls and explanations for 38 mostly traditional squares—27 patter calls and 11 singing calls—as danced in Smith's area at the time. Examples of breaks and patter. Glossary. 64 pp.

Community Dance Program. Pocono Pines, Pennsylvania: Callerlab, the International Association of Square Dance Callers, 1990.

The Community Dance Program, involving a list of 24 basic movements to be taught in a series of six two-hour lessons, was proposed by Callerlab as a way of attracting people who would like to

dance, but who cannot or will not invest the time required to learn full-fledged modern Western style square dancing. In many ways, it corresponds to the repertoire and philosophy behind traditional style square and contra dancing, but is built on the caller's existing knowledge of modern square dancing. This booklet outlines the program and provides suggestions for about 40 suitable squares, mostly based on specific recordings, as well as 11 mixers and progressive circles, 4 couple dances, 3 solo/line dances, 2 contras, and the Virginia Reel. No glossary. 42 pp.

Dalsemer, Bob. *New England Quadrilles and How to Call Them.* Baltimore, Maryland: Bob Dalsemer, 1985.

The purpose of this booklet is to encourage contra dance groups to embrace New England–style square dances as well—the term "quadrille" here denotes the highly structured/phrased type of square dance figures now common in New England style. Twelve good dances with an explanation of the basics about dancing and, especially, calling them. Includes a section on introductions, breaks and endings. No glossary. 13 pp.

Dalsemer, Robert G. *West Virginia Square Dances.* New York, N.Y.: Country Dance and Song Society, 1982.

Describes dance customs in five small, rural communities in West Virginia around 1980, including descriptions of about 50 main figures, plus intros, breaks, and transcriptions of typical calls. In contrast to most square dance books, which present the dances without regard to cultural context, this monograph includes thorough descriptions of the settings in which the dances exist. A valuable picture of dance traditions, their development and the surprising degree of variation from place to place within a relatively circumscribed area, as well as the attitudes of the dancers towards the activity. Music for six tunes, lists of often played tunes. Bibliography. No separate glossary. 86 pp.

Durlacher, Ed. *Honor Your Partner.* New York: Bonanza Books, 1949.

Calls and descriptions for 81 dances, mostly squares, but also a few contras, progressive circles, four waltz quadrilles, etc. Eleven of the dances are contributions from "guest callers"—well known callers of the day who were invited by Durlacher to choose one typical dance from their repertoires for inclusion in the book. Ed Durlacher was a popular caller during the square dance craze of the 1940s and 50s, and the book gives an interesting picture of the dances (mostly visiting couple figures) that were in use in the East before the new choreographic tendencies took root. Glossary and some good advice on calling technique and dance etiquette. Extensive bibliography and discography. Music for one tune for each dance. A unique feature is the "flipbook" illustrations at the back of the book, intended to show the basic movements in motion. 286 pp.

Durlacher, Ed. *Square Dances*. New York: Mills Music, Inc., 1946.

Calls, descriptions and music for 12 dances: 8 squares, 1 mixer, 1 progressive circle, a novelty dance and the Virginia Reel. Includes a short glossary with illustrations, and some advice for the caller and musicians. Most of the dances also appear in Durlacher's 1949 book *Honor Your Partner*, some under different names. 36 pp.

Everett, Bert. *Complete Calls and Instructions for Fifty Canadian Square Dances as Called by Bert Everett (2nd ed.)*. Toronto, Ontario: Can.-Ed Media Ltd., 1983.

First edition published in 1977. Complete calls for 49 dances, with clear explanatory comments and exact timing. Section one contains 19 mostly well known traditional figures, including a number of visiting couple dances. The 16 squares in section two are labelled "quadrilles" and are more along the lines of contemporary New England squares. Also three simple but interesting full set longways and a square, from French-speaking Canada; a mixer, a progressive circle and a simple dance-game from Newfoundland; and seven easy singing calls. No glossary. 142 pp.

Fischle, Heiner. *Leitfaden Contra Dancing/A Guide to Contra Dancing, Vol. 1*. Hannover, Germany: Heiner Fischle, 1983.

Written in both English and German, this book provides an introduction to contra dancing, with calls and descriptions for 37 contras. For each dance, a record is suggested. Fischle's goal was to promote contra dancing among the many German fans of modern Western style square dancing, so the terminology and orientation of the book are based on what they already know. Short bibliography, discography, list of book and record vendors in the United States and Europe. Additional volumes in the projected series have not been released to date. 48 pp.

Fix, Penn. *Contra Dancing in the Northwest*. Spokane, Washington?: Penn Fix, 1991.

Excellent summary of the historical developments leading up to the current popularity of contra dancing that, while it focuses on the Northwest, is largely applicable to other regions as well. Also includes much good advice about the roles of the caller, musicians, and experienced dancers in the success of an evening; advice about running one night stands and dance camp weekends; considerations when purchasing sound systems; and portraits of a traditional dance community and of some of the author's role models. Thirty-three contra dances by the author, 14 tunes by various composers, short bibliography, and directory of Northwest dance groups. No glossary. 132 pp.

Ford, Mr. and Mrs. Henry. *Good Morning: After a Sleep of 25 Years, Old-Fashioned Dancing Is Being Revived by Mr. and Mrs. Henry Ford*. Dearborn, Michigan: Dearborn Publishing Company, 1926.

In the early 1920s, Henry Ford began a crusade to reintroduce gracious old-time square and round dancing as a contrast to the increasingly popular and increasingly "wild" couple dancing done in the cities. He engaged a dancing master, Benjamin Lovett, and through him, made old-time dancing available not only in Dearborn, but to schools and other groups throughout the country. *Good Morning* was actually written by Lovett, and appears today as a quaint and charming manual on proper dance style and ballroom deportment. It includes directions for 17 quadrilles of four figures each, as well as four sets of Lancers; four "novelty quadrilles" employing waltz or polka steps; 17 contras, longways and progressive circles; a mixer; and a whole section on round dancing (couple or ballroom dances). The section on the Minuet is based on nineteenth century conceptions of that dance, not on the original style. Glossary. Helpful illustrations. 169 pp.

Foster, William A. *Favorite Square Dances*. Delaware, Ohio: Cooperative Recreation Service, n.d.

Pocket-size booklet with calls and descriptions for 42 traditional squares as called by William Foster. Probably published for the first time around the early 1940s. The descriptions are occasionally a little cryptic, and the term "right and left through" is often used where we would say "pass through." But the booklet gives us a picture of the typical repertoire of a rural caller who we are told has been active since 1928. Short introduction and glossary;

music for seven tunes. 37 pp. (Contents are also included in *Handy Square Dance Book* from the same press.)

Gotcher, Les, editor. *Book of Calls: Over 100 Excellent Square Dance Patter Calls*. Burbank, California?: n. pub., n.d.

Calls and explanations for 103 fairly complicated patter routines (squares), some devised by Les Gotcher but most by other callers, many of whose names are no longer familiar. Probably published in the mid- or late 1950s. Material relies heavily on certain calls that were new at the time but are now virtually part of the traditional repertoire, and seems to represent a stage at which the kind of choreographic complexity found in modern Western style square dancing today was being attempted with a smaller vocabulary of calls. No glossary or introduction. Some special calls no longer in the dance repertoire are defined as they occur, while others are taken for granted. 63 pp.

Gowing, Gene. *The Square Dancer's Guide*. New York: Crown Publishers, n.d.

Probably published around 1960. Carefully prepared text with an excellent glossary, many tips on dancing style, and lots of good advice about teaching and programming. Covers various regional variations and includes ideas about working with special groups (handicapped, etc.). Calls and descriptions for 28 squares, 12 contras, 6 figures for the running set, 4 progressive circles, 2 mixers, and the Oriental Lancers. Sample programs for various groups. 159 pp.

Greene, Hank. *Square and Folk Dancing: A Complete Guide for Students, Teachers & Callers*. New York, N.Y.: Harper & Row, 1984.

Historical overview and much sensible advice for aspiring leaders and callers. Calls and descriptions for 29 singing calls and 26 patter calls. In the case of the singing calls, the first 24 dances are extremely simple, old-fashioned warhorses, while the last five, abruptly, are complicated dances in modern Western style. A more suitable transition could have been made by including some contemporary dances in traditional style, but Greene seems unaware of their existence. In the patter call category, the final five selections are quite interesting and not as far removed from the other dances in the section. Dance descriptions are generally clear, but with occasional misinterpretations. Suggestions are made for recorded music, and there is music for

24 tunes. Also includes 28 folk dances and 6 mixers, glossary, bibliography, etc. 316 pp.

Greggerson, Herb. *Herb's Blue Bonnet Calls (6th ed.)*. El Paso, Texas: H.F. Greggerson, Jr., 1949.

First edition published in 1937. Traditional Southwestern figures as danced in the 1930s and 40s. Includes 53 squares—mostly of the visiting couple or single visitor type—and three traditional "icebreakers" or mixers. Explanations are generally good, but some could be clearer. Glossary; examples of patter for intros, breaks, and endings. 68 pp.

Gunzenhauser, Margot. *Country Dancing at School*. Croydon, Surrey, UK: Barn Dance Publications, Ltd., 1994.

See *Square Dancing at School*. For this British edition, an instructional videotape is available as a supplement.

Gunzenhauser, Margot. *Square Dance: Håndbog i Amerikansk Folkedans*. Lyngby, Denmark: Square Dance Partners Forlag, 1988.

Original Danish book on which the present work is based. Contains most of the same material. 289 pp.

Gunzenhauser, Margot. *Square Dance i Skolen*. Virum, Denmark: Square Dance Partners Forlag, 1991.

See *Square Dancing at School*. This Danish edition also includes an instructional videotape.

Gunzenhauser, Margot. *Square Dancing at School*. Virum, Denmark: Square Dance Partners Forlag, 1991.

Translated by the author from the Danish version (*Square Dance i Skolen*), this is a ring binder that offers 8 mixers, 7 full set longways dances, 10 progressive circles, 3 circle dances for trios, 10 squares, and 6 contras, accompanied by 12 appropriate, multi-purpose tunes on short cassette tapes. Also includes advice on teaching techniques and music, 9 suggested breaks for squares, an illustrated glossary, and a set of "puzzle pieces" as an aid to constructing one's own dances. 102 pp. (Has also been published in the United Kingdom in a slightly revised version as *Country Dancing at School*.)

Hall, J. Tillman. *Dance! A Complete Guide to Social, Folk and Square Dancing*. Belmont, California: Wadsworth Publishing Co., 1963.

Like many books that attempt to cover a great variety of material, this one bears some evidence of compromise. The survey of dance history and national dance characteristics should probably be approached with some skepticism, and the glossary includes some highly questionable definitions, particularly of square dance terms. The square dance section includes 12 patter calls (mostly well known traditional figures); 18 singing calls taken from the cue sheets to records available at the time; some suggestions for intros, breaks and endings; and transcriptions of four performance sequences used by the author's group. Dances are presented as calls, with few explanatory comments. The book also includes some good general teaching tips, exercises for practicing basic locomotor movements, and chapters on folk dancing, tap dancing, and ballroom dancing. 242 pp.

Handy Square Dance Book. Delaware, Ohio: Cooperative Recreation Service, 1955.

Instructions for about 85 dances from various regions of the country. This pocket-size booklet seems to have been created by reprinting several complete, smaller booklets within one cover. The descriptions vary from title to title in completeness and clarity, but cover a fair variety of material. No glossary. Music for 31 tunes. 146 pp.

Harris, Jane A., Anne M. Pittman, and Marlys S. Waller. *Dance a While: Handbook of Folk, Square, Contra, and Social Dance*. New York, N.Y.: Macmillan Publishing Co., 1988.

(6th ed. Earlier editions, titled *Dance a While: Handbook of Folk, Square, and Social Dance*, published 1950, 1955, 1964, 1968, 1978). Long considered the standard handbook for school and college dance teachers, *Dance a While* has evolved into an attractively presented collection of folk and social dance material. The appreciable expansion of the contra dance section in this edition, along with the extensive coverage of modern Western style square dancing (up to about the first 50 basics, thus substantially within the traditional movement repertoire) and traditional couple dances, novelty dances and mixers, makes the book valuable for anyone interested in American dance forms. Also includes chapters on dance history, instruction techniques, dance fundamentals, international folk dancing, and ballroom dancing; lists of periodicals, records, and record sources; extensive bibliography; and glossary. 464 pp.

Holden, Rickey. *The Contra Dance Book*. Newark, New Jersey: American Squares, 1956.

A catalog of all the contras and progressive circle dances the author could locate in American books published between 1850 and 1953, this book provides a valuable picture of the contra dance material extant in the United States before the recent explosion of new choreography. Good introductory sections on the background and character of the dances and how to teach and call them. Dances are classified according to the figures they include, a virtually unique feature in the literature. Includes calls, descriptions and commentary on 90 contras and 18 progressive circles, as well as cross references to a number of minor variations and alternate dance titles. Glossary. 126 pp.

Holden, Rickey. *Square Dances of West Texas: A Bit of History, the Structure, the Figures, and the Legacy of Bob Sumrall*. Austin, Texas: The Society of Folk Dance Historians, 1992.

Produced in connection with a projected series of workshops for reviving the West Texas dance style of the 1930s and 40s, this booklet includes descriptions of 21 squares, together with a discussion of intros, setups, figures, breaks, and getouts, and a somewhat personal history of square dancing in that area. Bibliography. No glossary, 32 pp.

Holden, Rickey, and Lloyd Litman. *Instant Hash*. Cleveland, Ohio: Lloyd Litman, 1961.

Reportedly the first attempt to analyze and categorize the many new calls and concepts that had started to appear in square dancing by the mid- and late 1950s and to offer tools to the caller for choreographic management. Many of the non-traditional movements mentioned are no longer current, even in modern square dancing, and the theoretical material may prove daunting to traditional style callers. However, the book also includes a large number of traditional and transitional dance figures, categorized by choreographic type, and it offers an interesting look at the status of square dancing at the time it was written. Glossary of less well known movements only. Various indices and tables. Bibliography. 116 pp.

Hunt, Paul, and Charlotte Underwood. *Eight Yards of Calico: Square Dance Fun for Everyone*. New York, N.Y.: Harper & Brothers, 1952.

Explanations of 50 squares, arranged in eight programs of increasing complexity. Starts with standard figures, and moves on through patterns largely based on older ideas to new material that was "state of the art" at the time. Explains the different styles of calling, with an unusual emphasis on the need for good rhythm and timing. Lots of teaching advice, both general and specific. List of recommended records. 114 pp.

Jennewein, J. Leonard. *Dakota Square Dance Book and Instructor's Manual*. Huron, South Dakota: J. Leonard Jennewein, 1950.

An intelligently written book aimed at dance leaders in the Dakota region and based on the author's knowledge not only of the then current dance practices, but of what was traditional for the region. Calls and explanations for 25 dances, including the Sicilian Circle, the Virginia Reel, and 23 squares, most of which are visiting couple dances or other traditional figures. Also has calls and explanations for 23 breaks, a detailed section on teaching techniques with a six-evening lesson plan, an analysis of various line, circle, star, and other formations that may be encountered (or created), and an analysis of various figures extant under the name dosido and how they differ. Annotated bibliography of 15 major books and a few magazines and sheet music collections. List of suggested records. Detailed glossary. 93 pp.

Jennings, Larry. *Zesty Contras*. Wellesley Hills, Mass.: New England Folk Festival Association, 1983.

Capsule descriptions of 500 dances, including almost 400 contras, 48 "triplets" for three couples in longways formation, and 59 dances in other formations, such as mixers, progressive circles, etc. (but no squares). Dance descriptions are written in a special shorthand, which looks more impenetrable than it actually is. The book has rapidly become a classic in the contra dance world, both because of the large amount of material it supplies and because of the introductory chapters, in which well known dance organizer Jennings expounds on the nature of the contra dance, contemporary dance practices in the Boston area (a hotbed of contra dancing today), music and musicians, how to organize a dance series, advice to callers, etc. A further valuable contribution is Jennings' notation of the places in a dance that are especially exciting or that require extra attention in dancing or teaching. 90 pp.

Jensen, Clayne R., and Mary Bee. *Square Dancing*. Provo, Utah: Brigham University Press, 1973.

Originally published in 1966 as *Beginning Square Dance*; intended as a high school and college text. About one-third of the book consists of explanations for the calls that made up the "basic" and "extended basics" programs of modern Western square dancing at the time. The 50 "basic" movements are almost all within the current repertoire of traditional style dancers, while on the other hand, about a third of the movements described as "extended basics" are no longer included in the modern Western Basic and Mainstream programs. Also contains calls for 18 patter call squares and 16 singing call squares. Of these, at least half are within the possibilities of traditional style with regard to the movements used. The remainder of the book deals with performance choreography, but there are also sensible sections on style, calling technique and teaching technique. Glossary, short bibliography and discographies. 159 pp.

Kennedy, Douglas, editor. *Community Dances Manual, Books 1–7*. Princeton, New Jersey: Princeton Book Company, 1986.

A collected reprint of seven booklets originally published in England in 1949, 1954, 1957, 1964, and 1967. Contains a total of 130 dances and 140 tunes from the English and American traditions, of which about one quarter are American. The new edition includes an introduction, glossary, bibliography and discography by respected New England dance leader Tony Parkes. 128 pp.

Kennedy, Douglas and Helen. *American Square Dancing*. London: English Folk Dance & Song Society, 1965.

Revised reprint of *Square Dances of America*. The main difference seems to be the omission of musical notation in the new edition. 16 pp.

Kennedy, Douglas and Helen. *Square Dances of America*. London: Novello & Co., n.d.

Probably published in the 1940s or 50s. Contains descriptions of about 35 figures for squares, of which about 20 can also be used for the Appalachian running set. Calls are included for about one-third of the figures. Aside from the fact that the English term "contrary" is used instead of "corner," the dance descriptions are quite clear. Music for 18 tunes. Glossary. 32 pp.

Kirkell, Miriam H., and Irma K. Schaffnit. *Partners All, Places All*. New York, N.Y.: E.P. Dutton & Co., 1949.

Calls and clear directions for 44 dances,

including 22 squares, 9 mixers and play party games, 6 couple dances, 3 full set longways, 3 line dances, and a "good night" dance, some of which are from countries other than the United States. Dances are mostly easy, as the book is intended for school and recreation use. Music for one tune for each dance; suggestions are for recorded music; suggestions for programming a whole dance evening. Glossary, bibliography, discography. 129 pp.

Kraus, Richard. *Square Dances of Today and How to Teach and Call Them*. New York, N.Y.: The Ronald Press Co., 1950.

Calls and clear descriptions for about 65 dances, including 40 squares, 12 mixers, 8 play party games, and a few miscellaneous dances. Introductory chapter with a little general background material and good advice about teaching and calling techniques. Illustrations help to clarify the dance figures. Music for 31 tunes. Glossary. 129 pp. (The record series *Let's Square Dance* is based on this book—see Annotated Discography.)

Lippincott, Peter and Margret. *Traditional Dance in Missouri, Vol. 1: Southern Missouri Jig Dancing*. St. Louis, Missouri: Childgrove Country Dancers, 1984.

Describes square dance figures, mode of dancing and social context as practiced in two rural Missouri communities in the early 1980s. Some of the ca. 20 figures are well known from other sources, while others are interesting local variants. Additional volumes in the projected series have apparently not been released to date. 27 pp.

Loy, Lawrence V. *Square Dances: As American as Corn Pone*. New York: Country Dance Society, n.d.

Small booklet, probably published around 1950, with calls and clear descriptions for eight easy singing squares popular at the time, some of which seem to be Loy's own variations on well known figures. 14 pp.

Lyman, Frank L., Jr. *One Hundred and One Singing Calls*. Fort Madison, Iowa: Frank L. Lyman, Jr., 1951.

Calls and occasional explanatory remarks for 101 singing call squares, including variants, most transcribed from the repertoires of specific callers. An interesting source of dance ideas for many popular old tunes, although music is not included. Glossary, discography, list of music books. 90 pp.

McNair, Ralph J. *Square Dance!* Garden City, New York: Garden City Books, 1951.

A well-written presentation by an author familiar with both twentieth century and nineteenth century dance customs. Includes sections on square dance history, calling technique, use of music, finding an appropriate hall, and basic square dance terms, as well as explanations of 38 squares and the Virginia Reel. Clear and helpful illustrations are supplemented in the dance descriptions by the unique idea of calling the four couples in the square by names starting with A, B, C, and D, respectively. No glossary, but terms are clearly described the first time they occur. 188 pp.

McVicar, Wes. *Wes McVicar's 75 Favorite Square Dance Calls for Dancers and Teachers*. Toronto: Gordon V. Thompson Ltd., 1949.

Calls for 62 squares and 13 mixers and couple dances. No separate glossary, but each basic movement is explained the first time it appears, and the most important explanations are indexed. The custom in Canada (and parts of the United States) at the time this book was written was to execute "tips" or "sets" of three dances or "changes" each, and certain guidelines were observed as to what types of figures were suitable for the first, second or third changes of a tip. Consequently, all the dances in this book are classified as either first, second, or third changes, which can be combined into tips at the caller's discretion. For each dance a tune is suggested. Most of these are pop tunes commonly used at the time for singing calls. 76 pp.

Mayo, Margot. *The American Square Dance*. New York, N.Y.: Sentinel Books, 1943.

General orientation, glossary, and instructions for 13 dances, mostly squares but also a mixer, a contra, a couple of full set longways, and a section on the big set. Helpful illustrations clarify the figures. Music for 11 tunes. Bibliography and discography. 120 pp.

Melamed, Lanie. *All Join Hands: Connecting People Through Folk Dance*. Montreal: Lanie Melamed, 1977.

Although the introductory remarks in this book are geared mainly toward teaching international folk dance, much of the material in the book is American. This includes 10 of the 13 play parties and singing games and 10 of the 21 dances in the "folk dance" section. Also covered are 5 squares, 5 contras, a short section on the big set, and a grand march. The explanatory sections could be clearer or better founded in some places; drawings, however, are clear and helpful. Glossary, list of record sources, short annotated bibliography and list of dance periodicals. 99 pp.

Meyers, Rick. *Traditional American Dance Book.* Portland, Oregon: Rick Meyers, 1983.

Intended mainly for primary school teachers who want to use authentic American folk dance material in the classroom. Most of the 55 dances are easy; in some cases, Meyers has adapted the material for use in the lower grades, but he makes his changes with respect for the dances' character, and gives the teacher good advice on execution. The introductory sections on dance history, etc., unfortunately do not live up to the dance material, and include some strange and unsubstantiated assertions. Similarly, the concluding chapter on clogging will be of limited use unless the reader already has some knowledge of this dance form, as it is virtually impossible to learn from written descriptions alone. Short bibliography. 131 pp. Two companion tapes contain instrumental and called music to go along with the book—see Annotated Discography.

Moody, Ed. *Swing Below: A Book Compiled by a Dancer for Square Dancers in Search of More Good Clean Fun, Subject "Contras."* n.p.: Ed Moody, n.d.

Apparently published around 1965 with the expressed intent of popularizing contra dancing among square dancers outside New England. Engagingly, if sometimes provocatively, written, with several dances diagrammed out figure by figure. Considering the author's harangues about the use of boring dances, a surprising number of the 50 contras presented are composed of the same "glossary" movements strung together in varying orders with few distinguishing characteristics. Includes music for four tunes and reprints of several poems by "Pat Pending" with ironic commentary on the square and contra dance scene. No glossary. 42 pp.

Muller, "Allemande" Al. *All-American Square Dances.* New York: Paull-Pioneer Music Corporation, 1941.

(Have also seen a copy published by Shawnee Press, Inc., Delaware Water Gap, Pa., also copyright 1941.) Calls and explanations for five "sets" of three changes (dances) each, with an explanation of the types of figures considered appropriate for the first, second, and third changes. Also includes 12 additional second change figures, three progressive

circle dances, five contras, and descriptions of the waltz, schottische and polka steps. Introductory section includes lots of sensible advice on dance style and etiquette for the "city slickers" who did not grow up with country dancing and are attempting it for the first time. Glossary shows that several terms had a different meaning in the Adirondack region in the 1930s than they have today. Music for 44 tunes. 48 pp.

Napier, Pat. *Kentucky Mountain Square Dancing (Running Set).* London: English Folk Dance and Song Society, 1982.

Based on Napier's *Kentucky Mountain Square Dancing.* Includes most of the same 20 figures, but with less explanatory material about the dance style, music and calling. The diagrams and glossary are also omitted. 24 pp.

Napier, Patrick E. *Kentucky Mountain Square Dancing.* Berea, Kentucky: Patrick E. Napier, 1975.

This book, by a long active Southern style caller affiliated with Berea College, was originally published in 1960. Includes short introductory sections on the history of Kentucky style square dancing and the way it is done today; calls and explanations for about 20 figures, mostly intended for the big set, but also including a few that are used only for the running set; and some suggestions for breaks and ending figures. Diagrams help to clarify the figures. Glossary. 49 pp.

Olsen, Ray and Arvid. *Musical Mixer Fun: 50 Easy Mixers for One Night Stands.* Moline, Illinois: Square Your Sets Enterprises, 1957.

Small booklet with 50 mixers, some of which are adaptations of well-liked square dance routines or couple dances, and some of which are more interesting than others. Sixteen square dance–type mixers, 18 based on the schottische or two-step, 5 in waltz time, and 11 miscellaneous others. Short glossary. 44 pp.

Osgood, Bob. *The Caller/Teacher Manual for the Basics and Mainstream Basics of American Square Dancing.* Los Angeles, California: Sets in Order American Square Dance Society, 1983.

Explicit teaching program for the Basic and Mainstream levels of modern Western square dancing. The first half of the book deals with material also used in traditional style and may be of use to traditional style callers. Book is a ring binder subject to periodic revision. 320 pp.

Osgood, Bob, editor. *Caller/Teacher Manual for the Basic Program of American Square Dancing.*

Los Angeles, California: Sets in Order American Square Dance Society, 1969.

Although written as a manual for those wanting to teach the first level of modern Western style square dance, this book covers only movements that today are a part of the traditional style repertoire. Its many drills, complete dances, and detailed teaching hints may therefore be a useful resource for traditional style callers, too. Unfortunately, the book is no longer in print, but the material was integrated in revised form into the *Caller/Teacher Manual for the Basics and Mainstream Basics of American Square Dancing*. 98 pp.

Osgood, Bob, and Jack Hoheisal. *Square Dancing for Beginners*. Los Angeles, California: Bob Osgood and Jack Hoheisal, 1949.

Calls and descriptions for 25 mostly traditional squares, plus four relatively complicated figures popular at the time. Glossary. 24 pp.

Osgood, Bob, and Jack Hoheisal. *Square Dancing for Intermediates*. Los Angeles, California: Bob Osgood and Jack Hoheisal, 1949.

Calls and descriptions for 38 squares, including many composed in the 1930s and 40s, plus four break figures popular at the time. Glossary lists only a few terms—for the rest, reader is referred to the same authors' *Square Dancing for Beginners*. 40 pp.

Osgood, Bob, and Jack Hoheisal. *Square Dancing: The Newer and Advanced Dances*. Los Angeles, California: Sets in Order, 1950.

Calls and descriptions for 46 squares and six popular break figures, most newly composed. No glossary. 48 pp.

Owens, Lee, and Viola Ruth. *Advanced Square Dance Figures of the West and Southwest*. Palo Alto, California: Pacific Books, 1950.

Descriptions, rhymed calls, and suggested music for 31 main figures and nine "trimming or chorus" figures for squares, representing the best of the advanced and exhibition figures that were being worked out in the Southwest (primarily Texas) up through the 1940s. Explanations of the sometimes complicated figures are surprisingly clear, considering that no diagrams or illustrations are used. Many are based on star patterns. Timing and phrasing are claimed to have been worked out carefully, but no timing of the movements is actually given. Presupposes an acquaintance with standard square dance movements and preferably also with material included in Owens' previous book, *American Square Dances of the West and Southwest*, which was more geared toward general social dancing. No glossary as such—only a few important movements are explained, but these very carefully, with attention to dancing style. 143 pp.

Owens, William A. *Swing and Turn: Texas Play-Party Games*. Dallas, Texas: Tardy Publishing Co., 1936.

Words, music and descriptions for 64 play party games (singing games) collected in Texas by the author. Cross references are given to similar games mentioned in a number of other written sources. Includes a useful introduction to the genre. Glossary and bibliography. 113 pp.

Page, Ralph. *An Elegant Collection of Contras and Squares*. Denver, Colorado: The Lloyd Shaw Foundation, 1984.

Calls and meticulous explanations for over 60 dances, mostly contras, but also some New England squares, quadrilles and lancers. Also includes commentary on the origin and background of each dance and quotes from late nineteenth century newspaper accounts of balls and dance assemblies. No glossary. Music for 48 tunes. 153 pp.

Page, Ralph. *The Ralph Page Book of Contras*. London: English Folk Dance and Song Society, 1969.

Instructions for 11 traditional and 11 contemporary contra dances, with music for 44 tunes. Origins of the individual dances are noted. Short introduction with good advice about dance style, music, etc. No glossary. 24 pp.

Piper, Ralph A. and Zora C. *Developing the Creative Square Dancer Caller*. Minneapolis, Minnesota: Ralph and Zora Piper, 1956.

A manual for aspiring callers, this book is not only well thought out and written, but is also unusual in presenting serious treatment and application of the New England contra dances side by side with predominantly Western style square dance calls. Covers the definitions of basic figures, choreographic design, timing of movements and calls, and elements of calling technique, and includes a list of 29 suggested exercises for developing calling and choreography skills. The material included would today be considered within the scope of traditional style dancing. Short bibliography. 159 pp.

Piute Pete. *Piute Pete's Down Home Square Dance Book*. New York: Grosset & Dunlap, 1977.

Descriptions of six play party games/mixers, six singing squares, six patter squares, and two full set longways dances, all on a very easy level.

Layout is clear, but text is often misleading, vague, inconsistent, or superficial. Lists of record companies and magazines, short bibliography. 96 pp.

Popwell, Shelia. *The Clogger's Book of Appalachian Square Dance Figures*. Huron, Ohio: Burdick Enterprises, 1983.

Good introductory sections on Appalachian dance styles, basic concepts, historical development of the dance, examples of complete dance sequences, and other supplementary information. Calls and clear descriptions for over 200 different figures for the big set and running set—probably the most extensive such collection in print. The inclusion of alternate names for the same figure and cross refernces between similar figures helps to provide an overview of the material. Glossary. 168 pp.

Rohrbough, Lynn. *American Folk Dances*. Delaware, Ohio: Cooperative Recreation Service, 1939.

Pocket handbook that combines two smaller booklets from the same publishers: no. 49, with ten dances from New England, the Midwest and the South, and no. 47, *Square Dances of the Smoky Mountains*, by Frank H. Smith, with about 20 figures for the big set. Some of the dance descriptions could be a little clearer, but the value of the book lies in the fact that especially the dances from the Southern states are described as they are done in specific localities, making comparison possible. The figures in Frank Smith's section are pretty much the same ones that appear in his later book, *The Appalachian Square Dance*. Music for nine tunes. Short glossary. 48 pp.

Rohrbough, Lynn. *Handy Play Party Book*. Burnsville, North Carolina: World Around Songs/Cooperative Recreation Service, 1968.

Pocket-size handbook originally published in 1940. Includes some general orientation, but consists primarily of instructions, including music and song texts, for about 100 play party games (singing games) from various sources. A good source of inspiration for simple mixers and party games, and useful as a concise introduction to this part of the Anglo-American dance repertoire. No glossary. 120 pp.

Ryan, Grace L. *Dances of Our Pioneers*. New York, N.Y.: A.S. Barnes & Co., 1939.

Originally published in 1926. Calls and descriptions for 6 complete "quadrilles," the form of square dance found in the Midwest at that time, consisting of three separate figures or "changes" per dance (today we would probably view them as three distinct dances making up a tip). Also includes 3 more figures suitable for the first change, 20 for the second change, 14 for the third change, 2 complete waltz quadrilles, 11 contra/longways dances, and about 15 couple dances and other miscellaneous dances. The book is clearly written and includes both well known and lesser known figures, giving a valuable peek at Midwestern square dance traditions of the 1920s. The contras, interestingly, are presented in an archaic form in which couples enter the dance progressively. Elegant illustrations. Glossary, list of recommended tunes for quadrilles, list of commonly played fiddle tunes, short discography. Music for 23 tunes. 196 pp.

Sannella, Ted. *Balance and Swing*. New York, N.Y.: Country Dance and Song Society, 1982.

Meticulously presented collection of 55 dances—contras, squares and "triplets," most choreographed by the author in traditional New England style. Since the death of Ralph Page in 1985, the role of "grand old man of New England dancing" has devolved on Ted Sannella, whose reputation is based not least on his talent for creating dances with excellent choreographic flow. Introductory chapters discuss the historical and contemporary New England country dance scene that forms the background for the dances in the book, as well as dance customs, style, and choreographic considerations. Dance descriptions are extremely clear and include helpful teaching and dancing tips. Specific tunes are suggested for each dance; music is included. Glossary and extensive discography. 156 pp.

Sannella, Ted. *Swing the Next*. Northampton, Mass.: Country Dance & Song Society, 1995.

Still in preparation, this volume is a follow-up to Sannella's first book, *Balance and Swing*, and will contain a similar collection of newly composed dances in New England style, both by the author and others, supplemented by teaching and dancing advice and comments on the contemporary dance scene.

Schild, Myrna Martin. *Square Dancing Everyone*. Winston-Salem, North Carolina: Hunter Textbooks, Inc., 1987.

Like several other books whose basic orientation is modern Western style square dancing, this one gives as traditional square dances only very traditional, mostly visiting couple, dances, although 8 of the 23 singing calls in the Appendix are also compatible with traditional style. There are very short sections on the big set, clogging, and "contras" (consisting of 2 full set longways only), but the main content is an explanation of the modern Western square dance figures up to Mainstream level, divided into movements for 2, 4, and 8 people. The book includes a lot of sound advice, but also some misconceptions, particularly with regard to traditional material. List of record companies, short bibliography. 120 pp.

Sharp, Cecil J., and Maud Karpeles. *The Country Dance Book, Parts 5 & 6*. East Ardsley, Wakefield, UK: EP Publishing Ltd., 1976.

The two volumes collected here were originally published in 1918 and 1922, respectively. Part 5 of Sharp's classic six-volume *Country Dance Books* describes Appalachian square dancing (which he called the "running set") as he and Maud Karpeles were shown it in Kentucky in the early 1900s. Sharp's reaction to Kentucky style square dancing was filtered through his interest in the English country dance, which he was in the process of researching and reviving, as well as through contemporary theories of folklore and cultural evolution. Some of his conclusions about the origin and character of the running set should therefore probably be taken with a grain of salt. The dance descriptions as such are, however, still useful, and include about 25 figures. 51 pp.

Shaw, Lloyd. *Cowboy Dances*. Caldwell, Idaho: Caxton Printers, Ltd., 1952.

Originally published in 1939. Lloyd Shaw, considered by many to be the father of modern Western style square dancing, was the superintendent of a private school in Colorado and began looking for indigenous folk dance material as a non-competitive physical activity for his students. Their performing group, as well as his book and the courses he and his wife later taught for educators and recreation leaders, ignited an interest in square dancing that fed into other developments of the 1940s and 50s. Aside from the introductory chapters, the book includes instructions for about 75 dances, which Shaw attempted to classify by type. The book is entertainingly written, if sometimes a little patronizing. Some of the stylistic details shown in photos of his Cheyenne Mountain Dancers were definitely intended for stage effect and should not be imitated for normal dancing. Glossary. Music for 30 tunes. 417 pp.

Silverman, Jerry. *Play Old Time Country Fiddle*. New York, N.Y.: Oak Publications, 1978.

Primarily a collection of tunes written out for fiddle, but includes calls and explanations for 25 traditional squares—mostly singing calls—suited to 25 of the 75 tunes in the book. Dances are taken from Ed Durlacher's 1949 book, *Honor Your Partner* and are clearly, but concisely, described. For singing calls, the original words to the songs are also given. 134 pp.

Smith, Frank H. *The Appalachian Square Dance*. Berea, Kentucky: Berea College, 1955.

Good introductory sections on the historical development of square dancing, status of square dancing in the United States in the mid–1950s, calling and teaching technique, and the basics of the Appalachian dance style. Calls and descriptions for 10 big circle figures, 15 small circle figures, and an additional 5 figures particularly well suited to the running set, with explanatory diagrams and photos. Strangely enough, not much is said about the specifics of how the running set is danced; otherwise, the book is very thorough. Music for 19 tunes. 86 pp.

Steele, Garland W. *The Running Set Book: Traditional Hoedown Figures for the Appalachian Four-Couple Running Set*. Doraville, Georgia: JoAnn Gibbs, 1985.

Besides a short introductory chapter on the dance style, the book contains about 80 traditional figures for Appalachian four-couple square dancing. Of these, about 20 figures are used as intros/breaks/endings and the rest as main figures. The diagrams may seem a little confusing at first glance, but are actually quite helpful if taken together with the explanatory texts. 108 pp.

Sumrall, Bob. *Do-Si-Do: Fifty-Five Square Dance Calls with Explanations (3rd ed.)*. Abilene, Texas: Bob Sumrall, 1949.

Revised and expanded version of book originally published in 1942. Calls and descriptions for about 55 squares, divided into categories such as visiting couple figures, single visitor figures, cumulative figures, split the ring figures, various types of exhibition figures, etc. Glossary and dance explanations are generally quite clear, with a few exceptions. Includes both local variants of well known figures and a number of more unusual dances. Also has a whole section with suggested patter for various situations. 110 pp.

Sweet, Ralph. *Let's Create "Old Tyme" Square Dancing*. Hazardville, Connecticut: Ralph Sweet, 1966.

Based on his knowledge of the square dance scene in his own region, Sweet gives an honest and interesting analysis of the growth and crises of modern Western style square dancing through the 1950s and 60s. It is interesting to note that many of the problems identified at that time, such as dancer attrition because of a too complicated system, are still being debated today. Sweet also goes through the developments within traditional style square dancing and analyzes good and bad points there. His conclusion is to propose a dance program called "old tyme" square dance, which in many ways resembles the repertoire danced by traditional style groups today, but which he intended as a bridge between the two types of square dancing. Includes specific dance recommendations for a 12-week basic course and instructions for about 70 dances. Discography, short bibliography, and music for about 10 tunes. 97 pp.

Tempelmann, Anne. *Nordost-amerikanische Contra Tänze und Mixer für internationale Volkstänzer/innen*. Witten, Germany: Anne Tempelmann, 1987.

Background and information in German on the origin and development of contra dances, as well as on music, calling and teaching techniques, and styles and customs of dancing in New England today, based on the author's travels in the United States and Canada in the mid–1980s. Calls and instructions are given in German and English for nine contras, four mixers, and three other dances, with the most detailed explanations in the German text. Glossary and short list of books and records. 33 pp.

Thomas, Charley. *Play as You Learn (Square Dancing in One Easy Lesson)*. Woodbury, New Jersey: American Squares, 1950.

A complete evening's program of 14 squares, 3 couple dances, 2 mixers, and the Virginia Reel, written out with explanatory comments exactly as the author would present them when working with a group of new dancers. No glossary. Annotated bibliography. 16 pp.

Tolman, Beth, and Ralph Page. *The Country Dance Book*. Brattleboro, Vermont: The Stephen Greene Press, 1976.

Reprint of a book originally published in 1937. An early classic, this work is mainly known for its lively descriptions of the New England dance scene in the early part of the twentieth century and for

the folksy illustrations by F.W.P. Tolman. Ralph Page was already a beloved caller when the book was published in 1937, and developed into a figurehead for country dancing in New England whose influence continued until his death in 1985. The book includes instructions for about 75 dances, mostly in the form of calls without too many explanatory comments—some descriptions may therefore prove puzzling or misleading. Many of the classic old contras are included, however, as well as squares, couple dances, etc. Glossary, suggested tunes for each dance, and music for five or six tunes. 198 pp.

Wilde, Nina. *Square Dancing at Sight: Handbook of the London Square Dance Association*. London: G. Bell and Sons, Ltd., n.d.

Probably published in the mid–1950s. Contains basic information for dancers and callers and a glossary of basic movements accompanied by step-by-step photos, as well as a few examples of typical, easy dances. 38 pp.

Woodchopper, Arkansas (Arkie). *Square Dance Calls with Music and Instructions*. Chicago, Illinois: M.M. Cole Publishing Co., 1940.

Complete calls and short explanations for about 30 traditional squares, with music for 30 tunes. Also includes "fan photos" of the author, who apparently was a popular singer at the time. Of interest mainly as a period document, since most of the dance material can be found in better form elsewhere. 66 pp.

Young, Israel G. *One Night Stands: En Square-Dance-Kväll med Izzy Young*. Stockholm, Sweden: Folklore Centrum, 1983.

Twenty-five mostly traditional, easy dances in various formations, including 8 squares, 2 mixers, 2 progressive circles, the Virginia Reel, Jessie Polka, a section on the big set, and calls only (in English) for 6 more squares. The rest of the book is in Swedish. Music for 3 tunes. No glossary. 40 pp.

Instructional books on historical dance forms

Included here are only a few representative works dealing with the direct American antecedents of today's square and contra dances. The 1976 Bicentennial celebration, with its focus on the customs and lifestyles of the late 1700s, provided the impetus for several of these publications.

Hendrickson, Charles Cyril, and Frances Cibel Hendrickson. *Early American Dance and Music: John Griffiths, Dancing Master. 29 Country Dances, 1788*. Sandy Hook, Connecticut: The Hendrickson Group, 1989.

Dance descriptions and music for the 29 country dances (in contra formation) found in Griffiths' 1788 booklet, "A Collection of the Newest and Most Fashionable Country Dances and Cotillions." Includes introductory information on the reconstruction process, tune selection, mode of dancing, steps, and certain possible adaptations of the dances. More information about Griffiths himself can be found in the companion volume by Kate Van Winkle Keller. Glossary and bibliography. 52 pp. Companion tape—see Annotated Discography.

Hendrickson, Charles Cyril, and Kate Van Winkle Keller. *Social Dances from the American Revolution*. Sandy Hook, Connecticut: The Hendrickson Group, 1992.

Clear descriptions of 15 country dances (in contra formation) and the Congress Minuet (a dance for one couple), including an explanation of the steps and deportment necessary to recreate the dance customs of the Revolutionary era. Most of the country dances, which were all originally triple minors, can be adapted to duple minor formation or as dances for sets of three or four couples. The dances and accompanying tunes were interpreted from the notebook of an officer in the Continental Army, George Bush, of whom a short biography is included. 48 pp. Companion tapes—see Annotated Discography.

Keller, Kate Van Winkle. *Early American Dance and Music: John Griffiths, Eighteenth Century Itinerant Dancing Master*. Sandy Hook, Connecticut: The Hendrickson Group, 1989.

Portrait of the dancing master who, in 1788, published the first known American country dance book. Includes a bibliography of early American dance sources and facsimiles of several pages from Griffiths' book. The dances themselves can be found in the companion volume by Charles Cyril Hendrickson. 27 pp.

Keller, Kate Van Winkle. *If the Company Can Do It: Technique in Eighteenth-Century American Social Dance*. Sandy Hook, Connecticut: The Hendrickson Group, 1991.

This meticulously researched treatise by a serious dance historian summarizes what can be gleaned from contemporary sources about the dance forms, steps, teaching practices, and customs of execution of social dance in the America of the late 1700s. Annotated bibliography. 48 pp.

Keller, Kate Van Winkle, and Ralph Sweet. *A Choice Selection of American Country Dances of the Revolutionary Era, 1775–1795*. New York, N.Y.: Country Dance and Song Society, 1976.

Instructions for about 30 eighteenth-century contra dances, based on the authors' research into old manuscripts. The authors have attempted to choose those dances that were most popular at the time, based on contemporary sources, and to locate the correct tune for each dance. Music for the tunes is included. Also includes a glossary and general orientation on the dances and the style in which they were executed. 53 pp. For the companion LP as well as a tape (*Sweet Richard*) produced in 1990, see the Annotated Discography.

Keller, Robert M. *Dance Figures Index: American Country Dances 1730–1810*. Sandy Hook, Connecticut: The Hendrickson Group, 1989.

Two thousand seven hundred thirty-eight early American country dances from a total of 82 printed and manuscript sources of the eighteenth and early nineteenth centuries were put into a computer database by the author. The dances were coded as to their sequence of figures, enabling him to produce tabular outputs sorted by dance title, by figure sequence, and by source. Although, as pointed out in the introduction, the dances cannot be reliably reconstructed in their entirety by the information given, nevertheless, this work represents a major research contribution for those interested in the choreography of early American dances. A complete bibliography of the sources is included. 120 pp.

Morrison, James E. *Twenty-Four Early American Country Dances, Cotillions & Reels for the Year 1976*. New York, N.Y.: Country Dance & Song Society, 1976.

Nicely presented collection of about 14 country dances (contra formation), three cotillions (French quadrilles), and three reels (dances for a specific, small number of dancers), with music for each. Descriptions are based on the author's research into printed and manuscript sources of the post-Revolutionary period, with an emphasis on finding dances that seemed exciting or unusual. Complementing the dance material are passages from contemporary journals and other manuscripts referring to dance customs and events. Glossary and bibliography. 72 pp. A companion tape (*Young Widow*) was produced in 1990—see Annotated Discography.

Page, Ralph. *Heritage Dances of Early America.* Colorado Springs, Colorado: Lloyd Shaw Foundation, 1976.

Instructions for 25 contra dances that Page researched from sources published during the period 1788–1817 and that would be suitable, for example, for bicentennial celebrations. Each dance description includes source information, the original directions, and Page's interpretation of the dance in modern terminology, including, in some cases, minor adaptations of the choreography. No attempt is made to interpret the dancing style of the period as such. Also included are a little general background information and music for 16 tunes. No separate glossary, but most terms are explained in detail where they occur. 64 pp.

Ticknor, Leland B. *Dances from George Washington's Birthday Balls.* Staunton, Virginia: Leland B. Ticknor, 1990.

Interpretations of 27 country dances from the late eighteenth and early nineteenth centuries as worked out for the George Washington's Birthday balls held in Williamsburg, Virginia, from 1979 to 1988. Includes musical notation for a tune for each dance. No glossary—the reader is referred to the step descriptions found in Keller and Sweet, *A Choice Selection of Country Dances of the American Revolutionary Era* and Morrison, *Twenty-Four Early American Country Dances.* Bibliography. 46 pp.

History and background

Blancke, Luc. *Kriskras door de Amerikaanse Dans: Overzicht van de Geschiedenis en Danstradities van de U.S.A.* Lovendegem, Belgium: Luc Blancke, 1990.

An admirable attempt (in spite of occasional misunderstandings) to summarize information about the historical development and current character of square and contra dancing. Includes a number of dance descriptions illustrative of the various types, as well as relevant illustrations and ten dance tunes, reproduced from other publications Text is in Dutch/Flemish. Bibliography. 94 pp.

Bohrer, Thomas M., editor. *Vic Kibler: Adirondack Fiddler.* Rochester, New York: Sampler Records, Ltd., 1992.

Issued in conjunction with Sampler Records cassette tape 8914 (see Annotated Discography). Contains transcriptions of the 31 tunes played by Kibler on the tape, together with an 11-page essay by James W. Kimball on Kibler's family and musical background, repertoire, and playing style, with numerous quotes from interviews with Kibler and other family members. Also includes photos, capsule biographies of the other people involved in the project, and a bibliography. Although Kibler's repertoire is rife with dance tunes, he always remained true to the promise made early in life to his mother, and never actually played for dancing. However, other family members and friends did, and their recollections are included in the essay.

Casey, Betty. *A Treasury of Texas Dance Memories.* n.p.: Texas State Federation of Square & Round Dancers, 1987.

Capsule biographies of important Texas square dance personalities, mostly callers who were active in the 1930s and 40s when Texas was a hotbed of square dance innovation. Also contains a short history of square dancing in Texas, some examples of typical Texas figures, and a short bibliography of square dance books by Texan authors. 56 pp.

Damon, S. Foster. *The History of Square Dancing.* Barre, Massachusetts: Barre Gazette, 1957.

Reprinted from the Proceedings of the American Antiquarian Society. A concise, mostly plausible account of the development of country dancing from the first edition of John Playford's *The English Dancing-Master* in 1651 until the mid–1950s in the United States, substantiated by copious references to dance books and literary sources. 54 pp.

Dart, Mary. *Contra Dance Choreography: A Reflection of Social Change.* Indianapolis, Indiana: Indiana University, 1992.

(University Microfilms, order no. 9231541.) This recent doctoral dissertation provides an invaluable look at the current contra dance scene through the eyes of its participants—callers, dancers and musicians. Discusses the process of composing new dances, the aesthetic criteria generally applied, the functional working of a contra dance event, as well as an analysis of the changes that have occurred both in the dances and the dancing over time. Appendices explain the formations and basic movements and offer capsule biographies of the informants and short descriptions of 20 dances. Bibliography. 362 pp.

Franks, A.H. *Social Dance: A Short History*. London: Routledge and Kegan Paul, 1963.

An apparently sober and trustworthy account of the history of social dance forms in Europe, taking into account the societal environments of the various periods, and making good use of quotes from primary sources. 233 pp.

Laufman, Dudley, and Corinne Nash. *Dick Richardson: Old Time New Hampshire Fiddler*. Keene, New Hampshire: Historical Society of Cheshire County, 1992.

Issued in conjunction with a privately produced tape by the same name (see Annotated Discography). The book is a kind of scrapbook of information related to Richardson's career as a fiddler and dance caller, including a chronological overview of his life; reminiscences by Richardson and Laufman, square dance calls from Richardson's notebook, a list of the tunes he frequently played as a member of the Ralph Page Orchestra, a list of jobs played in the 1930s and 40s, a Richardson discography, and numerous photos.

Marks, Joseph E., III. *America Learns to Dance: A Historical Study of Dance Education in America Before 1900*. New York: Dance Horizons, n.d.

(Unabridged republication of 1957 first edition, published by Exposition Press, N.Y.) Chronicles American attitudes toward the role of dance as a cultural and educational element through the seventeenth, eighteenth, and nineteenth centuries, drawing mainly on primary sources. Bibliography. 133 pp.

Nevell, Richard. *A Time to Dance: American Country Dancing from Hornpipes to Hot Hash*. New York: St. Martin's Press, 1977.

An entertaining survey of the various forms of square dancing as they were practiced in the United States in the mid–1970s. The author visited dance events and talked with dancers and callers in different parts of the country to obtain an impression of New England style, Appalachian style and modern Western club style. Also includes a section on the historical development of square dancing, some information on basic movements, and a few (not too useful) dance descriptions. Discography, extensive bibliography, and lists of periodicals, libraries, organizations, events, etc. 272 pp.

Sachs, Curt. *World History of the Dance*. New York, N.Y.: W.W. Norton & Co., 1937.

Classic work on dance history, including the role of country dancing.

Shaw, Dorothy. *The Story of Square Dancing: A Family Tree*. Los Angeles, California: Sets in Order, 1967.

An attempt at a chronicle of the social dance history leading up to contemporary square dancing, this pamphlet is charmingly written, but in many places more fanciful than accurate, with a "square dance-centric" perspective. Bibliography. 16 pp.

Tolman, Newton F. *Quick Tunes and Good Times*. Dublin, New Hampshire: William L. Bauhan, 1972.

Ralph Page, who was a friend of Tolman's, reviewed this book in the January 1973, issue of *Northern Junket*, saying: "This is a delightful and most entertaining book, written by a man who is a master of the square dance flute. ... It is not a history of square dance music, though I am afraid that many neophyte[s] will think that it is." Page points out that the book includes a number of wild and unsubstantiated assertions, a criticism in which I concur. It is, nonetheless, an entertaining and professionally written volume with a fair amount of useful information about country dancing and music in New England. Includes music for ten tunes. 109 pp.

Calling and teaching technique

Bolton, Charles. *So You Want to Be a Caller*. Evesham, Worcestershire, UK: Cotswold Music, 1992.

This booklet by a veteran English dance leader and choreographer is packed with good advice about teaching, programming, working with bands and sound equipment, and relating to your audience, while the technical aspects of calling per se are covered only very briefly. The emphasis is explicitly put on working with groups that already know how to dance, rather than the special skills needed for one night stands, but most of the advice given applies equally well to both situations. Readers not familiar with British dance traditions may need to know that the English do many more set dances for a specific number of couples than are done in the United States and that some of the points in the book relate to this. Otherwise the suggestions given transcend the Atlantic. 20 pp.

Edelman, Larry. *Square Dance Caller's Workshop (4th ed.)*. Baltimore, Maryland: D & R Productions, 1991.

Used by Edelman as a text for his calling workshops, this book concisely covers a number of topics related to calling technique, choreography, teaching, programming, and music. Includes calls for 32 squares of various types, interesting quotes from the works of other leaders, lists of resources and dance camps, and an extensive bibliography, but no glossary. 50 pp.

Holden, Rickey. *The Square Dance Caller*. San Antonio, Texas: Rickey Holden, 1951.

Valuable handbook for anyone wishing to learn how to call. Discusses both the technical and professional aspects of calling in some detail, with much good—and still relevant—advice. 48 pp.

Howard, Carole. *Just One More Dance: A Collection of Old Western Square Dance Calls*. Chelsea, Michigan: Carole Howard, 1989.

A large collection of rhymed patter gleaned from personal and printed sources. Howard's quite plausible theory is that old time Western callers evolved patter to help keep the rhythm when instrumentation was sparse. In this context, it is unfortunate that such great pains are taken to distance the Western style of calling from New England style, with no consideration of Southern style, which is more closely related. A plus is the re-use of the dynamic illustrations from Ryan's *Dances of Our Pioneers*. 69 pp.

Osgood, Bob, editor. *Planning and Calling One Night Stands*. Los Angeles, California: Sets in Order, 1969.

Detailed advice for planning, programming, and executing "one time only" dance events. Includes calls/directions for 28 suggested squares and seven mixers. Short bibliography. No glossary. 32 pp.

Parkes, Tony. *Contra Dance Calling: A Basic Text*. Bedford, Massachusetts: Hands Four Books, 1992.

This extensive manual by one of the most respected New England callers of the present generation is an indispensable guide for anyone interested in becoming a better teacher and caller of New England contras and squares. Parkes covers every

conceivable topic, including the historical development of contra dancing as an activity, calling and teaching techniques, choice of material, music and sound equipment, and how to organize dances and work with different types of groups. Part 2 analyzes all the basic movements with regard to execution, timing, transitions to and from other movements, and teaching tips. Finally, there are examples of circle dances, full set longways, contras, and squares, with calls. Extensive glossary. Annotated bibliography and discography. Lists of organizations, events, periodicals, recommended dances and tunes, and retailers. 300 pp.

Training Committee of the Square Dance Callers Association of Southern California. *Training Manual for Recommended Use by Callers and Teachers in Conducting Beginner Square Dance Classes (2d ed.)*. Glendora, California: Square Dance Callers Association of Southern California, 1958.

Lots of advice on teaching methods, use of sound equipment, organizing classes, plus suggestions for a 20-week course of study, including some round dances. Dance descriptions as such are not given—reference is made to books in which they can be found. Glossary. 97 pp.

Clogging

Although clogging is beyond the scope of this book, it is a fascinating dance form closely associated with certain kinds of square dancing. Listed here are only a few selected sources on the topic to serve as an appetizer.

Bernstein, Ira. *Appalachian Clogging and Flatfooting Steps*. Malverne, New York: Ira Bernstein, 1992.

Recommended resource for anyone with a basic knowledge of clogging technique who wants to learn more steps. Written by a versatile dancer and serious student of percussive dance, it contains 110 steps in unusually clear notation, plus useful background information. 164 pp.

Bonner, Charles X. *Clogging and the Southern Appalachian Square Dance*. Acworth, Georgia: The Bonner Company, 1983.

See "General instructional books."

Popwell, Shelia. *Everything You Always Wanted to Know About Clogging and Never Even Knew*

You Wanted to Ask. Huron, Ohio: Burdick Enterprises, 1975.

Although clogging is virtually impossible to learn from written descriptions alone, this booklet may be the best bet if you have no other choice. Popwell has an entertaining style and an unusual gift for explaining steps in terms of normal everyday movements. Explains the eight basic steps of precision style clogging and a number of step combinations, plus advice about practice techniques, equipment, etc. 38 pp.

Seeger, Mike. *Talking Feet: Buck, Flatfoot and Tap. Solo Southern Dance of the Appalachian, Piedmont and Blue Ridge Mountain Regions.* Berkeley, California: North Atlantic Books, 1992.

A unique and valuable project, consisting of a 100-min. videotape and accompanying 142-page book. Documents a wide variety of traditional solo step dancing styles from the Southern mountains of the United States. Straightforward, responsibly written, and easily read, the book includes detailed interviews and profiles for each dancer featured in the tape, style profiles and dance step notation that help clarify the differences among them, and advice and encouragement for those interested in doing similar fieldwork on their own.

Record leaflets

This section lists a number of leaflets and booklets designed to accompany phonograph records or tapes. In most cases, a description of the corresponding recording will be found in the Annotated Discography.

Allemande Left to the Calls of Two Members of the Canadian Old Tyme Square Dance Callers Association. n.p.: n.pub., n.d.

Probably published in 1970s. Instructions for 12 squares, mostly well known traditional figures but also a few more unusual ones. Directions are quite explicit in some places, but somewhat cryptic in others. Includes a glossary, which is quite clear. 16 pp.

Bannerman, Evelyn & Glenn. *Appalachian Clog Dancing and Big Circle Mountain Dancing: Instructions.* Freeport, New York: Activity Records, Inc., 1974.

Instruction booklet to go with AR 53 (see Annotated Discography). Instructions for the big set, including useful teaching and dancing hints, descriptions of a few simple big circle figures and two small circle figures, and a short bibliography. Also instructions for two basic clogging steps; unfortunately, neither text nor photos in this section are really very clear. 8 pp.

Bannerman, Evelyn & Glenn. *Big Circle Mountain Square Dance Instruction.* n.p.: Evelyn & Glenn Bannerman, 1972.

Instruction booklet to go with AR 52 (see Annotated Discography). Instructions for the big set, including useful teaching and dancing hints and descriptions for ten big circle figures and ten small circle figures, with calls for most. Short bibliography. 6 pp.

Bannerman, Evelyn & Glenn. *Mountain Dance Music Comes Alive: Teacher's Guide.* Freeport, New York: Educational Activities, Inc., 1978.

Instruction booklet to go with AR 82 (see Annotated Discography). Instructions for the big set, including useful teaching and dancing hints and descriptions of several big circle figures and 11 small circle figures, with calls for most of the latter. Also instructions for four clogging steps, which, however, will be of limited use to those who don't already clog. 8 pp.

Bannerman, Glenn. *Friday Night at the Barn: Teacher's Guide.* Freeport, New York: Educational Activities, Inc., 1978.

Instruction booklet to go with AR 81 (see Annotated Discography). Instructions for the big set, including useful teaching and dancing hints and descriptions and calls for a few simple big circle figures and five small circle figures. Plus instructions for the five novelty dances (solo or couple dances) on the record. 8 pp.

Bonuš, Jasan. *Country Dances 1.* Prague: Dvorana, 1994.

Descriptions in English of suggested dances for the music on Dvorana's tape *Country Tance I* (see Annotated Discography). Includes 3 squares, 1 mixer, 1 full set longways, 1 contra, 1 progressive circle, and directions for a grand march. No glossary. 12 pp.

Bonuš, Jasan. *Country Dances 2.* Prague: Dvorana, 1994.

Descriptions in English of suggested dances for the music on Dvorana's tape *Country Tance II* (see Annotated Discography). Includes 4 contras, 2 progressive circles, 2 mixers, 1 square, and 1 dance for 5 couples. Glossary. 24 pp.

Bradley, Sandy. *Potluck and Dance Tonite!* North Ferrisburg, Vermont: Alcazar Records, 1979.

Instruction booklet to go with Alcazar FR 202 (see Annotated Discography). Calls and directions for eight traditional squares as called by the author on the album. 4 pp.

Bucksnort Barndance Band. *Square Dance with Old-Time Southern Dance Music.* n.p.: Sunny Mountain Records, 1978.

Instruction booklet to go with Sunny Mountain Records EB 1008 (see Annotated Discography). Calls and directions for a big set sequence and three squares as called on the record, plus one more square and a slightly erroneous explanation of the Virginia Reel. Otherwise, the descriptions are fairly clear and include some good general advice. No glossary. 8 pp.

Clifton, Roy. *Square Dances with Calls.* New York, N.Y.: Folkways Records, 1959.

Instruction booklet for Folkways FW-8825 (see Annotated Discography). Introduction with general orientation on the manner of dancing employed in Clifton's home area, the southeastern part of Canada, and on his classification of the dances by type. Calls and explanations for the 12 squares called by Clifton on the record. Also includes a reprint of a description of dance customs in old-time Ontario, from Edwin C. Guillet's book *Early Life in Upper Canada*. On the record, the timing of some of the dances is incorrect, as dancers were not present during the recording session; the booklet may be of help in reconstructing the dances for those who want to try calling them. No glossary. 12 pp.

Cotten, Beverly. *Get Your Kicks Clogging.* Chicago, Illinois: Flying Fish Records, 1981.

Instruction booklet for 12 basic and intermediate clogging steps to go with *Clog-In Lessons* (FF 237—see Annotated Discography). Detailed photos and well-written instructions supplement the oral explanations on the record, creating a useful package. 12 pp.

Dalsemer, Bob. *Smoke on the Water: Square Dance Classics.* Baltimore, Maryland: Traditional Caller Productions, n.d.

Published in 1989 according to the author,

this booklet supplements his tape of the same name (see Annotated Discography). Describes ten singing call squares, including the tunes, the actual calls to be sung, explanatory remarks, and notation of the author's sources. No glossary, but a few movements that might be unclear to traditional style dancers are explained where they appear, and helpful teaching hints are included. Short bibliography; list of book and record dealers. 24 pp.

Dalsemer, Bob. *When the Work's All Done: A Square Dance Party for Beginners and Old Hands.* Baltimore, Maryland: Traditional Caller Productions, n.d.

Published in 1990, according to the author, to supplement a tape by the same name (see Annotated Discography). Calls and explanations, including helpful teaching hints, for nine squares, evenly divided between singing calls and patter calls; two mixers, and a progressive circle. Music for tunes for ten of the dances. Short bibliography; list of book and record dealers. 24 pp.

Gilmore, Ed. *Learn Square Dancing with Ed Gilmore.* n.p.: Decca Records, n.d.

Instruction booklet for Decca DL 9051 (see Annotated Discography), probably from about 1960. Text and illustrations supplement the record's oral explanations of basic movements. Also includes calls and descriptions for four intermediate-level squares called on the record by Gilmore. 8 pp.

Gilmore, Ed. *Square Dance Party with Ed Gilmore.* n.p.: Decca Records, n.d.

Instruction booklet to go with record album Decca DL 9052 (see Annotated Discography), probably from about 1960. Calls and descriptions for 12 squares as called by Gilmore—one of the most respected callers of his time—on the record. No glossary. 8 pp.

Gunzenhauser, Margot. *Square and Contra Dances with Calls.* Lyngby, Denmark: Square Dance Partners Forlag, 1988.

Instruction booklet to go with SQDP EP 8703 (see Annotated Discography). Calls and detailed descriptions for the four dances called on the record (two squares and two contras, of easy to intermediate difficulty, taken from the present work). Detailed glossary. Available in Danish or English. 12 pp.

Gunzenhauser, Margot. *Square Dance Fest.* Virum, Denmark: Square Dance Partners Forlag, 1991.

Instruction booklet to go with SQDP 9101 (see Annotated Discography). Directions for the 12 dances called on the tape (3 squares, 3 progressive circles, 2 contras, 2 full set longways, and 2 mixers, of easy to intermediate difficulty), presented in a clear, schematic form, with detailed, illustrated glossary and some general advice. Dances are taken from Gunzenhauser's *Square Dancing at School*. Available in Danish or English. 20 pp.

Gunzenhauser, Margot. *Square Dance Tonight Volume 1: Suggested Dances*. Lyngby, Denmark: Square Dance Partners Forlag, 1988.

Instruction booklet to go with SQDP LP 8701 (see Annotated Discography). Concise but clear directions for 3 squares, 3 progressive circles, 2 mixers, a contra, and a couple dance. Dances are taken from the present work and are of easy to intermediate difficulty. Includes detailed glossary with illustrations of the more complicated movements. 4 pp.

Gunzenhauser, Margot. *Square Dance Tonight Volume 2: Suggested Dances*. Lyngby, Denmark: Square Dance Partners Forlag, 1988.

Instruction booklet to go with SQDP LP 8702 (see Annotated Discography). Concise but clear directions for 3 squares, 3 contras, 2 mixers, and 9 figures for the big set. Dances are taken from the present work and are of easy to intermediate difficulty. Includes detailed glossary with illustrations of some of the movements. 4 pp.

Holden, Rickey. *Square Dancing Texas Style: A Guide to the Perplexed*. n.p.: Folkraft Records, 1949.

Instruction booklet to go with Folkraft set F-15. An unusually clear and instructive set of directions plus glossary for the eight Texas style squares found on the records. 16 pp.

Kraus, Richard. *Let's Square Dance, Vol. 1-5*. New York, N.Y.: RCA Records, 1955.

Five 8-page instruction booklets to go with a set of called records produced by Kraus (see Annotated Discography), a package of relatively easy dances intended for school use and divided into modules intended for the different age groups, starting with 3d to 4th graders and moving up through high school. Clear descriptions and diagrams. Material is based on Kraus' book, *Square Dances of Today and How to Teach and Call Them*.

Piute Pete. *Square Dance*. New York: Folkways Records, 1949.

Instruction booklet to go with Folkways FA 2001. Calls and explanations for four easy traditional squares and three play party games. Glossary unfortunately contains several errors and omissions. 8 pp.

Syllabi and compilations

The books listed here are either reprints of syllabi from dance camps and festival weekends—with or without general information to supplement the dance descriptions—or compilations of dances previously printed in magazines, etc.

Budnick, Hanny, editor. *Syllabus for Ralph Page Legacy Weekend III, January 12-14, 1990*. Cambridge, Massachusetts: NEFFA-RPLW, 1990.

Descriptions for a large number of dances, mostly contras and squares in New England style, both old and new, as presented at the third annual Ralph Page Legacy Weekend. Also includes music for 22 tunes and a few contributions on theoretical topics related to New England style dancing today. 74 pp.

Contra Dance Syllabus, 39th National Square Dance Convention. Memphis, Tennessee: National Square Dance Convention Contra Committee, 1990.

Contains the program for contra dance activities at the 39th annual National Square Dance Convention, held in Memphis, Tennessee, in June 1990. Includes descriptions of 40 dances, in most cases in the form of calls with a few supplementary comments. Since the dances are apparently presented unedited as submitted by the callers, there are a few cases of factual error or less than optimal choreography. Also included are a well written introduction to the contra dance form by Bob Krapf, using examples, and lists of record sources and contra dance leaders. No glossary. 35 pp.

Contra Dance Syllabus, 40th National Square Dance Convention. Salt Lake City, Utah: National Square Dance Convention Contra Committee, 1991.

Contains the program for contra dance activities at the 40th annual National Square Dance Convention, held in Salt Lake City, Utah, in June 1991. Includes descriptions of 67 dances (calls with occasional explanatory comments). Since the dances are apparently presented unedited as submitted by the callers, there are a few cases of factual error or less than optimal choreography. Also included are some remarks about the early Mormons' use of dance, and lists of book and record sources and contra dance leaders. A glossary gives clear definitions of some terms, but is less clear on others. 41 pp.

Howell, Bob, and Cathy and Stan Burdick. *Easy Level Squares/Mixers/Contras.* Huron, Ohio: American Squaredance Magazine, n.d.

This compilation, which presumably was published in the mid–1970s, contains about 200 dances that originally appeared in the "Easy Level" column of *American Squaredance* magazine. Almost half of the dances are squares. There are about 60 mixers, about 30 contras, and the rest are folk dances from other countries and line/solo dances. The label "easy level" is used as a kind of catch-all for everything from extremely simple mixers and solo dances to relatively complicated contras. The main criterion seems to be that the dances (in most cases) only make use of movements within the traditional repertoire. Some of the dances are more interesting or useful than others; most are described only in the form of calls. No glossary. 54 pp.

Knox, Roger C., editor. *Contras: As Ralph Page Called Them.* Ithaca, New York: Roger C. Knox, 1990.

Reprint of Ralph Page's syllabus of 109 contras and 31 New England squares published in 1957 by the Folk Dance Camp of the University of the Pacific in Stockton, California, where Page for several years appeared on the staff. An additional 90 contras are reprinted from Page's magazine, *Northern Junket,* forming an invaluable treasury of the dances Ralph himself used and liked. To the Stockton syllabus, Roger Knox has appended the names of the dances' authors, and he has added timing indications to all the dances, a big help for callers. The Stockton syllabus includes Page's treatise on the history of contra dancing, unfortunately somewhat superficial. Music for 55 tunes. Short annotated bibliography of contra dance books compiled by Roger Knox. No glossary. 109 pp.

Lloyd Shaw Foundation. *Syllabus for The Rocky Mountain Dance Roundup, July 4–10, 1993.* n.p.: Lloyd Shaw Foundation, 1993.

Compilation of many of the dances presented in 1993 at this annual week-long camp held near

Colorado Springs, including couple dances (round dances), clogging and line/solo routines, and English and Scottish country dances, as well as American contras, mixers, and historical dances. Also includes the program for the week, a list of participants, etc. Similar syllabi are presumably created each year. 64 pp.

Nisbet, Bob. *The Country Dance Database (V2.1).* Portland, Oregon: Bob Nisbet, 1986.

There are probably a lot of callers these days who have constructed databases of, in particular, New England style contra and square dances, since these dances continue to proliferate and have an easily tabulated choreographic structure. This is an early print-out of one such database, containing descriptions of 170 contras, 26 progressive circles, 23 squares, and 18 mixers. Also included are lists of the dances sorted alphabetically, by difficulty level, and by the presence of various often-recurring movements, with each dance's choreography given in capsule form on a single line. 116 pp.

Osgood, Bob, editor. *Double Square Dance Yearbook 1968: All the Square and Round Dances from the 1966-67 Issues of Sets in Order.* Los Angeles, California: Sets in Order, 1967.

One thousand sixty-nine squares dances, drills, and round dances in a format similar to that of the earlier Year Books. Includes 11 contra dances, some interesting workshop material (squares) by George Elliott, short biographies of 12 well known callers with some of their dance routines, an editorial about the practice of constantly introducing new calls, etc. No glossary. 96 pp.

Osgood, Bob, editor. *Double Square Dance Yearbook 1970: All the Square and Round Dances from the 1968-69 Issues of Sets in Order.* Los Angeles, California: Sets in Order, 1969.

One thousand one hundred forty-eight squares dances, drills, and round dances in a format similar to that of the earlier annual Year Books. Includes a large amount of square dance workshop material by George Elliott based on traditional calls and patterns, a section on one night stand material with 49 easy dances, etc. No glossary. 99 pp.

Osgood, Bob, editor. *Square and Round Dance Year Book 1964: More Than 500 Dances Taken from the 1963 Issues of Sets in Order.* Los Angeles, California: Sets in Order, 1963.

Five hundred twenty-three square dances, drills, and round dances reproduced from the magazine *Sets in Order* (later called *Square Dancing*). The square dance material is mostly in the form of calls only. Much of this material can be of use to an inquisitive traditional style caller. The singing calls are typically more straightforward than the patter routines, and there are also 13 contra dances and some useful drills and workshop material, including some examples of equivalent sequences and "zero" movement sequences based mostly on movements within the reach of today's traditional style dancer. No glossary. 111 pp.

Osgood, Bob, editor. *Square and Round Dance Year Book 1965: More Than 500 Dances Taken from the 1964 Issues of Sets in Order*. Los Angeles, California: Sets in Order, 1964.

Five hundred fifty-eight square dances, drills, and round dances reproduced from the magazine *Sets in Order* (later called *Square Dancing*). Similar format to the 1964 Year Book. Includes 12 contra dances, 11 routines in which new movements are broken down into their component parts and called directionally, a section on "tandem square" choreography, etc. No glossary. 103 pp.

Osgood, Bob, editor. *Square and Round Dance Year Book 1966: More Than 500 Dances Taken from the 1965 Issues of Sets in Order*. Los Angeles, California: Sets in Order, 1965.

Five hundred seventy-one square dances, drills, and round dances reproduced from the magazine *Sets in Order* (later called *Square Dancing*). Similar format to the 1964 Year Book. Includes 12 contra dances and some useful drills and workshop material. No glossary. 103 pp.

Programs of the Annual Festival of the Square and Folk Dance Leaders of the Delaware Valley, 1953, 1954, 1955, 1956, 1957. n.p.: n.pub., 1953–57.

Descriptions of the dances done at the association's annual festivals from 1953 to 1957, ranging from 43 to 55 dances in each booklet, including some round dances and a few foreign folk dances. Fascinating not only for the dance material, but also for the accompanying advertisements and notices. 24–32 pp. each.

Riley, Milly, editor. *Western Square Dancing from the Syllabi of the Lloyd Shaw Dance Fellowship 1955–1970*. Jacksonville, Illinois: Milly Riley, 1989.

Reproduces the square dance sections of the syllabi resulting from the first 16 sessions of the Lloyd Shaw Dance Fellowship, a week-long summer seminar for dance leaders. It includes not only the calls for a large number of traditional and transitional square dances, but also various sections on the theoretical aspects of good dancing, calling, and teaching. Lists of records. No glossary. 324 pp.

Glossaries and indexes

Knox, Roger, editor. *Index to Northern Junket, 1949–1984*. Ithaca, New York: Roger Knox, 1985.

Northern Junket was a magazine published approximately every other month for 35 years by Ralph Page. It was poorly mimeographed on coarse paper, but contained a good deal of interesting material for anyone concerned with country dancing. There were articles, dance descriptions, book and record reviews, music, editorials written in Page's inimitable style, recipes and household tips, folklore, and humor. After Page's death in 1985, publication was discontinued, and Roger Knox compiled this valuable index. The book also includes a short biography of Ralph Page and some information on the books and records that he produced or contributed to. Back issues of *Northern Junket* can be found in the major dance libraries, or contact the Country Dance and Song Society for possible availability. 132 pp.

MacGregor Records, editor. *Square and Round Dance Calls and Explanations*. Hollywood, California: C.P. MacGregor Company, n.d.

Probably published in the mid-1950s. Well-written glossary of basic and more advanced square dance movements, including descriptions of ten popular break figures. Also descriptions of some basic round dance positions and steps, with advice on proper dancing and styling. Bibliography. Lists of records on the MacGregor label. 20 pp.

Rogers, Peter. *Country Dance Index, 3d ed.* New York: Country Dance and Song Society, 1987.

Index of about 2000 English and American country dances and where to find descriptions and music (both sheet music and recordings) for them. Over 300 books and records are indexed. 150 pp.

Index